THE BIOLOGICAL
BASES
OF PERSONALITY
AND BEHAVIOR

THE SERIES IN CLINICAL AND COMMUNITY PSYCHOLOGY

CONSULTING EDITORS

Charles D. Spielberger and Irwin G. Sarason

Averill Patterns of Psychological Thought: Readings in Historical and Contemporary Texts
Bermant, Kelman, and Warwick The Ethics of Social Intervention
Brehm The Application of Social Psychology to Clinical Practice
Burchfield Stress: Psychological and Physiological Interactions
Cattell and Dreger Handbook of Modern Personality Theory
Cohen and Ross Handbook of Clinical Psychobiology and Pathology, volume 1
Cohen and Ross Handbook of Clinical Psychobiology and Pathology, volume 2
Friedman and Katz The Psychology of Depression: Contemporary Theory and Research
Froehlich, Smith, Draguns, and Hentschel Psychological Processes in Cognition
    and Personality
Iscoe, Bloom, and Spielberger Community Psychology in Transition
Janisse Pupillometry: The Psychology of the Pupillary Response
Kissen From Group Dynamics to Group Psychoanalysis: Therapeutic Applications of Group
    Dynamic Understanding
Krohne and Laux Achievement, Stress, and Anxiety
London Personality: A New Look at Metatheories
Manschreck and Kleinman Renewal in Psychiatry: A Critical Rational Perspective
Morris Extraversion and Introversion: An Interactional Perspective
Olweus Aggression in the Schools: Bullies and Whipping Boys
Reitan and Davison Clinical Neuropsychology: Current Status and Applications
Rickel, Gerrard, and Iscoe Social and Psychological Problems of Women: Prevention and Crisis
    Intervention
Smoll and Smith Psychological Perspectives in Youth Sports
Spielberger and Diaz-Guerrero Cross-Cultural Anxiety, volume 1
Spielberger and Diaz-Guerrero Cross-Cultural Anxiety, volume 2
Spielberger and Sarason Stress and Anxiety, volume 1
Sarason and Spielberger Stress and Anxiety, volume 2
Sarason and Spielberger Stress and Anxiety, volume 3
Spielberger and Sarason Stress and Anxiety, volume 4
Spielberger and Sarason Stress and Anxiety, volume 5
Sarason and Spielberger Stress and Anxiety, volume 6
Sarason and Spielberger Stress and Anxiety, volume 7
Spielberger, Sarason, and Milgram Stress and Anxiety, volume 8
Spielberger, Sarason, and Defares Stress and Anxiety, volume 9
Strelau, Farley, and Gale The Biological Bases of Personality and Behavior, volume 1:
    Theories, Measurement Techniques, and Development
Ulmer On the Development of a Token Economy Mental Hospital Treatment Program

IN PREPARATION

Auerbach and Stolberg Crisis Intervention with Children and Families
Diamant Male and Female Homosexuality: Psychological Approaches
Hobfoll Stress, Social Support, and Women
London The Modes and Morals of Psychotherapy, Second Edition
Munoz Depression Prevention Research
Spielberger and Diaz-Guerrero Cross-Cultural Anxiety, volume 3
Spielberger and Vagg The Assessment and Treatment of Test Anxiety
Spielberger and Sarason Stress and Anxiety: Sourcebook of Theory and Research, volume 10
Strelau, Farley, and Gale The Biological Bases of Personality and Behavior, volume 2:
    Psychophysiology, Performance, and Applications
Williams and Westermeyer Refugee Mental Health Issues in Resettlement Countries

THE BIOLOGICAL BASES OF PERSONALITY AND BEHAVIOR

VOLUME 1

Theories, Measurement Techniques, and Development

Edited by

Jan Strelau
University of Warsaw, Poland

Frank H. Farley
University of Wisconsin, Madison

Anthony Gale
University of Southampton, England

HEMISPHERE PUBLISHING CORPORATION

Washington   New York   London

DISTRIBUTION OUTSIDE THE UNITED STATES

McGRAW-HILL INTERNATIONAL BOOK COMPANY

*Auckland   Bogotá   Guatemala   Hamburg   Johannesburg
Lisbon   London   Madrid   Mexico   Montreal   New Delhi
Panama   Paris   San Juan   São Paulo   Singapore   Sydney
Tokyo   Toronto*

THE BIOLOGICAL BASES OF PERSONALITY AND BEHAVIOR, Volume 1:
Theories, Measurement Techniques, and Development

1 2 3 4 5 6 7 8 9 0   BR BR   8 9 8 7 6 5

Library of Congress Cataloging in Publication Data

Main entry under title:

The Biological bases of personality and behavior.

    (The Series in clinical and community psychology)
    Includes bibliographies and indexes.
    Contents: v. 1. Theories, measurement techniques, and
development – v. 2. Psychophysiology, performance, and
applications.
    1. Individuality–Physiological aspects. 2. Personality–
Physiological aspects. 3. Temperament–Physiological
aspects. I. Strelau, Jan. II. Farley, Frank H. III. Gale,
Anthony. IV. Series.
BF697.B48 1985   155.2   84-10802
ISBN 0-89116-314-X (v. 1)
ISSN 0146-0846

Contents

III
DEVELOPMENTAL ISSUES

Contributors

MARIE ÅSBERG, Karolinska Institute, Stockholm, Sweden
GORDON E. BARNES, University of Manitoba, Winnipeg, Manitoba, Canada
MICHELE CARLIER, University of Paris X, Nanterre, France
STELLA CHESS, New York University, New York City, New York, USA
ANDRZEJ ELIASZ, University of Warsaw, Warsaw, Poland
FRANK H. FARLEY, University of Wisconsin, Madison, Wisconsin, USA
J. A. FEIJ, Free University, Amsterdam, The Netherlands
EWA FRIEDENSBERG, University of Warsaw, Warsaw, Poland
ANTHONY GALE, University of Southampton, Southampton, UK
A. GAZENDAM, Free University, Amsterdam, The Netherlands
KIRBY GILLILAND, University of Oklahoma, Norman, Oklahoma, USA
J. F. ORLEBEKE, Free University, Amsterdam, The Netherlands
ARNOLD POWELL, University of Alberta, Edmonton, Alberta, Canada
PIERRE ROUBERTOUX, University of Paris V, Paris, France
JOSEPH R. ROYCE, University of Alberta, Edmonton, Alberta, Canada
DAISY SCHALLING, University of Stockholm, Stockholm, Sweden
JAN STRELAU, University of Warsaw, Warsaw, Poland
ROBERT E. THAYER, California State University, Long Beach, California, USA
ALEXANDER THOMAS, New York University, New York City, New York, USA
ANNE MARI TORGERSEN, University of Oslo, Oslo, Norway
R. F. VAN ZUILEN, Free University, Amsterdam, The Netherlands
MARVIN ZUCKERMAN, University of Delaware, Newark, Delaware, USA

Preface

The publication of *Pavlov's Typology* by J. A. Gray in 1964 introduced Western psychologists to the Pavlovian theory of nervous system traits. Particular attention was paid to the modifications proposed by B. M. Teplov and V. D. Nebylitsyn, who, unlike Pavlov, investigated human subjects and were able to enrich the theory with many novel ideas.

Recognizing the theory as an interesting attempt to account for the biological bases of personality, Western psychologists began to search for parallels between the Pavlovian nervous system traits, notably strength of nervous processes, and other dimensions of personality. An overture was Eysenck's address to the International Congress of Psychology in Moscow (1966) in which he drew our attention to certain affinities between his extraversion-introversion dimension and nervous system strength. There followed a series of comparative studies by G. L. Mangan disclosing the common elements in the dimensions of extraversion-introversion and neuroticism, on the one hand, and in the strength and mobility of nervous processes on the other.

Other milestones in the promotion of comparative research in this area, and in the popularization of the theory of nervous system traits in the West, were the volume of studies, *Biological Bases of Individual Behavior*, edited by Nebylitsyn and Gray (1972), and the publication in 1972 in English of Nebylitsyn's 1966 book, *Nervous System Properties in Man*.

The work of the Department of Psychophysiology and Individual Differences at Warsaw University has been closely related to the Pavlovian theory of nervous system traits ever since the laboratory was established in 1966.

Working on problems of nervous system typology since the late 1950s, and collaborating in this respect with Teplov and Nebylitsyn's laboratory (where I had a chance to work for six months in 1966), I focused my attention on the mechanisms underlying partial nervous system traits and on the methods of their investigation.

From this work there emerged a theory to which my collaborators and I have come to refer as the *regulative theory of temperament*. The theory leans heavily on Pavlovian typology, but at the same time it takes note of Western work on the biological determinants of personality dimensions, with special reference to activation theory.

In view of these affinities it was perfectly natural to seek an extended collaboration with investigators concerned with nervous system typology and the personality dimensions related to such a typology, just as much as with researchers interested in those behavioral dimensions that bear some relation to activation theory.

The idea of holding an international conference of psychologists working in this field grew in our laboratory in the early 1970s. Organized under the title *Temperament and Personality*, the conference took place in October 1974 in

Warsaw. The modest number of participants and the absence of both U.S. and Soviet researchers was a source of considerable concern at the time, but today the meeting may be safely assessed as a success: We had the opportunity to take a closer look at the theoretical work of some biologically oriented Western personality psychologists. This led to insights that could not fail to affect our subsequent research; and at the same time Western psychologists took note of our theoretical framework.

As we set out to organize the second international conference five years later, the interest shown by our colleagues abroad exceeded our expectations. In fact, our limited resources forced us to impose restrictions on the number of foreign participants. The meeting in September 1979 (the second Warsaw conference devoted to *Temperament, Need for Stimulation and Activity* and supported by the University of Warsaw and the Polish Academy of Sciences) was attended by 51 psychologists from 12 countries. Among the participants were some leading psychologists in the field.

In view of the role taken by the Department of Psychophysiology and Individual Differences at the University of Warsaw in preparing for and organizing the conference, it is appropriate to give a short account of the Department's work, to which all of our ten faculty members have contributed.

Broadly speaking, our investigations converge upon temperament, but the particular manifestations of temperament are studied from several points of view: in normative and pathological aspects, in developmental and general terms, in the laboratory and in practical school and work conditions, and in psychophysiological, psychomotor, psychometric, and comparative terms. We also conduct experiments on rats.

The following problems are encompassed by our research.

1. The notion of temperament and the structure of temperamental traits. Approaching temperament as a set of relatively stable and formal features of behavior that reveal themselves in the energy level and in the temporal characteristics of behavior, we tend to focus upon energy level, wherein we have come to identify *reactivity* and *activity* of behavior. We are particularly interested in temperament as one of the mechanisms that regulate mankind's relations with the world.

2. The role of reactivity in the regulation of a person's *need for stimulation* and the psychophysiological mechanisms associated with the demand for stimulation constitute another group of problems. Here we study situations of varying stimulation load. In addition to the stimulation load of the environment, where we pay attention to ecological aspects, we are concerned with the stimulation derived from behavior. The psychophysiological mechanisms of the need for stimulation are investigated in the rat.

3. Temperament and its interrelation with personality is studied on the assumption that *temperament is a product of biological evolution,* whereas personality is an outcome of sociohistorical conditions. The interdependence of the two concepts is investigated in a number of theoretical and experimental projects. Further research is in progress on anxiety level, neuroticism, extraversion-introversion, and their interdependence with some of the temperament traits we have identified, with special attention to reactivity and mobility of behavior.

4. Another problem we are interested in is temperament and *cognitive functioning.* This area involves the study of cognitive style, in particular the reflexive-impulsive dimension and its stimulation load, with a developmental orientation.

We are further interested in the relationship between certain abilities (flexibility and fluency of thinking) and temperamental traits, and also in the interaction of temperamental traits and general abilities as affecting creativity.

5. Exploring the effect of temperamental traits on the development of a person's *individual style of action*, we seek to determine the influence on this style of different types of activity, partly from a developmental perspective.

6. Studying the role of temperament traits in performance under difficult situations we expose subjects to extreme conditions that supply them either with exceedingly strong stimulation (resulting from overload, threat, emotional tension, and the like) or with very weak stimulation (sensory deprivation, monotonous work, and similar conditions). We are interested chiefly in the interrelation of temperament traits and *tolerance to stressing conditions as reflected in performance efficiency.*

7. The relation between temperamental traits and *mental disorders,* notably neurosis, neuroticism, and psychopathy, is another line of study. We have demonstrated the nonspecific effect of temperament traits on mental disorders. In psychopathy we are concerned with its physiological mechanisms and its association with the physiological mechanism of reactivity.

8. We are also concerned with techniques for diagnosing temperament and certain dimensions of personality. We have constructed the Strelau Temperament Inventory (TI) and a questionnaire for measuring the temporal characteristics of behavior. Several scales for estimating reactivity at different ages and a method for measuring reactivity in rats have been developed.

A rough picture of our activities emerges from the chapters written by the Warsaw group for inclusion in the present volumes.

Reverting again to the Second Warsaw Conference, we realize that the common desire of all the participants was to become familiar with investigations conducted in other parts of the world and to work out common ground and mutual understanding, in an effort to grasp the essence of the theories, concepts, and methods developed by the "other" side.

The conference contributors focused on such dimensions as nervous system strength, extraversion-introversion, arousability, activation, stimulus modulation intensity, sensation seeking, and reactivity, dealing either with the underlying physiological mechanisms, with the interrelations between the dimensions, or with how the dimensions relate to various aspects of human behavior.

Irrespective of their specific qualities these dimensions have certain elements in common; therefore the participants of the conference could freely communicate with each other. The common features are easy to enumerate:

1. They all conceptualize the relevant behaviors in terms of either dimensions or traits.

2. Among the focal notions employed in the analysis of the dimensions or traits is the notion of individual differences. Hence there is frequent reference to such categories as strong type-weak type, extravert-introvert, sensation seeker-sensation avoider, lower arousable-higher arousable, low activated-high activated, reducer-augmenter, low reactive-high reactive.

3. All contributors share the view that the dimensions under discussion are biologically determined; hence the many references to "biological dimensions of personality."

4. A fair number of people agree that the physiological mechanism of the

identified dimensions must lie in, among others, individual differences in activation and/or arousal.

While assertions about the breadth of the common ground may sound overly optimistic, there is no denying that the common ground is broad enough to ensure free traffic of ideas and mutual understanding.

A large number of the papers presented at the second Warsaw conference are presented in these two volumes. In addition, many papers from the first Warsaw conference were thought to be of considerable theoretical or empirical significance. We decided to include them, in updated form.

These two volumes would never have existed without the selfless devotion of my two colleagues, Anthony Gale and Frank Farley, who not only persuaded me of the practicability of the undertaking but also offered their generous editorial assistance. Their enthusiasm and diligence, as well as each contributor's responsible approach, is greatly appreciated. We are also grateful to Ms. Kerry Thompson for her vigilance and enthusiasm in checking the proofs of both volumes.

It is to be hoped that both volumes will strengthen the links between psychologists in the West and in the Socialist countries and that it will lead to a closer collaboration in the study of the biological bases of personality.

Jan Strelau

THE BIOLOGICAL BASES
OF PERSONALITY
AND BEHAVIOR

Introduction: Overview and Critique

Anthony Gale, Jan Strelau, and Frank H. Farley

This Introduction provides the reader with a guide to this work, published in two volumes. Each chapter is reviewed so as to present a critical framework for the evaluation of work in this field. We hope for another conference in a few years, when the issues covered in this work will have achieved a greater synthesis. The book provides an unusual opportunity for the reader to sample theory and research on individual differences -- results of work generated in laboratories across the northern hemisphere. We have here authors from the following countries: Canada, Czechoslovakia, England, Finland, France, West Germany, the Netherlands, Norway, Poland, Sweden, the United States, and the Soviet Union; at the original conferences there were delegates also from East Germany and Rumania. From the various Reference sections we see that the traffic of scientific knowledge appears to have been unidirectional; works by East European authors frequently cite work published by Western authors, but the reverse is rarely true. The contributors to this book no longer have a valid excuse for further neglect of their colleagues. Perhaps for the first time the Western reader may read work hitherto published in journals inaccessible to him. At a time when the world is in political turmoil, it is encouraging that psychologists, concerned as they are with the eternal qualities of the human spirit, unfettered by the vagaries of contemporary history, should see sufficient common ground in their enterprise to justify a cooperative and potentially collaborative venture of this nature.

What is remarkable is the communality of themes that runs through all the papers without exception, be they theoretical or empirical in style. The emphasis is on the biological determination of key elements that account for individual differences and the functional interaction of these elements with our physical and social environment, to produce elaborate and adaptive patterns of behavior. Within this central superordinate theme, the range of topics considered is unusually extended. The variables referred to in the papers include the following: genetic transmission of traits, biochemical correlates of personality, the early development of social behavior, feedback and mutual regulation, evolution of individual styles of action, self-stimulation in rats, the factorial structure of behavior, the factoring of psychometric instruments, interaction of cognitive and emotional factors in information processing, hemispheral specialization and other aspects of brain organization, physiological stressors, physiological indexes, biological energy, analysis of complex actions, anxiety, psychopathy, empathy and retaliatory aggression, sensory deprivation, hypoxia, subjective estimates of arousal, sedative drugs, addiction, hypertension, occupational choice, and environmental stress.

These topics provide a family of sets overlapping constructs, within which there is a subset of common terms and concepts: personality, biological factors,

1

arousal, the need for stimulation, and the regulation of activity. At another
level there is also communality in the use of psychometric instruments, commitment
to a transactional approach, and the use of empirical experimental means to test
aspects of theory. As one might expect in such a rich field of endeavor, there
is also a set of common faults in strategy, methodology, and interpretation. We
shall come to these faults at the end of this introduction, where we anticipate
future developments. First, however, we provide a brief introduction to each
chapter.

CHAPTER REVIEWS

Volume I (Theories, Measurement Techniques, and Development)

Theoretical approaches. Chapter 1, by Strelau, should be read before sampling
the contributions of the other East European authors, because he raises a number
of major conceptual issues and provides a background to much of the work in his
own laboratory and in those laboratories that have inherited the legacy of
Pavlovian typology. He draws a fundamental distinction between temperament
(basic properties of the nervous system of both animals and man), and personality
as a product of external social conditions and thus an essentially human phenomenon; this he suggests is the prevailing Soviet view. However, he points to the
difficulties involved in making such distinctions, for temperamental traits must
themselves be modulated by experience, and animals do not live in an unresponsive
world. Nevertheless, he suggests that many confusions would disappear if
"dimensions of behavior, which have a large physiological component and are a
result of a biological evolution, were considered an aspect of temperament,
whereas all the traits (mechanisms) that are mostly a product of social-historical
conditions were included under personality." This does not mean, of course, that
temperamental traits are impervious to environmental influence.

Strelau then identifies those traits in Eastern European and Western psychology
that can be treated as temperamental traits and shows how such apparently different constructs may be related both theoretically and in terms of existing
empirical data. He discusses, in particular, the long line of studies by Mangan
and his associates that were designed specifically to build bridges between the
two traditions. A correlation matrix is presented summarizing many studies
investigating relationships between excitation strength, inhibition strength,
mobility, and balance of nervous processes on the one hand, and extraversion-
introversion, neuroticism, and anxiety on the other. Excitation strength and
extraversion appear to be consistently well correlated in a positive direction,
whereas neuroticism correlates inversely with this measure. On the other hand,
extraversion-introversion seem to be unrelated to strength of inhibition, which,
as might be expected from the previous findings, relates to anxiety. The highest
correlation with extraversion holds for mobility, one of the traits that has
been neglected both theoretically and empirically. Correlations between mobility
and neuroticism or anxiety are low and trivial.

Strelau then turns to his own theoretical viewpoint, in which temperament is
seen as a set of relatively stable traits that are revealed in the energy level
of behavior and in the temporal characteristics of reaction. An important point
is that such traits are seen as formal since they have no content and do not
affect behavior directly; rather temperament, as a regulative mechanism, is
manifested in behavior, independent of its direction or content. For the Polish
group, energy level incorporates all traits that reflect individual differences
in the physiological mechanisms involved in the accumulation and release of
energy, that is, at endocrinal, autonomic, and brain stem levels, including
those corticial mechanisms that are integrated with lower centers in the regulation of excitation. These physiological mechanisms are seen as operating as

a system with stable characteristics and in which the contributory elements vary between individuals.

Two basic features of energy level are reactivity and activity. The former relates to a stable pattern of response to stimulus intensity in a person, as compared with others within the population; the latter refers to the intensity and frequency of aspects of performance. These two features, although seen as independent, interact in a complex fashion both as a function of individual development and of situational requirements. Highly reactive people are those who are particularly sensitive to stimulation and have a high stimulation-processing coefficient, which reflects a deficiency within physiological mechanisms that serve to suppress stimulation. Activity is related to the notion of optimal level of arousal in that the person acts to increase or decrease incoming stimulation to achieve the optimum. Thus we see how reactivity characteristics may interact with activity characteristics, such that weakly reactive people will seek additional stimulation, while highly reactive people will act to reduce it.

Strelau then provides a detailed discussion of the possible logical relations between temperament and personality, citing empirical data that support his theoretical position.

As the reader will discover from the remaining chapters written by members of the Warsaw laboratories, the empirical data are unique in their range, for they extend from detailed parametric studies of reactivity and activity in rats, to occupational choice and response to high- and low-stimulating environments in residential accommodation.

The development of the theoretical themes is taken up by Eliasz (Chapter 2), who explores in depth the nature of the functional characteristics of the mechanisms of temperament. Here we have a detailed discussion of the evolution of behavior in the individual and the ways in which the mechanisms described by Strelau, initially devoid of content, become elaborated into characteristic styles of individual behavior. Eliasz emphasizes regulatory activity, the constant interplay of a person with physical and social aspects of his environment, which in turn affects the behavior of other persons toward the individual. This view enables a retreat from deterministic concepts of temperament that predict a precise one-to-one relationship between traits and specific behavior patterns.

Eliasz then takes the concepts of reactivity and activity and shows how they may be used to predict aspects of behavior in natural settings. Thus complex interactions are demonstrated between temperament, occupation, sporting activities, and domestic accommodation, revealing the interplay between the person's actions, stimulation available within the environment, and the regulatory steps taken to ensure an optimal level of arousal. Such a challenging combination of real-life variables is rarely seen in Western personality research. The notion of defining situations by employing concepts and descriptors which are common coin in trait theory, provides a basis for the resolution of controversies relating to Trait × Situational interactions.

Farley (Chapter 3) sketches the outline of a model linking arousal and intellective and cognitive function, in which individual differences in arousability are presumed to have a moderating effect on the interrelatedness of cognitive processes. Thus, persons of low arousability show greater relatedness, in the correlational sense, among cognitive processes, than do persons of high arousability. It is proposed that cognitive processing associated with low arousability, as contrasted with cognitive processing associated with high arousability,

would show greater flexibility, stronger functional dependencies among cognitive
processes, greater transferability between modes of cognitive representation,
or perhaps "swapping" in computer terminology, more emphasis on simultaneous
than successive or sequential processing, more emphasis on parallel than serial
processing, and a general characteristic that Farley labels transmutative thought
-- an ease of transforming one mode of representation into another, as in hypostatizing the abstract into the concrete, or transmuting the concrete into the
abstract. The model is extended to a practical problem of immense social importance, but also one with significant theoretical interest, that of human creativity in general, and scientific creativity, discovery, and inventiveness in
particular. Farley argues that creativity, particularly scientific creativity,
requires to a substantial degree transmutative thought, and that such transmutative processes conducive to discovery and creativity are more characteristic of
low-arousable people than of people of higher arousability on a trait dimension
of arousability.

Although this arousal and cognition model is but barely outlined in the Farley
chapter, its implications for integrating some of the work on arousal with contemporary conceptions of cognitive processes seem substantial. In addition,
the implications for creativity and discovery in science, and other domains,
extends the reach of the psychobiology of personality to an important but
neglected area.

Farley reports a number of studies bearing on some of the foregoing ideas. He
uses the moderator design, traditionally applied to the more usual psychometric
instruments only, in identifying a biological moderator, that is, individual
differences in arousability, with the effects of this biological moderator on
the relatedness of the cognitive processes being examined. These studies show
that associative and conceptual processes are much more strongly correlated in
low- than in high-arousable persons. Similar, although less striking, results
were also obtained for verbal versus pictorial processing, and speed versus
accuracy in an intellective task. Some studies bearing on creativity are also
mentioned, although none directly concerns scientific discovery. The latter
aspects of the model await empirical consideration. One fascinating implication
of the model is that of a biological basis, at least in part, for creativity.

The chapter providing the most panoramic theoretical view of personality is
without doubt that of Royce and Powell (Chapter 4), who present us with a
universal factorial structure, or rather a conceptual program for integrating
past and future work. Within this complex model it is possible to assign pro-
portional variance to different levels, from sensory and motor systems
(heredity dominant) to style and value (environment dominant). Each level
within the factor hierarchy is itself multidimensional and hierarchical, and
integration occurs both within the six interacting systems and between them.
Within the general factorial structure that describes individual differences,
integrative principles operate on the basis of concepts derived from general
systems theory and information-processing theory . The inevitable complexity
of this theoretical approach is well characterized in the figures, which reveal
the inadequacy of an Occam's razor approach to individual-differences theory.

What is particularly striking is the constant endeavor to synthesize the two
traditions of personality and cognitive psychology. The reader will need to
return to the original chapters reviewed here to identify the precise nature
of the tests employed and the operationalization of the key constructs. Royce's
approach, which has a long and sustained history, is an immediate and pressing
challenge to those who would have us discard the psychometric tradition. At
the same time, it still raises the problem of how such complex theoretical
structures are to be tested empirically within the current framework of

experimental procedures, where even a triple interaction between factors stretches the explanatory power of the background theory.

Zuckerman (Chapter 5) reviews the early history of the development of the Sensation Seeking Scale (SSS). In an early formulation of his theory, the optimum level of arousal was a central concept, namely that sensation seekers look for stimulation to sustain the optimum. Thus individual differences in people are influenced by differences in optimum level of arousal. He reviews the evidence that leads him to reject this view, and the burden of his argument is that sensation seekers seek change and detest constancy of arousal level; thus some of the things they seek clearly reduce arousal. This is demonstrated in drug use, where there is little evidence of a preference for stimulants as such. Zuckerman then presents a metadiscussion of the nature of models designed to link psychobiology to behavioral traits, including a critique of sociobiology. Critics who challenge trait theory on the ground that it cannot predict specific behaviors are setting up a man of straw, since the trait represents averaged behaviors sampled across situations and time. Prediction is improved when the trait test refers to specific actions in specific contexts, and if the tasks offered to subjects are designed to reflect the theory in question. The SSS subscales and the empirical tests applied to them satisfy these requirements and yield good correlations. In reviewing the subscales of the SSS, Zuckerman points out that these reflect biological correlates when taken separately, rather than in combination, to yield a total sensation-seeking score. He then reviews the psychophysiological data, gonadal hormone data, and the more recent work on neurotransmitters and endorphins. The evidence here is novel and enticing and reveals potential links between sensation-seeking, activity, depression, and monoamine oxidase (MAO). MAO and its genetic determination play a central role in the most recent version of Zuckerman's theory. Gonadal hormones regulate MAO, which regulates dopamine and norepinephrine, which in turn are involved in approach behavior and reward mechanisms; reward affects the arousal systems and positive emotions. Zuckerman demonstrates how the systematic accumulation of data over a broad range of domains of description, based on a sound theoretical framework, may serve fully to exploit an essentially correlational approach. Nor is Zuckerman afraid to leap beyond the accumulating and coherent body of knowledge to push toward new avenues of enquiry.

Chapter 6, by Thayer, is particularly interesting because he allows us the privilege of looking over his shoulder as he develops new ideas. After reviewing standard criticisms of activation as a unitary dimension, he then proposes that at least two activation dimensions underlie behavior. He focuses in particular on the activating effects of exercise and the demonstration that exercise diminishes the activating effects of anxiety. He points to a number of paradoxes that illustrate the need to have more than one continuum: the tiredness associated with anxiety, the use of arousing drugs with hyperactive children, the presence of anxiety and tiredness after sleep deprivation, and tranquilizers that reduce anxiety yet do not make the patient tired. His two Activation Dimensions, A and B, are positively correlated at moderate levels of energy expenditure and negatively correlated at high levels. The two dimensions bear relationships both to different behavioral processes and to external and internal stimuli. Dimension A is seen as endogenous in nature and related to circadian rhythms in activity, whereas B is seen to be related to emergency reactions and the mobilization of energy. He then reviews studies showing differential effects of the two dimensions on a range of psychological variables. He concludes with a consideration of conscious awareness as "an excellent organismic integrating system." The reader should recall that it was subjective report that yielded the highest correlation with composite physiological scores in Thayer's early work. Apart from the fact that the reader is able to witness the evolution of

a new theoretical model, this chapter stands out as one that strongly emphasizes
the importance of subjective experience in the measurement of individual differences. It contrasts with many studies that seem to emphasize physiological and
performance measures, adding subjective report almost as an afterthought and
at a point in the development of the research design that makes it too late for
subjective measurement to determine the key features of the procedure.

Roubertoux (Chapter 7) provides an account of the rationale for behavioral
genetics, showing how genetic analysis (a field in which only few personality
theorists have been willing to engage) is appropriate to the study of individual
differences. This lucid account will be most valuable for those who are un-
familiar with alternative genetic analyses and inferential procedures. He provides examples of behavioral and pathological traits whose mode of genetic transmission is known. In the case of one disorder, a variety of muscular dystrophy,
Roubertoux is able to show that differential response in a conditioning procedure yielded a highly significant identification of different groups.

After a brief discussion of difficulties in estimating heritability and the
caution required in interpreting heritability studies, Roubertoux then goes on
to review twin-study findings. These have generally yielded higher correlations
for personality traits in monozygotic than in dizygotic pairs.   Although electroencephalogram (EEG) and average evoked potential (AEP) studies show evidence for genetic determination, autonomic nervous system measures yield more
equivocal data. He argues that low intercorrelations between autonomic variables need not imply their unsuitability for genetic study but rather their
sensitivity to situational variation. Modality of presentation and time within
the epoch appear to be differentially sensitive to genetic variation. If such
variation may be related to behavioral variation, then the dissociation within
the physiological indexes may be used to discriminate within behavioral processes.

Although Roubertoux claims his is not an exhaustive review, it provides an excellent and comprehensive introduction to this complex field of enquiry, providing
not only a justification for the approach but an account of the key methods
employed and some landmark studies.

Measurement aspects. Two detailed studies of the incorrelation among different
scales, by Carlier and by Gilliland, show that comparison between Western and
Eastern European scales is not a straightforward matter.

Carlier (Chapter 8) presents a thoroughgoing factor analysis of Strelau's scales,
relating them also to the Eysenck Personality Inventory (EPI) and Cattell's
Anxiety. The results of her careful and systematic analysis, like those of
Gilliland, cannot be a source of comfort to the Warsaw school. Strelau's Excitation and Inhibition scales, although they correlate well with extraversion-
introversion and neuroticism-stability/anxiety, respectively, may be considered
to be poor substitutes for these well-established scales. For Excitation also
loads on both neuroticism and anxiety, as well as Inhibition and Mobility.
There is, in addition, little evidence from Carlier's study for the integrity
of the Mobility factor. Given the intercorrelations between Strelau's constructs and the demonstrable orthogonality of Eysenck's constructs, there are
surely grounds for suggesting that studies based on the Strelau scales are
likely to be less reliable. If Mobility is a worthwhile theoretical construct,
it appears not to be embodied as a separate entity in the Strelau scales.
When the theory is subjected by Carlier to empirical test, it appears that
threshold for transmarginal inhibition is related to anxiety/inhibition qua
Gray (1964), rather than to excitation/extraversion, as claimed by both

Strelau and Eysenck. These data then provide insufficient support for the Warsaw School and at the same time yield contradictory evidence that is difficult to absorb into Strelau's theoretical framework.

Gilliland (Chapter 9) provides a brief introduction to Pavlovian typology and points to the paucity of Western studies either using the Pavlovian framework or exploring relations between it and Western scales. One problem is the complexity not only of the constructs but of the procedures employed to classify individuals. The Strelau scale presents a straightforward procedure. He describes the method of extinction with reinforcement as applied to EEG conditioning, which he suggests is one of the best measures of strength of the nervous system (excitation). He points to the similarity between strength and extraversion and reviews empirical findings that show parallels between the constructs (perception, reaction time, sustained attention, and drugs).

Gilliland presents data showing intercorrelations between scores on the EPI, the Eysenck Personality Questionnaire (EPQ), and the Strelau Scales. Like Carlier, he demonstrates the lack of independence of the Strelau scales, but in his case, there are more modest correlations between the Strelau and Western scales. Correlations with the Zuckerman scales are also modest. Finally, he shows that his EEG procedure fails, as a test of construct validity, to discriminate among the Strelau temperamental types. Gilliland urges caution in the use of the Strelau scales. The reader should find the comparison of tables in the Strelau, Carlier, and Gilliland chapters most instructive, since they do suggest some unity in factor structure albeit not wholly compatible with the theoretical views of either Strelau or Eysenck.

Barnes (Chapter 10) presents a review of studies using the Vando Reducing-Augmenting Scale, which he suggests presents the most straightforward technique available for measuring individual differences in stimulus intensity modulation. Correlation data from a variety of studies indicate that stimulus reducers in relation to augmenters are more tolerant to pain, more extraverted, less hypochondriacal, less guilty, and heavier smokers. Reducers are short sleepers; they are less socialized, more optimistic, and higher on ego strength than are augmenters. They internalize on locus-of-control measures; they are sensation-seekers (external) and risk takers. Reducers prefer stimulants (including marijuana and amphetamines), and they give less socially desirable responses in a faking test (although Barnes suggests this effect is not powerful enough to undermine the validity of the earlier findings).

Many of these findings are consistent with predictions from Petrie's original theory (1967), although some of the predictions concerning drug use are not. Barnes suggests that in the latter case, the fault may well be in the theory, since the reliability, construct, and discriminant validity of the Vando scale seem high. Thus Barnes shows (albeit in the absence of intercorrelations with many of the scales reported in these volumes) that the sensation-seeking construct may have useful applications in terms of habitual behaviors, aspects of self-concept, and modes of construing the world.

Schalling and Åsberg (Chapter 11) commence with an important assertion, that results relating to extraversion-introversion may be contradictory, and even self-defeating, if the investigator fails to distinguish impulsivity and sociability components. These not only give different results, but may yield findings in opposite directions. They cite Guilford's characterization of extraversion as "a shotgun marriage between impulsivity and sociability." Their own view is that impulsivity is more consistently associated with biological correlates. This has important implications for consideration elsewhere in the volume of the relationship between factors in scales developed in different countries and

different laboratories.   This is, of course, not a purely empirical issue, but
one of theoretical significance.

The main body of the chapter is devoted to a review of their laboratory's work
on impulsivity, based on their newly devised Impulsiveness and Monotony
Avoidance Scales.   It should be noted that the title of the latter scale emphasizes avoidance rather than sensation seeking.   Analyses using other scales,
however, show that it loads on thrill seeking, low conformity, and low anticipatory anxiety.   They report correlations between their scales and biochemical
and psychophysiological indexes in normal and clinical populations.   These correlations are then incorporated into neuropsychological models incorporating
central nervous system (CNS) and arousal constructs.   Thus the high impulsive
is dominated by the immediate environment, while the low impulsive "with his
greater involvement in processing of past events and future projects, is less
easily distracted."   This dependence on immediate stimulation will be associated
with behavior that ensures a varied pattern of incoming stimuli, that is, high
Monotony Avoidance.   They then suggest that such differences in cognitive style
might link up with alleged hemispheral differences in terms of holistic and
serial processing, although their own studies do not appear to employ the tasks
typically used in hemispheral specialization studies.   The second theoretical
notion is that high impulsives are low in arousal.

They then report biochemical studies using the new scales.   Monotony Avoidance
but not Impulsivity correlated with platelet MAO in a sample of depressive
patients .   A larger-scale study with students used several questionnaire
measures.   It will be seen from their Table 4 that although some significant correlations emerge for Monotony Avoidance, the relationship with Impulsivity is
complex and the Zuckerman Scales yield only one modest correlation.   This correlation, however, showing an inverse relation between MAO and Disinhibition
score, corroborates Zuckerman's findings.

Like Zuckerman, Schalling and Åsberg have already invested research effort into
biochemical studies.   The correlations obtained tend to be within the normal
range of magnitude for personality studies and the patterning of correlation
is complex.   The relationship between these neurotransmitter substances and
behavior is yet to be specified within a complex theoretical framework, but
these initial findings are clearly a sound basis for future work; and, as we
have seen, Zuckerman has already attempted an integration.

Feij et al. (Chapter 12) begin with a brief review of Zuckerman's research over
the last 15 years into sensation-seeking characteristics.   Zuckerman's four
scales (Thrill and Adventure Seeking, TAS; Experience Seeking, ES; Disinhibition,
Dis; and Boredom Susceptibility, BS) show some modest common variance, but are
best seen as independent constructs relating to different aspects of behavior.
They review briefly relations between sensation seeking as a construct with various scales, the Minnesota Multiphasic Personality Inventory (MMPI), 16PF, Kipnis,
and EPI; and its independence from anxiety and neuroticism.

In considering biological aspects of sensation seeking, they draw our attention
to certain key problems: (a) there is a need to be specific about the notion
of optimum level of arousal (i.e., is the optimum common for all people or does
it vary?);   (b) arousability is a characteristic of extraverts for Zuckerman,
but of introverts for Eysenck;   (c) similarly, for Zuckerman extraverts are
augmenters, while for Eysenck they are reducers;   (d) researchers need to specify
levels of stimulation used in experiments and to state in precise terms what
individual constructs mean, (as H. J. Eysenck has pointed out elsewhere (1981),
these views are not necessarily contradictory when one considers the curvilinear
relationship between level of stimulation and magnitude of response); (e) trans-

marginal inhibition may be a crucial characteristic for distinguishing groups and demonstrating parallel relationships between different personality constructs; and, (f) the important distinction drawn by Zuckerman between sensation seeking and arousal seeking, since there is no evidence from his work that prior to stimulation there is a difference between high and low sensation seekers in arousal level.

They then present their own data based on their specially developed question- naire. This has four traits (extraversion, emotionality, impulsiveness and sensation seeking) and uses Likert response mode rather than forced choice.

On the basis of their own factorial data and related studies, they conclude that "sensation seeking is related to two largely orthogonal dimensions: social extraversion and lack of constraint, that is, rejection of conventional norms and values." This construct is then related to several behavioral measures: more smoking, less sleep, and higher coffee intake. In the case of sleep habits, Feij et al. point to the complexities involved in making predictions and inter- preting data, particularly since emotionality is positively associated with sleep need.

The Amsterdam workers report that they obtain a factor structure for dimensions of sensation seeking similar to that of Zuckerman and report one of their psychophysiological studies, focusing on their equivalent of the disinhibition scale, since this, they believe, is most related to biological factors and closest to the notion of <u>strength</u>. Using Galvanic Skin Response (GSR) and heart rate (HR), they predict that high disinhibitors (strong nervous system, stimulus augmenting) will show cardiac deceleration (orienting responses) while low disinhibitors will show acceleration (defensive responses). Both groups will show equal GSR responses; but <u>general</u> sensation seekers will be more respon- sive to stimuli, yield higher GSRs, and habituate quicker. Generally speaking, their predictions were confirmed.

The papers by Schalling and Åsberg and Feij et al., like that of Zuckerman, review extended programs of work, based on similar conceptual frameworks and thus demonstrate the universality of their key constructs. They also show how specific predictions may be made not only within a correlational model, but within highly controlled laboratory investigations.

<u>Developmental issues</u>. The paper by Thomas and Chess (Chapter 13) is a brief historical account of their work and the thinking that went behind it, including a comment on the resistance of their early contemporaries to the notion of longitudinal studies, designed to be interactional in nature, at a time when (a) cross-sectional data was considered to be supreme, and (b) the heredity/ environment controversy and the polarization of viewpoint it fostered was at its peak. This brave strategy, in the face of the prevailing <u>zeitgeist</u>, has clearly paid dividends, as witnessed by the richness of the data produced by the New York study and its clear implications for developmental theory and per- sonality theory. They provide a detailed discussion of the crucial problem of measuring consistency of behavior over time, the need to see every action within its social context, and the constant interplay between people and their social environments. The value of their work is clearly demonstrated in the longitudinal study by Torgersen (Chapter 14), which owes its essential strategy and methodology to the pioneering foresight of Thomas and Chess. The thrust of the argument is reflected in many of the remaining papers.

Torgersen presented a paper at both Warsaw conferences and thus was able to provide a follow-up study of her unique sample of identical and nonidentical twins. It is difficult to overestimate the importance of this study. Using the nine Thomas and Chess behavioral categories, she studied her sample at three time periods: shortly after birth, at 6 months, and at 6 years. A striking feature of this study is not only the range of measures taken, but the care taken to ensure reliability. The reader must go to Chapter 14 for a precise account of all the findings. The study clearly supports a genetic determination of temperamental aspects of behavior, showing the relative importance of genetic factors for different aspects of behavior at different ages. Torgersen provides a subtle discussion of her data in terms of the interaction of genetic and environmental factors in the determination of observed patterns of behavior. This includes consideration of interuterine conditions that may have served to mask characteristics at the time of her earliest observations. She points to the difficulty of teasing out causal sequences from correlational data, a common source of controversy in the heredity/environment debate. One particularly fascinating outcome is that characteristics associated by Thomas and Chess with the "difficult child syndrome" are low on heritability and thus most easily modified by environment. Torgersen's painstaking and extended work reveals the benefits to psychological theory of longitudinal studies carried out within an adequate conceptual framework and reinforces again the benefits of twin study in genetic research.

Friedensberg (Chapter 15) employs a constructional task to study developmental trends in style of action, that is, the proportion of basic and auxiliary actions. High reactives show a greater proportion of auxiliary actions in adult populations. Friedensberg's sample ranges from 6 to 16 years. This age range must necessitate use of tasks of varying levels of complexity, a problem encountered in several developmental studies, so that the data shown for different age groups in her tables are not, strictly speaking, comparable. The most powerful source of variance in her study appears to be intelligence, as measured by the Progressive Matrices. Taking high- and low-reactive groups separately, however, it is in the latter group that intelligence correlates with a variety of performance indexes. She also shows an age trend toward deliberate and controlled operations, rather than corrective actions. This study reveals a number of problems of interpretation in this field and, in particular, difficulties involved in discovering variables that may be confounded. In two of her five age groups, Matrices score and Reactivity are related, high reactives being less intelligent. The task employed resembles the Koh's block task, used in the Wechsler Intelligence Scale for Children (WISC) and the Wechsler Adult Intelligence Scale (WAIS), and the operations involved in solving the Matrices bear some resemblance to the dependent variables studied. At the same time, there must be a confounding between the measures of performance, because a speedy solution reduces the opportunity for occurrence of subsidiary operations. Friedensberg employs a variety of extreme group and correlational statistics, each treated independently; it may be that a multivariate analysis would be more appropriate to the clarification of the complex relationships between age, intelligence, and the development of style of action. Also, generalizability of the findings would be more certain if a variety of tasks were employed; for example, would an analysis of performance of classroom students yield similar findings? The power of developmental studies of this nature is that they enable us to examine basic processes before the person has acquired strategies to compensate for performance discrepancies.

Volume 2 (Psychophysiology, Performance, and Applications)

Psychophysiological studies. Gale (Chapter 1), in reviewing EEG studies of extraversion-introversion, appeals for a change of direction in research. Of the 30 or more studies he identifies in the literature, most are almost theory free, resting quite simply on the hope that there will be a correlation between personality, as measured by questionnaire, and cortical activity, as measured by the EEG. Even so, measurement of personality and EEG in these studies leaves much to be desired. He shows that the discrepant findings in the literature can be reconciled by use of a post hoc hypothesis derived from H. J. Eysenck's (1967) theory, the notion of sensation seeking in extraverts, and the characterization of the testing situation as one of extreme monotony, in which subjects are obliged to devise different strategies to comply with ambiguous experimental instructions. He draws attention to a number of confounding variables and potential sources of measurement error, and claims that the absence of performance data makes interpretation of results difficult. It is clear from other chapters that the means are available for following Gale's advice and that, indeed, many of the Soviet workers appear to have established a long tradition of integrated research in which personality, performance, and electrocortical measurement share common paradigms. One feature of Gale's paper, however, that has general application is his brief analysis of the experimental situation itself as a context in which several sources of arousal may combine to confound personality research. Such confusion exists particularly in those areas that emphasize sensation seeking, the effects of novelty, fear of evaluation or punishment, and personal regulation of stimulus input. Thus notions of regulation and cost emphasized by the Warsaw group -- and, in particular, the strategy of focusing on process as well as outcome -- would be seen by Gale to apply to the experimental situation per se and the coping strategies used by the subject to handle a threatening or ambiguous stimulus field. In general, Gale indicates that little has been achieved in the West in relating EEG characteristics to extraversion-introversion.

Bodunov (Chapter 2) presents a considerable contrast; it is clear from his work that the use of well-structured performance tests and a thoroughgoing analysis of EEG parameters can demonstrate the relationship between brain function and individual differences. Moreover, references cited by both Bodunov and Danilova show that such studies have an established tradition of sustained research behind them. Bodunov focuses on the detailed analysis of the dynamics of activity, which he demonstrates must be explored in a multidimensional fashion, because different indexes of activity do not necessarily intercorrelate. Thus, he devises three groups of tests measuring individual tempo, persistence under pressure, and variety seeking. Principal-components analysis was used to derive factors whose reliability were established on a second sample. He demonstrates that the relationships between the different parameters of activity are complex, for example, yielding a curvilinear function between tempo and variety seeking. This demonstrates the multidimensional but interactive nature of the components of activity. The EEG parameters were also subjected to factor analysis, yielding four factors. In the final stage of the work the activity variables are related to the EEG variables. Many of the loadings obtained in the final-factor table are of considerable magnitude and far exceed those obtained in Western work, even at its very best (see Rösler, 1975). Thus the strategy, supported in Zuckerman's paper, of being specific about the tasks to be correlated with other (psychometric and physiological) measures is clearly vindicated. A point made by Bodunov and by other contributors is that well-designed studies of individual differences provide an adequate data base for the construction of general models in psychology and, in this case, of brain function. It is to be hoped that workers in the West will examine studies of this nature and follow Bodunov's example, not only in terms of methodology but in terms of theoretical orientation; the concept of activity is clearly central to any model of brain function that purports to explain the constant feedback and regulatory actions that occur between the organism and its environment.

Näätänen's contribution (Chapter 3) is important in several respects. Given the ease with which evoked brain potentials may now be measured and quantified, there is little excuse for those investigators who persist in focusing on peripheral indexes which, apart from heart rate, are sluggish and nondiscriminating. He shows that by designing a series of carefully devised and logically rigorous experiments, one can show which aspects of the evoked potential are sensitive to which aspects of the task. He concludes by locating the neuronal mismatch aspect of Sokolovian neural model orienting-response (OR) theory, at the neuronal mismatch negativity (N2) stage of the evoked potential. Moreover, he suggests that at this stage of information processing, one is witnessing electrocortical events at a preconscious level. The basic paradigm involves a sequence of homogenous and repetitive stimuli among which occasional stimuli, deviant in physical characteristics, are interspersed. By taking us through the experimental sequence, he argues as follows.

The repeated stimulus sets up the neuronal model, the N2 component show a difference in amplitude. Yet in a dichotic listening task, N2 fails to differentiate attended and nonattended stimuli, although they are discriminated at P300. The first major negative deflection (N1) and N2 are different in similar style for latency. Thus he claims the N2 mismatch occurs at a preattentive level, whereas stimulus "significance" must wait for a positive deflection of P300 to show effects. He summarizes further evidence to show (a) that N2 to standards is small (thus is distinguishable from afferent input effects); (b) N2 is sensitive to stimulus omission (showing the temporal aspect of the mismatch process); (c) in contrast to N1, which shows strong generalization of habituation, N2 displays a vigorous response to slight stimulus change and also responds even when the subject misses the deviant; (d) N2 fails to distinguish misses and hits (thus is preattentive); (e) although N1 covaries with input (reducing with reduced intensity), N2 increases with any slight change; (f) N1 shows a decrement after the first stimulus, while N2 is not responsive; (g) N2 is responsive to the probability and magnitude of stimulus deviance; (h) the N2 has foci frontally and in specific sensory modality regions (raising the possibility not only of a locus of neuronal mismatch, but also of multiple-level vertical representation from hippocampus upward); and, finally, (i) a more difficult aspect to determine unequivocally, N2 is insensitive to stimulus evaluation of significance.

Näätänen argues that his techniques and the style of research study he advocates could serve rapidly to get to the heart of some of the issues that currently dominate OR research and, in particular, the controversy as to whether the stimulus has to be appraised as significant before the OR occurs. Given the temporal characteristics of the evoked potential and its power to discriminate among task parameters, it is clear that long-latency peripheral measures like heart rate and skin conductance represent merely a gross amalgamation, which in principle could never serve to discriminate among the early stages of information processing. Though Näätänen is modest in his evaluation of the evidence, a clear conclusion must be that future OR studies must include electrocortical measures as a sine qua non whatever other measures are taken. We have devoted considerable space to Näätänen's contribution because its importance should not be underestimated. It has the potential to influence future thinking even more than did his excellent and much-cited review (1975) of evoked potential studies. At the same time, the psychophysiologist must surely acknowledge that his linear model of information processing is conceptually far removed from contemporary approaches to attention, as exemplified by the Attention and Performance series.

The Näätänen paper is not addressed directly to personality research. However, as O'Gorman shows (1977), the OR and its habituation has been a popular tool for personality research, has been limited almost exclusively to noncortical measures, and has yielded equivocal results. The lesson is surely clear.

Changes in the Contingent Negative Variation (CNV) are studied by Werre (Chapter 4) in a reaction time procedure, in which several subject variables were controlled for (extraversion, action preparedness, neuroticism, and intelligence) and the data handled by means of factor analysis. He demonstrates a complex pattern of relationships that alter as a function of time in task and treatment conditions. In a second study, stimulants, sedatives and white noise were used. Both studies demonstrate the sensitivity of the CNV to a variety of conditions. Its relationships with <u>action preparedness</u> are, of course, of significance in a work devoted to activity and its part in the regulation of stimulation and feedback. This study demonstrates a number of fundamental points: (a) the relation between activation and performance is curvilinear; (b) temporal analysis is a powerful source of data in psychophysiological studies; (c) slight variations in procedure can shift relationships, even in an opposite direction; and, finally, (d) the practiced subject employs different strategies from those of the naive subject. At the same time, the study shows that multiple determinants of physiological arousal may be combined in one study and interpreted within a unitary framework. Werre reports that future studies in this newly developing field will include subjective reports as well.

The study by Danilova (Chapter 5) explores evoked potential and heart rate changes in subjects with strong and weak nervous systems (Strelau questionnaire) during the learning of temporal discrimination of light-flash stimuli. Differences are obtained in performance, basal physiological indexes, and in the interrelationships among the variables for the two groups. She interprets her findings both in terms of individual differences in the patterning of general and localized orienting responses, and in the alleged differences between subjects with strong and weak nervous systems in cognitive style (verbal and nonverbal) and arousability. Danilova adopts the strategy of repeated measures within a small experimental population, representing extreme scores for personality trait. The remarkably high correlations obtained may attest to the wisdom of this strategy. Again, this study by a Soviet worker reveals how well advanced are Soviet studies in the integration of personality, performance, and physiological measures.

Uherík (Chapter 6) sees the individual as a complex and open psychophysiological feedback system, and personality is defined in terms of characteristic modes of interaction with the environment. Activation and conscious regulation are seen as crucial and interacting features. Personality integrates these features. He reviews work at the Bratislava laboratory directed at the comparison of Russian and Western personality traits. Using skin conductance responses as a dependent variable, a number of experiments were set up comparing responses in criterion groups selected on the basis of the EPI, the MAS and other Western instruments. Experimental variables include performance under stress, stimulus-intensity judgments, sleep deprivation, transmarginal inhibition, self-stimulation and relaxation, the Stroop test, autogenic training, and hypnosis. Other studies involved schizophrenic patients in whom Uherík provided one of the first demonstrations of extreme bilateral asymmetry, foreshadowing the work of Gruzelier (1976). He summarizes many studies and provides a detailed discussion of error sources. The chapter includes a valuable bibliography which will enable the Western reader to seek out detailed procedural aspects from the original papers.

Strelau, Sosnowski and Oniszczenko (Chapter 7) report a detailed study of the effects of hypoxia and sensory deprivation on psychophysiological indexes and state anxiety. Scores on the Strelau scale and measures of trait anxiety were also included. The study demonstrates how a relatively straightforward set of questions can lead to complex data, particularly when trends over time are

considered. There is no doubt that the key experimental manipulations affected
the dependent measures: one difficulty demonstrated here is that variance attributable to <u>treatments</u> can wash out intersubject effects or, at least, interact
with them in a particularly complex fashion. The authors provide a sensitive
discussion of error sources and the problems associated with designs that call
for partitioning of novelty effects.

<u>Personality and performance</u>. In one of her two contributions to this volume,
Klonowicz (Chapter 8) draws our attention to the notion of psychological and
psychophysiological <u>costs</u>. Following Tomaszewski, she states that performance
depends on "the equilibrium between the acting subject, the task, and the working
environment." These elements have to be balanced; and in successful performance,
one aspect is compensated for by another. That is why we do not often find differences in performance between criterion groups selected for particular traits;
subjects compensate for the mismatch between temperamental characteristics and
task or situational requirements. In her own study, she confirms that subjects
selected on the basis of reactivity perform equally well. When a cost index
is devised, however, it appears that in stressful environments, high-reactive
subjects are required to exercise additional actions to maintain performance.
Thus, though her measure of <u>quality</u> differentiates conditions, but not subjects,
temperament groups are differentiated for a number of <u>operations</u> and <u>plasticity</u>
(corrective operations). This elegant and simple task demonstrates a problem
that runs through many of the experimental studies reported in this volume,
namely, that of selecting the theoretically appropriate variables for examination. Here we see that groups selected for different traits nevertheless
achieve identical outcomes, but by employing different strategies. It is the
notion of <u>cost</u> that Klonowicz refers to when she talks of "the third side of
the coin."

Studies of the relationship between individual differences and memorial processes have been greatly stimulated in the West by the publication of
M. W. Eysenck's volume, <u>Human Memory: Theory, Research and Individual Differ-
ences</u> (1977). Such work sets the scene for a rapprochement between traditional
areas of concern in experimental psychology on the one hand and psychophysiology
and individual differences on the other. Thus the chapter by Halmiová and
Šebová (Chapter 9) is likely to be received with considerable interest by
Western workers, because these authors manipulate task difficulty in working
memory in one experiment and word frequency (familiar and rare surnames) in
another, to explore memorial performance in subjects selected for strength and
weakness of the excitatory process (Strelau scales) in the first study, and a
law-of-strength reaction-time procedure in the second. Although the authors
appear to be not wholly satisfied with the outcome, their data are reminiscent
of Western studies manipulating item arousal and individual differences; strong
subjects perform better, particularly under difficult and stressful conditions.
They interpret this as a reflection of a lower working capacity in weak subjects.
Analysis of skin-conductance measures differentiates the groups as a function
of relationships between activation and performance, weak subjects being more
activated at the outset and showing a parallel change in performance and reactivity.
These studies demonstrate again the value of experiments designed to test specific
predictions against a background of established data on performance and a coherent theory.

A brief chapter by Haase (Chapter 10) focuses on the notion of stimulus overload,
providing details of his Polychronicity Scale, which measures subjective report
of experienced disturbance under intense levels of informational input. The
polychronic style is one that fails to structure action in a manner that reduces

perceived stress. He presents a number of intercorrelations between the subtests of his scale and scores on the Strelau questionnaire.

Nosal (Chapter 11) provides an empirical study of strategies used in problem solving, using a naturalistic task. Subjects are studied while they learn elementary aspects of computer programming. Temperament and scores on intelligence scale subtests are among the independent variables; the dependent variables, in relation to program initiation, checking on errors, and time scores, enable him to construct a model of the interaction between temperamental and cognitive variables to produce individual styles of information processing. The data are subjected to a sophisticated multivariate analysis, which enables Nosal to partial out different sources of variance and attribute proportions of overall variance to them. This sort of approach enables a precise measurement of style of action (see Friedensburg, Chapter 15, Volume 1) enabling the investigator to explore the microstructure of problem-solving strategies along the lines of artificial intelligence studies. He identifies three basic styles of cognitive activity, all reflecting an interaction between temperament and intellect: (a) a conservative style, characterized by delays and a concern for long-term consequences of actions; (b) an impulsive style, in which control is imposed after action; and (c) a balanced approach representing a compromise between the processes involved in (a) and (b). A characteristic of this task, which personality researchers would do well to note, is that the task, like those used by the Schönpflug group (Chapter 18), has meaning and ecological validity for the subject; thus opportunities for uncontrolled error variance in the form of subject interpretation of demand characteristics, lack of involvement, or even withdrawal of attention, are minimized. At the same time, the task is not so uncontrolled and free running that it cannot provide a basis for comparison of strategies between subjects, in spite of wide differences in their approach.

An early study of stimulus hunger in humans carried out by one of the present authors revealed how difficult it is to distinguish stimulus intensity, stimulus change, activity, and activity cost effects, without detailed parametric studies (Gale, 1969). Matysiak (Chapter 12), by using rats as subjects, is able to overcome many of the problems raised, in an economic and rigorous fashion. Of course, he cautions us against ready extrapolation to humans. His approach has an additional advantage of allowing the use of populations bred for certain characteristics. Intensity of stimulation, modality of stimulation, sensory deprivation, and sensory overload may all be studied within one design, providing answers to a number of important questions. Thus he enables us to ask (a) whether need for additional stimulation is correlated with scores for reduction of stimulation under overload (a crucial problem for many participants in the volume); (b) whether stimulation from different modality sources has equivalent effects and whether there can be cross-modality additivity; and (c) how intensity of stimulation, change within or between stimulation sources, and amount of activity incurred are interrelated (again a central issue). Because researchers of the Warsaw school, following the Pavlovian tradition, believe that temperamental characteristics are seen in nervous systems as such, the use of nonhuman species to test particular hypotheses and to find complex interrelationships is clearly justified. At the same time, Matysiak's studies provide a model for human studies that personality theorists might do well to imitate. The question must be asked whether the limits to systematic and parametric work in humans are not truly logical, technical, or ethical, but stem rather from a tradition of experimental sloppiness that reflects a zeitgeist in the history of our discipline, rather than a well-thought-out strategy. Many issues raised in this volume call for a careful accumulation of basic data, filling in all the cells logically generated by the implications of theory.

A possible basic paradigm for parametric studies is devised by Hockey (Chapter 13),

who presents an ingenious study in which subjects were tested in threes. One
subject (introvert or extravert) determined the level of noise during a vigilance
task, and the yoked subjects were one introvert and one extravert. Extraverts
chose higher levels of extraneous noise during the task, and both groups increased their call for noise as the task proceeded. Introverts performed better,
and extraverts performed worse, when paired with an introvert noise control.
Introverts were relatively unaffected by task conditions. The power of the results using this paradigm indicates that it might be developed further, for it
allows for parallel measures of performance, sensation seeking, and physiological
response. It also demonstrates nicely the effects of regulatory behavior on
arousal and efficiency and the disruptive influence of stimulus conditions
that are ill-matched to the individual characteristics of the subject. This
theme is also one take up by Klonowicz (Chapter 8).

Applied implications. Hare and Jutai (Chapter 14) preface their discussion on
sensation seeking in psychopaths with a cautionary note on problems of diagnosis
and classificaton, indicating that the then current American Psychiatric Association's Diagnostic Manual was likely to yield a high false-positive rate (more than
doubling the estimate of psychopathy in one sample, compared with the procedures
devised by Hare & Cox, 1978). Their own early procedures, on their own admission,
involve considerable experience and judgment which of course undermines their
psychometric purity. They report preliminary findings on a new 22-item checklist;
even here the reader may observe that many of the characteristics are not defined behaviorally ("glibness", "lack of sincerity"), whereas others would seem
to guarantee the reported overall correlations with global measures they report
(i.e., one item is "previous diagnosis as psychopath (or similar)"; another is
"lack of affect and emotional depth"). Hare and Jutai then review evidence for
high levels of sensation seeking in psychopaths. Again the authors express
caution, because several studies reviewed indicate statistically significant
but small correlations between scores on Sensation Seeking scales and psychopathy in prison populations. They are particularly concerned with response sets
that are adopted by prison populations. In contrast with psychometric studies,
however, experimental studies and case histories do indicate support for a model
proposed by Farley (1973) in which delinquency might result from the combination
of stimulation-seeking behavior and an absence of socially acceptable channels
for the expression of such behavior. Hare and Jutai then report studies of
coping strategies in psychopathic subjects. It is clear that the problem of
psychopathy will continue to challenge the ingenuity of both theoreticians and
experimentalists.

Two empirical studies follow that explore aspects of aggressive behavior in relation to neurotics, psychopaths, and high and low reactives. Ciarkowski and
Fraczek (Chapter 15) explore in a subtle fashion the complex interrelationships
between individual characteristics (neuroticism and psychopathy) and frustration,
exposure to aggressive stimuli, conditioning to stimuli of positive and negative
emotional value, anger, and expressed aggression. There is evidence that both
neuroticism and psychopathy modulate the interpretation of incoming stimuli
associated with aggression. Neuroticism appears to facilitate the release of
anger. Levels of psychopathy seem to interact in a complex fashion with task
conditions, since highly psychopathic subjects appeared to be impervious to
opportunities for increased aggression in the presence of stimuli that evoked
negative emotion. The authors conclude with an appeal to researchers to employ
measures that reveal cognitive mechanisms operating on the structural and dynamic
properties of interpersonal aggression. Such measurement would presumably have
to apply to several data sources: (a) reports from subjects of their response
to life situations; (b) subject responses (including social desirability effects,
as warned by Hare and Jutai) to instruments designed to measure emotional and

and psychopathic traits, and (c) cognitive evaluations of the experimental procedures per se, their demand characteristics, and, in particular, the unusual
context of procedures inviting public expression of anger and retaliatory
aggression. Studies of this nature capture the methodological and interpretative dilemmas faced by those who wish to measure emotion in the laboratory.

H. Eliasz and Reykowski (Chapter 16) provide an interesting analysis of empathy
in terms of Strelau's theory. High reactives are more susceptible to social
influence and adjust their responses to others while showing reduced adjustment
to features of the physical environment; thus their behavior is selectively tuned
to people. Such a sensitivity is presupposed by the expression of empathy toward
others. The empathic response, however, will be regulated by the degree of emotional experience perceived in another, since that determines the level of stimulation provided by another's suffering. Eliasz and Reykowski are able to make
specific predictions concerning retaliatory aggression under conditions in which
empathy is manipulated. At the same time, aggressive acts may be seen as a means
of increasing stimulation and thus provide a means of stimulus regulation for
the low reactive.

Thus, Eliasz and Reykowski predict that low reactives will not respond empathet-
ically to low levels of suffering in others. Even when empathy does occur, it
may serve to increase arousal and thus lead to increased aggression toward the
victim.

The reverse holds for high reactives, who will experience empathy at low levels
of suffering in others, and will reduce aggressive acts as a means of lowering
incoming stimulation.

Thus aggression and empathy are not seen as primary traits but as aspects of
regulation of stimulation that depend on higher-order needs.

Klonowicz, Ignatowska-Świtalska, and Wocial (Chapter 17), as in the earlier
chapter by Klonowicz (Chapter 8) provide a clear demonstration of individual
differences in strategy -- in this case, coping with stress. Hypertensive and
normal subjects are exposed to noise stress, and measures are taken of subjective activation and output of prostaglandin, adrenaline, and noradrenaline.
Again, performance of continuous arithmetic did not vary for the two groups for
correct additions, yet did vary for errors and the dynamics of errors. Hypertensives were less accurate under noise stress, making most errors at the start
of the task. Though normals decreased in perceived activation as time pro-
gressed, the reverse held for hypertensives (Thayer Deactivation Scale) who were
continuously at a higher level. Whereas healthy subjects showed increased
adrenaline, hypertensives started at a higher level and did not increase. We
select only a few of the findings here; the reader must go to the chapter for
the full discussion. A good feature of this paper is its attempt to integrate
performance, biochemical, and experiential data within one theoretical framework.

The chapters by Schönpflug and Mundelein (Chapter 18) and Shulz (Chapter 19)
are considered together here because they come from the same laboratory and are
based on a number of common conceptions and research procedures. Using a computer both to present problems and to store data concerning the subject's pattern of response, they are able to simulate realistic tasks, generate detailed
and continuous records of complex behaviors, and combine these with measures
of subjective report and physiological change. A taxonomy of actions is presented that enables the analysis of regulatory behavior. One study (Schönpflug
and Mundelein) centers on the simulation of an insurance office in which subjects
(unemployed, experienced clerical workers) are required to check insurance

claims against the claimant's file, ascertaining whether premiums have been paid,
time since the last claim, and so on. The authors are able to explore the subjects' working strategies, that is, care taken in checking work, need to refer
to stored information, rest behaviors, response under work pressure, and fatigue
over extended periods of work.

The Shulz study provides the subjects with a number of problems to be solved
and a variety of information sources with which to solve them. Again, a detailed
analysis is possible of the structuring of the subjects' performance, their responses to the task, and their reactions to stress. In both studies, high and
low reactives (measured by Strelau questionnaire) are seen to perform differently
This work clearly has an affinity of objectives with that of Nosal (Chapter 11)
and enables a rapprochement between personality theory and artificial intelligence studies, demonstrating yet again that studies of individual differences
can themselves provide a base for devising models of performance in general experimental psychology. One aspect of the work is that it generates a tremendous
quantity of data. Only a small sample is provided here; nevertheless it is more
than sufficient to tantalize the reader into further study of the work of the
Free University of Berlin group.

RECURRENT THEMES

A set of recurrent themes runs throughout these theoretical and empirical
studies.

1. Individual variation is, in part, attributable to biological factors.
2. Such factors are transmitted through genetic mechanisms.
3. There is a constant interplay between biologically determined dispositions
    and physical, biochemical, and social events.
4. The individual is seen as regulating crucial aspects of this interplay.
5. The principles of regulation are themselves derivable from the biological
    dispositions and their interaction with the external world.
6. Factors that play an important role in the regulation of behavior are
    arousal level, optimal levels of arousal, optimal levels of stimulation,
    changes in stimulation, and activity. All these constructs are in some
    sense related to the input and output of energy.
7. The dispositional variables may be tapped by use of psychometric instruments.
8. Because of the range of identified dispositional variables and because each
    person evolves within a constantly emerging feedback system, it is not ex-
    pected that there will be a simple one-to-one relation between trait vari-
    ables and behavior, even where the number of traits specified by the theory
    is limited.
9. The appropriate description of the individual will encompass behavioral,
    psychophysiological, and experiential domains of description.
10. The understanding of personality structure is impossible without considera-
    tion of dynamics; therefore experimental studies are obliged to focus on
    process as well as outcome.
11. There are no grounds for sustaining the historical division between the
    psychology of individual differences and general experimental psychology,
    nor between physiological, cognitive, and social psychological approaches.
    Indeed, the psychophysiology of individual differences has the power to
    integrate these various fields. Data derived from studies of individual
    differences may provide a base for describing general processes.
12. The examination of individual differences and the patterning of behavior
    is therefore of heuristic value in all branches of psychology.
13. In examining data derived from experiments, the investigator must be aware
    that individual differences will determine not only the patterning of

response, but the <u>individual's response to the experimental situation per se.</u>

15. It is the recognition of the biological nature of temperamental characteristics that enables a cross-mapping of constructs devised in both Western
and Eastern laboratories, and thus provides for the evolution of a common
language for the description of crucial aspects of human behavior.

CRITIQUE: AN ATTEMPT AT CONSTRUCTIVE CRITICISM

It would be an abuse of our twin roles as contributors and co-editors if we were
to appear to criticize our colleagues in their absence. All the critical points
made here were stated either in individual papers, or in the lengthy discussions
(here unpublished) that followed each paper session at the Conferences. We
attempt therefore to draw them together in a coherent fashion.

As a preliminary statement of formal requirements for theory in personality research, let us return to the criteria set out by Hall and Lindzey in the first
edition of their classic text <u>Theories of Personality</u> (1973). (a) The key
constructs of the theory should be clearly stated, as must be the domains of
behavior they seek to describe and explain. (b) Because most theories have
several key constructs, there should be interaction rules for relating the constructs, so that we might see how they interact, as well as their relative
importance in different contexts. (c) Rules are also required for translating
the constructs into observable phenomena, either in the natural world or in the
experimental context; without such empirical definitions, the theory can have
no factual basis. (d) There should be internal consistency, for an internally
inconsistent theory may be used to predict any observation. All the issues
raised by these simple requirements have been considered in this volume.

Constructs

There is a handful of constructs that clearly are crucial for contributors:
excitation, inhibition, strength, mobility, arousal, activation, regulation,
reactivity, activity, optimum arousal, anxiety, sensation seeking, dynamism,
and energy exchange. It is surely clear that if the works presented here are
to progress as an integrated endeavor, then there must first be a thoroughgoing
theoretical evaluation of these constructs, their logical limits, and their
degree of dependence or independence. Thus we really do need to know whether
workers in different laboratories are using common constructs only at the most
superficial level, whether there is true cross-mapping of meaning and content,
or whether they are talking of different entities. The investigation of this
communality of constructs must be conducted at the theoretical level before much
more empirical work is done; otherwise, the work will diverge in different directions, and an opportunity for synthesis will be lost.

Such an analysis must presuppose a detailed consideration of the internal structure of the concepts themselves. We have seen, for example, how the notion of
optimum level of arousal has been used in several ways. The optimum is viewed
as a biologically determined factor common for all individuals, or varying
between individuals, or acquired by individuals, or required by particular task
demands. At the same time arousal, activation, arousability, arousal threshold,
stress-induced arousal, and pathological states of hyperarousal or hypoarousal,
are all confounded. Thus a basic concept, which is probably referred to by all
our authors, requires urgent elucidation. This must also be true for most of
the variables to which arousal is said to relate. The temptation to oversimplify
is challenged by several of our authors, who point to the need to be specific in

the use of subscales and in the specification of conditions under which hypotheses are to be tested. Such empirical rigor is incompatible with conceptual
sloppiness.

Mind and Body

A perennial problem, and one that must be tackled by investigators who report
data on biochemistry, electrophysiology, performance, subjective report, and
psychometric scale scores, all within one study, is the challenge of interre-
lating these domains of discourse within a conceptual framework that allows for
cross-mapping or translation across the domains. It is difficult for personality
theorists with both a biological emphasis and an emphasis on information processing
and conscious regulation, to avoid the mind-body problem in its modern manifestation. These problems are hinted at in several chapters; but there is no formal
recognition of the need to tackle the logical problems that psychophysiological
approaches to personality and behavior must raise. In a sense, this may be considered by some to be the central issue in psychology; but to be close to a
central issue does not imply that we should so regulate our thinking as to
devise strategies to avoid it.

Instruments of Measurement

A good proportion of the data reported here is directly related to test scores
and intercorrelations between them, or is based on criterion groups selected
by psychometric instruments. The former are perhaps the most crucial empirical
data in the two volumes, because failure to demonstrate the validity of a scale or
failure to show strong intercorrelations with scales devised to measure allegedly
related constructs must surely cause us to stop and think. Even when intercorrelations hold in the predicted direction, they are often modest in magnitude
and account for only a small proportion of the variance. Moreover, several of
our authors, given the set of looking for corroborative data, often fail to comment on obtained correlations within their matrixes, which, according to theory,
should not occur. The principle of selectivity applies to all of us, but it
must not be allowed to distort the perceptions of scientists. Despite the
studies reported here, there is still a gap to be filled, within which all the
scales used by our contributors may be cross-related in the style of approach
adopted by Carlier (Chapter 8, Vol. 1). Again the crucial question must be,
Are we examining similar factors? And are the factors we examine themselves
valid? The multivariate, hierarchical factor structure of Royce and Powell
(Chapter 4, Vol. 1) stands in stark contrast to the two- and three-dimensional
models of many of the contributors.

Standardizing Procedures

Just as there is a need to explore systematically the nature of the theoretical
constructs employed, so also should there be an agreed taxonomy of the varying
tasks employed in different laboratories. The temptation to devise a new procedure or experimental paradigm is symptomatic for all branches of psychology;
but it does not aid comparisons between laboratories, particularly when they
are based in different countries where conventions for reporting procedural and
methodological detail seem to vary. An attempt to force all workers into a
common approach would be sterile and would stifle creativity; however, it should
be possible, at least, to provide a classification of tasks and to specify the
parameters that Laboratory A would wish to see included in studies carried out
by Laboratory B. For example, we have not thought it proper to tamper with
terminology employed by contributors; but in psychophysiology, for example, there
appears to be some agreement in the West on terminology to be used and the characteristics of devices employed to measure psychophysiological response. This is

not a tyranny, but merely an attempt to create a language of common discourse.
Similarly, Western workers would benefit from a clear explication of procedures
employed for measuring the neo-Pavlovian indexes of temperamental traits, so
that these may be incorporated in future studies.

Autonomic or Cortical Measures?

Näätänen (Chapter 3, Vol. 2) raises some fundamental issues. He suggests quite
baldly that autonomic indexes, which are typically sluggish and gross in nature,
are too far removed from central processes in both location and time to be of
much use in testing hypotheses about information processing. The cognitive element in the regulation of behavior is mentioned by several authors; thus, there
seems to be a prima facie case for focusing on the central nervous system in
our exploration of the physiological correlates of regulatory and, specifically,
cognitive strategies. Bodunov (Chapter 2, Vol. 2), Danilova (Chapter 5, Vol. 2),
Näätänen (Chapter 3, Vol. 2), Werre (Chapter 4, Vol. 2), and Farley (Chapter 3,
Vol. 1) all demonstrate how this is possible, and how rich the data may prove
to be. It is surely the brain that is the final common path for information
within the nervous system.

Appropriate Statistical Models

Nosal (Chapter 11,Vol. 2) reveals how necessary it is when dealing, as experimental personality studies do, with very many variables, to employ a multivariate
approach. The repeated use of several t tests and the accumulation of many
separate correlations is both wasteful of the parent data and an abuse of the
data sampled. In addition, when studies must be correlational, but reasonably
well-developed and coherent theory is available, greater use of quantitative
techniques of causal modeling is recommended. Use of path analysis, structural
equations, maximum likelihood methods, and analysis of covariance structures
might well be examined. Given the important role of measurement and psychometric
instrument development in this area, such technqieus as latent trait analysis,
Rasch scaling, and other important developments should be considered.

CONCLUSIONS

The preparation of this work leaves us with a sense of great optimism. We may
look forward to a revival in the fortunes of personality research, at a time
when the sense of direction has perhaps been lost for many workers in the West.
It is particularly pleasing that a basis for future work should be provided by
the meeting of minds from different cultures and the discovery of so many re-
freshingly original and productive approaches. If we have seemed unduly critical
in the foregoing section, it is only because our enthusiasm is accompanied by
caution. We believe that the program for future work, if it acknowledges some
of the difficulties to which we have referred, will surely thrive.

REFERENCES

Eysenck, H. J. (1981). General features of the model. In H. J. Eysenck (Ed.),
   A model for personality. Berlin: Springer Verlag.

Eysenck, H. J. (1967). The biological basis of personality. Springfield, IL:
   Charles C Thomas.

Eysenck, M. W. (1977). Human memory: Theory, research and individual differences.
   Oxford: Pergamon Press.

Farley, F. (1973, September). A theory of delinquency. Paper presented at the meeting of the American Psychological Association, Montreal, Canada.

Gale, A. (1969). Stimulus hunger: Individual differences in operant strategy in a button-pressing task. Behaviour Research and Therapy, 7, 265-274.

Gray, J. A. (1964). Pavlov's typology. Oxford: Pergamon Press.

Gruzelier, J. (1976). Clinical attributes of schizophrenic skin conductance responders and non-responders. Psychological Medicine, 6, 245-249.

Hall, G. S., and Lindzey, G. (1973). Theories of personality. New York: Wiley.

Hare, R. D., and Cox, D. N. (1978). Clinical and empirical conceptions of psychopathy and the selection of subjects for research. In R. D. Hare and D. Schalling (Eds.), Psychopathic behavior: Approaches to research. Chichester, NY: Wiley.

Näätänen, R. (1975). Selective attention and evoked potentials in humans. A critical review. Biological Psychology, 2, 237-307.

O'Gorman, J. (1977). Individual differences in habituation of human physio-logical responses: A review of theory, method and findings in the study of personality correlates in non-clinical populations. Biological Psychology, 5, 257-318.

Petrie, A. (1967). Individuality in pain and suffering. Chicago: University of Chicago Press.

Rösler, F. (1975). Die abhangigkeit des electroenzephalogramms von den person lichkeitsdimentionen E und N sensu Eysenck und unterscheidlich aktivierenden situationen. Zeitschrift für Experimentelle und Angewandte Psychologie, 12, 630-667.

I

THEORY AND MODEL

1

Temperament and Personality: Pavlov and Beyond

Jan Strelau

DELINEATING TEMPERAMENT AND PERSONALITY

As in most cases of psychological inquiry, it seems worthwhile to recall the ancient philosophers when considering the relation between temperament and personality. Galen -- the most remarkable physician of those times, after Hippocrates -- developed the first typology of temperament in his well-known dissertation "De temperamentis," referring to the conception of his predecessor. This very first typology is popular to this day.

Galen's phenomenal conception, stating the proportion of four "cardinal humors" that form the nature of the body and hence the physiological basis of behavioral traits, has been partially confirmed in contemporary endocrinological and psycho-pharmacological research. Hippocrates and Galen were persistent in searching for the clue to individual differences in the human psyche within the internal factors of the human body or, more precisely, in its hormonal system. Thus, their theory of temperament is a classical example of endogenic conceptions of human nature.

Ancient philosophers were also responsible for the idea that human nature depends on factors residing outside the organism. As an example of such exogenic conception, let us recall the theory of Theophrastus -- a colorful description of types of human behavior (types of personality as we would refer to them today) -- presented under the distinctive title of "Characters."

Although undoubtedly much simplified, popular opinion still holds that individual differences in behavior, determined by physiological factors of the organism, belong to the sphere of temperament, and that the typical behavior exhibited by a person and determined by external conditions is denoted by personality.

This view has also been emphatically upheld by Pavlov, the author of a popular conception of nervous system types. Pavlov's typology, most fully and consistently presented in "general types of higher nervous activity in animal and man" (Pavlov, 1952),[1] is well known (see Gray, 1964; Nebylitsyn, 1972; Strelau,

---

The research reported here was supported by the Polish Academy of Sciences, Grant 11.8.

[1]Quotations from Pavlov's works are taken from the Polish translation, since this was the only version available.

1975, 1983) and requires no comment.   This chapter refers to some of its aspects of direct relevance to the problem.   In his description of the properties
of the nervous system -- strength, mobility, and balance of nervous processes
(their combination forming the type of nervous system) -- Pavlov maintained that
his four types of nervous system correspond to the classical four types of temperament as defined by Hippocrates and Galen.   Being strongly influenced by
those philosophers, Pavlov assumed that the types of nervous system established
in animal research can be extended to the human race.   "The mentioned types are
what we call temperament in humans" (Pavlov, 1952, p. 389).   Pavlov stated ex-
plicitly that the type of nervous system is innate and barely susceptible to
environmental or rearing influences; he called it genotype.[2] Instead, phenotype
was believed by Pavlov to correspond to character, as meant by psychologists.
As argued by Pavlov (1952, p. 594):

> From the moment an animal is born, it is subject to a variety of
> environmental influences to which it must respond by certain actions,
> and those actions often become ultimately consolidated for the rest
> of the animal's life -- therefore, the ultimate type of the animal's
> nervous activity is a composition of the properties of its type and
> changes elicited by the environment -- it is the phenotype, the
> character.

In conclusion, temperament, according to Pavlov, is the innate type of the nervous system or, putting it mildly, the typical behavioral traits of a person
that are conditioned by the innate type of his nervous system.   Character is,
in a way, a result of the influence of external factors on the innate type of
the nervous system.   If we identify external factors with environment in its
broadest sense, including the physical environment, then we must say that character, according to Pavlov, is a property of humans as well as of animals, even
at low phylogenetic levels.   Such a definition of character is at variance with
the idea of psychologists at the time of Pavlov, who treated character as a
typically human property.

Pavlov's views on temperament and character and their interrelationship had a
large impact on Soviet psychology.   For instance, Teplov and his followers,
being strongly attached to the Pavlovian notion of the innate nature of the basic
nervous system properties (strength, mobility, and balance), demanded that these
traits were to be investigated so as to distinguish the innate from the acquired
(Nebylitsyn, 1972; Teplov, 1961).   According to Teplov and Nebylitsyn, laboratory
research based primarily on measurement of psychophysiological or conditioned-
reflex reactions was the right method.

Rubinstein (1946), the leading postwar Soviet psychologist, as well as other
Soviet psychologists (e.g., Levitov, 1969; Merlin, 1973) conceived of temperament as the dynamic aspect of personality.   Unfortunately, they never arrived
at a precise definition of dynamism.   Still, it was most often understood as
strength and speed of reaction, which were, by the way, used even by Wundt (1911)
for distinguishing four types of temperament, his classification stemming from
the study of emotions.

The prevailing opinion in Soviet psychology, formed mostly under the influence of
Pavlov and current even today, says that the innate type of the nervous system
constitutes the physiological basis of temperament.   Personality is more and more

---

[2]Pavlov's concept of genotype, comprising innate traits in addition to hereditary
ones, is inconsistent with the definition of Johannsen accepted in genetics.
The same concerns phenotype, conceived by Pavlov as character, no matter how we
would define character.

often (recently even unequivocally) conceived by Soviet psychologists (e.g., Leontev, 1975; Shorokhova, 1974) as a product of external conditions of a specific character, namely social conditions. In fact, such an opinion is becoming more and more popular among personality theorists (see Reykowski, 1977). For this, if for no other reason, they strongly reject conceptions of temperament that point at the hereditary or innate nature of temperamental traits and, at the same time, relate them to the content, the goals of behavior. A crass example is Kretschmer's typology of temperament and the even more extreme constitutional typology of Conrad (1963), who says that the variety of body structure and the relation between body structure and temperament in man can be explained only by referring to specific dominant genes, determining the type of body structure and related temperamental traits. Another conception of this kind is Sheldon's typology of temperament, once popular in the USA.

Investigators like Thurstone (1951) or Guilford (Guilford & Zimmerman, 1956), known as authors of tools for measuring temperament, treated properties that definitely develop under the influence of social conditions also as temperamental. For instance, we can mention Guilford's objectivity, friendliness, and personal relations, listed among other traits as temperamental.

Such a situation made a majority of personality psychologists discard conceptions of temperament, which in this form not only held back progress in the science of psychology, but also did a great deal of harm, serving, for example, as a pseudoscientific legitimation of racist attitudes.

Certainly, personality psychologists cannot ignore the fact that people do differ when it comes to various behavioral traits that can be no more considered a matter of physiology and yet can hardly be treated as a product of social-historical conditions. Thus, new concepts have emerged, for example, the dynamic aspect of personality, the intensity dimension of behavior, individual differences in activation level, and biologically conditioned personality dimensions. The last one seems to comprise such dimensions as extraversion-introversion, neuroticism, anxiety, and sensation seeking. These dimensions are often discussed at meetings and in books under this kind of title (e.g., Mangan, 1982; Nebylitsyn & Gray, 1972; Powell, 1979).

If we assume, in accordance with the common tradition in psychology, that personality is a typically human phenomenon (Latin persona -- actor's face, mask, character, person) and a product of conditions that are specific for human development (i.e., social-historical conditions), then the previously mentioned dimensions hardly can be treated as personality ones, for they exist in animals, too. They are, in a way, a product of biological evolution, which certainly does not mean that such dimensions as extraversion-introversion, neuroticism, anxiety, or sensation seeking cannot acquire a different content in humans. Their determination is not purely by the physical environment alone; the social environment also undoubtedly modifies these dimensions, making them more complex as well.

Yet they are largely determined by the functioning of certain mechanisms that exist in humans as well as in other animals. And so, Eysenck assumes the reticular formation-cortex loop to be the basic mechanism of the extraversion-introversion dimension. The limbic system is presumed by this author to underly the neuroticism dimension (Eysenck, 1967). Referring to Hull's conception, Spence (1960) explained the formation of trait anxiety by pointing to the physiological mechanism responsible for the speed (facility) of conditioning to negative stimuli. Recently, the limbic system and, particularly, the neurohormones operating in this system (catecholamines, norepinephrine, and dopamine) have been indicated by Zuckerman (1979) as factors that, operating together, determine sensation seeking.

If these dimensions of behavior, which have a large physiological component and are a result of biological evolution, were considered an aspect of temperament, whereas all the traits (mechanisms) that are mostly a product of social-historical conditions were to be included under personality, as proposed by Leontev (1975), then we would avoid much misunderstanding in psychology.

Certainly, when we speak of temperament as a psychological phenomenon resulting from biological evolution, we do not mean that it is stable or independent of external factors. On the contrary, there is no trait or behavior that would not result from the interaction of hereditary and environmental factors. There can be no doubt, however, that for temperament, the hereditary and particularly the innate physiological properties of the organism, determining the energy level, are important. However, these properties develop and change under the influence of the environment (e.g., nutrition, temperature, and noise). Of course, such changes never occur in a rapid, dynamic way. Once they take place, they usually remain stable for some time.

NERVOUS SYSTEM PROPERTIES AND BIOLOGICALLY BASED PERSONALITY DIMENSIONS

Dimensions of behavior such as extraversion-introversion, neuroticism, anxiety, and sensation seeking are very close to the concept of temperament, conceived as a result of biological evolution, or may even form temperament. Thus, comparative studies on the relation between particular nervous system properties (as distinguished by Pavlov, mainly strength of excitation) and the behavior dimensions (investigated mostly by West European and American psychologists) began to attract interest in the mid-1960s.

Even Pavlov, in studies of nervous system type in dogs, found that one mode of behavior that makes the weak type differ from the strong one is fearfulness and cowardice. The weak type often shows the passive-defensive reflex, i.e., fear, marking its whole behavior.

In the 1940s and 1950s, new studies appeared, based on laboratory research on dogs (Kolesnikov, 1953; Krushinsky, 1947) indicating that the absence of the passive-defensive reflex is, in nearly all cases, a property of the strong type. References to the relation between nervous system strength and anxiety level can be found also in other works (see Marton & Urban, 1966; Nebylitsyn, 1959). A theoretical analysis justifying such a relation is contained in one of my earlier papers (Strelau, 1969).

The question of the relation between nervous system strength and extraversion-introversion was posed for the first time at the International Congress of Psychology in Moscow in 1966 (Eysenck, 1966). Referring to the physiological bases of the two dimensions and to their indexes, Eysenck suggested that extraversion corresponds to the strong nervous system type, whereas a weak system is typical of introverts. Ever since, the number of studies on the relation between traits of nervous system type, especially strength, and behavior dimensions has been growing (see Mangan, 1982; Strelau, 1969, 1970, 1983).

Several studies on the relationships among extraversion-introversion, neuroticism, and strength of nervous system have been conducted by Mangan and co-workers (Mangan, 1967c; Mangan & Farmer, 1967; Paisey & Mangan, 1979); the results, however, are not unequivocal. Besides, Mangan also presented some evidence for an interrelation between strength and mobility of nervous processes on the one hand, and sensation seeking (Paisey & Mangan, 1979), activation level (White & Mangan, 1972), and flexibility (Mangan, 1967b, 1967c, 1978), on the other.

Also, in the present book, the reader will find studies concerned with a comparative analysis of particular nervous system properties (according to Pavlov) and
other dimensions of behavior (see Carlier and Gilliland in this volume and Haase
in Volume 2).

In the past 15 years, we obtained data in our laboratory that illustrate the
relationships among excitation strength, inhibition strength, mobility, and
balance of nervous processes on the one hand, and extraversion-introversion,
neuroticism (both dimensions measured by Eysenck's MPI), and anxiety level
(measured by Taylor's MAS or Spielberger's STAI) on the other. Basic nervous
system properties were measured by Strelau's Temperament Inventory (STI) (see
Strelau, 1972a, 1983). Our findings are presented in Table 1.

TABLE 1. Basic Nervous System Properties Measured by Strelau's Temperament
Inventory, and Extraversion-Introversion, Neuroticism, and Level of Anxiety

Reference [a]	Behavior dimension		
	Extraversion-Introversion	Neuroticism	Anxiety [b]
	Excitation strength		
1	.444***	-.378***	-.481***
2	.476***	-.557***	-.554***
3	.381***	-.538***	-.617***
4	.504***	-.442***	-.467***
5	.548***	-.426***	-.394**
6	.349***	-.504***	--
	Strength of inhibition		
1	-.080	-.246**	-.202*
2	.028	-.526***	-.359***
3	.052	-.588***	-.581***
4	.160	-.496***	-.489***
5	.156	-.545***	-.332*
6	.165	-.396**	--

	Mobility of nervous processes		
1	.694***	-.174	-.177
2	.652***	.215*	.289**
3	.563***	-.209*	-.282**
4	.536***	-.141	-.226*
5	.448***	-.173	-.224
6	.517***	.296*	

	Balance of nervous processes		
1	.350***	-.080	-.190*
3	.356***	.108	.002
4	-.413*	.112	.043
5	-.504***	-.020	.140

[a] 1. Strelau (1983), Ns (males and females are as follows, by behavior dimension columns:

    Excitation strength: 171, 169, and 148.

    Strength of inhibition: 183, 178, and 159.

    Mobility of nervous processes: 178, 177, and 157.

    Balance of nervous processes: 199, 197, and 200.

2. Strelau (1970), N = 159 males and females.

3. Terelak (1974), N = 115 males.

4. Zarzycka (1980),   N = 174 males.

5. Zarzycka (1980),   N = 59 males.

6. Ciosek & Oszmiańczuk (1974), N = 70 males.

[b] Anxiety levels for References 1–3 were measured by Taylor's MAS; for References 4–6 by Spielberger's STAI = X2.

*p < .05

**p < .01

***p < .001

Even a cursory examination of Table 1 reveals certain regularities that can be summarized as follows. All six studies provided positive correlations (ranging from .349 to .548) between excitation strength and extraversion. These findings concur with Eysenck's (1966) hypothesis.

Furthermore, all studies indicated a negative correlation between excitation strength and anxiety (ranging from -.394 to -.617). As mentioned before, research on dogs has shown that the weak type exhibits a high level of anxiety. Thus, our findings have fully confirmed our expectations.

The fact that level of anxiety and neuroticism are positively correlated is well known. Thus, the negative relation between neuroticism and excitation strength (-.378 to -.557) should not be surprising.

If we consider the relation between strength of inhibition and the behavioral dimensions in question, we must admit that the results virtually suggest the lack of a relation between extraversion-introversion and inhibition strength. I have already pointed out that conditioned inhibition according to Pavlov (such inhibition is meant here when speaking of inhibition strength) differs from Eysenck's conception of inhibition (Strelau, 1970). That makes the lack of correlation between the two variables more understandable.

Comparing inhibition strength with anxiety level and neuroticism, we find that the coefficients are negative in both cases, with no exception, and have a similar value ranging from -.202 to -.588. Thus, the regularity observed in the case of excitation strength has reappeared here. But to explain the negative correlation between inhibition strength and anxiety level, and between inhibition strength and neuroticism, we need more extensive investigations -- the fact of positive correlation between excitation and inhibition strength is not sufficient.

Mobility of nervous processes correlated with extraversion positively (.448 - .692) in all studies. The correlation coefficients are highest among all those reported. In our early studies (Strelau, 1969) the relation was likewise quite conspicuous, reaching the value of r = .669. As far as I know, the relation between mobility of nervous processes and extraversion has never been theoretically analyzed. The task is also difficult at the physiological level, because so far we have not got at the core of the physiological mechanism of mobility. Considering, however, that mobility is behaviorally manifested mainly in the capability of reacting quickly and adequately to changing conditions, it can be assumed that this property is present in people who are externally oriented, that is, focused on events occurring in the environment. Such orientation corresponds to extravertive patterns of behavior. Perhaps the two properties can also be linked in that persons with high mobility of nervous processes show a pronounced need of stimulation resulting from changes of surroundings, conditions, and behavior. As we know, extraverts require more stimulation than do introverts (Zuckerman, 1979).

A comparison of mobility of nervous processes with neuroticism and anxiety level (Table 1) does not give grounds for far-reaching conclusions. In either case our studies have revealed, with one exception, low negative correlations. The relation between balance of nervous processes and extraversion-introversion seems to be the least clear one. In two studies, significant and moderately high positive correlations have been obtained, whereas in two other studies, even higher, but negative, correlations have been found. These results are not conclusive.

The comparison of balance of nervous processes on the one hand, and neuroticism and anxiety level on the other, has produced negative results; these variables appeared to be virtually unrelated.

Having acquainted the reader with some dependencies between broadly understood temperamental traits, I shall now present the conception of temperament developed in our laboratory in the past 15 years. Then, we shall return to the main problem -- the relation between temperament and personality.

THE CONCEPT OF TEMPERAMENT

We assume that temperament is a set of formal, relatively stable traits revealed in the energy level of behavior and in the temporal characteristics of reaction. We use the term formal traits to show that temperament as such has no content and that it does not determine the content of behavior in a direct way. That does not rule out the possibility of indirect influences.

As one of the regulative mechanisms of behavior, temperament is manifested in all kinds of reactions (actions) independent of their direction or content. As conditioned by structural and functional properties of a person, it affects the course of action by determining, alone or together with other factors, the energy level and the temporal characteristics of action.

In our research, we paid heed mostly to the energy level of behavior: it seems that the temperamental features related to this aspect of behavior bear a special impact on human activity.

The growing concern with the energy level of human behavior, particularly with relatively stable individual differences in this respect, stems mostly from the fact that the conditions of life as molded by our civilization frequently give rise to situations of highly stimulating qualities (overload, deprivation, monotony, and various kinds of stress). The individual trait influencing the way the same objective settings are perceived as more or as less stimulating seems to be an important regulator of human actions, especially in extreme situations. It is responsible for the variability of responses to such situations, revealed in the mode of behavior and in efficiency.

The property termed as the energy level of behavior includes all the traits delineated by individual differences in physiological mechanisms responsible for the energy level of an organism -- for the accumulation as well as the release of stored energy. These physiological mechanisms include certain features of the endocrine system; the autonomic nervous system; the nervous centers located in the brain stem (and especially the reticular activating system); and, finally, properties of the cortex, which collaborates with lower nervous centers and with the endocrine system in the process of regulating the level of excitation. As has been indicated elsewhere (Strelau, Klonowicz & Eliasz, 1972), these systems, being closely conjugated, operate as a unit, possessing a fairly stable structure. Through mutual influence, these systems delineate the features of behavior comprised by temperament. It should be stressed, however, that persons differ in the level of functioning of each system within the unit, which is the cause of well-known and widely described partial differences observed in particular temperamental traits (Nebylitsyn, 1972b; Strelau, 1972b).

One may distinguish two basic temperamental features when the energy level of behavior is considered, namely: reactivity and activity of behavior. Reactivity in a person is marked by a relatively stable and typical intensity of response to stimuli. To measure this property, the intensity or the magnitude of an individual response is estimated by comparing it with the intensity of reactions of other persons to the same stimulus. It is assumed here that the administered stimulus has a similar value for each person, or else is neutral. We conceive reactivity described thus as a dimension. It extends from extreme sensitivity (sensory, emotional) to resistance or efficiency, understood here as similar to

Pavlov's concept of nervous system strength, that is, the capability of responding adequately to high-intensity, or long-term, or repetitive stimulation
(Pavlov, 1952). As studies on nervous system strength carried out by Soviet
psychologists (Teplov & Nebylitsyn, 1963) indicate, there is a relatively stable
relationship between sensitivity and efficiency.

The weaker the stimulus that elicits a perceptible response (the higher the sensitivity) and the weaker the stimulus that starts to lower efficiency (the lower
the resistance), the higher is an individual's reactivity; conversely, a low-
reactive person is marked by low sensitivity and high resistance.

Without delving into the details of the physiological mechanism of reactivity,
we can say that, in highly reactive people, this mechanism reinforces stimulation. That is, certain stimuli received from outside as well as inside the
organism evoke stronger responses in these persons in comparison to weakly reactive persons. According to Matysiak (1980), highly reactive people are marked
by a high stimulation processing coefficient (SPC). In low-reactive people, on
the other hand, this physiological mechanism suppresses stimulation, which
means that stimuli of given strength elicit in them a lesser reaction than
in high-reactive people. In other words, weakly reactive people have a low SPC.
Coefficient values denoting the physiological mechanism of energetic stimulation
processing are most likely distributed according to a Gaussian curve. Therefore,
we speak of a high versus low SPC, to emphasize the difference
respect between individuals (groups).

Besides reactivity, a second feature is distinguished, associated with the behavioral energy level. This property is activity, whereby individuals vary in
the intensity or frequency of different kinds of tasks they undertake. To
clarify this trait, we shall invoke the concept of optimal activation introduced by Hebb (1955) and initially incorporated into our theory by Eliasz (1974).
According to this concept, a person supplies himself with stimuli until he
attains an optimal level of arousal. A person who is excessively stimulated,
however, undertakes activities to reduce this arousal to an optimal level.
Maintenance of such a level becomes a kind of need that develops in ontogenesis.
Disturbance of the equilibrium in this respect elicits in the person the motivation to act in such a way as to ensure (provide or maintain) an optimal level
of activation.

The sources of stimulation evoking a certain degree of excitation may be various,
for example, situations, tasks, and surroundings. Stimulations can also result
from the person's own reactions and behavior -- on the basis of the well-known
mechanism of feedback afferentiation. Behavior that arouses certain emotions
for the performed action itself possesses a particular stimulating capacity,
since the factor evoking a state of excitation is the emotional process accom-
panying a given action. Activities thus may be a source of stimulation chiefly
because they generate certain emotions, which in turn directly elicit a certain
state of activation. Activities that carry threats of various intensity are a
good illustration here -- the magnitude of threat evokes certain emotional
tension.

Reactive persons, in whom the physiological mechanism is marked by a high SPC,
have a low need of stimulation required for attaining optimal activation. On
the other hand, less reactive persons, having a low SPC, provide themselves with
a larger number of stimuli to maintain the optimal level of activation, and thus
they show a high need of stimulation.

Therefore, highly reactive people avoid situations and activities that bring
along strong stimulation, whereas less reactive persons undertake activities
and look for situations that possess a high stimulating capacity. In consequence,

weakly reactive people are generally more active, and highly reactive ones show lowered activity. This statement seems to be confirmed by results obtained by Sosnowski (1978) in his study of verbal activity of persons with varied reactivity in small, task-oriented groups.

The activity of a person is initially nonspecific in character; only later, as a result of certain environmental influences, does it become directed. Still, the direction (content) of activity is not related to the level of a person's reactivity.

Studies on rats carried out at our laboratory by Matysiak (1979) provide evidence suggesting that regularity concerning the relation of level of activity to reactivity is confined to activities that produce stimulation in a direct way (through feedback afferentiation or by generating emotions). It appears that highly reactive individuals may manifest a great deal of activity in their behavior, providing the goal of their activity is to reduce or avoid stimulation. In such cases, as Matysiak says, positively oriented activity (stimulation seeking) or negatively oriented activity (stimulation avoidance) occurs.

A discussion of the relation of reactivity to activity of behavior, as well as a detailed presentation of the theoretical approach including a temporal characteristic of behavior and indication of how our concept of reactivity relates to the Pavlovian strength of the nervous system can be found elsewhere (Strelau, 1974, 1983).

BASIC RELATIONS BETWEEN TEMPERAMENT AND PERSONALITY

With a few exceptions (e.g., Thomas & Chess, 1977; Thomas, Chess & Birch, 1968), the psychological literature does not provide any evidence on the relations and dependencies between temperament, meant as a result of biological evolution, and personality, conceived as a result of social-historical conditions that affect an individual. The problem attracted our interest many years ago. Some generalizations we arrived at in this respect are presented necessarily in a brief form. The more inquisitive reader is referred to more extensive works (Eliasz, 1974; Strelau, 1978, 1983).

As we believe, the relation between temperament defined in the preceding section and personality reveals itself in at least four ways.

From the day a child is born, his temperamental traits affect his family environment, mainly his mother, or father, or others taking care of him, thus modifying their behavior. At first, these traits appear in a very primitive form, such as intensity and duration of crying and laughing and more or less expansive motor activity. These yet primitive forms of responding are not indifferent to people in the child's environment, who devote more or less time to the child, depending on the intensity and duration of his reactions; the caretaker responds in a calm way or with irritation and shows positive or negative attitudes toward the child. All these reactions of the family environment are not without meaning for the development of the child's personality, as has been persuasively demonstrated by Thomas and Chess.

In the course of development, temperamental traits start to reveal themselves in more and more complex and diverse reactions, inciting others to interact with the child in accordance to the type of his temperament. This regularity can be presented as follows:

$$T \rightarrow E \rightarrow P \tag{1}$$

which means that the individual's temperament (T) induces changes in the environment (E), which in turn has certain consequences for the development of the individual's personality (P).

Temperament may also affect personality development in that any environment (having objectively a common value) gains a specific, subjective value for an individual possessing certain temperamental traits. For instance, a person showing a high sensitivity and low efficiency will react to the same difficulties, obstacles, and other people's behavior, differently from a person who is highly efficient and hence not overly sensitive. The fact that temperamental traits have a modifying effect on environmental influences cannot be insignificant in personality development. This modified influence of the environment with respect to temperamental traits becomes more comprehensible if one considers the conception of <u>situation</u>. "Each situation," states Tomaszewski (1977, p. 18), "is delineated by its component elements, their features, the state of particular elements at a given moment, and by mutual relations that exist between the elements at the moment, in the first place." A person's state (mental and physical) and all the traits that at the moment codetermine the variability of behavior, can be an element of a situation. A person's temperament is an element, too. It modifies the environment (remaining objectively the same) according to individual differences in this respect.

This regularity is illustrated by studies conducted by Merlin and his collaborators on the effect of negative grades on the behavior of pupils differing in strength of nervous system. Merlin (1955) found that pupils with a strong nervous system (equivalent to low reactivity on the basis of indexes) react to negative grades with high arousal and behavior leading to improvement of schoolwork. In contrast, pupils with a weak nervous system (equivalent to high reactivity) in the same situation (response to low grades), withdraw and tend to give up further activity. This difference in response to low grades in pupils differing in nervous system type (reactivity) was borne out in later studies (Utkina, 1964).

This relation between temperament and personality can be presented as follows:

$$E \rightarrow T \rightarrow P \tag{2}$$

The environment (E) may differ in its effect on individuals, depending on their temperamental traits (T), which in turn indirectly affects the formation of personality (P).

The relation between temperament and personality that has attracted considerable interest in our laboratory and that has been backed up by empirical evidence is the relation involving the activity of a person -- the modulator of stimulation demand as related directly to reactivity. In accordance with the level of reactivity, which determines stimulation demand, a person undertakes activities or prefers surroundings to make the current level of activation come closer to the optimal one. The choice of activities or surroundings with specific stimulating qualities is important for personality development. The regularity can be presented as follows:

$$T \rightarrow A_B \rightarrow P \tag{3}$$

which means that temperamental traits (T) determine activity (A) aimed, among others, at modulating stimulation by choice of adequate activity (B) or environment (E). These preferences of activities and environment, acquiring some stability in the course of ontogenesis, affect personality development (P).

Finally, the fourth relation between temperament and personality runs in the opposite direction. Namely, traits or mechanisms of personality (P), independently

of their content or superior regulative function, may become a source of stimulation (S) and thus may indirectly affect the temperamental traits (T) of a
person:

$$P \;\rightarrow\; S \;\rightarrow\; T \hspace{6cm} (4)$$

Because personality traits are, in fact, secondary to temperament in terms of
time, the regularity shown in Equation 4 cannot be easily verified by empirical
means.

EMPIRICAL VERIFICATION

For reasons of space, our evidence on the relation between temperament and personality is presented in rough outline only. The bulk of our research is concerned with the third type of relationship between temperament and personality,
where a person's demand for stimulation as determined by his or her temperamental traits is met by repeating activities or choosing situations that eventually
result in the consolidation of certain mechanisms or dimensions of personality.
Five experiments are briefly described here.

Self-Regulation Style

The first experiment aimed at examining this relation was conducted by Eliasz
(1974), who tested the relationship between self-regulation style conceived
according to Nuttin (1965) and reactivity level. Eliasz hypothesized that
people with low reactivity will prefer so-called active self-regulation styles,
whereas those with high reactivity will prefer passive styles.

Active self-regulation was conceived as a process of bringing about changes by
the organism itself, leading to reduction of the discrepancy between the organism and the environment. This is manifested in behavior requiring active improvement of one's abilities or leading to a modification of the environment.
The opposite type of behavior was thought to manifest itself in passive self-
regulation.

In Eliasz's experiment, realistic goals and their successful and persistent pursuit were adopted as indexes of active self-regulation, whereas the indexes of
passive self-regulation were excessive or depressed aspirations in comparison
to the person's potentialities and low effectiveness and lack of perseverance
in their realization. Reactivity was measured by means of STI. The results
supported the author's hypotheses. The relationship failed to reach statistical
significance only in the case of level of aspirations.

Level of Aspiration

Outside of our laboratory, Król (1977) studied the relation between nervous
system strength as measured by Kraepelin's modified test[3] and level of aspiration; his results (obtained from 121 subjects: 37 male and 84 female) have confirmed Eliasz's hypotheses. Level of aspiration was measured, among others, in
a game requiring skill. Working with the goal divergency index (difference
between level of aspiration and previous performance), Król found people with
a strong nervous system (i.e., low-reactive) to show high goal consistency
(lack of divergency). Weak individuals (highly reactive) exhibited goal

---

[3]This task was adopted in one of my experiments on the phenomenon of partial
 nervous system traits (see Strelau, 1969) for measuring nervous system strength.

divergency either in a positive (excessive aspiration) or negative form (depressed aspiration).

Preference of Value Versus Likelihood

In an experiment conducted by Kozłowski (1977) we were concerned with the relation between level of reactivity and safe and risky attitudes as indicated by preference of value versus likelihood of winning in a decision game involving uncertainty. The hypothesis was that low-reactive persons will prefer value to likelihood (risky attitude), whereas highly reactive people will prefer likelihood to value (safe attitude).[4]

A risky situation is a source of emotional tension; it raises activation and leads to a higher intensity of stimulation. That is why low-reactive persons prefer risk. The opposite is true for highly reactive people, who avoid situations of risk and thus do not have to experience such high emotional tension.

Activity level was measured in this study by Strelau's STI. Risk preference was determined experimentally on the overall score in five different decision games (e.g., card games and roulette). The likelihood of winning ranged in each game from 1 in 6 to 5 in 6. The study consisted of two series differing only in the winnings. Two extreme groups (36 highly reactive and 36 low-reactive subjects) participated in the study, being selected from a larger group of 144 men (aged 18-21 years). The results revealed that the low-reactive group comprised more risky persons, while the conservatives predominated in the highly reactive group. In the first series, where the stakes were lower, this was just a tendency ($\alpha < .10$), whereas in the second series, where the stakes were higher, the predominance of risky versus conservative subjects in the two groups was statistically significant ($\alpha < .05$).

Resistance to Group Pressure

There is evidence to show that inconsistency of information input with expectancies is a source of emotional tension (Festinger, 1957; Reykowski, 1974). Therefore, it can be assumed that highly reactive people organize their activities to avoid larger inconsistencies of this kind, or that they at least try to reduce it as much as possible. The opposite tendency would be expected in low-reactive people who, due to their high stimulation demand, would have no reason to avoid situations of inconsistency between their own expectancies and information input.

The dependency between tolerance to inconsistency of information input with cognitive expectancies and temperamental traits has been investigated in an experiment conducted by Białowąs. A situation of group pressure was arranged. Yielding to group pressure was adopted as a measure of conformist attitude, and resistance to such pressure was adopted as an index of independency (see Strelau, 1983).

Proceeding from the assumption of the stimulating capacity of dissonance, we hypothesized that highly reactive people would tend to submit to group pressure

---

[4]Besides reactivity we measured stimulation requirement, just as in the studies conducted by Eliasz (1974). A high stimulation requirement was indicated by low reactivity and low neuroticism as measured by the MPI. Low stimulation requirement was indicated by high reactivity and high neuroticism. This measure of stimulation requirement was first used by Eliasz (1974), where the reader will find a more detailed justification.

(conformists), and low-reactive people would rather resist group opinions, such resistance favoring the development of an independent attitude. Using the STI, Białowąs selected 24 highly reactive and 25 low-reactive subjects from a group of 148 women (aged 18-21 years). The two groups were examined to measure their resistance to group pressure in a situation resembling Asch's classical experiment. The women evaluated eight pictures of a child's face. Yielding to group pressure was indicated by agreeing with group opinion in six cases. In addition, state and trait anxiety were measured with Spielberger's STAI, among others.

The results revealed that there were more highly reactive people than low-reactive ones among those yielding to group pressure ($\alpha < .01$). Furthermore, highly reactive, submissive persons exhibited significantly less state anxiety than did resistant people. This is indirect evidence that resistance to group pressure carries more emotional tension. Highly reactive people, no matter whether they yielded, experience more anxiety in the experimental situation than low-reactive persons ($\alpha < .001$). If state of anxiety were to be regarded as a measure of psychophysiological cost, then one could say that highly reactive people had to pay more than did low-reactive subjects for being in the experimental situation. In conclusion, the results confirmed our expectations.

Machiavellian Attitude

In the experiment conducted by Mirkowska (1976) we were interested in the relation between reactivity level on the one hand and the Machiavellian attitude, revealed in the tendency to deliberately manipulate others, and facility of reducing such an attitude in others.

According to Christie and Geis (1970), the two extremes of the Machiavellian attitude can be described as follows:

1. The cool syndrome is typical of strong Machiavellian tendencies. It comprises such traits as resistance to social infleunce and external pressures, high ability to function efficiently in situations evoking emotional tension, and the tendency to initiate and control situations.

2. The soft-touch syndrome is typical of weak Machiavellian tendencies. It comprises susceptibility to social influence, submittance to the pressures of others, concentration on the partner of interaction, tendency to submit to the demand of a situation, and activity that does not go beyond certain accepted rules.

In this study, aimed primarily at investigating the influence of sensitivity training in reducing the Machiavellian attitude, a hypothesis was set up that the cool syndrome would be more frequently found in low-reactive people, whereas the soft-touch syndrome would be more frequent in highly reactive persons. In the light of our earlier arguments about reactivity, these hypotheses seem quite justified.

The results obtained on a group of 47 executives aged 22-45 years supported our expectations. It turned out that among 12 highly reactive people, selected on the basis of the quarter deviation of STI scores, there were significantly more individuals with weak Machiavellian tendencies ($\alpha < .005$), while among 12 low-reactive subjects, those with strong Machiavellian tendencies predominated. Machiavellian tendencies were measured by the Mach IV and Mach V scales developed by Christie.

Recapitulating, we believe that the concept of temperament, though often abandoned in psychology, mostly because of the constitutional-typological tradition of investigating this phenomenon, is clearly justified. Temperament, being an effect of biological evolution, has a specific denotation of its own and cannot be reduced to the concept of personality. The latter concept is more and more often viewed by psychologists as an outcome of social-historical conditions. There are specific interrelations between temperament and personality conceived in this way. A closer examination of these relationships must be undertaken if we want to explore the nature of temperament and to discover the optimal conditions of personality development.

REFERENCES

Christie, R., & Geis, F. (1970). Studies in Machiavelianism. New York & London: Academic Press.

Ciosek, M., & Oszmiańczuk, J. (1974). Właściwości procesów nerwowych a ekstrawersja i neurotyzm. (Nervous system properties and extraversion and neuroticism). Przeglad Psychologiczny, 17, 235-246.

Conrad, K. (1963). Der Konstitutionstypus. Theoretische Grundlegung und praktische Bestimmung (2nd ed.). Berlin: Springer Verlag.

Eliasz, A. (1974). Temperament a osobowość (Temperament and personality). Wroclaw: Ossolineum.

Eysenck, H. J. (1966). Conditioning, introversion of extraversion and the strength of the nervous system. Paper presented at the meeting of the International Congress of Psychology, Moscow.

Eysenck, H. J. (1967). The biological basis of personality. Springfield, IL: Charles C Thomas.

Festinger, L. (1957). A theory of cognitive dissonance. Stanford, CA: Stanford University Press.

Gray, J. A. (1964). Pavlov's typology. Oxford: Pergamon Press.

Guilford, J. P., & Zimmerman, W. S. (1956). Fourteen dimensions of temperament. Psychological Monographs, 70, 10, 1-26.

Hebb, D. O. (1955). Drives and the CNS (conceptual nervous system). Psychological Review, 62, 243-254.

Kolesnikov, M. S. (1953). Material on the description of the weak type of nervous system. Trudy Instituta Fiziologii im. I. P. Pavlova, 2, 120-135 (in Russian).

Kozłowski, C. (1977). Demand for stimulation and probability preferences in gambling decisions. Polish Psychological Bulletin, 8, 67-73.

Król, T. Z. (1977). The relation between nervous system strength and aspiration level. Polish Psychological Bulletin, 8, 99-105.

Krushinsky, L. V. (1947). Inheritance of passive-defensive behavior (cowardice) as connected with types of nervous system in the dog. Trudy Instituta evolucionnoj Fiziologii i Patologii im. I. P. Pavlova, 1.

Leontev, A. N. (1975). Activity, consciousness, personality. Moscow: Izdatelstvo politicheskoi literatury.

Levitov, N. D. (1969). Problems of the psychology of character. Moscow:
   Prosvesqhcheniye.

Mangan, G. L. (1967a). Studies of the relationship between neo-Pavlovian properties of higher nervous activity and Western personality dimensions: II. The
   relation of mobility to perceptual flexibility. Journal of Experimental
   Research in Personality, 2, 107-116.

Mangan, G. L. (1967b). Studies of the relationship between neo-Pavlovian properties of higher nervous activity and Western personality dimensions: III. The
   relation of transformation mobility to thinking flexibility. Journal of Experimental Research in Personality, 2, 117-123.

Mangan, G. L. (1967c). Studies of the relationship between neo-Pavlovian properties of higher nervous activity and Western personality dimensions. IV.
   A factor analytic study of extraversion and flexibility, and the sensitivity
   and mobility of the nervous system. Journal of Experimental Research in Personality, 2, 124-127.

Mangan, G. L. (1978). The relationship of mobility in inhibition to rate of
   inhibitory growth and measures of flexibility, extraversion, and neuroticism.
   The Journal of General Psychology, 99, 271-279.

Mangan, G. L. (1982). The biology of human conduct. East-West models of
   temperament and personality. Oxford: Pergamon Press.

Mangan, G. L., & Farmer, R. G. (1967). Studies of the relationship between neo-
   Pavlovian properties of higher nervous activity and Western personality dimen-
   sions: I. The relationship of nervous strength and sensitivity to extraversion.
   Journal of Experimental Research in Personality, 2, 101-106.

Marton, L., & Urban, J. (1966). The relationship between typological personality
   traits and characteristics of the process of elaboration and extinction of
   conditioned links. Voprosy psikhologii, No. 2, 92-100.

Matysiak, J. (1979). Activity motivated by sensory drive. Polish Psychological
   Bulletin, 10, 209-214.

Matysiak, J. (1980). Różnice indywidualne w zachowaniu zwierząt w świetle
   konceptji zapotrzebowania na stymulację (Individual differences in animal
   behavior in the light of the need of stimulation theory). Wrocław: Ossolineum.

Merlin, V. S. (1955). The role of temperament in emotional reaction to school
   grades. Voprosy psikhologii, No. 6, 62-71.

Merlin, V. S. (Ed.). (1973). Outline of the theory of temperament (2nd ed.).
   Perm: Permskoye knizhnoye izdatelstvo.

Mirkowska, A. (1976). Posiom reaktywności i skłonność do zamierzonego
   oddziaływania na innych. Podatność na zmiany w nasileniu tych skłonności
   (Level of reactivity and tendency toward deliberate acting upon others.
   Susceptibility to changes in these tendencies). Unpublished Master's thesis,
   University of Warsaw, Poland.

Nebylitsyn, V. D. (1959). An investigation of the connection between sensitivity
   and strength of the nervous system. In B. M. Teplov (Ed.), Typological features
   of higher nervous activity in man (Vol. 2). Moscow: Izdatelstvo Akademii pedagogicheskikh Nauk RSFSR.

Nebylitsyn, V. D. (1972a). Fundamental properties of the human nervous system. New York & London: Plenum Press.

Nebylitsyn, V. D. (1972b). The problem of general and partial properties of the nervous system. In V. D. Nebylitsyn & J. A. Gray (Eds.), Biological bases of individual behavior. New York & London: Academic Press.

Nebylitsyn, V. D., & Gray, J. A. (Eds.). (1972). Biological bases of individual behavior. New York & London: Academic Press.

Nuttin, J. (1965). La structure de la personnalité. Paris: Presses Universitaires de France.

Paisey, T. J. H., & Mangan, G. L. (1980). The relationship of extraversion, neuroticism and sensation-seeking to questionnaire-derived measures of nervous system properties. Pavlovian Journal of Biological Science, 15, 123-130.

Pavlov, I. P. (1952). Dwadzieścia lat badań wyższej czynności nerwowej (zachowania się) zwierząt (Twenty years' experience in objective studies of higher nervous activity (behavior) of animals). Warszawa: Państwowe Zakłady Wydawnictw Lekarskich.

Powell, G. E. (1979). Brain and personality. Farnborough: Saxon House.

Reykowski, J. (1974). Eksperymentalna psychologia emocji (Experimental psychology of emotion) (2nd ed.). Warszawa: Książka i Wiedza.

Reykowski, J. (1977). Osobowość jako centralny system regulacji i integracji czynności (Personality as a central system regulating and integrating activity). In T. Tomaszewski (Ed.), Psychologia (Psychology) (3rd ed.). Warszawa: Państwowe Wydawnictwo Naukowe.

Rubinstein, S. L. (1946). Fundamentals of psychology (2nd ed.). Moscow: Institut filosofii Akademii Nauk SSSR.

Shorokhova Ye. V. (Ed.). (1974). The theoretical problems of psychology in personality. Moscow: Izdatelstvo Nauka.

Sosnowski, T. (1978). Reactivity, level of stimulation and some features of verbal behavior in small, task-oriented groups. Polish Psychological Bulletin, 9, 129-137.

Spence, K. W. (1960). Behavior theory and learning. Selected papers. Englewood, NJ: Prentice Hall.

Strelau, J. (1969). Temperament i typ układu nerwowego (Temperament and type of nervous system). Warszawa: Państwowe Wydawnictwo Naukowe.

Strelau, J. (1970). Nervous system type and extraversion-introversion. A comparison of Eysenck's theory with Pavlov's typology. Polish Psychological Bulletin, 1, 17-24.

Strelau, J. (1972a). A diagnosis of temperament by nonexperimental techniques. Polish Psychological Bulletin, 3, 97-105.

Strelau, J. (1972b). The general and partial nervous system types -- data and theory. In V. D. Nebylitsyn & J. A. Gray (Eds.), Biological bases of individual behavior. New York & London: Academic Press.

Strelau, J. (1974). Temperament as an expression of energy level and temporal features of behavior. Polish Psychological Bulletin, 5, 119-127.

Strelau, J. (1975). Pavlov's typology and current investigations in this area. Netherlands Tijdschrift voor Psychologie, 30, 177-200.

Strelau, J. (1978). Rola temperamentu w rozwoju psychicznym (The role of temperament in mental development). Warszawa: Wydawnictwa Szkolne i Pedagogiczne.

Strelau, J. (1980). The temperament Inventory: A Pavlovian typology approach. Unpublished manuscript. Available from J. Strelau, Institute of Psychology, University of Warsaw, 00-183 Warsaw, Poland

Strelau, J. (1983). Temperament - personality - activity. London: Academic Press.

Strelau, J. (1982). Temperament a osobowość : związki i zależnosci (Temperament and personality: Relationships and dependencies). In J. Strelau (Ed.), Regulacyjne funkcje temperamentu (The regulating functions of temperament). Wrocław: Ossolineum.

Strelau, J., Klonowicz, T., & Eliasz, A. (1972). Fizjologiczne mechanizmy cech temperamentalnych (Physiological mechanisms of temperament traits). Przegląd Psychologiczny, 15, 25-51.

Teplov, B. M. (1961). Problems of individual differences. Moscow: Izdatelstvo Akademii pedagogicheskikh Nauk RSFSR.

Teplov, B. M., & Nebylitsyn, V. D. (1963). The study of basic properties of the nervous system and their significance in psychology of individual differences. Voprosy psikhologii, No. 5, 38-47.

Terelak, J. (1974). Reaktywność mierzona indeksem alfa a cechy temperamentalne (Alpha index as a measure of reactivity and temperamental features). In J. Strelau (Ed.), Rola cech temperamentalnych w działaniu (The role of temperamental traits in activity). Wrocław: Ossolineum.

Thomas, A., & Chess, S. (1977). Temperament and development. New York: Brunner/Mazel.

Thomas, A., Chess, S., & Birch, H. G. (1968). Temperament and behavior disorders in children. New York: New York University Press.

Thurstone, L. L. (1951). The dimensions of temperament. Psychometrika, 16, 11-20.

Tomaszewski, T. (1977). Człowiek i otoczenie (Man and his surroundings). In T. Tomaszewski (Ed.), Psychologia (Psychology) (3rd ed.). Warszawa: Państwowe Wydawnictwo Naukowe.

Utkina, N. S. (1964). Typological differences in influence of school grades on some features of attention. In V. S. Merlin (Ed.), Typological investigations in personality and industrial psychology. Perm: UDOP & PGPI.

White, K. D., & Mangan, G. L. (1972). Strength of the nervous system as a function of personality type and level of arousal. Behaviour Research and Therapy, 10, 139-146.

Wundt, W. (1911). Grundzüge der physiologischen Psychologie (6th ed., Vol. 3). Leipzig: Verlag von Wilhelm Engelmann.

Zarzycka, M. (1980). Rola cech temperamentu i osobowości w powodowaniu wypadków przez maszynistów PKP (The role of temperamental and personality traits in railroad accidents). Unpublished doctoral dissertation, University of Warsaw.

Zuckerman, M. (1979). Sensation seeking: Beyond the optimal level of arousal. Hillsdale, NJ: Lawrence Erlbaum.

2

Mechanisms of Temperament: Basic Functions

Andrzej Eliasz

For many years, studies of temperament were purely academic, in the pejorative sense, contributing little to psychological practice. Some changes for the better, however, are envisaged.

Presented here is the development of Pavlovian conceptions of temperament from an exclusively deterministic approach to a conception that also emphasizes the regulative functions of temperament. Changes in Pavlovian conceptions of temperament have gone far enough for us to consider current conceptions as neo-Pavlovian. While describing some general regularities, we shall indicate their relevance to the activities of the individual in everyday life.

TRADITIONAL DETERMINISTIC APPROACH

Interest in temperamental characteristics goes back to ancient times, when temperamental types were distinguished. The terminology used then still appears in many temperament theories and in common language. The meanings of the terms, however, have often changed. Notions relating to the physiological mechanism underlying temperament have altered most of all. But despite all these changes of the conception of temperament and its mechanisms, the traditional approach still weighs heavily on contemporary views and also on the work of Pavlov's followers.

The traditional way of analyzing temperamental features was deterministic. Researchers tried to answer the question "Why do certain phenomena occur?" Inquiries have never gone beyond the problem of causation; nobody has ever raised the question of the function of the phenomena themselves. As a consequence, temperament studies have amounted to no more than the statement of differences, among people and animals, in certain features and physiological mechanisms of behavior. Enquiries into minute-aspect causality, indicating certain physiological mechanisms conditioning the character of behavior, have made Pavlovian followers narrow the concept of temperament down to dynamic qualities, that is, certain formal aspects, of behavior.

Today, both theoretical studies and empirical evidence seem to justify such an approach, accepted even by those who apparently have not followed Pavlov's ideas. By narrowing the concept of temperament down to formal aspects of behavior, however, Pavlovians have isolated these characteristics from those

Some research reported in this paper was supported by Grant 11.8 from the Institute of Philosophy and Sociology of the Polish Academy of Sciences.

pertaining to the contents of behavior. Thus analytical reasoning has not been followed by synthesis. Temperamental traits were believed to be unrelated to personality traits, since no questions were asked about the function of given features and mechanisms of behavior. It has been assumed that physiological mechanisms cannot have any effect on the formation of personality traits, the latter being conceived as conditioned by socio-historical factors.

Temperamental traits were presumed to be innate. This assumption has led to a conviction that neither personality traits nor environment during postnatal development can modify the physiological mechanism of temperament and, thus, temperament itself -- the dynamic quality of behavior. It has been assumed that experience, in the broad sense, may merely disguise actual traits. All these assumptions have led to the distinctions between genotype and phenotype. Attempts to distinguish temperamental features, that is, the genotype, from phenotypical features have prompted Pavlovians to examine the most simple involuntary reactions of an organism to stimuli and to research simple conditional responses. Certainly, animals are most convenient for such purposes, thus the great popularity of animal studies among Pavlovians. But the tradition of animal studies in temperament research has only served to reinforce Pavlovians' beliefs concerning the separation of temperament and personality.

Western European and American conceptions of temperament, not derived from Pavlov's theory, have acknowledged the relationship between the dynamic qualities of behavior (its formal aspects) and its content. Such an approach has been revealed in various conceptions in which temperament has been broadly defined. Eysenck's (1981) conception of extraversion, neuroticism, and psychoticism is the best example.

The limitation of temperament studies to an entirely determinist paradigm has resulted in the view that temperamental mechanisms are variables that mediate strength and speed of reaction. Therefore, the concept of temperament has been reduced to the dynamic qualities of respondent behavior.

New perspectives were brought to Pavlovian ideas by studies conducted by Leites, Merlin, Klimov, Teplov, Baimetov, and others in the Soviet Union (see Strelau, 1984). Soviet researchers were concerned with such correlates of temperament and its mechanisms as tolerance to stress and individual work style. Unfortunately, their line of reasoning was totally deterministic. Therefore, they found that nervous system strength (the physiological property that determines sensitivity to weak stimuli and resistance to strong stimuli) determines weaker or stronger resistance to stress (strong stimuli) and that individual work style was associated with individual reaction to working conditions. Such a view is circular. Findings on emotional resistance to stress have been no surprise: such resistance is simply a direct empirical indicator of the temperamental feature in question defined precisely in terms of sensitivity to weak stimuli and resistance to strong stimuli.

Strelau's study of the student's work style (Strelau, 1970) is an evident sign of a break from the deterministic approach to temperament. Strelau hypothesized that work style protects an individual from the fatigue and excessive tension associated with difficult situations. Strelau pointed to the compensatory function of work styles; individuals differing in reactivity -- ceteris paribus -- may show similar efficiency, thanks to an adjustment of their work styles to given circumstances and their own potential. Later studies conducted by Klonowicz (1974) demonstrated the psychophysiological costs of working under conditions that were inadequate to individual temperament features, without any opportunity for compensation through adopting an individualized work style.

BASIC REGULATIVE FUNCTIONS OF THE PHYSIOLOGICAL MECHANISMS OF TEMPERAMENT

Reactivity Mechanism and Stimulation Requirement

The reactivity mechanism is an important factor that affects regulation; it is aimed at maintaining optimal stimulation and, thus, optimal activation. [1]

The physiological mechanism of reactivity determines individual arousability. Stimuli of the same strength may evoke different levels of arousal in the central nervous system, depending on individual reactivity (see Gray, 1964). If one also agrees with Hebb (1965), Leuba (1965), Berlyne (1960), Fiske & Maddi (1967), who say that people tend to maintain optimal activation, then it is clear that the amount of stimulation that is required for maintaining the optimum depends on individual arousability. It has been assumed, therefore, that people differing in reactivity will require different amounts of stimulation to maintain the optimal level of activation. Thus, the physiological mechanism of reactivity is a fundamental determinant of stimulation requirement. A detailed theoretical argument is presented elsewhere (Eliasz, A., 1972, 1973a, 1974, 1981).

Zuckerman's studies (e.g., 1979) clearly demonstrated the great role of stimulation need [2] in human development. Such a concept was based not only on experimental or questionnaire studies. There were also some findings on differences in everyday behavior between people with low- versus high-stimulation requirements. Similar data on criminal behavior of institutionalized delinquent girls were reported by Farley & Farley (1972).

Need for stimulation. The following are empirical findings showing that behavior in natural settings, exhibited by people differing in reactivity, is indicative of differences in stimulation need. The findings also show how great the role of temperament traits is in life.

It has been hypothesized that level of reactivity may affect preferences concerning type of occupation and sporting activity. Naturally, strivings for maintaining optimal stimulation are not unrelated to other human needs that often determine the choice of occupation or sporting activity. When a given activity is high or low stimulating in the extreme, however, striving for the maintenance of optimal stimulation probably becomes stronger and more important, compared with other needs. Certainly, when it comes to jobs, a person will not always make a good choice with respect to stimulation requirement. Moreover, in case of a bad choice, the person may not quit the job soon enough because of his involvement in the job, high wages, or some other reason. Nevertheless, the employee may still be removed because of deteriorating health and frequent absences, lower efficiency in comparison with other employees, and injuries at work. A similar, negative, selection probably takes place in sports.

---

[1] The concept of optimal activation as a standard of activity, the range of optimal activation on the activation continuum, and possible specification of general optimal activation are issues discussed elsewhere (Eliasz, A., 1981). This work also showed the differences and similarities in defining the concept, as found in works by Berlyne (1960), Hebb (1965), Leuba (1965), Duffy (1962), Fiske & Maddi (1967), and others.

[2] Zuckerman's research was concerned with a phenomenon called sensation seeking. According to Zuckerman, sensation seeking ought to be distinguished from the intellectual type of stimulation (Zuckerman, 1979).

Such reasoning suggests that occupational preferences and the process of negative selection results in a different distribution of high- and low-reactive
people when working conditions differ considerably in their stimulation load.
Occupations and sports carrying large amounts of stimulation (high load) should
have a higher proportion of low-reactive persons, whereas activities carrying
low stimulation (no load) should be chosen by high-reactive individuals. No
disproportion was expected in the moderate load group.

Stimulation load in occupational groups was indicated by the degree of social
threat, as rated by competent judges. Studies were conducted by Danielak (see
Eliasz, A., 1974). Stimulation load in sporting activities was indicated by
the degree of physical threat in studies conducted by Popielarska (see Eliasz, A.,
1974).

The hypothesis was fully confirmed in the case of high load groups, in which
low-reactive subjects significantly predominated (reactivity was measured with
Strelau's Temperament Inventory). However, our expectancies have failed us
in the case of no load groups.

Neuroticism (measured with Eysenck's MPI) was another variable considered apart
from reactivity. When extreme groups, with regard to the assumed stimulation
requirement (low-reactive nonneurotic subjects versus high-reactive neurotic
subjects), were compared, significant differences appeared in both high load
and no load groups. Low-reactive nonneurotic subjects predominated in the
high load groups, whereas high-reactive neurotic subjects prevailed in the
no load groups. The regularity appeared for both social threat and physical
threat (Eliasz, A., 1974).

Similar studies were carried out on physical workers at an old foundry, where
the working conditions in some sections were particularly severe (or heavy).
For purposes of reducing the variability of social factors, a comparative group
working under much lighter conditions was selected within the same foundry.
The stimulation load associated with work in a given section, indicated by
noise, physical threat (type and frequency of injuries in a section), and temperature, was rated by competent judges. Thus, a few heavy sections could be
fairly easily distinguished. There were also some relatively lighter sections.
Furthermore, stimulation provided by the living macroenvironment was considered.
Two groups were distinguished: one living in a large industrial city's central
district (dense traffic, noise, accident risk; also novelty and variety of
stimuli), the other living in the suburbs (little traffic, quiet, peace).

The reactivity of workers in relatively light and heavy sections was compared
within groups living in similar macroenvironments. No differences were found
within the group living in the suburbs. However, our analysis yielded differences within the group living in highly stimulating districts of the city. The
results suggest that job preferences and the process of negative selection are
more pronounced when high stimulation load associated with work coincides with
high stimulation provided by the living macroenvironment. This finding is consistent with our assumption that the more difficult and stimulating everyday living conditions are, the more important is the right choice of activities, tasks,
and situations associated with the stimulation they carry. Moreover, negative
selection becomes more stringent than with a person who takes a job that exceeds
his or her potential (Eliasz, A., 1981).

Modulation of behavior. The preceding findings suggest that, depending on reactivity, people prefer situations of various stimulation load. Still, a question
arises whether people also modulate their behavior adequately to the stimulation
provided by their surroundings. Modulation of behavior seems to be particularly
important when the environment is inadequate to the person's need for stimulation,

and stimulation cannot be reduced by withdrawal from the situation or by simple removal of stimuli. In the following study, boys aged 14-15 years with average IQs were examined. The sample was homogeneous for economic status, housing, parents' education, and family structure. Boys attended schools of similar educational standard and similar equipment. Access to cinemas, libraries, and sports clubs was equal. The boys, however, came from two districts in Warsaw that differed in stimulation load. As in the previous study, stimulation provided by living macroenvironment was indicated by traffic, noise, and casualty risk, as well as novelty and variety of stimuli associated with traffic. The comparatively quiet and peaceful living district of one group of boys, being distant from the city center and isolated from traffic, was considered a low-stimulating living macroenvironment. On the other hand, the central living district of the remaining boys, being located between a railway overpass and a bridge carrying heavy traffic, including particularly noisy trams, was considered a highly stimulating living macroenvironment.

Apart from variables associated with environment, we also distinguished reactivity as an individual variable. The dependent variables were as follows: amount of sleep, ways of spending free time, and amount of time spent on recreation. School achievements, regularity of work, and time devoted to study at home were also registered. Information on recreation and time devoted to study at home was derived from daily schedules. Data on school achievements and regularity of work, that is, stability of grades, were obtained from school records.

A combination of the two independent variables -- the environmental and the individual factor -- yielded two categories. The first category, comprising subjects living in $\underline{A}$ conditions, i.e., adequate to stimulation needs, consisted of low-reactive subjects from the highly stimulating environment, and high-reactive subjects from the low-stimulating environment. The other category of subjects, living in inadequate conditions ($\underline{I}$), consisted of low-reactive subjects from the low-stimulating environment (likely to be understimulated) and high-reactive subjects from the highly stimulating conditions (likely to be overstimulated).

Overstimulated subjects spent significantly more time on play than their peers who were understimulated or lived in adequate conditions.

As for sleep, there was no significant difference between inhabitants of the two districts. Moreover, the need for stimulation -- an individual variable -- was not decisive for sleep time in the supposedly adequate conditions. In inadequate conditions, understimulated subjects slept 1 hour longer ($\overline{X} = 9.8$ hr) than did overstimulated subjects ($\overline{X} = 8.8$ hr). The difference was significant. According to Rofwarg & Muzio (1966), the average sleep time for people 14-18 years of age is 8.5 hours. The sleep time of our subjects from adequate conditions was about the same (8.6 hr) and a little longer (8.8 hr) in the overstimulated group. Understimulated-group results (9.8 hr), however, were different, suggesting that the crucial factor for sleep at age 14-15 years is not overstimualtion, but understimulation.

As for school grades, no differences were found between groups. Yet it appeared that almost the same results were attained at school with differing amounts of time devoted to study at home: subjects living in conditions that were adequate to their traits studied more than did subjects living in inadequate conditions. Thus, the effort required to achieve the same results were greater in group A than in I. It seems plausible that favorable conditions (A) can be simply wasted, at least partially, by less systematic work. Such an explanation is suggested by differences in stability of grades; a wider dispersion of grades was noted in group A. In addition, systematic subjects were found to predominate in group I, whereas the number of systematic and nonsystematic students in group A was equal (the distinction between systematic and nonsystematic students was based on stability of grades). Only when students were understimulated or overstimulated did systematic study gain some role in the process of stimulation control. These results suggest that subjects from group I were more economical than were students from group A who wasted their energy (Eliasz, A., 1974a).

An array of both empirical and experimental evidence indicates that people with different mechanisms of reactivity prefer different situations as far as stimulation load is concerned. Their behavior also depends on the amount of stimulation. An analysis has shown that the role of behavior is to compensate for overload or deficiency of stimulation, as compared with individual stimulation requirement.

Physiological Mechanism of Reactivity and Development of Stimulation Regulators at the Level of Temperament and Personality

The mechanism of transforming stimulus strength into excitation strength determines the dynamic quality of respondent behavior, that is, stimulus-evoked behavior (reactivity). The same mechanism also determines, in a more indirect way, the dynamics of operant behavior (activity)[3].

By determining stimulation requirement, the physiological mechanism of reactivity results in the reinforcement of different dynamic qualities of operant behavior, namely, those that facilitate the attainment of optimal stimulation and, thus, optimal activation. Therefore, the dynamic qualities of operant behavior, as well as its desired effects, will recur (Eliasz, A., 1973a). Activity is conceived here as the typical intensity and duration of a person's behavior that is organized so as to maintain optimal activation. As has been indicated, formal features of behavior, revealed in its energetic level, are determined by two closely related mechanisms:

- Reactivity - by the mechanism that transforms stimulus strength into strength of central excitation. The mechanism, though hereditary in its origin, is modified by the environment during ontogenesis.

- Activity - by the mechanism acquired through learning. This mechanism controls the dynamics of behavior and, thus, regulates activation. It also supports the physiological mechanism in the regulation of activation level. Because the dynamics of operant behavior are determined by a mechanism that is complementary to the regulative functions of the physiological mechanism of reactivity, the intensity of operant behavior (activity) must remain in a reverse proportion to reactive behavior (reactivity) (Eliasz, A., 1973a). Such a relationship between reactivity and activity was demonstrated by Matysiak (1980).

Research studies indicate that people prefer those dynamics of operant behavior, situations and styles of activity, that facilitate fulfillment of their stimulation requirement as determined by their reactivity mechanism. For the same reason, people may prefer behavior of a certain content more than other activities that give more

---

[3]Activity is conceived here in line with Strelau (1974). In an earlier work, different terminology was used for describing dynamics of respondent and operant behavior (Eliasz, A., 1973a). The terminology is still different at a time when the necessity of distinguishing the two concepts has only just emerged (Eliasz, A., 1972).

or less stimulation. Though initially performed to provide required stimulation, such behaviors may become autonomous. Some activities are strongly stimulating through feedback, such as a persistent pursuit after personal goals and choice of realistic goals followed by activities that enable their effective attainment. This feedback may provide the desired amount of stimulation. Such stimulating activities also lead to certain feelings of success, and this is conducive to developing the need for achievements (Eliasz, A., 1973b, 1974b).

A functional analysis of various behaviors from the perspective of their stimulating capacity enables us to predict the relationship between reactivity and various personality traits (Reykowski, 1976; Strelau, 1982, 1984). These two studies were concerned with the extent to which temperamental mechanisms affect development of different personality traits, by determining the strength of stimulation needs. Certainly, temperamental mechanisms are not the only determinants of personality development; they may only favor or hamper formation of given mental traits. The role of social influence and ecological conditions cannot be denied (Eliasz, A., 1973b, p. 575).

The specificity of the reactivity mechanism may also influence personality development in another way. An environment full of novel and varied stimuli may be overstimulating for highly reactive people, inducing them to withdraw. The same environment may evoke curiosity in low-reactive people, inducing them to explore the world around them. For these low-reactive persons, however, abundance of such stimuli may lead to development of cognitive structures. As a result, comparatively less stimuli will evoke a strong reaction of surprise, which induces a person to withdraw from the environment (Eliasz, A., 1981).[4]

Ability of Acquiring Means for Fulfilling Stimulation Requirement

Both theoretical premises and empirical findings justify an assumption that the reactivity mechanism determines stimulation requirement. Can we say, however, that people having the same stimulation requirement will make the same efforts to meet it? An analysis of the behavior of some people may give the impression that they have no definite optimal standard of stimulation. Most of all, such an impression is given by psychopaths who show large needs of stimulation that are hard to satisfy (Quay, 1965, 1977). In a way, they resemble Pavlov's dogs with a particularly strong nervous system that slept when bored, but became animated in a strongly stimulating situation without losing efficiency. One could say that the activity of such dogs is externally determined. People also often adjust their activity to external stimulation, without making any efforts to increase or reduce stimulation. Such behavior seems quite natural, but only when specific intentions lie behind it, such as a desire to relax. Quay interpreted the chronic understimulation in psychopaths as being an extraordinarily large need of stimulation, satisfied from time to time through, for example, violent destructive activity. Such a large need of stimulation, however, can be satisfied through many socially approved activities. People need to acquire

---

[4]The physiological mechanism may also indirectly influence formation of personality traits. Children differing in temperament elicit different reactions in others. Modulation of social influence with respect to the child's temperament may mean that children from the same social environment are brought up differently. Thomas, Chess & Birch (1968), and Thomas & Chess (1977) have shown that the parent's attitudes toward a child can be largely affected by the child's temperament. According to Rothbart & Derryberry (1979), the new interest in temperament stems from the discovery of the child's active role in shaping child-parent interactions.

an appropriate functional mechanism for fulfilling the need for stimulation.
In the course of development, people must learn to recognize and associate
internal stimuli and external stimuli with regard to their capacity for satisfying needs (Reykowski, 1970). Reykowski illustrates the process of acquiring
functional mechanisms for satisfying needs by referring to the alimentary need.
According to Reykowski, human needs associated with the biological structure of
an organism are only the basis for developing drives. A need of something necessary for normal functioning and development is not sufficient to build up a
drive. An organism must also develop certain means for satisfying the need.

Gray's findings lead to a hypothesis that the ability of acquiring a functional
mechanism for regulation of stimulation, just as the magnitude of stimulation
need itself, depends on the properties of the physiological mechanism of reactivity (Eliasz, A., 1981). According to Gray, extraverts are much less sensitive to punishment than are introverts (Gray, 1972a, 1972b, 1981), which can
be explained in terms of reactivity; the physiological mechanisms of both these
behavioral dimensions are similar. Results obtained by Gray suggest that low-
reactive people are marked by higher tolerance to punishment than that of highly
reactive persons. This fact may bear serious consequences for the process of
acquiring abilities of modulating stimulation and, thus, activation as well:
the divergence between optimal and actual activation can be viewed as punishment.
Therefore, it seems plausible that low-reactive people will exhibit more tolerance to this divergence and thus probably will have weak motivation for reducing
it, leading to worsened learning of stimulation control. If that were so, then
development of the mechanism for satisfying the stimulation need would be more
difficult in low-reactive people, compared with those who are highly reactive.
People with such deficient functional mechanisms would not be able to protect
themselves against a severe drop or excessive growth of activation in response
to deficient or excessive stimulation. They could be perceived as externally
controlled, that is, as adjusting their activities to external stimulation and
to the day and night rhythm in a passive way.

Certainly, the physiological mechanism of reactivity does not necessarily lead
to such specifically understood external control, but it still may. The likelihood of external control is particularly high when strivings for maintaining
optimal activation are aroused only by strivings for having a sense of well-
being. If a low-reactive person, however, acquires more specific standards of
activity, then optimal activation will also be desired as a prerequisite of
success. Specific standards of activity can be formed through social interactions. Paradoxically, lower reactivity accompanied by weak motivation for
maintaining optimal activation, that has to be reinforced by specific standards,
correlates also with high resistance to social influence (see Eliasz, A., 1981;
Strelau, 1982). [5] When specific standards of activity are nevertheless acquired,
despite resistance to social influence, then positive reinforcement associated
with the maintenance of optimal activation becomes a significant reinforcer of
motivation for maintaining optimal activation needed for the accomplishment of
tasks and for other activities. Such positive reinforcements probably are
more important in stimulation control the lower reactive people are. The conclusion is drawn out from Gray's model of relations between extra- and introversion and susceptibility to reward and punishment.

In summary, we have observed the following phenomena: the lower the reactivity
of a person, the higher is his or her need of stimulation, but then acquisition
of appropriate operations for effective stimulation control is probably more

---

[5] The fact that socialization occurs in two senses, through emotional and cognitive processes, is not denied here.

difficult. Thus, the mechanism of reactivity manifests dialectical "unity of opposites" in the course of developing a system of stimulation control.

Furthermore, it appears that discrepancies between actual and optimal stimulation, being punitive in a way, are likely to evoke too weak a motivation for accurate stimulation control in low-reactive people and too strong a motivation in high-reactive ones. Since the social environment is a primary source of stimulation for people (cf. Spielberger, 1972), those with low stimulation requirements and strong motivation for accurate stimulation control should be most likely to learn to regulate stimulation provided by this source. H. Eliasz's study (1980) on the role of empathy in the dynamics of aggression yielded data that correspond with this assumption. The author failed to elicit empathy toward a suffering victim in low-reactive subjects, whereas the experimental manipulation was effective in the high-reactive group.

Strong motivation for accurate regulation of stimulation, as any other strong motivation, may narrow attention to certain stimuli, leaving out less important cues. Research indicates that high-reactive teenage boys are mostly "person specialists," to use Little's (1976) phrase. Such boys adjust their behavior to social demands, but they do not modulate their way of life with respect to the physical aspects of their living macroenvironment (i.e., amount of stimulation and spatial character of their habitation area). On the contrary, low-reactive boys are mostly "thing specialists"; they adjust their activity to the physical qualities of their living macroenvironment and are relatively resistant to social influence (Eliasz, A., 1981).

Differences in stimulation requirement cannot be considered the only reason for such adjustments of activity, just as psychopathic behavior cannot be explained simply in terms of an extraordinarily high stimulation requirement. Rather, we recall our hypothesis that the reactivity mechanism not only determines stimulation requirement, but also the ability of acquiring operations for fulfilling this requirement. This hypothesis still requires direct examination.

Stimulation Control at the Level of the Physiological Mechanism of Reactivity

The physiological mechanism of reactivity transforms the energy of a stimulus into a certain level of activation; it determines the amount of required stimulation, necessary for maintaining optimal activation. This transformer is believed to be stable, despite the growing number of voices stating that even hereditary traits may change during a lifetime.

Data cited in the literature allow us to assume that a person counteracts decreases or increases of activation, resulting from deficient or excessive stimulation, not merely by adjusting his behavior to the situation. It appears that the physiological mechanism of reactivity also plays an active role in the process of regulating stimulation and, hence, activation. Several findings suggest that sensitivity to stimuli increases when stimulation is deficient; conversely, sensory sensitivity decreases, while resistance to strong stimuli increases when stimulation is excessive (see Eliasz, A., 1979). This type of stimulation control is based on negative feedback. If both higher stimulation regulators and the basic type of regulation associated with functioning of the physiological mechanism of reactivity fail, then negative feedback may give way to positive feedback, which is revealed in maladaptive changes at a given level of functioning; sensitivity starts to decrease under deficient stimulation, and it shows an increase under excessive stimulation. In such a situation, a person must make some fundamental changes within his higher stimulation regulators. This might require radical re-evaluation of the most general goals in life. Only then, the maladaptive changes at the physiological level will not lead to

self-destruction. The above hypotheses are confirmed by data on the effect of
ecological conditions on the level of reactivity in adolescents and adults.

The effect on reactivity of living in strongly stimulating central districts
was examined, compared with living in low-stimulating suburbs of the same large
city. Adolescents living in highly stimulating central districts exhibited
lower reactivity than did adolescents from low-stimulating suburbs. The opposite
was found for adults who worked under relatively light (low-stimulating) conditions. No differences appeared in the group of adults working under highly
stimulating conditions, which has probably resulted from job preferences and
negative selection (see section "Need for Stimulation"). In both studies, reactivity was measured by Strelau's Temperament Inventory (Eliasz, A., 1981).

Since the studies were cross-sectional, the effect of ecological conditions on
level of reactivity could be determined only after taking for granted the random
distribution in samples of genetic factors that undoubtedly codetermine level
of reactivity. It has been further assumed that the stimulation requirement,
which is largely determined by reactivity, has little if any effect on people's
choice of living district in Poland. This assumption is confirmed by data obtained for adults; the findings would be quite opposite if personal preferences
associated with stimulation requirement were actually conclusive for their
choice of living district. Namely, low-reactive people would outnumber high-
reactive ones in the highly stimulating macroenvironment, and the opposite would
be found in the low-stimulating macroenvironment. Such a distribution would
certainly affect the average reactivity level of inhabitants in the two districts. For adolescents, the effect of preferences on choice of living district
was assumed of little importance for other reasons. At first glance, our data
confirm the relationship between preferences associated with stimulation requirement in teenagers and parents' choice of living district. It is hard to believe,
however, that adolescents could have any influence on their parents' decision,
which is even more obvious considering that families moved into the districts
at least 5 years before our study was run -- subjects were then no more than
9-10 years of age (a tenancy of 5 years was a minimum).

Finally, many variables were kept constant: certain individual factors, family
characteristics, structure of social environment, and school conditions. It
seems that the procedure has considerably reduced the effect on level of reactivity of uncontrolled nonecological factors, with the exception of variables
that simply cannot be controlled in cross-sectional studies in natural settings.
Naturally, we still cannot be certain whether the effect of such an ecological
factor as the stimulation carried by a living macroenvironment is direct, without any particular transmission as highly punitive child rearing resulting from
overstimulation of parents and other patrons in given macroenvironment conditions.

Our demonstration showing that changes in reactivity may result from ecological
factors shows that such changes are not rare, as has been supposed, but rather
common.

Two basic problems arise during an analysis of changes in functioning of the
physiological mechanism of reactivity: What are the factors that determine how
fast these changes occur and can situation-induced changes remain permanent?

It seems that rapidity of reactivity changes depends on the product of the
extent to which the system of stimulation regulators is loaded and the duration
of loading. At a certain value of this product, higher regulation fails;
and adaptive changes in functioning at the level of the physiological mechanism of reactivity must take place to help stimulation control. If the
active participation of this mechanism also proves insufficient, however,
then regulation based on negative feedback may switch to positive feedback.

Most likely, such change takes place at higher values of the loading times duration product.

It was stated previously that reactivity changes are determined by the extent to which stimulation regulators are loaded, among others. The load may be a joint effect of stimulation that is inadequate to requirements, inability to follow rapid changes in the environment (too weak mobility; the opposite case is rather seldom), and too little elasticity of personality traits. A combination of factors probably determines the final stimulation load.

Earlier findings indicated that a person may arrange his surroundings at work and may prefer certain types of work with respect to his reactivity. Today we can state the opposite, that the environment may elicit reactivity changes.

By determining resistance to strong stimuli and, hence, emotional tolerance to stress, the reactivity mechanism bears an influence on the degree of mobility as defined by Strelau (1974, p. 125). The opposite also seems true. We have hypothesized that all the mechanisms that determine slow reactions (inertness, rigidity, perseverance and arrhythmicity -- in general a weak mobility) can lead to strong emotional excitation in situations requiring considerable mobility. Low mobility may thus load a person with additional stimulation resulting from his inability to follow rapid changes in the environment. Although these assumptions require empirical justification, data collected so far are supportive (Eliasz, A., 1981).

The effect of the physiological mechanism of reactivity on formation of personality traits has been shown. One could presume that several personality traits that are first developed for their facilitating effect on stimulation control may inhibit this regulation when the environment changes, after they gain autonomy. It may also happen that personality traits, unfavorable to stimulation control, are inculcated in a child from the very beginning by people who disregard the child's potential. It can be expected that stimulation load, being determined by personality features, affects not only the level of activity conceived as a temperamental trait (Strelau, 1978, p. 124) but also the functioning of the physiological mechanism of reactivity.

We suppose that any loading of the system of stimulation regulators may lead to changes in functioning of the reactivity mechanisms -- change similar to those resulting from loading with ecological factors.

As has been emphasized, reactivity changes are the joint effect of several factors; even strong environmental stimulation does not lead to changes in functioning of the physiological mechanism of reactivity, if only a person is capable of adjusting activity to his living conditions. We also pointed to the two-way relationships between particular elements of the system of stimulation regulators and the reactivity mechanism. We must finally stress that multilateral relations seem to exist between particular elements of the system of stimulation control.

Permanence of reactivity changes. Short-term pressure of the given situation leads to changes in reactivity. Such changes in reactivity may pass away together with their causes. Transsituational instability of reactivity is associated with changes in functioning of the physiological mechanism of reactivity only. Such variability can be compared with psychosomatic functional changes that spontaneously pass away, together with their causes.

Changes in reactivity of the "temporal" type may appear gradually; for example, changes that at first are barely perceptible may build up when stimulation is permanently deficient or excessive as regards requirements. We cannot exclude, however, the possibility of abrupt changes in the reactivity mechanism that may be due to traumatic events just as changes in personality traits can occur in response to trauma.

For psychologists, the primary indicator of the temporal changes is their stability and inertness. In such cases, a psychologist would perceive these changes as "structural." That does not necessarily mean anatomical changes, but it may indicate relatively stable changes in the organization of systems belonging to this mechanism, that is, the endocrine system, the autonomic nervous system, the reticular formation, and the cortex (Strelau, Klonowicz & Eliasz, 1972).

Temperamental features have been traditionally defined in psychology by referring to behavior. Strelau (1969, 1974, 1978, 1982) follows this tradition. His definition, adopted in this paper, gives the concept of temperament a descriptive status.[6] As a consequence of adopting such terminology, one must admit that reactivity may change transsituationally and temporally. Transsituational changes, however, are connected with altered functioning (reactivity changes); only changes of the temporal type indicate changes within the reactivity mechanism itself. Therefore, the definition of reactivity ought to be reformulated. The present definition, stressing that reactivity is revealed in relatively stable and typical dynamic qualities of a person's respondent behavior, is actually true only for the reactivity mechanism.

A MODEL OF TEMPERAMENT

An attempt has been made here to illustrate the interrelatedness of stimulation regulators. Arguments have been presented suggesting a higher complexity of the system than has been presumed. While describing these relationships, we tried to show that bilateral, rather than unilateral, relationships exist between the physiological mechanism of reactivity on the one hand, and the mechanisms of mobility, personality traits, and environment on the other. It has also been stated that these two-way relationships affect the condition of the whole system of stimulation control, which in turn affects particular elements of the system and their relations. The system of stimulation control has been supposed to consist of features and mechanisms of temperament, as well as of personality traits.

Such a complex system of relationships is called transactional. The term is used by those clinical and environmental psychologists who attach importance to the environmental origin of changes in human behavior. Thus, the postulated model of temperament has been labeled transactional to point out the environmental conditioning of temperamental features.

The model of temperament and the whole system of stimulation control can be also viewed from another angle. We have just pointed to the transactional character of relationships; that is, we have postulated an all-unity model consisting of mutual dependencies between the temperament mechanisms on the one hand, and personality traits and environment on the other. We have earlier indicated, however, the instability of temperament and its mechanisms. We have also described those physiological properties of the reactivity mechanism that must lead to "internal contradictions" in the course of developing a system of stimulation control (see the section "Ability of Acquiring Means for Fulfilling Stimulation Requirement"). Our way of conceiving the role of temperamental mechanisms in this system corresponds with the basic theses of dialectics. The theses stress

---

[6]Strelau (1984) changed his definition of temperament in this respect in his recent book. He defined temperament in explanatory, not descriptive, terms.

the "relatedness of all beings," their constant instability, and the struggle of internal contradictions. The applied implications of the proposed model of temperament have been suggested by a presentation of findings that referred mostly to real behavior, determined by the functions of the mechanisms of temperament, and factors in natural settings.

REFERENCES

Berlyne, D. E. (1960). Conflict, arousal, and curiosity. New York: McGraw-Hill.

Choynowski, M. (1968). The development of the Polish adaptation of Eysenck's "Maudsley Personality Inventory"; Polish results and international comparisons. Biuletyn Psychometryczny, 2, 51-95.

Duffy, E. (1962). Activation and behavior. New York: J. Wiley.

Eliasz, A. (1972). Reaktywność a styl samoregulacji. [Reactivity and style of self-regulation]. Unpublished doctoral dissertation, University of Warsaw.

Eliasz, A. (1973a). Temperament traits and reaction preferences depending on stimulation load. Polish Psychological Bulletin, 4 (2), 103-114.

Eliasz, A. (1973b). Zapotrzebowanie na stymulację a potrzeba csiagnięć [Need for stimulation and need of achievement]. Psychologia Wychowawcza, 16 (5), 562-579.

Eliasz, A. (1974a, October). Techniques of adaptation to an environment inadequate as to the individual demand for stimulation. Paper presented at the International Conference on Temperament and Personality, Warsaw.

Eliasz, A. (1974b). Temperament a osobowość. [Temperament and personality]. Wrocław: Ossolineum.

Eliasz, A. (1979). Temperament and transsituational stability of behavior. Polish Psychological Bulletin, 10(3), 187-198.

Eliasz, A. (1981). Temperament a system regulacji stymulacji [Temperament and the system of stimulation control]. Warsaw: Państwowe Wydawnictwo Naukowe.

Eliasz, H. (1980). The effect of empathy, level of reactivity and anxiety on interpersonal aggression intensity. Polish Psychological Bulletin, 11 (3), 169-178.

Eysenck, H. J. (Ed.). (1981). A model for personality. Berlin, Heidelberg, New York: Springer-Verlag.

Farley, F. H., & Farley, S. V. (1972). Stimulus-seeking motivation and delinquent behavior among institutionalized delinquent girls. Journal of Consulting and Clinical Psychology, 39 (1), 94-97.

Fiske, D. W., & Maddi, S. R. (1967). A conceptual framework. In D. W. Fiske & S. R. Maddi (Eds.), Functions of varied experiences. Homewood: The Dorsey Press, pp. 11-57.

Gray, J. A. (1964). Pavlov's typology. Oxford: Pergamon Press.

Gray, J. A. (1972a). The psychophysiological nature of introversion-extraversion: a modification of Eysenck's theory. In V. D. Niebylitsyn & J. A. Gray (Eds.), Biological bases of individual behavior. New York: Academic Press.

Gray, J. A. (1972b). Learning theory, the conceptual nervous system and personality. In V. D. Niebylitsyn & J. A. Gray (Eds.), Biological bases of individual
behavior. New York: Academic Press.

Gray, J. A. (1981). A critique of Eysenck's theory of personality. In H. J.
Eysenck (Ed.), A model for personality. Berlin: Springer-Verlag, pp. 246-276.

Hebb, D. O. (1965). Drives and C. N. S. (conceptual nervous system). In
H. Fowler (Ed.), Curiosity and exploratory behavior. New York: Macmillan,
pp. 176-190.

Klonowicz, T. (1974). Reactivity and fitness or the occupation of operator.
Polish Psychological Bulletin, 5 (3), 129-136.

Leuba, C. (1965). Toward some integration of learning theory: the concept of
optimal stimulation. In H. Fowler (Ed.), Curiosity and exploratory behavior.
New York: Macmillan, pp. 169-175.

Little, B. R. (1976). Specialization and the varieties of environmental experi-
ence: Empirical studies within the personality paradigm. In S. Wapner, S. B.
Cohen, & B. Kaplan (Eds.), Experiencing the environment. New York: Plenum
Press.

Matysiak, J. (1980). Roznice indywidualne w zachowaniu zwierzat w swietle
koncepcji zapotrzebowania na stymulacje [Individual differences in animal
behavior in light of the stimulation requirement conception]. Wrocław:
Ossolineum.

Pavlov, I. P. (1929). Lectures on conditioned reflexes: Twenty-five years of
objective study of higher nervous activity (behavior) of animals. New York:
Int. Publishers.

Quay, H. C. (1965). Psychopathic personality as pathological stimulation-
seeking. American Journal of Psychiatry, 122, 180-183.

Quay, H. C. (1977). Psychopathic behavior: Reflections on its nature, origins
and treatment. In I. C. Užgiris & F. Weizman (Eds.), The structuring of
experience. New York: Plenum Press.

Reykowski, J. (1970). Natura ludzka a potrzeby [Human nature and needs].
Etyka, 6, 31-49.

Reykowski, J. (1976, July). Intrinsic motivation and intrinsic inhibition of
aggressive behavior. Paper presented at the Conference on Psychological Issues
in Changing Aggression, Warsaw.

Rofwarg, H. P., & Muzio, J. N. (1966). Ontogenic development of human sleep-
dream cycle. Science, 152, 604-619.

Rothbart, M. K., & Derryberry, D. (1979, September). Theoretical issues in
temperament. Paper presented at Symposium on Developmental Disabilities in
the Preschool Child, Chicago, IL.

Spielberger, C. D. (1972). Anxiety as an emotional state. In C. D. Spielberger
(Ed.), Anxiety: Current trends in theory and research. New York: Academic
Press.

Strelau, J. (1984). Temperament - personality - activity. New York: Academic
Press.

Strelau, J. (1969). Temperament i typ układu nerwowego [Temperament and type of nervous system]. Warsaw: Państwowe Wydawnictwo Naukowe.

Strelau, J. (1970). Indywidualny styl pracy ucznia a cechy temperamentalne [A pupil's individual work habits and temperamental traits]. Kwartalnik Pedagogiczny, 15 (3), 59-77.

Strelau, J. (1974). Temperament as an expression of energy level and temporal features of behavior. Polish Psychological Bulletin, 5 (3), 119-127.

Strelau, J. (1978). Rola temperamentu w rozwoju psychicznym [The role of temperament in mental development]. Warsaw: Wydawnictwa Szkolne i Pedagogiczne.

Strelau, J. (1982). Temperament a osobowość: Zwiazki i zależności [Temperament and personality: Relationships and dependencies]. In J. Strelau (Ed.), Regulacyjne funkcje temperamentu [The regulating functions of temperament]. Wrocław: Ossolineum.

Strelau, J., Klonowicz, T., & Eliasz, A. (1972). Fizjologiczne mechanizmy cech temperamentalnych [Physiological mechanisms of temperament traits]. Przeglad Psychologiczny, 15 (3), 25-51.

Thomas, A., & Chess, S. (1977). Temperament and development. New York: Bruner/Mazel.

Thomas, A., Chess, S., & Birch, H. G. (1968). Temperament and behavior disorders in children. New York: New York University Press.

Zuckerman, M. (1979). Sensation seeking: Beyond the optimal level of arousal. New Jersey: Lawrence Erlbaum.

3

Psychobiology and Cognition: An Individual-Differences Model

Frank H. Farley

The focus of this chapter is on the implications of individual differences in arousability for aspects of cognition and creativity; and some applications to education are outlined. The organizing scheme for the chapter will be a provisional model of arousability and thought -- particularly, the possibility that two important modes of thought may be identified that are related differentially to extremes of cortical arousability.

One topic that has been too much ignored in the study of arousal, the need for stimulation and activity, is that of cognitive processes. The model proposed here should contribute to an amelioration of this problem and, perhaps, contribute even slightly to discussions on the nature of human cognition. Individual differences in cognition are an important consideration, as well as scientific creativity. Moreover, it is hoped that the model will be influential in educational matters. Despite the fact that we are in the midst of a "cognitive revolution" in psychology, the role of stimulation-seeking, arousal, and related concepts in cognitive function continues to be little understood or studied.

By way of propaedeutics, I should state my beliefs, after Galileo, that the goal of science is application. That is, all science should be applied science. Galileo defined the sole purpose of science to be "to lighten the toil of human existence." It seems to me that a central goal for psychology should be to improve the human condition. Not just understand it (a formidable task in its own right), but improve it. I further believe that one of the areas with the greatest potential to accomplish this grand task is education, by improving the comprehension and creativity of succeeding generations.

As a further introductory point, I would like to here support the notion of simplicity in theory and research. There is an ancient principle of art applicable to science: In complexity, simplicity; in diversity, unity. A modern version of this idea is that underlying many phenotypes are few genotypes. Or, to cast it into a more pithy form, one might propose what could be called Lord Rutherford's dictum. Rutherford, a leading British physicist, allegedly once proposed that, and I paraphrase, "If you can't explain your theory to your local bartender, it has almost no chance of being proved true."

The author gratefully acknowledges the support of the Spencer Foundation and the University of Wisconsin Graduate School for his work on psychobiology, cognition, and individual differences.

Before discussing our research and theoretical work, I will note that I will not get into what might be called the "arousal wars," referring to the extensive contemporary discussion concerning the validity of the arousal concept, or the correct number of arousal systems required to account for relevant available psychological, physiological, and biochemical data. Thayer (Chapter 6 in this volume) has reviewed many of the issues here. I will for present purposes treat arousal and arousability as simply as possible, using trait-like cortical and autonomic measures that are simple, reliable, transportable indexes of the major ascending reticular activating system (ARAS) source of arousal.

AROUSABILITY

The studies described here have attempted to identify psychophysiological indicators that show strong relationships to components of cognitive tasks. Productive interfaces between cognitive psychology and neuroscience are increasingly being identified. In our research, the main methodological model is the moderator design (Saunders, 1956), in which physiological and psychophysical variables are employed as moderators of the interrelatedness of cognitive processes and measures. Such a conception of biological moderators is a particularly useful one for the analyses of individual differences. It allows for at least a weak inference of cause, despite the absence of an experimental manipulation.

Some issues involving the arousal concept require consideration so as to provide background for our work (see Thayer, this volume, for a more detailed discussion). It is almost certain that there is more than one arousal system. Some are as follows: (a) the Lacey (1967) proposal of electrocortical, autonomic, and behavioral arousal; (b) the cognitive versus organismic arousal of Blum and colleagues (1967); (c) arousal versus activation versus effort of Pribram and McGuinness (1975); (d) Broadbent's (1971) Lower Level system versus Upper Level system; (e) Thayer's (this volume) Activation Dimension A versus Activation Dimension B; (f) Routtenberg's (1968) two-arousal model, consisting of Arousal System I, related to the Reticular Activating System, and Arousal System II, related to the limbic midbrain area; and (g) Farley's (1981) Intrinsic versus Extrinsic Arousal. Arousal, for better or worse, is a major psychophysiological concept, somewhat akin to the ability concept in psychometrics, and, like ability as reflected in conceptions of intelligence, it is a productive, and controversial, idea.

The physiological measures and markers we have generally used have reflected both cortical and autonomic function. In some studies, only one or two of which are directly relevant to our topic, we have employed real-time polygraph measures, including electrodermal response, blood volume, and heart rate. Generally, however, we have measured such variables as cortical arousability or autonomic arousability with indexes that we treat rather like trait indicators, in which we look for such items as reliability of measure and intertester correlations. We have often employed the two-flash threshold (Maaser & Farley, 1980) as a measure of individual differences in cortical arousability. This measure (Venables, 1963a, 1963b) is not to be confused with the older critical flicker fusion. The former is defined as the interflash interval at which two flashes are seen as one. Its validation as a cortical arousal index lies in electro-encephalographic (EEG) studies (Venables & Warwick-Evans, 1967), studies of the effects of centrally active stimulant and depressant drugs (Kopell, Noble, & Silverman, 1965), and correlations with other trait-like arousal indexes (Farley, Osborne, & Severson, 1970). It has significant test-retest reliability (Heller, 1979). We have used both classical psychophysical methods for its assessment, as well as signal-detection procedures. With sufficient trials (> 40) in the signal-detection paradigm, we have obtained a correlation of .80 (p < .01) between the threshold assessed with a modified method of limits and sensitivity assessed with the signal-detection procedure, suggesting that these two methods yield quite similar results (see Maaser & Farley, 1980).

For an autonomic arousability index we have used the "sweat bottle technique" of Strahan and colleagues (Strahan, Todd, & Inglis, 1974). The rationale for the sweat bottle technique is as follows: a small bottle of distilled water is inverted over the palm for a few seconds; thus a sweat sample is obtained. The more sweat entering the bottle, the more ions there will be, with a resulting increase in the measureable electrical conductivity of the bottle's contents. Multiple measures can be taken over time, and the conductivity scores averaged, among other possible uses of this index. Retest reliability estimates by Strahan et al. (1974) have ranged from .7 to .8 . We have obtained stability estimates of from .6 to .8 .

Another autonomic arousability measure we have used in a wide range of settings and samples is a salivary measure (referred to in our laboratory as the "drool tool"), that is a variant of a cotton swab technique reported by Razran (1955), Corcoran (1964), and others. White (1977) has recently reviewed work using such measures. We have found retest reliability of .8 , with intertester correlations of .9 .

DIFFERENCES IN COGNITIVE PROCESSES

It is proposed that lower or less arousable people differ in cognitive processes from higher or more arousable people in systematic ways, such that two types of organization of cognitive processes might be postulated. The cognitive processes held to be dominant in low-arousable persons are what might be provisionally called correlative thought, in contrast to the cognitive processes held to be dominant in high-arousable persons, which may be called uncorrelative thought.

Low-arousable people may be characterized by a greater interrelatedness of cognitive processes, greater transferability among modes of cognitive representation and cognitive processes, perhaps greater functional dependencies among cognitive processes, greater emphasis on parallel as contrasted with serial processing of information, greater simultaneous versus successive/sequential processing, and more efficient hypostatization and transmutative (e.g., translating abstract to concrete and vice versa) processes. The low-arousable persons may have more highly interrelated associative nets in memory, greater functional relationships among memory storage processes, and so on.

The high-arousable person, on the other hand, may be characterized by lesser interrelatedness of cognitive processes, lesser functional dependencies, greater emphasis on serial as contrasted with parallel processing of information, greater successive/sequential versus simultaneous processing, and less efficient hypostatization and transmutative processes. The high-arousable person may have less interrelated associative nets in memory, lesser functional dependencies among memory storage processes, and so on.

This presently rather vague and general model of individual differences in arousal and cognition requires a major assumption. The assumption is that a complex of related cognitive processes and functions can be identified and can be considered in terms of stable, individual differences in dominant modes of cognitive functioning. It is proposed that these dominant modes of cognitive functioning are moderated by individual differences in the physiological dimension of arousability.

Intelligence

Before discussing studies that have contributed to the development of this provisional model, let us look first at that most vexing of psychological concepts,
that Hamlet on the stage of psychometrics, the concept of intelligence.

In the past decade, a "New Look" in research into intelligence has taken place,
based on contemporary information-processing theory and cognitive theory, focusing mainly on process analyses of intellective performance (Sternberg, 1981).
Pellegrino and Glaser (1979) and Sternberg (1981) have categorized the recent
approaches to the study of intelligence as cognitive correlates, cognitive components, cognitive training, and cognitive contents. The first relates performance on intelligence tests to performance on tasks supposedly reflecting
basic information-processing abilities (e.g. Hunt, 1978; Jensen, 1979). The
cognitive components approach develops cognitive process models of tasks taken
from standard intelligence tests (e.g., Roger, 1971; Sternberg, 1980). Cognitive training teaches people a particular skill and determines its effects on
subsequent performance (e.g., Feuerstein, 1979). The cognitive contents approach
studies the knowledge structures that differentiate experts from novices (Larkin,
McDermott, Simon, & Simon, 1980), although this approach has not yet been directly applied to the study of intelligence. This New Look in research on intelligence may be contrasted with the traditional technology of intelligence testing, involving prediction or selection uses of tests that were constructed generally without theoretical understanding of the cognitive processes involved
in test performance or underlying test scores. The recent process analyses are
primarily concerned with understanding the cognitive processes involved in intellectual accomplishment.

These process analyses are laudatory. Indeed, they fit nicely into the search
for explicable psychobiological correlations, for they provide, on the psychological side, some differentiated cognitive processes that separately, or within
a scheme, can be related to differentiable biological or physiological indexes.

An analysis of intelligence that has received substantial attention in recent
years is the two-dimensional model of Jensen (1974). Jensen's model of mental
abilities consists of associative processes (Level I intelligence) and conceptual processes (Level II intelligence). Associative processing is defined by
Jensen (1974) as "the capacity to register and retrieve information with fidel-
ity. It is characterized essentially by a relative lack of transformation, conceptual coding, or other mental manipulation intervening between information
input and output." Conceptual processing, on the other hand, involves the elaboration and transformation of the stimulus input before an overt response occurs,
and is "characterized by mental manipulation of inputs, conceptualization,
reasoning, and problem solving; it is essentially the general intelligence (g)
factor common to most complex tests of intelligence" (Jensen, 1974). From the
point of view of our provisional cognitive model, one of the most interesting
features of Jensen's proposal is the relationship between Level I and Level II
abilities. Jensen (1973) has proposed that this relationship may be influenced
by population characteristics. For example, for low socioeconomic status (SES)
groups, correlations between Level I and II ranged from .10 to .20, whereas in
middle and higher SES groups they ranged from .60 to .80. To what might such
differences in correlations be attributed? Jensen (1974) argued:

> The most reasonable hypothesis at this point would seem to be that
> the correlation is due only slightly to functional dependence of
> Level II upon Level I and mostly to a common genetic assortment
> on both factors, that is, a genetic correlation in the population
> between two broad classes of ability with different genetic under-
> pinnings.

Differing from Jensen, I find the hypothesis of differential functional dependence rather more interesting. Perhaps functional dependence might vary within SES groups as well as between SES groups, being influenced by a major psychophysiological dimension (given the putative neural basis of mind) such as arousal. We explored this question, employing a moderator design, in which the physiological variables were studied as moderators of the relatedness of associative and conceptual processing. In a study undertaken with Jakubowsky, 85 middle-class college student undergraduates were administered Jensen's main Level I measure, digit span, and his main Level II measure, the Advanced Progressive Matrices. A cortical arousal measure, the two-flash threshold, and an autonomic measure, the salivation test, were administered to all students. Individuals were identified who were extreme on both arousal indexes, and Pearson correlations were computed between Level I and Level II performance separately within the resulting high-arousable and low-arousable groups. For the former, the correlation was a nonsignificant .1; for the latter, however, the correlation was a highly significant .7 (p < .01). The difference between the two correlations was also tested and found to be significant (p < .01). Thus, among low-arousable students, the associative and conceptual measures had almost 50% of variance in common, whereas among high-arousable students there was no significant common variance. These analyses were repeated separately for the cortical and the autonomic measures. The results were the same, but the differences were not as strong.

This almost textbook demonstration of a moderator effect seemed to open up a new range of possibilities for the psychobiological analysis of cognitive function.

Another approach to intelligence that is, not unlike Jensen's, perhaps somewhat more in the psychometric than information-processing or cognitive-process-analysis domain is the three-dimensional model described by Furneaux (1973). Furneaux has argued that there are three main determinants of score in intelligence assessment. These three presumably independent factors are mental speed, accuracy, and persistence. The first of these, mental speed, has been of interest to psychologists since Sir Francis Galton (Eysenck, 1973; Jensen, 1980). The Furneaux model offers a multidimensional approach that may be useful in relating arousability to differentiated cognitive functions. Furneaux has developed measures for each of this three dimensions. The basic item that he uses is a variant of the Thurstone letter series item.

In a study undertaken with David Goh, we examined the moderating effect of individual differences in arousability measured by the two-flash threshold on the interrelatedness of the three factors of speed, accuracy, and persistence, measured by Furneaux' test, employing college students as subjects. Greater interrelatedness of the measures was found in the low-arousable as compared with high-arousable students. We also studied the effects of an experimental manipulation presumed to influence arousal. Here, there was a slight effect toward increased arousal, leading to a lower intercorrelation among the three cognitive dimensions.

Further research on arousability as a biological moderator of intelligence and mental ability should be directed at more process-oriented cognitive tasks, such as those reported by Sternberg (1977), Snow (1979), and others. Such measures that more clearly represent specific aspects of cognitive processing would provide effective means of examining our individual-differences model of arousability and cognition in its applicability to intelligence.

Learning and Memory

Another major domain of cognitive analysis is that of learning and memory. One issue here is the nature of cognitive representation, and notions of encoding and memory processing. One major issue concerns the role in memory and comprehension of pictorial versus linguistic presentation of information. Paivio (1978) has proposed a dual-coding theory of memory representation, consisting of imagery (a nonverbal symbolic system) and a linguistic or verbal system. This theory provides a relatively straightforward analysis of memory representation into the two aspects which would allow, for our present purposes, the study of moderating effects of arousability on the relatedness of these two codes in a statistical, correlational sense. One interesting question in the literature is the relatedness of imaginal versus linguistic processing, and the psychometric aspects of these, as in "imagery ability" (e.g., Ernest, 1977).

In a preliminary analysis of the possible moderating effect of arousability on the correlation of imaginal and linguistic performance, Marc Braverman and I considered as part of a larger study of film comprehension in college students (Braverman & Farley, 1978) the correlation between performance on imaginal (nonverbal pictorial) and linguistic aspects of the film as moderated by arousability. Here, analyses employing a cortical measure (two-flash threshold) indicated that, for high-arousable persons, the relationship between imaginal and linguistic items was not significant, whereas for low-arousable persons, the relationship was significant. The Pearson correlation for the former was 0.1, and for the latter 0.4 (p < .01). Here, again, a moderating effect of arousability is suggested. This study opens up a wide range of possibilities for the study of brain/cognition relationships in the arena of memory research and theory.

Taken together, the foregoing studies of arousability and cognition implicate at least individual differences in cortical arousability as a moderator of the relationships among cognitive tasks and processes. Further studies bearing on our model of arousability and cognition should examine measures directly reflecting currently evolving conceptions of cognitive processes (cf. Anderson, 1980).

There are a number of applied implications of our general model. One is for the study of schizophrenia. A number of writers have proposed that schizophrenia may be, in part, a disorder of overarousal. Our model of the possible unrelatedness of cognitive function in highly arousable persons might constitute a rough analogue for one form of schizophrenic thought, and would be in accord with an overarousal generalization.

CREATIVITY

It is proposed that one of the fundamental processes of creative thought is that of hypostatization and transmutation. It is proposed that this cognitive process is significantly involved in scientific creativity, discovery, and inventiveness, as well as in many areas of artistic creativity. Another term that might well capture the cognitive function we are referring to is flexibility. The translation between and among cognitive processes, the ability to transfer, swap, tradeoff, translate, or otherwise flexibly relate one cognitive process to another. Scientific creativity probably involves hypostatization and transmutation at many stages, where abstract conceptualizations and abstract problems cannot be solved without hypostatizing the problem into some concrete form. For example, one may use a physical representation or physical model, which suggests aspects of a solution not attainable abstractly; then one may transmute "back to" the abstract and then complete the mathematical representations. This flexible process of hypostatization and transmutation is an ongoing process during creative work. It allows a basis for insight, for fresh perspectives, for new ways of looking at a problem, for varied representations of a problem. Hypostatization and transmutation include techniques of metaphor, simile, and analogy, all of which represent major kinds of nonliteral and elaborative thought. Introspective

evidence consistent with the present view of scientific creativity has been suggested in the extensive report of a major contemporary scientific discovery,
that of the DNA structure (Watson, 1968). The discovery of the benzene ring
by Kekule is another example consistent with our analysis.

If our analysis of creativity is even in part correct, then it would be expected
that low-arousable people would generally be more creative than high-arousable
people. To pursue this prediction, it will be necessary to consider briefly
the notion of arousal and the need for stimulation. In our analysis, it is
accepted that the primary psychological notion based on arousal is the need for
stimulation. Sensation seeking or avoiding/reducing is a primary means of
modulating ARAS arousal. It is proposed that sources of arousal can be categorized as <u>intrinsic</u> or trait arousal (being characteristic and trait-like in
nature, as <u>individual</u> differences in arousability) and <u>extrinsic</u> (the manipulable
component of arousal, as, for example, the effects of <u>stimulus</u> characteristics).
Sources of extrinsic arousal may be mental (e.g., fantasy) or behavioral (e.g.,
overt stimulation seeking). These sources are of course not mutually exclusive,
segregated categories. It is argued that extrinsic sources of arousal are reflected in such attributes of stimuli as their intensity, uncertainty, novelty,
variety, complexity, and so on -- attributes like the collative properties
described by Berlyne (1972). The general relationship between ARAS arousal and
performance is accepted as being in the form of an inverted-U function. We have
generalized the performance construct to include "effective psychological functioning." The relationship between intrinsic arousal (arousability) and the
need for stimulation is considered to be generally negative and linear. People
who are low in arousability will seek to increase stimulation (extrinsic arousal)
so as to increase their overall arousal to optimal levels. Thus, they will be
expected to seek variety, novelty, complexity, intensity, and risk. This modulation of stimulation and attempt to achieve optimal arousal levels is assumed to
be significant for survival of the organism.

The implications of the foregoing for creativity lie in the expectation that
arousability and the need for stimulation will be related to creativity. In
addition to the proposed correlative thought processes in creativity, and their
association with low arousability, there are other reasons to believe that stimulation seeking will be positively related to creativity. The seeking of novelty,
variety, and uncertainty; the taking of risks; the motivated exposure to perplex-
ity, ambiguity, and conflict -- all will be expected to increase the probability
of new and creative solutions to problems, of new perceptions, rejection of the
usual perceptions, and of acheivement of unusual and original artistic and scientific perspectives.

Support for our biologically based model of creativity has been extensive
(Farley, 1974, 1981). To examine the relatedness of creativity tasks and individual differences in arousability are concerned, we undertook a recent analysis with Gordon Nelson, employing a large sample of adolescents. Methods were
the two-flash threshold, used as an arousability index, as well as widely used
measures of verbal and figural (pictorial) creativity. This study showed greater
relatedness of the tasks in the low- over high-arousable subjects. In a series
of studies, it has been shown that the need for stimulation is one of the best
personality and motivational predictors of creativity (e.g., Davis, Peterson, &
Farley, 1974; Farley, 1974, 1981).

We have undertaken a breakdown of creativity into three provisional categories
(Farley, 1974). The first represents instrumental, utilitarian, productive creativity, that is, <u>useful or potentially useful</u> creativity, as in inventions or
increased conceptual understanding or power. The second category is <u>expressive</u>
creativity, that is, creativity with no clear practical or conceptual use, value,
or goal, as in much of the arts. Our third category refers to <u>creative</u> personality,

by which we mean a persona and perhaps a life style that is open and flexible
and tolerant of variety, change, and uncertainty, with a positive regard for creativity.   The person with a creative personality may or may not be a direct
contributor to creative activity in the first two categories, although it is
expected that he or she will be. Obviously, these three categories are not
mutually exclusive, and are used here mainly for heuristic purposes.

Our research strongly supports a contribution of the need for stimulation to
both expressive creativity and the creative personality. We have not undertaken sufficient research on tasks reflecting more utilitarian forms of creativity, particularly in areas of scientific creativity and inventiveness, to
allow for strong conclusions.

One means of assessing expressive creativity is through the study of artistic
products, including visual art, sculpture, and various constructions, rating
these as to their evidence of creativity, and relating these ratings to arousability measures or the need for stimulation. We have done this in a number of
studies, employing children, adolescents, and young adults, finding correlations
between creativity ratings and measures of the need for stimulation ranging from
.34 to .66 (e.g., Davis et al., 1974).

A number of characteristics of the creative personality have been identified.
Independence of judgment is one, as is preference for complexity (Barron, 1963).
High energy level, risk taking, nonconformity, and tolerance of ambiguity have
also been identified (e.g., Smith & Schaefer, 1969; Torrance, 1972). Our model
views all these characteristics as in part deriving from or serving the sensation-seeking motive; and in a large number of studies, the strong positive relationship of sensation seeking to these personality attributes has been demonstrated (Farley, 1974, 1981). This relationship between sensation seeking and
creativity might be diagramed in a levels-of-science model (Figure 1), with creative characteristics including high energy, preference for complexity, variety
of interests, nonconformity, and risk taking. The model proposes a biological
basis for creativity, including creative personality and creative artistic
accomplishment.

For our category of instrumental, utilitarian, and productive creativity, not
a great deal of evidence is presently available. Some standard tests of creativity, however, seem to reflect this facet of creativity, including tests
from the widely used Torrance battery (Torrance, 1966), such as the Product
Improvement Test and Unusual Uses Test; and some studies have reported significant positive relationships between these measures and sensation seeking (Farley,
1974), although results in these studies are by no means clear (Farley, 1976).

Additional measures of creativity, which may not fit handily into our heuristic
three-part scheme, have been shown to be related to the need for stimulation.

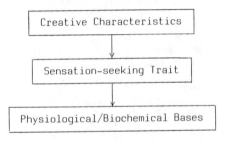

FIGURE 1.   Creativity: A levels-of-science model.

This includes teachers' global ratings of students' creativity (Farley, 1974), peer rankings of creativity, and measured imagery ability (our unpublished data). Zuckerman (1979) has reported other studies. The imagery finding, employing the Galton Breakfast Table test of imagery and Zuckerman's Sensation Seeking Scale, with a correlation of .41 (p < .01), is of particular interest to the hypostatization aspect of our cognitive model, supporting the likelihood of more efficient hypostatization processes in sensation seekers.

Further studies bearing on the creativity implications of the model might well consider directly the processes of scientific discovery and creativity in relation to arousal and the need for stimulation. One approach could examine closely the cognitive processes involved, considering hypostatization, transmutation, and other processes postulated to be involved in scientific creativity, employing scientific problems as the tasks. In addition, the recent work on the knowledge structures and cognitive processes differentiating expert from novice physicists, for example (Larkin et al., 1980), might be considered from the psychobiological perspective of the present model.

EDUCATIONAL IMPLICATIONS

One of the principal educational implications of the model is for individualization, adaptive education, and the notion of aptitude x treatment interaction (ATI) (Cronbach & Snow, 1977; Farley, 1981). Related to this would be a wide range of implications for education of the gifted, talented, and creative child, as well as education in specific subject matter areas such as science, mathematics, and the arts.

The educational implications are treated briefly here: many of them have been considered at length elsewhere (Farley, 1981). One major possibility is the adaptive one, of adapting instruction to biological differences among learners. Adaptive education has become a major theme in contemporary educational research in many countries, wherein instructional methods are adapted to differences among learners (Cronbach & Snow, 1977). Typically the individual differences have been of the traditional aptitude categories, such as verbal intelligence, special intelligence, and fluid and crystallized intelligence, or personality indexes such as anxiety and need for achievement (Shuell, 1981; Tobias, 1981). The researcher attempts to find ATIs that will suggest maximally effective treatment and trait combinations for desired educational outcomes.

Considering aptitudes from a biological viewpoint, we might propose biological aptitudes as a basis for adaptive education. Such biological aptitudes, if shown to interact with treatments in educationally important ways, might have a number of advantages over traditional aptitude and personality measures. If their measurement could be made relatively simple and transportable, then these aptitudes could be assessed in practical situations, with learners of all ages, including possibly the preliterate; the aged; and people of differing races, cultures, and language groups. The possibility would be raised of circumventing at least some of the glaring problems of traditional psychometric assessment of educationally relevant aptitudes, in the face of biases concerning race, age, sex and linguistic background. The measurement of biological aptitudes could contravert the relative remoteness of the traditional methods to measurement from the putative brain bases of cognition and learning. In addition, an advantage of biological aptitudes measures might lie in their high compatibility with the increasing role of microcomputers in education. Thus, an interactive, real-time, computer-mediated learning module or environment could ideally measure in a nonreactive way, via telemetry or other related means, such candidates for biological aptitudes as arousability, cortical augmenting and reducing, orienting reaction, biological cycles, event-related potentials, autonomic

lability, and electrocortical coherence. There could be continuous monitoring
during learner-computer interactions of ongoing electrophysiological changes,
pupillometry, and so on. To the extent that the biological aptitudes and ongoing electrophysiology were shown in research to be related to educationally
relevant learning, cognition, and motivation, then this information could be
taken into account by the computer in the ongoing content selection and sequenc-
ing of instruction. For ethical reasons and considerations of learner freedom,
great care and openness would be required in the use of this process, with
learner control and freedom to choose being central features. With the foregoing caveat, however, the wedding of computers and neuroscience in the general
manner suggested could represent a revolution in education waiting to occur.

For the biological aptitude central to the model presented in this chapter,
arousability, a number of ATIs (one might say, arousability x treatment
interactions) could be hypothesized. Treatments could be considered in at
least three categories -- instruction, the environment for learning, and teacher
characteristics. The arousal value or extrinsic arousal of these three educational factors could be measured and their relationship to learner arousability
considered in an ATI framework. It would be predicted, for instance, that the
arousal seeking of low arousable youngsters would be best served for optimal
educational outcomes by instruction, teachers, and learning environments of high
arousal value, with the opposite being true for high-arousable youngsters. In
addition, the proposed dominant correlative thought processes of low-arousable
people would be best served by complex, varied, multifaceted instruction, so
as to most effectively engage the correlative capabilities of the learner, with
other forms of instruction being required for high-arousable learners. These
proposals from our general model are testable in ATI designs; indeed, some
studies are now available supporting aspects of it (Farley, 1981).

CONCLUSIONS

An individual-differences model of arousal and cognition has been sketched out,
in which the nature of cognitive function is moderated by individual differences in arousability. Low-arousable persons are seen as having more strongly
correlative, transmutative cognitive processes than are high-arousable persons.
Research bearing on this simple model is discussed, and implications for schizophrenia, human creativity, and education are proposed. The model is seen as providing one scheme for investigating brain-cognition relationships -- a process
that has significant practical implications.

REFERENCES

Anderson, J. R. (1980). Cognitive psychology and its implications. San Francisco,
    CA: Freeman.

Barron, F. (1963). Creativity and psychological health. Princeton, NJ: Van
    Nostrand.

Berlyne, D. E. (1972). Aesthetics and psychobiology. New York: Appleton-Century-
    Crofts.

Braverman, M. T., & Farley, F. H. (1978). Arousal and cognition: The stimulation
    seeking motive and structural effects in the comprehension of film. Educational
    Communication and Technology Journal, 26, 321-327.

Broadbent, D. E. (1971). Decision and stress. London: Academic Press.

Corcoran, D. W. J. (1964). The relationship between introversion and salivation. American Journal of Psychology, 77, 298-300.

Cronbach, L. G., & Snow, R. E. (1977). Aptitudes and instructional methods. New York: Irvington.

Davis, G. A., Peterson, J. M., & Farley, F. H. (1974). Attitudes, motivation, sensation-seeking, and belief in ESP as predictors of real creative behavior. Journal of Creative Behavior, 8, 31-39.

Ernest, C. (1977). Imagery ability and cognition: A critical review. Journal of Mental Imagery, 1, 181-216.

Eysenck, H. J. (Ed.). (1973). The measurement of intelligence. Lancaster, PA: Medical and Technical Publishers.

Farley, F. H. (1974, August). A theoretical-predictive model of creativity. Paper presented at the American Psychological Association Annual Meeting, New Orleans, LA.

Farley, F. H. (1976). Arousal and cognition; Creative performance, arousal and the stimulation-seeking motive. Perceptual and Motor Skills, 43, 703-708.

Farley, F. H. (1981). Basic process individual differences: A biologically based theory of individualization for cognitive, affective, and creative outcomes. In F. H. Farley & N. J. Gordon (Eds.), Psychology and education: The state of the union. Berkeley, CA: McCutchan.

Farley, F. H., & Gordon, N. J. (Eds.). (1981). Psychology and education: The state of the union. Berkeley, CA: McCutchan.

Farley, F. H., Osborne, J. W., & Severson, H. H. (1970). The reliability and validity of salivation as a measure of individual differences in intrinsic arousal. (Working Paper No. 51). Madison, WI: Wisconsin Research and Development Center for Cognitive Learning, University of Wisconsin.

Feuerstein, R. (1979). Instrumental enrichment: An intervention program for cognitive modifiability. Baltimore, MD: University Park Press.

Furneaux, W. D. (1973). Intellectual abilities and problem-solving behavior. In H. J. Eysenck (Ed.), The measurement of intelligence. Lancaster: Medical and Technical Publishers.

Heller, C. H. (1979). Criminal behavior and arousal: Test of a theory. Unpublished doctoral dissertation, University of Wisconsin, Madison.

Hunt, E. B. (1978). Mechanics of verbal ability. Psychological Review, 85, 109-130.

Jensen, A. R. (1973). Level I and Level II abilities in three ethnic groups. American Educational Research Journal, 10, 263-276.

Jensen, A. R. (1974). Interaction of Level I and Level II abilities with race and socioeconomic status. Journal of Educational Psychology, 66, 99-111.

Jensen, A. R. (1979). g: Outmoded theory or unconquered territory? Creative Science and Technology, 2, 16-29.

Jensen, A. R. (1980). Chronometric analysis of mental ability. Journal of Social and Biological Structures, 3, 103-122.

Kopell, B. S., Noble, E. F., & Silverman, J. (1965). The effect of thiamylal and methamphetamines on the two-flash fusion threshold. Life Sciences, 4, 2211-2214.

Lacey, J. I. (1967). Somatic response patterning and stress: Some revisions of activation theory. In M. H. Appley & R. Trumbull (Eds.), Psychological stress: Issues in research. New York: Appleton.

Larkin, J. R., McDermott, J., Simon, D. P., & Simon, H. A. (1980). Models of competence in solving physics problems. Cognitive Science, 4, 317-345.

Masser, B. W., & Farley, F. H. (1980). Procedural and statistical methods in the use of the two-flash threshold. Bulletin of the Psychonomic Society, 15, 188-190.

Paivio, A. (1978). Dual coding: Theoretical issues and empirical evidence. In J. M. Scandura & C. J. Brainerd (Eds.), Structural process models of complex human behavior. Leiden, The Netherlands: Nordhoff.

Pellegrino, J. W., & Glaser, R. (1979). Cognitive correlates and components in the analysis of individual differences. In R. J. Sternberg & D. E. Detterman (Eds.), Human intelligence: Perspectives on its theory and measurement. Norwood, NJ: Ablex.

Pribram, K. H., & McGuinness, D. (1975). Arousal, activation and effort in the control of attention. Psychological Review, 82, 116-149.

Razran, G. (1955). Conditioning and perception. Psychological Review, 62, 83-95.

Routtenberg, A. (1968). The two arousal hypothesis: Reticular formation and limbic system. Psychological Review, 75, 51-80.

Roger, F. L. (1971). Information processing of visual figures in the digit symbol substitution task. Journal of Experimental Psychology, 87, 335-342.

Saunders, D. R. (1956). Moderator variables in prediction. Educational and Psychological Measurement, 16, 209-222.

Scandura, J. M., & Brainerd, C. J. (Eds.). Structural/process models of complex human behavior. Leiden, The Netherlands: Nordhoff, 1978.

Shuell, T. J. (1981). Dimensions of individual differences. In F. H. Farley & N. J. Gordon (Eds.), Psychology and education: The state of the union. Berkeley, CA: McCutchan.

Smith, J. M., & Schaefer, C. E. (1969). Development of a creativity scale for the adjective check list. Psychological Reports, 25, 87-92.

Snow, R. E. (1979). Theory and method for research on aptitude processes. In R. J. Sternberg & D. K. Detterman (Eds.), Human intelligence: Perspectives on its theory and measurement. Norwood, NJ: Ablex.

Sternberg, R. J. (1977). Intelligence, information processing, and analogical reasoning: The componential analysis of human abilities. Hillsdale, NJ: Erlbaum.

Sternberg, R. J. (1980). Sketch of a componential subtheory of human intelligence. Behavioral and Brain Sciences, 3, 573-584.

Sternberg, R. J. (1981). Testing and cognitive psychology. American Psychologist, 36, 1181-1189.

Sternberg, R. J., & Detterman, D. K. (Eds.). (1979). Human intelligence: Perspectives on its theory and measurement. Norwood,NJ: Ablex.

Strahan, R.F., Todd, J. B., & Inglis, G. B. (1974). A palmar sweat measure particularly suited for naturalistic research. Psychophysiology, 11, 715-720.

Tobias, S. (1981). Adaptation to individual differences. In F. H. Farley & N. J. Gordon (Eds.), Psychology and education: The state of the union. Berkeley, CA: McCutchan.

Torrance, E. P. (1966). Torrance Tests of Creative Thinking: Directions manual and scoring guide. Princeton, NJ: Personnel Press.

Torrance, E. P. (1972). Some validity studies of two brief screening devices for studying the creative personality. Journal of Creative Behavior, 5, 94-103.

Venables, P. H. (1963a). Selectivity of attention, withdrawal, and cortical activation. Archives of General Psychiatry, 5, 94-103.

Venables, P. H. (1963b). The relationship between level of skin potential and fusion of paired light flashes in schizophrenic and normal subjects. Journal of Psychiatric Research, 1, 279-287.

Venables, P. H., & Warwick-Evans, L. A. (1967). Cortical arousal and two-flash threshold. Psychonomic Science, 8, 231-232.

Watson, J. D. (1968). The double helix: A personal account of the discovery of the structure of DNA. New York: Atheneum.

White, K. D. (1977). Salivation: A review and experimental investigation of major techniques. Psychobiology, 14, 203-212.

Zuckerman, m. (1979). Sensation seeking: Beyond the optimal level of arousal. Hillsdale, NJ: Lawrence Erlbaum.

4

An Overview of Multifactor-System Theory

Joseph R. Royce and Arnold Powell

The study of individual differences in psychological functioning has a long history in the field of psychology (e.g., Boring, 1950), and individual differences have provided the backbone of the applications of psychological science. Even so, the study of individual differences has remained at the periphery of modern experimental-theoretic psychology. This bifurcation of approaches has resulted in the overlooking of many important insights (Cattell, 1966; Cronbach, 1957; Royce, 1950, 1977a). In what follows we present an overview of a variety of individual-difference variables and general psychological processes.

Multifactor-system theory is a general theory of individual differences and integrative personality in which the interacting components are identified via factor analysis, and the principles of integrative functioning are derived from general system and information-processing theory (Powell, Royce, & Voorhees, 1982; Royce, 1973, 1983; Royce & Buss, 1976; Royce & Powell, 1983).

INTEGRATIVE PERSONALITY

The total personality, or the suprasystem, is postulated to be composed of six interacting systems. The cognitive (Diamond & Royce, 1980; Powell & Royce, 1982) and affective (Royce & McDermott, 1977) systems are conceptualized as central

Different versions of this paper have been presented at the 1977 Annual Meeting of the Society of Multivariate Experimental Psychology, Colorado Springs, Colorado; at the University of California, Berkeley, 1977; at the University of California, Santa Cruz, 1977; at the University of Ottawa, 1978; at the Demodata Seminar of Latin American and Canadian Scholars, University of Alberta, May 23-30, 1979; as part of a symposium entitled "A General Theory of Individual Differences," American Psychological Association, held in September 1979, in New York; and as an invited presentation at the International Conference on Individual Differences, University of Warsaw, and Polish Academy of Sciences, September 10-14, 1979, in Warsaw. A longer version of this chapter has appeared as three papers in the Journal of Personality and Social Psychology entitled "An overview of a multi-factor-system theory of personality and individual differences: I. The factor and system models and the hierarchical factor structure of individuality; II. System dynamics and person-situation interactions; III. Life-span development and the heredity-environment issue." In addition, an extended version is appearing in Royce, J. R., & Powell, A. D. (1983), A theory of personality and individual differences: Factors, systems, processes, Englewood Cliffs, NJ: Prentice-Hall.

processing units, which function as information transformers.   The style (Wardell & Royce, 1975, 1978) and value (Schopflocher & Royce, 1980). systems are also central processing units, but they function more as personality integrators. Finally, the sensory (Kearsley & Royce, 1977) and motor (Powell, Katzko, & Royce, 1978) systems are more peripheral processing units, which function as input-output transducers, encoders, and decoders. These six systems are organized as a multilevel, hierarchical, system (Mesarovic, Macko, & Takahara, 1970), in which there is a controlled-process layer or stratum (sensory, motor), a learning-adaptive layer (cognitive, affective), and an integrative layer (styles, values). In turn, each of the individual systems is conceptualized as a multilevel, hierarchical, system, where the elements of the hierarchies are identified via factor analysis.

The individual systems and major system interactions that are postulated to constitute integrative personality are diagrammed in Figure 1. The major subsystems within each of the six personality systems are also depicted in this figure (for example, the cognitive system is composed of the perceiving, conceptualizing, and symbolizing subsystems, while the subsystems of the motor system are spatiality and temporality). These subsystems can also be described as higher-order factors or dimensions of individual differences. To be more specific, the various subsystems depicted in Figure 1 are identified via thirdorder factors that subsume a variety of second and first-order (or primary) factors. In our research on the structure and dynamics of the various systems of integrative personality, approximately 200 factors have been identified as

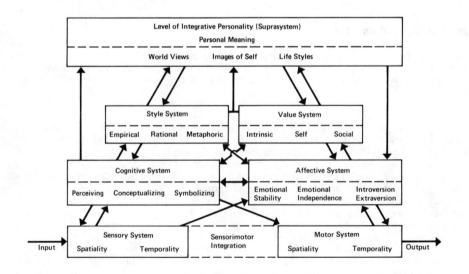

FIGURE 1.   Integrated personality and subsystem interactions. From "Paths to Being, Life Style, and Individuality" by A. Powell and J. R. Royce, 1978, Psychological Reports, 42, 987-1005. Copyright 1978 by Psychological Reports. Reprinted by permission.

viable dimensions of individual differences.[1] The system interpretation of
these factors emphasizes their role as psychological processors (Royce, 1963;
Royce, Kearsley, & Klare, 1978), that transform and integrate psychological
information.

Integrative personality has been conceptualized as being hierarchically organized, because there are systems that intervene in the functioning of other,
lower level, systems. For example, there are control-decision units, such as
cognition or value, which provide coordinating inputs (Mesarovic et al., 1970;
Royce, 1977b) into lower level systems, such as motor and affective. Such coordinating inputs are depicted in Figure 1 as arrows pointing from higher to
lower level systems, whereas feedback and other inputs (e.g., feedforward) are
represented by the arrows that point toward the higher level systems.

An additional point needs to be made with respect to the postulated structure
of integrative personality. That is, the suprasystem, as well as its component
central processing systems, is construed as a goal-seeking system (Mesarovic
et al., 1970; Sommerhof, 1969; von Bertalanffy, 1955, 1962) with internal norms for
evaluating positive and negative feedback information. Furthermore, the goals
of the system are hierarchically decomposable; for example, plans can be decomposed into strategies and strategies into tactics (Miller, Galanter, & Pribram,
1960; Royce, 1977b; Singer, 1975). At the highest level of personality, the
system goal is to optimize personal meaning, which involves such subtotal goals
as establishing a satisfactory life style and evolving an adequate world view
(see Figure 1). But life style entails coordination of the value and affective
systems (Powell & Royce, 1978) and world view involves coordination of the
style and cognitive systems (Royce, 1974, 1975).

STRUCTURE AND DYNAMICS OF INDIVIDUAL DIFFERENCES

The basic units of analysis in individuality theory are the dimensions of individual differences, which have been identified via the theory and methodology of
factor analysis. More precisely, a factor is conceived as a theoretical construct which (a) accounts for observed covariation when viewed in the context of
the factor model (Royce, 1963), and (b) identifies processing components when em-
bedded in the conceptual framework of system-information theory (Royce & Buss,
1976; Royce et al., 1978). In either case the conceptual focus is on factors as
O variables rather than S or R variables. Thus, at the dimensional level, we are
describing the trait or behavior phenotypic properties of organisms.

In this section we provide a highly compressed summary of individuality structure. We begin with our conception of the total psychological or behavioral
system. The psychological system (or personality) is defined as a hierarchical
organization of systems, subsystems, and traits that transduce, transform, and
integrate information. As described in Figure 1, this complex suprasystem is
composed of six major subsystems, each of which is further decomposed into
multileveled, multidimensional subsystems.

Because of space limitations, however, we cannot describe all six systems. We
can define each of the systems; further, we can exemplify them. And, since the
structure of these hierarchies is similar, the lack of detail will not affect
the reader's comprehension of the total theory. We begin with the definition
of four multidimensional, hierarchical systems:

---

[1]The current inventory of dimensions for the total psychological system breaks
down as follows: Sensory = 19, Motor = 46, Cognitive = 32, Affective = 30,
Style = 15, and Value = 43.

1. The sensory system transduces physical energy into psychological information.
2. The motor system transduces psychological information into physical energy.
3. The style system integrates and modulates information by coordinating cognition and affect and by selecting particular modes of processing.
4. The value system integrates and modulates information by coordinating cognition and affect to achieve specifiable goals, by satisfying specifiable needs, or by selecting specifiable informational content.

The Cognitive and Affective Systems

Because of the relative strength of the available empirical findings, along with their central role in understanding personality, we provide details for the two transformational systems, cognition and affect, indicated in Figures 2 and 3 respectively. Both are multidimensional, hierarchical systems, as were the previous four:

1. The cognitive system transforms information in order to detect environmental invariants.
2. The affective system transforms information into arousal states.

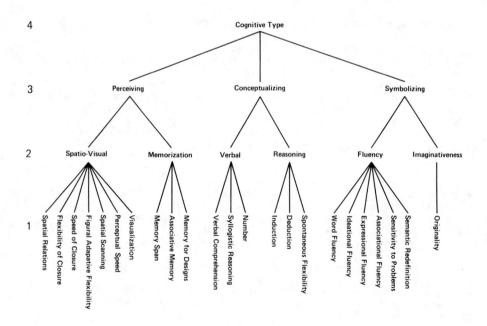

FIGURE 2. The hierarchical structure of the cognitive system. From "Cognitive Abilities as Expressions of Three 'Ways of Knowing'" by S. Diamond and J. R. Royce, 1980, Multivariate Behavioral Research, 15, 31-56. Copyright 1980 by Multivariate Behavioral Research. Reprinted by permission.

Individual differences in these two domains are the most thoroughly researched
of the six systems. This means, for example, that the case for factor invariance is stronger for these two systems than it is for the remaining four,
particularly at the primary level. The case for invariance is equally strong
at the third order of the affective system, however, primarily because of the
extensive experimental research of Eysenck. There is also less extensive
confirmation of the second-order factors of the cognitive domain, and the
factorial evidence for the third-order cognitive constructs is minimal.
Despite this deficiency, the cumulative, nonfactorial, experimental literature
provides a compelling empirico-inductive basis for these higher order constructs.
It would be surprising if categories akin to these were not eventually fac-
torially confirmed. The second-order constructs of the affective domain, on
the other hand, are much less secure. Although there is weak empirical evidence
for each of them, it would be surprising if all of these factors are eventually
confirmed. Factorial clarification of the second stratum of the affective
domain is the most critical structural deficiency of these two systems.

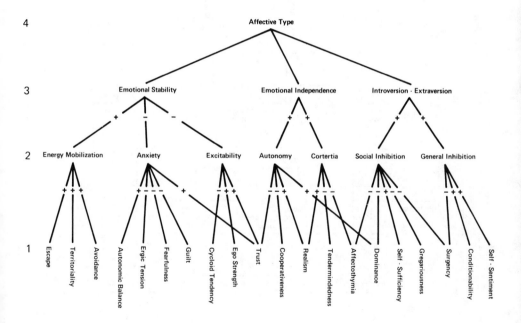

FIGURE 3. A hierarchy for the affective system. From "A Multi-dimensional
System Dynamics Model of Affect" by J. R. Royce and J. McDermott, 1977,
Motivation and Emotion, 1, 193-224. Copyright by Plenum Publishing Corporation.
Reprinted by permission.

SYSTEM DYNAMICS

The system dynamics aspect of individuality theory is dealt with via a comprehensive description of functional interactions of relevant dimensions during
different phases of information processing. This approach is based on the
biological principle that function is dependent on structure. Thus, whereas
Figures 1-3 indicate the structural interrelationships between the dimensions,
what follows focuses on their functional interactions. The point is that understanding of the dynamics of individuality or general functioning requires an
information-processing account of both component interactions and the temporal
sequentiality of these interactions. We have chosen the cognitive system as
an example. Figure 4 provides a model of human cognition as a complex information processing system in which the role of individual differences has been
incorporated (Powell & Royce, 1982). As can be seen, there is a multilevel,
hierarchical organization where the decision-control processes are conceived
as coordinating the activity of the three principal cognitive subsystems.
These subsystems coordinate the activity of the various transformational
processes of the subsumed levels. The percepts, concepts, propositions, and
symbols are viewed as having a direct coordinating impact on the lower level

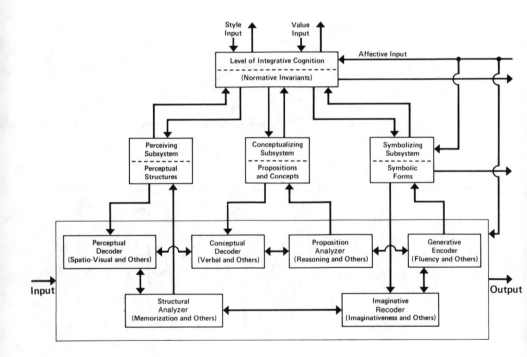

FIGURE 4. Cognition represented as a complex information-processing system.
From "Cognitive Information Processing: The Role of Individual Differences in
the Search for Invariants" by A. Powell and J. R. Royce, 1982, Academic
Psychological Bulletin. Copyright 1982 by Academic Psychological Bulletin.
Reprinted by permission.

processing (transformations and encodings). Moreover, given that there are
feedforward and feedback relations operative between higher level subsystems
and components, the ongoing processing activities also modify the perceptual,
conceptual, and symbolic structures of the system. This latter relationship
is analogous to the standard information-processing notion that information can
be stored in long-term memory. But, as in Neisser's more recent model (1976;
see also Bransford, Franks, McCarrel, & Nitsch, 1977), the present theory views
the problem of long-term memory as more of a problem of modification of existing
schemata than as a problem in storage.

It is obvious that the cognitive system is goal directed, and certainly knowledge
of the world is a cognitive goal. Furthermore, knowledge critically involves
the discovery of invariants (Powell & Royce, 1982). Another aspect of the goals
of the cognitive system (or the maintenance of a steady state) can be expressed
in terms of the regulation or management of uncertainty (Jung, 1965). But it is
necessary to produce uncertainty (i.e., perform transformations whose results
are uncertain beforehand) in the available information in order to discover invariants. Thus, the management of uncertainty and the search for invariants
are different sides of the same coin.

A variety of factors influence the amount of uncertainty a person will tolerate
and the specific transformations produced. In addition to cognitive abilities,
for example, a person's profile of styles and values affects the management of
uncertainty. Styles select for specific modes of processing (Wardell & Royce,
1978), whereas values select for specific informational content (Schopflocher
et al., 1980). Furthermore, the various effects of affective arousal must also
be considered (Royce & McDermott, 1977).

A TOTE hierarchy for describing the decision-control processes of the cognitive
system is presented in Figure 5. The important normative match in the case of
human cognition relates to the extent to which a person's perceptual, conceptual,
and symbolic schemata express sufficient invariance about the environment for
the current adaptive requirements to be met. Whether a given discrepancy
between current norms and existing cognitive schemata can be ignored is related
to the affective and evaluative characteristics of the organism. For example,
inhibition (Royce & McDermott, 1977) is one affective characteristic that is
important in this regard. Affective characteristics would also influence the
extent to which people will temporarily increase uncertainty in order to reduce
long-range uncertainty (e.g., emotional stability is critical here). Values are
also relevant; for example, a person who is higher on an intrinsic evaluative
orientation will be more likely to engage in the manipulation of conceptual
uncertainty and less likely to ignore conceptual discrepancies. A person with
a social value orientation would be more likely to focus on perceptual invariants (Royce & Diamond, 1980). But cognitive styles influence the selection
of processing modes and parameters, as when persons who are higher on empirical
style give greater emphasis to perceiving as a mode of processing, and persons
higher on rational style emphasize conceptualizing as a mode of processing
(Wardell & Royce, 1978).[2]

Life-Span Development of Factors

The prototypic, quantitative, life-span developmental curve for factor growth
is shown in Figure 6. The abscissa is chronological age and the ordinate is

---

[2]There are, of course, similar linkages for the empiric and metaphoric styles
as well. See Wardell and Royce (1978) for details.

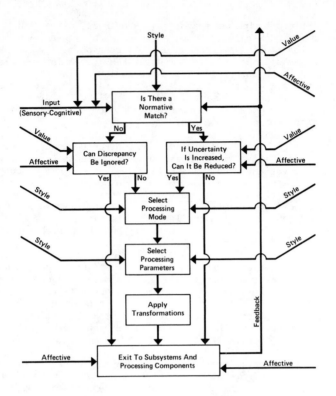

FIGURE 5. A TOTE hierarchy describing the decision-control processes of the cognitive system. From "Cognitive Information Processing: The Role of Individual Differences in the Search for Invariants" by A. Powell and J. R. Royce, 1982, Academic Psychological Bulletin. Copyright 1982 by Academic Psychological Bulletin. Reprinted by permission.

the scaled score on a given factor. There are three parameters of psychological interest: K_1, K_2, and K_3. On the age dimension, maturity (M), or maximum performance, is indicated by K_2, and the onset of senility (S), or performance level before death, is indicated by K_3. The location of the y intercept, K_1, indicates the extent of prenatal development, or the degree to which the factor is present at birth (B). The value of the parameter K_2 indicates the maximum factor performance level (P) which occurs at maturity (M). If a factor does not reach optimal developmental level in the life span of a person (i.e., continues to either increase or decline over the entire life span), the value of K_1 will take the value of the factor score at birth or death (for a decrease or increase, respectively). The curve segment $K_1 - K_2$ indicates the rate of developmental change during childhood, adolescence, and early adulthood. The parameter K_3 represents the factor score at the onset of senescence (S) (or death if there is no senescent period). It is to be expected that factor scores will always decline in any postsenescence measurement. The segment of development

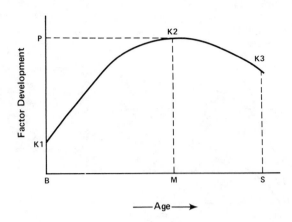

FIGURE 6. The generalized life-span development curve. The parameters K₁ to
K₃ indicate performance (P) levels at birth (B), maturity (M), and senescence
(S). Adapted from "The Conceptual Framework for a Multi-factor Theory of
Individuality" by J. R. Royce, 1973, in J. R. Royce (Ed.), <u>Multivariate Analysis</u>
<u>and Psychological Theory</u>, London: Academic Press. Copyright 1973 by Academic
Press. Reprinted by permission.

represented by the K₂ - K₃ portion of the curve is, of course, factor change over
the major part of the life span of the person. Empirical examples of quantitative changes in the cognitive domain are presented in Kearsley, Buss, and Royce
(1977). Changes in the other domains are summarized in Powell, Holt, and Royce
(1979).[3]

Let us now take a closer look at the relationships between heredity, environment,
and development. Note, for example, that the actual performances depicted so
far are due to both heredity and environment. Hence, it will be necessary to
tease out exactly how such effects are operating. The two classes of factors,
<u>heredity-dominant</u> and <u>environment-dominant,</u> and shown in Figures 7 and 8. The
solid-line curve in Figure 7 shows the performance level for a particular genotype in interaction with a specified environment. To the extent performance
can be shifted in either direction from this genetic baseline, we get environmental effects. If the effect of environment is severe, performance level will
be drastically changed, as in the case of the two dotted-line curves labeled
environment dominant. If the effect is minimal, there will be no significant
departure in observed performance; hence the solid line curve is labeled
heredity dominant. Similar effects concerning age of maturity are shown in
Figure 8. Environmental effects can speed up or retard or have no effect on

---

[3]A complete analysis of multivariate development must include both quantitative
(shifts in any one factor) and qualitative (shifts in the organization of factor subsets) change. It also includes an analysis of shifts in the functioning
of the six systems and their subsystems. But space limitations preclude a full
exposition. We have, therefore, confined the present exposition to quantitative multivariate development.

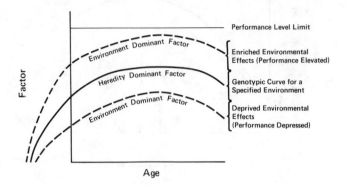

FIGURE 7. Heredity- and environment-dominant factors in terms of performance.
From "The Conceptual Framework for a Multi-factor Theory of Individuality" by
J. R. Royce, 1973, in J. R. Royce (Ed.), Multivariate Analysis and Psychological
Theory, London: Academic Press. Copyright 1973 by Academic Press. Reprinted
by permission.

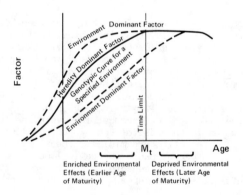

FIGURE 8. Heredity- and environment-dominant factors in terms of age and
maturity. From "The Conceptual Framework for a Multi-factor Theory of Individuality" by J. R. Royce, 1973, in J. R. Royce (Ed.), Multivariate Analysis and
Psychological Theory, London: Academic Press. Copyright 1973 by Academic
Press. Reprinted by permission.

age of maturity. Those factors (dotted-line curves) that are highly susceptible to such effects have been labeled environment dominant, whereas the solid-line curve has been labeled heredity dominant.

Thus, a heredity dominant factor is a primarily genetically determined dimension with a developmental curve highly resistant to environmental effects. It is statistically definable in terms of relatively small variations from the genotype curve despite attempts to induce environmental effects. An environment dominant factor is a dimension with a primarily environmentally determined developmental curve that is relatively uninfluenced by hereditary effects. It is statistically definable in terms of a relatively large variation from the genotypic curve as a result of attempts to induce environmental effects.

It should be obvious that these are idealized extremes, and that most cases, being subject to both environmental and genetic influences, will fall in between.[4] We have designated such interaction cases as partial hereditary dominance or partial environmental dominance, in accordance with the direction of the major effect. Furthermore, it should be apparent that complete or partial hereditary or environmental dominance may occur in connection with either or both genetic-environment limits. The point of immediate importance is that this analysis provides a plausible theoretical foundation for empirically finding out the extent to which various factors are heredity dominant or environment dominant.

The Factor-Gene Model

In Figure 9 we have depicted the most probable linkage between the multiple factors of behavioral variation and the underlying multiplicity of genes, linked via a variety of unspecified, intervening biological mechanisms (labeled psychophysiological genetics). Note that in both the behavioral and genetic domains, many elemental factors account for a complex. On the behavioral side, many different factors (both first-order factors, such as Space and Memory, and higher order factors such as g1 and g2) or behavioral phenotypes account for the complex we call intelligence. On the genetic side, various combinations of many genes account for a particular behavior phenotype such as Space or Memory. Thus, a person may inherit all of the capital letter forms of the gene pairs of the Space factor (i.e., AA, BB, CC, DD, EE, FF, GG). Because this means that the person has the maximum number (seven chosen arbitrarily) of capital letter genes for this particular genotype, and assuming optimal environmental conditions, we would expect him to perform at the highest possible level in tasks involving the perception of spatial relationships. If another person inherited genes f, g, h, i, j, k, l, and m from the available gene pairs of the Memory factor, we would expect a minimal performance on pure memory tasks.

Note that the hereditary correlate for each factor is polygenic, and that the usual genetic mechanisms, such as dominance, epistasis, pleiotropy, and sex linkage, are operative, depending on the factor in question. It is important

---

[4]We should anticipate the fact that few factors will behave in complete accordance with these idealized curves for the simple reason that it is impossible for either σ_H^2 or σ_E^2 to equal zero. That is, there will always be some variance due to environment in the case of heredity-dominant factors, and vice versa. This is true because there is always an interaction going on between heredity and environment; it is impossible for genes to function independently of environment, and it is impossible for environment to determine phenotype independently of gene effects.

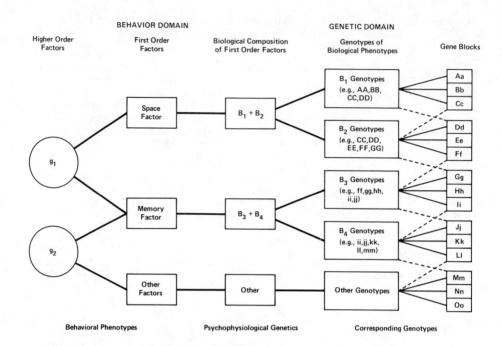

FIGURE 9. The revised version of the most probable linkage between the multi-factor theory of psychology and the multiple-factor theory of genetics. From "The Factor-gene Basis of Individuality" by J. R. Royce, in J. R. Royce & L. P. Mos (Eds.), Theoretical Advances in Behavior Genetics, Leyden, The Netherlands: International Publishing. Copyright 1979 by Martinus Nijhoff Publishers (for International Publishing). Reprinted by permission.

to note that the factor-gene model does not imply a one factor-one gene linkage, as erroneously claimed by Fuller and Thompson (1960). Nor does the model imply that there are mutually exclusive blocks of genes with corresponding uncor-related factorial phenotypes. Rather, it implies that specifiable subsets of the gene pool account for the hereditary variation and covariation of factors. For example, gene pairs Aa through Gg combine, via biological phenotypes B_1 and B_2, to account for hereditary variation on the Space factor, and gene pairs FF through Mm combine, via biological phenotypes B_3 and B_4, to account for heredi-tary variations on the Memory factor. Covariation of phenotypes, however, is attributed to gene subsets that are common to two or more phenotypes. These include gene pairs Cc, Dd, Ff, Gg, Ii, Jj, Ll, and Mm. Only four gene pairs, however, are relevant to correlated behavior phenotypes, namely Ff and Gg (as the hereditary basis for the correlation between the Memory and Space factors) and Ll and Mm (as the hereditary source of correlation between Memory and Other factors). The other gene pairs, Cc, Dd, Ii, and Jj, constitute the hereditary basis for those biological phenotypes (i.e., the full range of psychophysiology, such as brain function, hormone function, and biochemical mechanisms) that are relevant to specifiable first-order factors (gene pairs Cc and Dd account for the covariation of B_1 and B_2 and gene pairs Ii and Jj account for the covariation of B_3 and B_4).

Although the factor-gene model was first put forward over 20 years ago (Royce, 1957), the supporting evidence is limited to two of the six systems -- cognition and affect (Royce, 1979a). Most studies involve monozygotic and dizygotic twin samples and classical heritability estimates. The remaining studies involve a range of family resemblance strategies. The findings indicate that there is a significant hereditary effect for 10 (Thurstone's Primary Mental Abilities plus three others) of the 32 factors (around 31%) of the cognitive system. The hereditary effect is particularly strong for three factors -- verbal comprehension, spatial relations, and word fluency. The evidence is only moderately strong, however, in the case of memorization, perceptual speed, inductive reasoning, and number factors; and the evidence is weakest for the associative memory, associational fluency, and ideational fluency dimensions.

The research on the hereditary basis of factor-identified behavioral phenotypes in the affective domain is more extensive. The methods include Cattell's Multiple Abstract Variance Analysis, classical heritabilities, or some form of biometric analysis. Briefly summarizing, there is evidence for a significant hereditary effect for 25 of the 30 factors (i.e., 83%) of the affective system.[5] The strong-evidence factors include all three third-order factors (introversion-extraversion, emotional stability, and emotional independence) and six primaries (surgency, fearfulness, escape, territoriality, avoidance, and autonomic balance). The moderate-evidence factors include three second-order factors (social inhibition, cortertia, and anxiety) and eight primaries. The minimal-evidence factors include two second-order factors (autonomy and excitability) and three primaries.

Factor-Learning Model

The key to how learning affects factors lies in how we conceive of learning. Traditional treatments of learning are not adequate for our purposes, because they were not developed in the context of factor-system theory. Thus, we will define <u>learning</u> as any change in psychological structure (i.e., factors and their relationships) due to experience (e.g., practice effects).

---

[5] The most convincing experimental confirmation of factor-gene model comes from the affective domain. The research in question involved 42 measures, 6 inbred mouse strains, and their F_1 offspring, and a total of 775 subjects (Poley & Royce, 1973; Royce, Holmes, & Poley, 1975; Royce, Poley, & Yeudall, 1973). A diallel analysis (Mather & Jinks, 1971) was carried out in each of 15 factors. The most pervasive finding is that the genetic correlate for each factor is polygenic, and, in general, in the direction of complete dominance effects. A major point of this investigation, however, is that mode of inheritance depends on the factor in question. For example, factors related to escape and avoidance -- the avoidance, territorial marking, fearfulness, audiogenic reactivity, and escape components -- are governed by complete or over (i.e., heterotic) dominance effects. Furthermore, in three of these cases -- escape, audiogenic reactivity, and territorial marking -- there is evidence of directional dominance. Factors related to undifferentiated arousal, such as autonomic balance, motor discharge, and activity level, showed either partial or no dominance effects (i.e., an intermediate or blending form of inheritance) (Royce, 1979b).

This conception of learning puts the focus on the psychological structure which underlies change in performance per se and it applies to all structural levels and facets, such as cognitive structure and affective structure, and all their individual components. Thus, changes at the higher order levels of psychological structure would represent shifts in style or world view, changes in cognitive structure relate to the usual school learning or general fund of knowledge a person has acquired, and changes in affective structure refer to temperament shifts. All are manifestations of acculturation -- shifts in psychological structure due to cultural learning. The implication is that different cultures or environments will maximize different combinations of structural components. For example, the environmental-cultural forces of relatively primitive societies will reinforce those cognitive and affective components that are consistent with such activities as hunting, fishing, agriculture, and other basic survival behavior. Similarly, more developed cultures will require that its participants learn a great deal about numbers and words, in some cases to the extent of developing experts in knowledge specialties such as the humanities or the sciences. In short, differential reinforcement is probably the learning principle that can best account for the acculturation process. But note one important difference between the present account and the traditional socialization account. The standard view reinforces responses; in this view, the change in underlying psychological structure is important (Buss, 1973a, 1973b; Royce, 1973).

There are two general classes of structural change in the factor-learning model, quantitative and qualitative. Quantitative change is a modification in the performance level of any one factor. Qualitative change is a modification in the relationships (e.g., the correlations) between two or more factors. For example, if reinforcement simultaneously elevates the performance levels on two previously uncorrelated factors, it constitutes an example of a qualitative change due to learning. The best empirical demonstrations of quantitative change due to learning involve a progressive change in the contributions of various cognitive and motor factors to performance on a complex motor task (Fleishmann, 1972, 1975).

Heredity, Environment, and Individuality

What conclusions can be drawn concerning the relative roles of heredity and environment as sources of observed psychological variation? We hypothesize that the sensory and motor systems are heredity dominant, that the cognitive and affective systems are partially heredity dominant, and that the style and value systems are environment dominant. These hypotheses receive support on both empirical and theoretical grounds. The empirical grounds have been summarized in Royce (1979b), and the theoretical grounds have to do with the evolutionary-adaptive significance of living information-processing systems (Royce & Mos, 1979).

Elsewhere, we have elaborated on the transductive information-processing role of the sensory (Kearsley & Royce, 1977) and motor (Powell et al., 1978) systems. This kind of information processing occurs at the interface between the organism (the psychological system) and the environment (the organism's suprasystem); it is, therefore, critical to species survival. That is, organismic survival is presumed to be impossible without some kind of input-output structure (Miller, 1978). Evolutionary theory implies that species with ineffective input and output transducers are weeded out via natural selection. In short, because the sensory and motor systems are the most biologically primitive of the six systems, it is not surprising that heredity should play a greater role than environment in these two systems.

It is hypothesized, on the other hand, that the cognitive and affective systems are only partially heredity dominant. This means that heredity is more important than environment, but only slightly -- perhaps in the neighborhood of 55-60% of the variance attributable to heredity and the remainder attributable to environment. How does this square with the evolutionary-adaptive role of the organism? According to individuality theory, these two systems are information transformers. This means they take the transduced information provided by the sensory system and change it into some other psychologically meaningful form, such as cognitions (i.e., percepts, concepts, and symbols) and affects (i.e., the emotions). We have argued elsewhere that the major role of the cognitive system is to interpret or understand the environment. More specifically, this means identifying environmental invariants -- that is, perceptual, conceptual, and metaphoric invariants (Powell & Royce, 1982). Because such invariances constitute human constructions of "the way things are," they are also critical components of world views (Royce, 1974, 1975). The affective system plays a similar role, but the transformational process is focused on preparing the organism for action via a variety of arousal mechanisms (Royce & McDermott, 1977). The affective system is organized for coping with the daily stresses of life (Royce & Diamond, 1980) as well as providing a basis for life style (Powell & Royce, 1978). In short, the argument is that the cognitive and affective systems have been selected for adaptive flexibility. Biologically, flexibility implies the capacity to adapt to the widest possible range of ecologies. Thus, such reactions as fixed action patterns and rigid perceptions would be inconsistent with optimizing flexibility. The implication is that cognitive and affective behavior would be too rigid with extreme genetic determination, too flexible with extreme environmental determination, but optimally flexible with near equivalent genetic-environment determination.

Finally, we come to the hypothesis that the functioning of the style and value systems is environment dominant. This means that environment is more important than heredity in such cases. Why should this be true? According to individuality theory, these two systems are primarily concerned with integration -- that is, the coordination and synthesis of information and personality. However, integration clearly requires prior informational inputs and transformations. But it seems equally clear that there will be a wide range of possible syntheses, depending on what information has been previously stored, how it has been transformed, and the particular styles and values that have guided the synthesizing process. The point is that nature has not evolved a genetic-evolutionary mechanism for transmitting informational content (an acquired characteristic) from one generation to the next. Thus, biological evolution appears to be irrelevant in the case of styles and values. But cultural evolution is critical, for cultural evolution has to do with those styles and values that have been institutionalized. The institutionalization of styles and values refers to "how" and "what" commitments that were so adaptive in a given time and place that it was thought they might be equally adaptive in another time and place. Thus, styles and values are passed on from one generation to the next via the culture. Furthermore, they constitute the major building blocks for such molar behavioral complexities as world view, life style, and self image. In short, styles and values are relevant to the big questions of existence -- the nature of reality, the key to self identity, and how we should live our daily lives. Psychological questions of this magnitude are clearly beyond the ken of genes. The genes have enough burden to bear in accounting for variations in the sensory, motor, cognitive, and affective systems.

PERSON-SITUATION INTERACTIONS

It is clear that behavior is a function of both the person and the situation. Furthermore, it is possible that an even more significant proportion of behavioral variation is attributable to person-situation interactions (e.g., Bowers, 1973). In what follows, we analyze the relationships between personality traits and situational demands in terms of a factor based typology of both persons and situations.[6] By <u>personality type</u> we mean the profile of the total psychological system, where the term profile refers to performance level on the total set of dimensions that defines personality. It follows from this that profile type is a composite profile of the six systems.

Similarly, we refer to environmental or situational demands as the situational template. <u>Situational template</u> means the profile of psychological requirements for adapting to a specifiable situation, where the term profile refers to performance level requirements on the total set of dimensions that psychologically define the situation. Thus, situational profile is a composite profile of a situation in terms of the relevant dimensions of the six psychological systems.

The concepts of situational template and personality type are highly compressed conceptions of the information processing required for coping with environmental demands.[7] These two concepts are, in fact, the key to understanding individuality-systems processing. The implication is that the degree of overlap between situational and personal profiles is a crucial determinant of psychological functioning. Thus, if the corresponding profiles are exactly the same (i.e., the same components and beta weights), performance should be perfect. If, on the other hand, the profiles are totally different (i.e., they involve entirely different component subsets), then performance should be impossible. Since neither of these two logical extremes are possible in practice, we must look to the range of mismatches in between for relevant empirical realities.

Combining the concepts of personality type and situational template leads to the concept of <u>type-template match</u>. This refers to the degree of alignment between the situation and person profiles. A perfect alignment would mean that a particular personality type was optimally matched to the demands of the situation.[8] The obvious consequence of a personality type-situation template

_____

[6] We are aware of the theoretical troubles that traditionally have accompanied the concept of personality type. It should be noted that our usage does <u>not</u> follow the traditional practice of regarding two or more points on a continuous distribution as types. This approach violates at least two critical points: it arbitrarily categorizes a distribution that is clearly continuous, and it fails to take the multidimensionality of personality into account. See Diamond, Voorhees, and Royce (1981) for a more complete exposition of our multidimensional conception of personality type.

[7] The concepts of situational template and personality type have also been simplified because of space constraints. The full exposition of these concepts would include temporality -- the temporal organization of a given personality type on the one hand, and the sequential properties of a situational profile on the other.

[8] It is our view that process sequentiality is primarily determined by the demands of the situation, particularly if the situation is highly structured. The less structured the situation, on the other hand, the greater the role of personality type in determining process sequence. This follows logically because of the diminished role of situational determinants whenever there is ambiguity. Furthermore, how a situation is actually dealt with, regardless of the degree of situational structure, is dependent on personality type. Clearly, different types will invoke different components and different temporal sequences. The role of the situation in determining behavior has

mismatch is <u>compensatory functioning</u>, that is, adapting to situational demands in terms of the available personality type. Since no single personality type can be optimal for all situations, it follows that some compensatory function- ing is an inevitable characteristic of normal functioning. If the mismatch is primarily due to the demands of the situation, one form of adaptation is for the person to switch to a less discrepant environment. If the situational demands are minimal, however, adaptation will occur via some mix of assimilation or accommodation.

Type-template match, which refers to the degree of alignment between situation- al template and personality type, should not be confused with normative match. <u>Normative match</u> refers to the degree of alignment between a specifiable norm (i.e., a psychological construction such as a goal or purpose) and the environ- mental input. When there is a close match (within a specifiable tolerance), no adjustments in either the environment or the person are required. In these cases, the conclusion is that the norm has assimilated the demands of the situ- ation. Normative adjustments are required, however, when there is a mismatch. If the normative shift subsequently leads to a match, we refer to such changes as accommodation.

Suprasystem plans and system programs provide the basis for assessing the degree of match or mismatch. For example, a plan or program that is identical with the situational template (i.e., completely replicates the task demands) would constitute a perfect type-template match. It should be noted, however, that optimal performance would require a perfect normative match as well. Since actual plans and programs will usually not result in optimal performance, it can be concluded that this is due to mismatches in either normative or type- template matching. For example, a perfect normative match accompanied by poor performance would mean the right plan but the wrong personality type -- a type- template mismatch. A perfect type-template match accompanied by poor per- formance, on the other hand, would mean the right personality type but the wrong plan -- a normative mismatch.

Both type-template and normative matches are suprasystem constructs; they refer to the total psychological system as the functioning unit (see level 4 in Figure 1). However, there are important functional differences. The major difference is that normative match is focused on interactions between the organism and the environment and type-template match is focused on system interactions within the organism. Thus, normative match is externally oriented and type-template match is focused on system interactions within the organism. Thus, normative match is externally oriented and type-template match is inter- nally oriented. More specifically, in terms of process, type-template matching is focused on the central processing of information in terms of environmental demands. Normative matching, on the other hand, involves comparing (via assim- ilation and accommodation) psychological constructions with the demands of the environment.

----

been referred to as the principle of context dependency. When this principle is combined with other multidimensional system properties, such as the causal properties of macrodeterminism, multiple determination, and interdeterminism, we see why the standard sequentiality of billiard-ball causality will not work for complex phenomena such as individual differences. The point is that billiard-ball causality would only be able to account for the behavior of rigid robots. That is, its limitation to closed systems renders it incapable of accounting for the behavior of flexible persons (Powell, et al., 1982).

Personality integration involves a delicate balance of interaction components at all levels of the psychological system -- interactions between elemental components, subsystems, and the six systems. The most encompassing indicator of personality integration at a given moment in time is the dynamic balance between the assimilative and accommodative functioning of the total system.

ACKNOWLEDGEMENTS

We wish to acknowledge the grant support provided by the National Research Council, the Alberta Human Resources Research Council, and the University of Alberta. But we are especially indebted to Canada Council for the generous and extended financial backing provided to J. R. Royce since 1968. This includes a Sabbatical Leave Grant for the year 1972-1973. The Individuality Project constitutes a unique experiment in theory construction in that it is the product of a group effort. The Project Director is particularly indebted to Arnold Powell, Senior Research Associate. We are also indebted to the other major contributors to the project -- Stephen Diamond, Research Associate; Burt Voorhees, Mathematical Research Associate; and Donald Schopflocher, Graduate Research Assistant. Other collaborators include Research Associate Allan Buss and Graduate Research Assistant Gregory Kearsley, both of whom made important contributions during the early stages of the project. Others who have contributed include Research Associates George Kawash and Warren Klare and Graduate Research Assistants Michael Katzko, John McDermott, and Douglas Wardell. Other contributions have been made by Research Assistants Peter Holt, Kenneth Meehan, Steve Nicely, and John Wozny. Finally, we are indebted to the following Center Staff for continual critical feedback over the past 15 years: Richard Jung, W. W. Rozeboom, Herman Tennessen, Kellogg Wilson, and Teddy Weckowicz. However, we owe a special indebtedness to Leendert Mos, Center Professional Officer, who has contributed directly to several empirical aspects of the project, and who has also interacted with us in our weekly individuality seminars as a friendly and constructive critic.

REFERENCES

von Bertalanffy, L. (1955). General systems theory. Main Currents in Modern Thought, 11, 85-93.

von Bertalanffy, L. (1962). General system theory: A critical review. General Systems, 7, 1-20.

Boring, E. G. (1950). A history of experimental psychology (2nd ed.). New York: Appleton-Century.

Bowers, K. S. (1973). Situationism in psychology: An analysis and a critique. Psychological Review, 80, 307-336.

Bransford, J. D., Franks, J. J., McCarrell, N. S., & Nitsch,K. E. (1977). Toward unexplaining memory. In R. Shaw & J. Bransford (Eds.), Perceiving, acting, and knowing: Toward an ecological psychology. Hillsdale, NJ: Lawrence Erlbaum.

Buss, A. R. (1973a). A conceptual framework for learning effecting the development of ability factors. Human Development, 16, 273-292.

Buss, A. R. (1973b). An extension of developmental models that separate ontogenetic changes and cohort differences. Psychological Bulletin, 80, 466-479.

Cattell, R. B. (1966). Guest editorial: Multivariate behavioral research and the integrative challenge. Multivariate Behavioral Research, 1, 4-42.

Cronbach, L. J. (1957). The two disciplines of scientific psychology. American Psychologist, 12, 671-684.

Diamond, S., & Royce, J. R. (1980). Cognitive abilities as expressions of three "ways of knowing." Multivariate Behavioral Research, 15, 31-56.

Diamond, S., Voorhees, B., & Royce, J. R. (1981). Factor fulfillment model and the concept of multivariate personality type. Personality and Individual Differences, 2, 181-189.

Fleishman, E. A. (1972). On the relation between abilities, learning, and human performance. American Psychologist, 27, 1017-1032.

Fleishman, E. A. (1975). Toward a taxonomy of human performance. American Psychologist, 30, 1127-1149.

Fuller, J. L., & Thompson, W. R. (1960). Behavior genetics. New York: John Wiley & Sons.

Jung, R. (1965). Systems of orientation. In D. M. Kochen (Ed.), Some problems in information science. New York: Scarecrow Press.

Kearsley, G. P., Buss, A. R., & Royce, J. R. (1977). Developmental change and the multi-dimensional cognitive system. Intelligence, 1, 257-273.

Kearsley, G. P., & Royce, J. R. (1977). A multifactor theory of sensation: Individuality in sensory structure and sensory processing. Perceptual and Motor Skills, 44, 1299-1316.

Mather, K., & Jinks, J. L. (1971). Biometrical genetics: The study of continuous variation (2nd ed.). London: Chapman & Hall.

Mesarovic, M. D., Macko, D., & Takahara, Y. (1970). Theory of hierarchical, multi-level, systems. New York: Academic Press.

Miller, J. G. (1978). Living systems. New York: McGraw-Hill.

Miller, G. A., Galanter, E. H., & Pribram, K. H. (1960). Plans and the structure of behavior. New York: Holt.

Neisser, U. (1976). Cognition and reality. San Francisco: Pergamon Press.

Poley, W., & Royce, J. R. (1973). Behavior genetic analysis of mouse emotionality: II. Stability of factors across genotypes. Animal Learning and Behavior, 1, 116-120.

Powell, A., Holt, P., & Royce, J. R. (1979). The life-span development of individuality. Unpublished manuscript, Center for Advanced Studies in Theoretical Psychology, University of Alberta, Edmonton, Canada.

Powell, A., Katzko, M., & Royce, J. R. (1978). A multi-factor-systems theory of the structure and dynamics of motor function. Journal of Motor Behavior, 10, 191-210.

Powell, A., & Royce, J. R. (1978). Paths to being, life style, and individuality. Psychological Reports, 42, 987-1005.

Powell, A., & Royce, J. R. (1982). Cognitive information processing: The role of individual differences in the search for invariants. Academic Psychological Bulletin, 4, 255-289.

Powell, A., Royce, J. R., & Voorhees, B. (1979). Personality as a complex information processing system: Properties and principles. Behavioral Sciences, 27, 338-376.

Royce, J. R. (1950). A synthesis of experimental designs in program research. Journal of General Psychology, 43, 295-303.

Royce, J. R. (1957). Factor theory and genetics. Educational and Psychological Measurement, 17, 361-376.

Royce, J. R. (1963). Factors as theoretical constructs. American Psychologist, 18, 522-528.

Royce, J. R. (1973). The conceptual framework for a multi-factor theory of individuality. In J. R. Royce (Ed.), Multivariate analysis and psychological theory (pp. 305-407). London: Academic Press.

Royce, J. R. (1974). Cognition and knowledge: Psychological epistemology. In E. C. Carterette & M. P. Friedman (Eds.), Handbook of perception, Vol. 1, Historical and philosophical roots to perception (pp. 149-176). New York: Academic Press.

Royce, J. R. (1975). Epistemic styles, individuality and world-view. In A. Debons & W. Cameron (Eds.), NATO Conference on Information Sciences (pp. 259-295). Leyden, The Netherlands: International Publishing.

Royce, J. R. (1977a). Guest Editorial: Have we lost sight of the original vision for SMEP and MBR? Multivariate Behavioral Research, 12, 135-141.

Royce, J. R. (1977b). Meaning, value and personality. In The search for absolute values: Harmony among the sciences. The Fifth International Conference on the Unity of the Sciences, Washington, D. C.

Royce, J. R. (1979a). The factor-gene basis of individuality. In J. R. Royce (Ed.) Theoretical advances in behavior genetics. Leyden, The Netherlands: International Publishing.

Royce, J. R. (1979b). The genetic correlates of emotionality. Manuscript submitted for publication.

Royce, J. R. (1983). Personality integration: A synthesis of the parts and wholes of individuality theory. Journal of Personality, 51, 683-706.

Royce, J. R. & Buss, A. R. (1976). The role of general systems and information theory in multi-factor individuality theory. Canadian Psychological Review, 17, 1-21.

Royce, J. R. & Diamond, S. (1980). Toward a multifactor-system theory of emotion: Cognitive-affective interaction. Motivaton and Emotion, 4, 263-297.

Royce, J. R., Holmes, T. M., & Poley, W. (1975). Behavior genetic analysis of mouse emotionality: III. The diallel analysis. Behavior Genetics, 5, 351-372.

Royce, J. R., Kearsley, G. P., & Klare, W. (1978). The relationship between factors and psychological processes. In J. M. Scandura & C. J. Brainerd (Eds.), Structural/process theories of complex human behavior, NATO Advanced Study Institute. Leyden, The Netherlands: Sijthoff International Publishing.

Royce, J. R., & McDermott, J. (1977). A multi-dimensional system dynamics model of affect. Motivation and Emotion, 1, 193-224.

Royce, J. R., & Mos, L. P. (Eds.). (1979). Theoretical advances in behavior genetics. The Netherlands: Sijthoff & Noordhoff.

Royce, J. R., Poley, W., & Yeudall, L. T. (1973). Behavior genetic analysis of mouse emotionality: I. Factor analysis. Journal of Comparative and Physiological Psychology, 83, 36-47.

Royce, J. R. & Powell, A. (1983). Theory of personality and individual differences: Factors, systems and processes. Englewood Cliffs, NJ: Prentice-Hall.

Schopflocher, D., & Royce, J. R. (1980). The structure of values: A multi-factor theory. Unpublished manuscript, Center for Advanced Study in Theoretical Psychology, University of Alberta, Edmonton, Canada.

Singer, R. N. (1975). Motor learning and human performance: An application to physical education skills (2nd ed.). New York: MacMillan.

Sommerhof, G. (1969). The abstract characteristics of living systems. In F. E. Emery (Ed.), Systems thinking: Selected readings. Harmondsworth, England: Penguin.

Wardell, D. & Royce, J. R. (1975). Relationships between cognitive and temperament traits and the concept of "style." Journal of Multivariate Experimental Personality and Clinical Psychology, 1, 244-266.

Wardell, D. & Royce, J. R. (1978). Toward a multi-factor theory of styles and their relationships to cognition and affect. Journal of Personality, 46, 476-505.

5

Biological Foundations
of the Sensation-Seeking Temperament

Marvin Zuckerman

NEED FOR STIMULATION AND ACTIVITY

The first Sensation Seeking Scale (SSS) (Zuckerman, Kolin, Price, & Zoob, 1964) was devised to predict individual differences in response to the experimental situation of sensory deprivation. Our assumption was that such response differences might be based, in some part, on individual needs for stimulation and activity. In the first use of the SSS as a predictor in a sensory deprivation experiment (Zuckerman et al., 1966), we attempted to predict stress reactions and general restlessness of subjects exposed to two conditions: confinement in sensory-deprivation conditions, and confinement in nonsensory-deprivation conditions. The high sensation seekers showed a greater amount of restlessness, as indicated by measured body movements, than did the low sensation seekers in both conditions of confinement. The restlessness was not correlated with measures of subjective stress or anxiety, and high and low sensation seekers did not differ on these types of measures. Anxiety trait measures did predict these latter types of reactions. In this study, as in many later studies, trait measures of sensation seeking and general anxiety or neuroticism were not correlated (Zuckerman, 1979a).

Providing an operant response lever that produces visual or auditory stimulation as reinforcement for pressing the lever is one way of measuring "need for stimulation" in sensory deprivation (Jones, 1969). Using this operant method, we were unable to find any differences in response rates between high and low sensation seekers after 6 hours of sensory deprivation (Zuckerman & Hopkins, unpublished study). Lambert and Levy (1972), however, provided their subjects access to the stimulation lever immediately at the two-hour period of sensory deprivation and did find differences in response rates between high and low sensation seekers. Although the highs and lows started at the same rate of response, by the second hour of sensory deprivation, the high sensation seekers were responding at a significantly higher rate than the lows. We might be tempted to interpret these results as evidence of a greater need for external stimulation in the high sensation seeker, but there are other possible interpretations. Bar pressing was the only activity allowed people in this study, and the high rate of response of high sensation seekers might reflect more of a need for activity than for visual stimulation.

Hocking and Robertson (1969) allowed their subjects to choose between visual, auditory, and kinesthetic stimulation, the latter consisting of a 15-s period during which the person could move freely on the bed or get up and move around. Although the high sensation seekers had a higher overall rate of response for all three types of reinforcement, their rate of responding was lower than that

of the low sensation seekers for visual stimulation, and relatively higher for
the kinesthetic (movement) reinforcement.

We have generally found that the movement-restriction aspect of sensory deprivation constitutes a major part of the stress and autonomic arousal produced by
this experimental situation (Zuckerman, Persky, Link, & Basu, 1968a). It certainly seemed to be the most stressful part of the procedure to the high sensation seekers in the Hocking and Robertson (1969) study, where the need for
activity overrode the need to look at the visual stimuli. But even before this
study, we had realized that the trait we were measuring had to do more with the
internal effects of stimuli rather than a simple need for external stimuli of
any kind. High sensation seekers are not compulsive television watchers (Brown,
Ruder, Ruder, & Young, 1974), although they do like to listen to music, read
fiction, and attend movies (particularly the X-rated ones that contain explicit
portrayals of sexual activity). High sensation seekers are _more_ likely than
lows to volunteer for activities or experiments such as meditation training
(Myers & Eisner, 1974), sensory deprivation, and hypnosis (Zuckerman, Schultz, &
Hopkins, 1967), which offer little in the way of _external_ stimulation, but
which promise new kinds of _internal_ sensations and complex experiences. High
sensation seekers prefer abstract designs that are more complex (Griffin, S. R.,
personal communication, 1972; Looft & Baranowski, 1971; Zuckerman, Bone, Neary,
Mangelsdorff, & Brustman, 1972) than those preferred by lows.

There is another type of complex stimulation that appears to be somewhat aver-
sive to low sensation seekers, but is generally positive for the highs: social
stimulation. Zuckerman, Persky, Link, and Basu (1968b) correlated the SSS with
stress reactions to three conditions of confinement: (a) sensory deprivation,
(b) social isolation, and (c) confinement with another person in the same
cubicle used for the first two conditions. There were no relationships found
between SSS scores and responses to the first two conditions, but many stress
variables correlated _negatively_ with the SSS in the third condition. High sensation seekers seemed to enjoy this condition of confinement with another person
for 8 hours with access to stimulation (music and slides) and freedom to converse with the other person. Low sensation seekers in this condition reported
feelings of depression and hostility, somatic complaints, tedium, and feelings
of unreality. The lows also had greater levels of 17-ketosteroids in their
urine compared with their levels in a control condition. High sensation seekers
tend to dominate in unstructured social situations, such as leaderless discussion groups (Ozeran, 1973), and the SSS correlates positively with dominance as
a measured trait (Zuckerman, 1979a). Sensation seeking is correlated low to
moderately with extraversion (E), as measured by Eysenck's scale (Eysenck, S., &
Zuckerman, 1978; Zuckerman, 1979a).

It is likely that sensation seekers obtain most of their day-to-day stimulation
from social interactions. This type of sensation seeking is best assessed by
the Disinhibition subscale of the SSS, which is also the one that correlates
most consistently with Eysenck's E scale, as well as with certain biological
correlates of sensation seeking, such as augmenting of the average evoked potential and gonadal hormones.

Social stimulation, particularly from approaches of strangers, can be very
arousing to the brain, as related by Gale in his chapter in Volume 2 of the
present work. An earlier version of the theory of sensation seeking (Zuckerman,
1969) maintained that the seeking of stimulation depended on the capacity of
the stimulation to activate the brain or, as Berlyne (1971) called it, the
"arousal potential" of stimuli. Novel, intense, and complex stimuli were
thought to be preferred by high sensation seekers because they had more arousal
potential than did familiar, low intensity, or simple stimuli. As the theory

was formulated in 1969, sensation seekers sought stimulation that maintained a high optimal level of arousal (cortical arousal).

OPTIMAL LEVEL OF AROUSAL

The optimal level of arousal (OLA) was described by Hebb (1955) as the level of cortical arousal, on a continuum from sleep to highly excited states, where performance was most effective. The theory (Zuckerman, 1969; Zuckerman et al., 1964) suggested that people differed reliably in their OLAs, and that those with high OLAs need more stimuli with high arousal potential (high optimal level of stimulation, or OLS) to feel good and function better. The trait of sensation seeking was assumed to be directly related to both the OLS and the OLA. A similar theory was formulated by H. J. Eysenck (1967) for the trait of extraversion.

Over the intervening years, we have had difficulty in verifying the OLA theory of sensation seeking. There is no question of the high sensation seeker's greater propensity to search for novel and complex experiences, but these are not necessarily arousing experiences. On the basis of an OLA theory, it is not difficult to see why sensation seekers would volunteer for encounter groups (Stanton, 1976), but it is difficult to understand why they would volunteer for meditation training where the main point is to reduce external and internal stimulation and arousal (Myers & Eisner, 1974). Sensation seekers take all kinds of risks to experience the sensations produced by drugs, but attempts to show a preference for stimulant over depressant drugs have yielded only weak results (Carrol & Zuckerman, 1977). High sensation seekers are typically multidrug users; they use stimulant, hallucinogenic, and depressant drugs. They sometimes go up and sometimes go down. What they cannot stand is constancy in arousal level or experience.

Carrol et al. (1982) posed an experimental test of the OLA theory. They selected first-year medical students scoring at both extremes of the SSS distribution and, on different occasions, gave each student a placebo or d-Amphetamine, or Diazepam. Amphetamine stimulates the reticular activating system and cortex, whereas the tranquilizer Diazepam has opposite effects. According to the OLA hypothesis, the high sensation seeker should feel and function better after taking the stimulant and the low sensation seeker should feel and function better under the low arousal conditions produced by the depressant drug. Mood scales and performance tests were used as dependent variables. The predicted interaction between personality and drug effects was not found, although a significant main effect for drugs was found. Both high and low sensation seekers felt better and functioned better with d-Amphetamine than with the placebo or Diazepam.

DEVELOPING A COMPARATIVE PSYCHOBIOLOGICAL MODEL

Figure 1 outlines an approach to the development of a psychobiological model for a behavioral trait. Too often such models depend on a mixture of metaphor, analogy, and unadulterated anthropomorphism. Sociobiology provides many examples of inappropriate leaps between animal and human behavior patterns. Causal factors are placed in the evolutionary past; thus, they cannot be verified. A post hoc explanation of natural selection can be invented for almost any current human trait. In this respect, sociobiology resembles psychoanalysis, where adult traits are attributed to hypothetical, and largely intrapsychic, events of early childhood that are also unverifiable. What is needed is a model that permits verification in current living organisms and specification of the biosocial communalities of humans and other species.

Whether we start from the human or animal level is certainly important, because the constructs in the theory may be shaped by the limitations of species

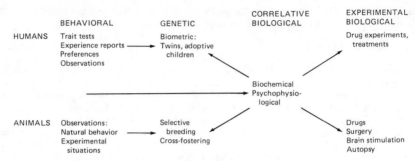

FIGURE 1. A model for comparative study of a trait.

characteristics that may be too specific to be extended up or down the phylogenic scale. Eysenck and I have evolved our constructs from the human level
down, whereas Gray (1973) and Stein (1978) have built their theories from the
rodent level up. Our hope is that we will find common biological structures
serving similar kinds of behavior in the different species.

Behavioral Studies

If we choose to start at the human level, we can use the unique capacity of
humans to describe their own responses, some of which are unobservable to others,
as well as their impressions of the responses of other persons. Although trait
tests and the idea of a trait have been criticized by social learning theorists
(Bandura, 1977; Mischel, 1968), these researchers have offered no viable operational alternatives to assess the role of the person in the person-situation
interaction. The criticisms of the trait construct center around the issues of
situational specificity and the lack of consistency in specific behaviors, as
opposed to the demonstrated reliability of trait measures, tests, and ratings.
But it is a mistaken notion that traits should predict the isolated behavioral
event with any large degree of preciseness. Trait measures can only be expected
to predict the averaged or cumulated behaviors sampled across time and within
specified classes of situations (Zuckerman, 1979b). When persons report their
own responses or those of others, there is an implicit averaging of such events
that eliminates, to some extent, the narrower specificities of isolated situations.

It cannot be disputed that most general trait tests are of little use in predicting specific behavior from the entire distribution of the trait measure;
that is why we often select subjects from the extreme ranges of the trait distribution for a theoretical, as opposed to an applied, study. These persons
may be expected to be more predictable and consistent in their behavior if
(a) we make the prediction with careful attention to the theory from which the
test is derived; (b) we select the proper situation and dependent variables on
the basis of the theory; and (c) our test is reliable and valid. Broad trait
tests are of more theoretical than applied use. If the primary goal of a test
is to predict specific behavior, then a narrow or situation-specific test is
generally (but not always) more accurate (Zuckerman, 1979b). The SSS is a test
designed for construct validity rather than specific predictive validity
(Cronbach & Meehl, 1955), although in some situations it seems to do as well
as more specific trait tests in predicting behavior (Mellstrom, Cicala, &
Zuckerman, 1976).

Direct reports of experience constitute a much underutilized form of measure in humans. Some trait tests use such reports, but rarely in a systematized, focused manner. A trait test item might read: "I enjoy sex." While this kind of generalized self-report may have some value for trait assessment when combined with other types of items, a sex experience scale (e.g., Zuckerman, 1973) asks more specific questions, such as what kind of sex activity, with whom, and how many times? Such scales generally avoid the more subjective aspects of the experience such as "How did it feel?" Using such experience scales, we have been able to show consistent relationships between the SS scales and the extent of sexual and drug experience (Zuckerman, 1979a, Chapter 10; Zuckerman et al., 1972; Zuckerman, Tushup, & Finner, 1976). These are important areas of life activities that are difficult to study in the laboratory with humans.

Stimulus preferences, such as those shown in reactions to designs (Zuckerman et al., 1972), provide another way of studying temperament. I have already alluded to the preferences of high sensation seekers for complexity, and the lows for simplicity, shown using this method.

Observations of humans in preselected and controlled situations may also provide meaningful data if we select situations that are meaningful for the personality construct involved. The SS scales predict some aspects of response to sensory deprivation experiments, as previously described; and the Thrill and Adventure Seeking subscale predicts behavioral reactions to selected fear situations (Mellstrom et al., 1976). Volunteering for unusual activities as well as reactions to such activities also may be predicted by the SSS.

We are in a much better position to observe behavior directly when we study animals. We may study natural behavior in a colony of animals; or we can study behavior in constructed situations, such as exposure to novel stimuli or situations (e.g., the open-field arena).

Genetic Studies

Genetic studies of a trait in humans most often use the twin comparison strategy or the method of comparing adopted children with biological and adopting parents. Fulker, Eysenck, and Zuckerman (1980) compared the similarity of pairs of identical and fraternal twins on the SSS using the same twin population as was used for the Eaves and Eysenck (1975) study of the genetics of the extraversion trait. Using the sophisticated biometrical method of Jinks and Fulker (1970), we found an uncorrected heritability of 58%, which is high for a personality trait and higher than the 42% found for extraversion. It may be that relatively narrower traits, such as sensation seeking, which are in part components of broader traits, such as extraversion, may lie closer to the genotypes on which both kinds of traits are based.

Using animals, we have recourse to the methods of selective breeding and cross-fostering to explore the genetics of a behavioral trait. McClearn and DeFries (1973, pp. 215-217) and Royce, Holmes, and Poley (1975) have demonstrated the heritability of activity in the open-field arena using selective breeding in the former study and diallel cross-mating in the latter study. Broadhurst (1967) selectively bred rats for the emotional reactivity in the open field and found that he had also produced high-activity rats; the rats that were low in emotional reactivity were high in ambulation or exploration of the open field. Despite this genetic link between emotional reactivity and activity, Royce (1977) and Whimbey and Denenberg (1967) have shown that these are two relatively independent factors in open-field behavior.

Biological Correlates

If we can assume that a behavioral trait in humans and what we assume to be its
analogue in animals have a common biological correlate, we can move a giant step
beyond anthropomorphic speculation. Before beginning this discussion of the
biological correlates of sensation seeking in humans and analogous traits in
animals, I must describe the SS scales. Some of the biological correlates are
primarily related to a particular subscale rather than the General or Total
scales.

The current form (V) of the SSS was developed from factor analytic studies of
both male and female samples in the United States and England (Zuckerman, 1971;
Zuckerman, Eysenck, & Eysenck, 1978). The first scale developed (form II,
Zuckerman et al., 1964) contained a General scale with a broad range of item
content derived from the unrotated factor. The later factor analyses revealed
four primary factors in the populations sampled:

· Thrill and Adventure Seeking (TAS) items reflect desires to engage in sports
and other activities involving some physical risk, such as parachuting, diving,
flying, and driving at high speeds. People who actually engage in these activities generally score quite high on all of the SS scales, not just on the TAS,
showing the generality of the trait.

· Experience Seeking (ES) items represent the seeking of stimulation through
the mind and senses, through travel, music, and art, and through unconventional
social behavior and friends. We used to call it the "hippie" factor before that
term became anachronistic. It is the most culturally influenced of the subscales, being related to national, educational, and racial factors, but does not
yield sex differences (Zuckerman & Neeb, 1980).

· Disinhibition (Dis) items are characterized by the seeking of social and
hedonistic stimulation through parties, sexual variety, drinking, and gambling.
It is the most culture-free of all of the scales, but usually shows the largest
sex differences, with males scoring higher than females. Along with TAS it
also shows the largest age declines (Zuckerman et al., 1978; Zuckerman & Neeb,
1980).

· Boredom Susceptibility (BS) items reflect an intolerance for sameness and
routine situations or people, and restlessness when such situations or persons
cannot be avoided.

In the latest SSS form (V) we have a scale consisting of four balanced scales
based on the four factors, with 10 items in each scale, and a total score that
is the sum of the subscale scores and is based on all 40 items.

Sex and age constitute the two strongest demographic influences on SSS scores
(Zuckerman, 1971, 1979a; Zuckerman & Neeb, 1980). Scores decline from the
late teens on, and males are higher than females at all ages in the U. S. and
English samples. The Total scores are very close in English-speaking male samples, whereas the females show more international variation. Both age and sex
differences are greatest for the TAS and Dis scales.

Orienting Reflex (OR). The first psychophysiological studies of sensation seeking were done using the electrodermal OR. Two studies by Neary and Zuckerman
(1976) found that high sensation seekers have stronger initial ORs to novel
visual and auditory stimuli, but the differences in the magnitudes of the ORs
disappear on the second presentations of the stimuli and do not reappear until
a new stimulus is presented.

Cox (1977) compared the responses of high and low sensation-seeking males to 110-dB and 70-dB tones. A 110-dB tone is loud enough to elicit a preponderance of <u>defensive reflexes</u> (DRs). ORs cannot be differentiated from DRs on skin conductance response (SCR) measures, but can be on heart rate response; the OR is characterized by the deceleration of heart rate, while the DR is related to heart rate acceleration in the first few seconds following stimulus presentation. Cox found that the low sensation-seeking group had a larger heart rate acceleration to this intense stimulus than did the low sensation seekers. There was no difference in electrodermal response to this tone.

The 78-dB tone was in the range where some persons show ORs and others show DRs. In response to this tone, the high sensation seekers showed stronger ORs, as indicated by greater deceleration of both heart and respiratory rates, whereas the low sensation seekers had stronger DRs, as indicated by increases of heart and respiratory rates. Again, the SCR showed no differences, possibly because it confounds the OR and DR measures.

The chapter by Feij et al. in this volume describes a study that supports and extends the findings of differences in ORs and DRs as a function of sensation seeking. Using an 80-dB tone, they replicated the finding from the Neary and Zuckerman (1976) study showing a relationship between scores on the General SSS and the magnitude of the SCR to the first stimulus presentation. When comparisons were made between persons scoring high and low on the SSS-Disinhibition scale, differences in heart rate were found that are similar to the results of Cox (1977). High sensation seekers tended to show heart rate deceleration (ORs), whereas low sensation seekers showed heart rate acceleration (DRs).

The results of these three studies suggest that sensation seeking has something to do with the biological trait of <u>arousability</u> in response to stimuli of moderate to high intensities. There is some evidence that the SSS factors are differentially related to the OR and DR, with the General and TAS factors related to the OR response to novelty, and the Disinhibition factor related to the OR-DR differential response to intensity of stimulation.

None of these studies shows differences in basal, or rest period, levels of arousal. Cox's study used the EEG in addition to skin conductance, heart rate, vasomotor, and respiration measures. There is little evidence from these or other studies to support a hypoarousal theory of sensation seeking of the type that has been proposed for a psychopathic personality (Hare, 1970). High sensation seekers start from the same baseline of arousal as lows, but they tend to respond more strongly to novel stimuli, and show less defensive arousal than the lows in response to intense stimuli.

Pavlov (1927, 1960) called the OR the "investigatory" or "what is it?" reflex and thought it was related to the state and trait of curiosity. Both animals and humans with strong ORs seem more alert and attentive to their environments. Either too little or too much basal arousal, as in anxiety neurotics (Lader & Wing, 1966) or normals in a state of anxiety (Neary & Zuckerman, 1976), seems to weaken the electrodermal OR. Persons with strong ORs perform·better on certain types of verbal learning and conditioning tasks (Maltzman & Raskin, 1965). The strength of the initial electrodermal OR is related to intelligence in children (DeBoskey, Kimmel, & Kimmel, 1979). Studies of the relationship between the OR amplitude and the trait of extraversion have yielded an inconsistent picture (Orlebeke & Feij, 1979). Generally the results suggest that the OR amplitude, as a trait, is related to the capacity for focused attention and resistance to distractibility at high levels of arousal. Anxiety and sensation seeking seem to be the two most relevant traits, with the former dampening the OR and the latter amplifying it.

Evoked Potentials. The work on the OR and DR suggests that the biology of sensation seeking may involve physiological mechanisms for stimulus regulation, particularly at high levels of stimulation. Another psychophysiological measure related to sensation seeking is the augmenting or reducing of the amplitude of the cortical average evoked potential (AEP) in response to stimuli of high intensity. This method, devised by Buchsbaum and Silverman (1968), consists of presenting persons with stimuli covering a range of intensities and measuring the P1-N1 component of the AEP in response to each intensity of stimulation. Augmenting-reducing is defined by the relationship between stimulus intensity and AEP amplitude for the individual. Augmenters are those who show a linearly increasing AEP amplitude with increasing intensity of stimulation; reducers either show no marked change in AEP amplitude or actually show significant decrease (reducing) of the AEP at the highest stimulus intensities. It should be emphasized that augmenters and reducers are not types, but represent extremes on a continuum defined by the AEP-stimulus-intensity relationship.

Zuckerman, Murtaugh, and Siegel (1974) demonstrated a substantial relationship between augmenting of the AEP, in response to visual stimuli, and one of the SS subscales, Disinhibition. High disinhibitors were generally augmenters, and lows were usually reducers. This finding has been replicated by von Knorring 1981, using a Swedish translation of the SSS. The augmenters in this study scored significantly higher than reducers on the Disinhibition subscale, and the differences on the General and two other subscales approached significance. Coursey, Buchsbaum, and Frankel (1975) found a relationship between augmenting of the AEP in response to auditory stimulation and the SS General scale.

Not only humans show reliable individual differences in augmenting-reducing. Cats also show this as a reliable trait (Buchsbaum, 1971). Two studies of the behavioral correlates of augmenting-reducing in cats have shown that augmenter cats are exploratory, active, aggressive, and highly reactive to novel stimuli, while reducer cats are socially avoidant and unreactive to novel stimuli (Hall, Rappaport, Hopkins, & Griffin, 1970; Lukas & Siegel, 1977).

Gonadal Hormones. The consistent finding of sex differences on the SS scales, particularly Thrill and Adventure Seeking and Disinhibition, prompted us to study the relationships between gonadal hormones and sensation seeking. Suggesting that trait differences between men and women might have some biological basis has become politically dangerous in the United States, but we decided to investigate this problem anyway. We used primarily males in these studies because the levels of sex hormones vary with the menstrual cycle in females, and this would be a major source of unreliability in individual comparisons. In the first study (Daitzman, Zuckerman, Sammelwitz, & Ganjam, 1978), we correlated androgens with the SS scales and found a significant correlation with one of them, Disinhibition. You may recall that this is the subscale that reflects an impulsive-extraverted type of hedonism, shows strong sex differences, and is the scale most highly correlated with augmenting of the AEP. In the second study, which used a larger sample of males and a small sample of females, we also measured estrogens in addition to androgens. Both androgens and estrogens correlated significantly with Disinhibition in males. The same results were found in females, and the results were significant even though the sample size was low.

In a third study, Daitzman and Zuckerman (1980) selected males scoring high or low on the Disinhibition scale and compared them on plasma levels of the androgen, testosterone and the estrogens, 17-B estradiol and estrone and progesterone. Replicating our previous results, we found that the high male disinhibitors were significantly higher than the lows on testosterone, estrone, and estradiol. The groups did not differ on progesterone.

In this last study we also correlated testosterone with other traits in the sample of males. Those high in testosterone also tended to be high on extra-

version, sociability, self-acceptance, dominance, and activity scales. The results of a factor analysis show testosterone loading positively on a dimension
that could be called stable extraversion versus neurotic introversion. Males
who were low on testosterone tended to be neurotic, introverted, unsociable,
submissive, and inactive. Males with high estradiol levels tended to score high
on scales from the Minnesota Multiphasic Personality Inventory (MMPI) measuring
deviancy and psychotic types of psychopathology. Those with low levels of
estradiol tended to score more normally, but overcontrolled, conventional, and
somewhat defensive. We labeled this dimension in the factor analysis as social
deviancy versus control. Persons who were high in both testosterone and estradiol tended to be sensation seeking, extraverted, and impulsive.

Testosterone has been related to aggressive and dominant behavior in males of
other species. There is only some evidence for a link between more severe kinds
of aggression in man and high levels of testosterone (Rose, 1975). Testosterone
declines with age, particularly in males. Sensation seeking, particularly Disinhibition and Thrill and Adventure Seeking, also declines with age (Zuckerman
et al., 1978; Zuckerman & Neeb, 1980). Is it possible that the increasing
conservatism of age is a function of biological factors, such as gonadal hormones, that regulate the risk-taking propensities? Considering some of the less
desirable traits that may be governed by testosterone, it may be fortunate that
this hormone's production falls off with age in males (Harman, 1978). "Time
wounds all heels," particularly the male ones. The link between testosterone
and extraversion (sociability) suggests that this trait must also decline with
age, and indeed it does (Eysenck, H. J., & Eysenck, S. B. G., 1975).

Monoamine Oxidase (MAO). The most interesting findings on biological correlates
of sensation seeking are those by a group at the National Institute of Mental
Health (NIMH) in Bethesda, MD, which link a neural enzyme called monoamine
oxidase (MAO) with the trait measure of sensation seeking. MAO is contained
in the neurons of the brain. The type B MAO found in the platelets of blood
is quite similar in structure to that found in the primate brain, and it reacts
to MAO-inhibiting drugs that lower brain MAO as well. The primary function of
MAO in the brain seems to be the deamination or reduction of the neurotransmitters: norepinephrine, dopamine, and serotonin. Norepinephrine seems to be of
crucial importance in the reward pathways of the limbic system originating in
the locus coeruleus (norepinephrine) and substantia nigra (dopamine). These
pathways yield high rates of self-stimulation in rats; Stein (1978) has shown
that self-stimulation in these areas is dependent on the supply of their neurotransmitters.

The MAO inhibiting (MAOI) drugs are used in the treatment of depression. These
drugs elevate levels of brain catecholamines and serotonin by inhibiting the
MAO and thus reducing this biochemical control over levels of the neurotransmitters in the neuron. The effect on unipolar depressive disorders is to return
them to normal levels of activity and interest. But in a substantial proportion
of patients in the depressive phase of a bipolar disorder, the MAOIs may pre-
cipitate a manic episode (Bunney, 1978). It is suggested that the MAOIs do this
by increasing the levels of functional monoamines in these susceptible patients.
MAOIs may also cause brief manic-like episodes in normal volunteers and patients
with medical disorders such as tuberculosis (Murphy, 1977a). These drugs also
increase activity in animals (Murphy, 1977b).

Because the lowering of MAO levels results in increases in activation and manic-
like behavior, we would be led to the prediction that MAO levels would be low in
high sensation seekers and high in low sensation seekers. Two studies (Murphy
et al., 1977; Schooler, Zahn, Murphy, & Buchsbaum, 1978) have been done in which
platelet MAO levels have been correlated with the SSS in normal college students
of both sexes. MAO correlated negatively and significantly with the General SSS

in both male samples and in one of the two female samples in these two studies. As expected, the high sensation seekers are low in MAO, and the converse is found for the low sensation seekers.

Let us consider the correlates of platelet MAO in behavior and age and sex differences to see if they are congruent with the inverse relationship found between MAO and sensation seeking. Females' mean platelet MAO levels are about 20% higher than those of males, and the difference is found at all ages from 11 to 60 years (Murphy et al., 1976). This is consistent with the finding that males are higher on sensation seeking than are females at all ages (Zuckerman et al., 1978). Although an earlier study by Robinson, Davis, Nies, Ravaris, and Sylvester (1971) had reported that MAO increases with age, a finding consistent with the decrease of sensation seeking with age, Murphy et al. (1976) could not replicate this finding.

Coursey, Buchsbaum, and Murphy (1979) studied persons selected from a normal population on the basis of high and low MAO levels. The low-MAO types of both sexes are more socially active than the high-MAO people. The low-MAO males are more likely to have had convictions for criminal offenses and psychiatric contacts. The low-MAO males also reported more cigarette smoking and drug use, consistent with the association of sensation seeking with smoking and drug use (Zuckerman, 1979a, Chapter 10; Zuckerman et al., 1972).

The differences found between high- and low-MAO types in sociability in humans have also been found in monkeys whose behavior was studied in their natural habitat on an island colony in the Caribbean. Redmond, Murphy, and Baulu (1979) found that high-MAO monkeys of both sexes spent more time alone than did low-MAO monkeys. Low-MAO males spent more time in social activities, particularly of a dominant-agonistic type (aggressive and sexual behaviors), and in play. Low-MAO females received more grooming, a sign of high status, than did high-MAO types. The behavioral parallels with trait and experience correlates of human sensation seeking are striking.

Among human psychiatric patients, low MAO levels are found in bipolar affective disorders (manic-depressives) (Murphy & Weiss, 1972), and in their well relatives (Leckman, Gershon, Nichols, & Murphy, 1977). Sensation seeking is also related to mania, both as a trait (Hypomania scale of the MMPI, Zuckerman et al., 1972) and as a diagnosis (Zuckerman & Neeb, 1979).

Endorphins. The recent discovery of endogenous morphine-like peptides, or endorphins, in the brain has led to studies of their role in protection against pain and excessive stimulation, mood regulation, and schizophrenia. A group of Swedish investigators (Johansson, Almay, von Knorring, Terenius, & Åström, 1979) compared the SSS scores of patients with high and low levels of endorphins measured from cerebrospinal fluid. The patients with low levels of endorphins were significantly higher on all of the SS scales than were the patients with high endorphin levels. The inverse relationship between endorphins and the SS scales was most pronounced for the Disinhibition and Boredom Susceptibility scales. No age or sex differences were found in this study. Endorphins did not correlate with Eysenck's extraversion scale, but did correlate positively with the neuroticism scale. This last correlation may have been produced because the authors' sample consisted of patients complaining of pain, and patients with psychogenic pain (presumably more neurotic) had higher levels of endorphins than those with organic pain syndromes. The two types of patients did not differ in sensation-seeking scores.

MAO, Endorphins, and AEP Augmenting-Reducing. Things related to the same thing are not necessarily related to each other, as any student of logic knows. The fact that endorphins, MAO, and reducing of the AEP are all negatively related to the sensation-seeking trait does not necessitate that they have any correlation with each other, unless of course there are some involvements of these brain chemicals in the inhibitory response of the brain to excessive stimulation. Endorphins have been shown to be involved in sensitivity to pain, and augmenters have been shown to be more pain sensitive than reducers. It is not so surprising, therefore, that von Knorring, Almay, Johansson, and Terenius (1979) have found a relationship between augmenting-reducing and endorphins. Augmenters had significantly lower levels of endorphins than reducers. It remains for experiments to show how endorphins may actually effect the inhibition of cortical response in reaction to intense stimulation.

In the case of MAO, a negative relationship has been found between platelet MAO and augmenting of the AEP in people with affective disorders (Buchsbaum, Landau, Murphy, & Goodwin, 1973) or "normals" with tendencies toward such disorders (Haier, Buchsbaum, Murphy, Gottesman, & Coursey, 1980); but no relationship was found between these two variables in normal controls without psychiatric disturbance. The authors (Haier et al., 1980) have proposed a model that suggests that the combination of low MAO and augmenting will result in overarousal and pathological expressions of sensation seeking, as in mania, whereas the combination of high MAO and reducing would lead to underarousal and low sensation seeking, as seen in unipolar depression. The other two combinations of MAO and augmenting-reducing would lead to balanced arousal (high sensation seeking with high sensory protection and low sensation seeking with low sensory protection) and therefore normal expressions of high or low sensation seeking. This is an interesting model, which seems to be based on the assumption that sensation seeking is related to MAO, but not correlated with augmenting-reducing.

A NEW BIOLOGICAL MODEL FOR SENSATION SEEKING

The first model for sensation seeking (Zuckerman, 1969; Zuckerman et al., 1964) was based on the idea of the optimal level of arousal, determined by the excitatory-inhibitory balance within the reticulo-cortical activating system. The current model, described more fully in my book, goes "beyond the optimal level of arousal" in an attempt to incorporate the various biological correlates of sensation seeking that have been discovered in the ensuing 10 years.

It is assumed that genetic influences play an important role in determining levels of brain monoamines directly, or through levels of gonadal hormones and MAO. There is evidence that gonadal hormones influence brain MAO with lowered gonadal levels increasing levels of MAO (Broverman, Klaiber, Kobayashi, & Vogel, 1968; Murphy, 1976). Such an influence could partly explain sex and age differences in sensation seeking. Brain MAO regulates the available supply of the neurotransmitters dopamine and norepinephrine. According to the theory of Stein (1978), dopamine is the transmitter of a system involved in pursuit or approach behavior, whereas norepinephrine guides response selection and regulates reward systems. I would suggest that the sensitivity of these activity and reward systems is the basis for the sensation-seeking temperament. The sensation-seeking organism is active in exploration of its environment and approaches novel stimuli with the expectation of reward. The reward systems may regulate arousability through their effects on the reticular activating system, and result in a more direct arousal of the cortex through the "second arousal system" described by Routtenberg (1968). Arousal through this second system is more likely to be associated with the OR and positive emotions, in contrast to arousal originating in the punishment system associated with negative affect (fear) and the DR.

This is a highly speculative theory based largely on correlational data. Ellison (1977) has shown that rats with chemically depleted levels of norepinephrine show behavioral deficits in social dominance, positive reinforcement susceptibility, and goal-directed approach behavior. It is difficult, if not impossible, to do these kinds of crucial experiments on humans; this is why I have proposed a parallel phylogenic approach that leans heavily on correlational studies of humans.

No science has ever been eliminated through reductionism, because phenomena may be profitably studied at all levels. But Skinner's "empty box" organism is no longer excusable on the basis of a lack of information from the neurosciences. The box is partly open (or partly closed if one is a pessimist) and we must peer into it if we are to advance a science of personality and correctly align our trait variables with their underlying genotypes. Hypothetical structures, such as traits, types, or genes, are useful at an early stage of science; but they inevitably must give way to more precisely defined variables. Historically, the greatest advances in science have taken place at their interfaces with bordering sciences. The behavior of organisms must be studied as a function of the biology of organisms as well as the external stimuli and consequent events controlling the behavior.

SUMMARY

The Sensation Seeking Scale was developed to assess individual differences in the needs for stimulation and activity, on the assumption that such needs were a source of a general trait that could predict reactions to the experimental situation of sensory deprivation. The construct of sensation seeking was originally based on the idea that the need for stimulation served a biological need for nonspecific arousal of the cortex. This theory proved untenable in the face of conflicting data.

A comparative psychobiological model is described, which approaches the social behavior of humans and animals by searching for common biological correlates of similar behaviors across species. Biological correlates of high sensation seeking in humans with analogues in other species include (a) strong orienting reflexes and weak defensive reflexes; (b) augmenting of the average evoked potential (reducing in lows) in response to high levels of stimulation; (c) high levels of gonadal hormones; (d) low levels of the enzyme monoamine oxidase (MAO); and (e) low levels of endorphins.

A new biological model of sensation seeking suggests that the trait is based on the sensitivity of limbic reward systems as regulated by brain catecholamines and the enzyme MAO, which regulates the monoamines. Gonadal hormones are assumed to play a role in the regulation of MAO. Genetic control over the biochemistry of these systems is assumed. Substantial genetic control of the sensation-seeking trait, as measured by the Sensation Seeking Scale, has been shown in biometric twin studies.

REFERENCES

Bandura, A. (1977). Social learning theory. Englewood Cliffs, NJ: Prentice-Hall.

Berlyne, D. E. (1971). Aesthetics and psychobiology. New York: Appleton-Century-Crofts.

Broadhurst, P. L. (1967). The biometrical analysis of behavioral inheritance. Science Progress, Oxford, 55, 123–139.

Broverman, D. M., Klaiber, E. L., Kobayashi, Y., & Vogel, W. (1968). Roles of activation and inhibition in sex differences in cognitive abilities. Psychological Review, 75, 23–50.

Brown, L. T., Ruder, V. G., Ruder, J. H., & Young, S. D. (1974). Stimulation seeking and the change seeker index. Journal of Consulting and Clinical Psychology, 42, 311.

Buchsbaum, M. S. (1971). Neural events and the psychophysical law. Science, 172, 502.

Buchsbaum, M. S., Landau, S., Murphy, D., & Goodwin, F. (1973). Average evoked response in bipolar and unipolar affective disorders: Relationship to sex, age of onset, and monoamine oxidase. Biological Psychiatry, 7, 199-212.

Buchsbaum, M. S., & Silverman, J. (1968). Stimulus intensity control and the cortical evoked response. Psychosomatic Medicine, 30, 12-22.

Bunney, W. E., Jr. (1978). Psychopharmacology of the switch process in affective illness. In M. A. Lipton, A. DiMascio, & K. F. Killam (Eds.), Psychopharmacology: A generation of progress. New York: Raven Press.

Carroll, E. N., & Zuckerman, M. (1977). Psychopathology and sensation seeking in "downers," "speeders," and "trippers": A study of the relationship between personality and drug choice. International Journal of Addictions, 12, 591-601.

Carrol, E. N., Zuckerman, M., & Vogel, W. H. (1982). A test of the optimal level of arousal theory of sensation seeking. Journal of Personality and Social Psychology, 42, 572-575.

Coursey, R. D., Buchsbaum, M. S., & Frankel, B. L. (1975). Personality measures and evoked responses in chronic insomniacs. Journal of Abnormal Psychology, 84, 234-244.

Coursey, R. D., Buchsbaum, M. S., & Murphy, D. L. (1979). Platelet MAO activity and evoked potentials in the identification of subjects biologically at risk for psychiatric disorders. British Journal of Psychiatry, 134, 372-381.

Cox, D. N. (1977). Psychophysiological correlates of sensation seeking and socialization during reduced stimulation. Unpublished doctoral dissertation, University of British Columbia.

Cronbach, L. J., & Meehl, P. E. (1955). Construct validity in psychological tests. Psychological Bulletin, 52, 281-302.

Daitzman, R. J., & Zuckerman, M. (1980). Disinhibitory sensation seeking, personality, and gonadal hormones. Personality and Individual Differences, 1, 103-110.

Daitzman, R. J., Zuckerman, M., Sammelwitz, P. H., & Ganjam, V. (1978). Sensation seeking and gonadal hormones. Journal of Biosocial Sciences, 10, 401-408.

DeBoskey, D., Kimmel, E., & Kimmel, H. D. (1979). Habituation and conditioning of the orienting reflex in intellectually gifted and average children. In H. D. Kimmel, E. H. van Olst, & J. F. Orlbeke (Eds.), The orienting reflex in humans. Hillsdale, NJ: Lawrence Erlbaum.

Eaves, L., & Eysenck, H. J. (1975). The nature of extraversion: A genetical analysis. Journal of Personality and Social Psychology, 32, 102-112.

Ellison, G. D. (1977). Animal models of psychopathology: The low-norepinephrine and low-serotonin rat. American Psychologist, 32, 1036-1045.

Eysenck, H. J. (1967). The biological basis of personality. Springfield, IL: Charles C Thomas.

Eysenck, H. J., & Eysenck, S. B. G. (1975). Manual of the Eysenck Personality Questionnaire. London: Hodder & Stoughton.

Eysenck, S., & Zuckerman, M. (1978). The relationship between sensation seeking and Eysenck's dimensions of personality. British Journal of Psychology, 69, 483-487.

Fulker, D., Eysenck, S. B. G., & Zuckerman, M. (1980). The genetics of sensation seeking. Journal of Personality Research, 14, 261-281.

Gray, J. A. (1973). Causal theories of personality and how to test them. In J. R. Royce (Ed.), Multivariate analysis and psychological theory. New York: Academic Press.

Haier, R. J., Buchsbaum, M. S., Murphy, D. L., Gottesman, I. I., & Coursey, R. D., (1980). Psychiatric vulnerability, monoamine oxidase, and the average evoked potential. Archives of General Psychiatry, 37, 340-345.

Hall, R. A., Rappaport, M., Hopkins, H. K., & Griffin, R. B. (1970). Evoked response and behavior in cats. Science, 170, 998-1000.

Hare, R. D. (1970). Psychopathy: Theory and Research. New York: Wiley.

Harman, S. M. (1978). Clinical aspects of aging of the male reproductive system. In E. L. Schneider (Ed.), The aging reproductive system (Aging, Volume 4). New York: Raven Press.

Hebb, D. O. (1955). Drives and the CNS (conceptual nervous system). Psychological Review, 62, 253-154.

Hocking, J., & Robertson, M. (1969). The Sensation-Seeking Scale as a predictor of need for stimulation during sensory restriction. Journal of Consulting and Clinical Psychology, 33, 367-369.

Jinks, J. L., & Fulker, D. W. (1970). Comparison of the biometrical genetical, MAVA, and the classical approaches to the analysis of human behavior. Psycho logical Bulletin, 73, 311-349.

Johansson, F., Almay, B. G. L., von Knorring, L., Terenius, L., & Åström (1979). Personality traits in chronic pain patients related to endorphin levels in cerebrospinal fluid. Psychiatry Research, 1, 231-239.

Jones, A. (1969). Stimulus-seeking behavior. In J. P. Zubek (Ed.O, Sensory deprivation: Fifteen years of research. New York: Appleton-Century-Crofts.

von Knorring, L. (1981). Visual evoked responses and platelet monoamine oxidase inpatients suffering from alcoholism. In H. Begleiter (Ed.), The biological effects of alcohol. New York: Plenum Press.

von Knorring, L., Almay, B. G. L., Johansson, F., & Terenius, L. (1979). Endorphins in CSF of chronic pain patients, in relation to augmenting-reducing response in visual averaged evoked response. Neuropsychobiology, 5, 322-326.

Lader, M. H., & Wing, L. (1966). Physiological measures, sedative drugs and morbid anxiety (Maudsley Monograph No. 14). London: Oxford University Press.

Lambert, W., & Levy, L. H. (1972). Sensation-seeking and short term sensory isolation. Journal of Personality and Social Psychology, 24, 46-52.

Leckman, J. F., Gershon, E. S., Nichols, A. S., & Murphy, D. L. (1977). Reduced platelet MAO activity in the first degree relatives of patients with bipolar affective disorders. Archives of General Psychiatry, 34, 601-606.

Looft, W. R., and Baranowski, M. D. (1971). An analysis of five measures of sensation seeking and preference for complexity. Journal of General Psychology, 85, 307-313.

Lukas, J. H., & Siegel, J. (1977). Cortical mechanisms that augment or reduce evoked potentials in cats. Science, 196, 73-75.

Maltzman, I., & Raskin, D. C. (1965). Effects of individual differences in the orienting reflex on conditioning and complex processes. Journal of Experimental Research in Personality, 1, 1-16.

McClearn, G. E., & DeFries, J.C. (1973). Introduction to behavioral genetics. San Francisco, CA: W. H. Freeman & Co.

Mellstrom, M. Jr., Cicala, G. A., & Zuckerman, M. (1976). General versus specific trait anxiety measures in the prediction of fear of snakes, heights, and darkness. Journal of Consulting and Clinical Psychology, 44, 83-91.

Mischel, W. (1968). Personality and assessment. New York: Wiley.

Murphy, D. L. (1976). Clinical, genetic, hormonal, and drug influences on the activity of human platelet monoamine oxidase. In Monoamine oxidase and its inhibition (Ciba Foundation Symposium 39). Amsterdam: Elsevier.

Murphy, D. L. (1977a). The behavioral toxicity of monoamine oxidase-inhibiting anti-depressants. In S. Garattini, A. Goldin, F. Hawking, & I. J. Kodin (Eds.), Advances in Pharmacology and Chemotherapy (Vol. 14, pp. 71-105). New York: Academic Press.

Murphy, D. L. (1977b). Animal models of mania. In I. Hanin & E. Usdin (Eds.), Animal models in psychiatry and neurology. New York: Pergamon Press.

Murphy, D. L., Belmaker, R. H., Buchsbaum, M. S., Martin, N. F., Ciaranello, R., & Wyatt, R. J. (1977). Biogenic amine related enzymes and personality variations in normals. Psychological Medicine, 7, 149-157.

Murphy, D. L., & Weiss, R. (1972). Reduced monoamine oxidase activity in blood platelets from bipolar depressed patients. American Journal of Psychiatry, 128, 1531-1357.

Murphy, D. L., Wright, C., Buchsbaum, M. S., Nichols, A., Costal, J. L., & Wyatt, R. J. (1976). Platelet and plasma amine oxidase activity in 680 normals: Sex and age differences and stability over time. Biochemical Medicine, 16, 254-265.

Myers, T. I., & Eisner, E. J. (Oct. 31, 1974). An experimental evaluation of the effects of karate and meditation (Report No. 43800 [P-391X-1-29]). Washington, DC: American Institutes for Research.

Neary, R. S., & Zuckerman, M. (1976). Sensation seeking trait and state anxiety, and the electrodermal orienting reflex. Psychophysiology, 13, 205-211.

Orlebeke, J. F., & Feij, J. A. (1979). The orienting reflex as a personality correlate. In H. D. Kimmel, E. H. van Olst, & J. F. Orlebeke (Eds.), The orienting reflex in humans. Hillsdale, NJ: Lawrence Erlbaum.

Ozeran, B. J. (1973). Sensation-seeking as a predictor of leadership in leader-less task oriented groups. Unpublished master's thesis, University of Hawaii, Honolulu.

Pavlov, I, P. (1927, 1960). Conditioned reflexes: An investigation of the physiological activity of the cerebral cortex (G. V. Anrep, Trans. & ed.). New York: Dover Publications.

Redmond, D. E., Jr., Murphy, D. L., & Baulu, J. (1979). Platelet monoamine oxidase activity correlates with social affiliative and agonistic behaviors in normal rhesus monkeys. Psychosomatic Medicine, 41, 87-100.

Robinson, D. S., Davis, J. M., Nies, A., Ravaris, C. L., & Sylvester, D. (1971). Relation of sex and aging to monoamine oxidase activity of human brain, plasma, and platelets. Archives of General Psychiatry, 24, 536-539.

Rose, R. M. (1975). Testosterone, aggression, and homosexuality: A review of the literature and implications for future research. In E. M. Sachar (Ed.), Topics in endocrinology. New York: Grune & Stratton.

Routtenberg, A. (1968). The two-arousal hypothesis: Reticular formation and limbic system. Psychological Review, 75, 51-81.

Royce, J. R. (1977). On the construct validity of open-field measures. Psychological Bulletin, 84, 1098-1106.

Royce, J. R., Holmes, T. M., & Poley, W. (1975). Behavior genetic analysis of mouse emotionality, III. The diallel analysis. Behavior Genetics, 5, 351-372.

Schooler, C., Zahn, T. P., Murphy, D. L., & Buchsbaum, M. S. (1978). Psychological correlates of monoamine oxidase in normals. Journal of Nervous and Mental Diseases, 166, 177-186.

Stanton, H. E. (1976). Hypnosis and encounter group volunteers: A validational study of the Sensation Seeking Scale. Journal of Consulting and Clinical Psychology, 44, 692.

Stein, L. (1978). Reward transmitters: Catecholamines and opioid peptides. In M. A. Lipton, A. DiMascio, & K. F. Killam (Eds.), Psychopharmacology: A generation of progress. New York: Raven Press.

Whimbey, A. E., & Denenberg, V. H. (1967). Two independent behavioral dimensions in open-field performance. Journal of Comparative and Physiological Psychology, 63, 500-504.

Zuckerman, M. (1969). Theoretical formulations: I. In J. P. Zubek (Ed.). Sensory deprivation: Fifteen years of research. New York: Appleton-Century-Crofts.

Zuckerman, M. (1971). Dimensions of sensation seeking. Journal of Consulting and Clinical Psychology, 36, 45-52.

Zuckerman, M. (1973). Scales for sex experience for males and females. Journal of Consulting and Clinical Psychology, 41, 27-29.

Zuckerman, M. (1979a). Sensation seeking: Beyond the optimal level of arousal. Hillsdale, NJ: Lawrence Erlbaum.

Zuckerman, M. (1979b). Traits, states, situations, and uncertainty. Journal of Behavioral Assessment, 1, 43-54.

Zuckerman, M., Bone, R. N., Neary, R., Mangelsdorff, D., & Brustman, B. (1972). What is the sensation seeker? Personality trait and experience correlates of the Sensation Seeking Scales. Journal of Consulting and Clinical Psychology, 39, 308-321.

Zuckerman, M., Eysenck, S., & Eysenck, H. J. (1978). Sensation seeking in England and America: Cross-cultural, age and sex comparisons. Journal of Consulting and Clinical Psychology, 46, 139-149.

Zuckerman, M., and Hopkins, T. R. Unpublished manuscript.

Zuckerman, M., Kolin, E. A., Price, L., & Zoob, I. (1964). Development of a Sensation-Seeking Scale. Journal of Consulting Psychology, 28, 477-482.

Zuckerman, M., Murtaugh, T. M., & Siegel, J. (1974). Sensation seeking and cortical augmenting-reducing. Psychophysiology, 11, 535-542.

Zuckerman, M., & Neb, M. (1979). Sensation seeking and psychopathology. Psychiatry Research, 1, 255-274.

Zuckerman, M., & Neb, M. (1980). Demographic influences in sensation seeking and expressions of sensation seeking in religion, smoking, and driving habits. Personality and Individual Differences, 197-206.

Zuckerman, M., Persky, H., Hopkins, T. R., Murtaugh, T., Basu, G. K., & Schilling, M. (1966). Comparison of stress effects of perceptual and social isolation. Archives of General Psychiatry, 14, 356-365.

Zuckerman, M., Persky, H., Link, K. E., & Basu, G. K. (1968a). Responses to confinement: An investigation of sensory deprivation, social isolation, movement, and set factors. Perceptual and Motor Skills, 27, 319-334.

Zuckerman, M., Persky, H., Link, K. E., & Basu, G. K. (1968b). Experimental and subject factors determining responses to sensory deprivation, social isolation and confinement. Journal of Abnormal Psychology, 73, 183-194.

Zuckerman, M., Schultz, D. P., & Hopkins, T. R. (1967). Sensation seeking and volunteering for sensory deprivation and hypnosis experiments. Journal of Consulting Psychology, 31, 358-363.

Zuckerman, M., Tushup, R., & Finner, S. (1976). Sexual attitudes and experience: Attitude and personality correlates and changes produced by a course in sexuality. Journal of Consulting and Clinical Psychology, 44, 7-19.

6

Activation (Arousal): The Shift from a Single to a Multidimensional Perspective

Robert E. Thayer

Theoretical scientists are fond of developing general principles and models. To the extent that these theories are valid, meaningful organization is imposed on otherwise diverse and seemingly unrelated phenomena. In the psychological sciences, one such general theoretical model divides behavior into two basic aspects: direction and intensity. That is, at any one time we may characterize behavior in terms of its direction, approach, or withdrawal (not necessarily overt), and also in terms of its intensity, activation, or arousal. This language was proposed by Elizabeth Duffy (1962) primarily in connection with her observations of peripheral physiological systems, but similar intensity and directional categories have been put forth by others working mainly from central neurophysiological and behavioral observations (see Malmo, 1959).

It seems to me that the existence of one or more intensity continua, which directly affect most, if not all, behavior, is indisputable. For example, following the sleep-wakefulness cycle, on most days of our lives we move inexorably from quiescence to activity and back again to quiescence. Also, among our common emotions, mild states are clearly related to strong reactions by an intensity continuum. These aspects of bodily activation act as predispositional states. As such, they are not the sole determinants of behavior, but their presence makes certain behaviors more likely. We usually respond differently in the same situation when we are energetic than we do when we are tired. Common situations elicit different reactions when we are extremely afraid than they do with mild apprehension.

In dispute for a modern viable activation theory are clear demonstrations of the exact way that these intensity variations affect other behavioral processes (e.g., psychomotor activity, information processing, and learning). Also in dispute is the assumption of some theories that there is a unitary activation continuum that underlies and energizes behavior. As will be seen, the dimensionality of activation is one of the central issues of this chapter. I believe that at least some emotional variations are mediated by a different intensity continuum from what underlies the sleep-wakefulness cycle.

MEASUREMENT OF ACTIVATION STATES: THE CONCEPT OF LEVELS OF ABSTRACTION

Early activation theorists such as Elizabeth Duffy, Harold Schlosberg, and Donald Lindsley relied on a physiological substrate for the measurement of the bodily intensity continuum. Influential critics challenged these conceptualizations with demonstrations of low intercorrelations among commonly employed measurements of autonomic and central nervous system reactivity (e.g., Lacey, 1967). Critics asked, if individual systems do not become activated together, how can the concept of general activation be valid?

These criticisms were well answered by Duffy (1962), when she indicated that individual physiological subsystems could not be expected to intercorrelate highly with employment of the usual single-occasion, interindividual research designs. It is clear that individual bodily systems have different response latencies and that each probably has its own homeostatic balancing mechanism that could result in temporary antagonistic actions with other systems. Furthermore, individual- and situational-response specificities would contribute additional error variance to the measurement process. Still, if the intensity continuum is to be useful for scientific research, there must be valid measures of its variations.

We need reliable measures to demonstrate the basic variations in intensity that seem obvious. I believe that the problem with the development of an influential activation theory has to do with the level of abstraction in measurement. One approach is to use intraindividual designs and to combine individual physiological systems in appropriate ways so as to reduce the error variance arising from response specificities. Unfortunately, the appropriate combination methods have not yet been demonstrated. Furthermore, this kind of measurement is extremely costly, and it imposes often unacceptable constraints of artificiality on the behavior under study.

Another measurement approach is to use bodily variations, which by their nature and function are good indications of the most basic intensity continua. Although conscious awareness and its product, controlled self-report, is associated with numerous methodological measurement problems, it usually represents a high level of organismic integration. If a person with some verbal facility is asked to describe his momentary state of activation, he can introspect and use a number of simultaneously functioning bodily systems. It is not known how awareness occurs, but it is at least probable that the summation of information from many of these systems leads to a person's awareness of any given intensity variation (see Davitz, 1969). Furthermore, reliable data suggest that self-report provides a better indication of basic intensity variations than does any one of the commonly used psychophysiological measures (Thayer, 1967, 1970). Therefore, if integrated organismic functioning is to be assessed, self-report would appear to be an excellent practical index.

The activation model to be described is largely based on self-report data obtained with the Activation-Deactivation Adjective Check List (AD ACL). This test, as it was originally constructed, included four separate activation factors; at the time, these were thought to represent all elements of a single nondirectional activation continuum (Thayer, 1967). There has now been a major revision of the test (Thayer, 1978a), and the four factors as they currently stand are General Activation (energetic, vigorous, lively, full of pep, active, peppy, and activated); Deactivation-Sleep (tired, sleepy, drowsy, wide-awake, and wakeful); High Activation (tense, anxious, jittery, clutched-up, fearful, intense, and stirred-up); and General Deactivation (still, quiet, placid, at rest, calm, leisurely, and quiescent).

PROBLEMS WITH A UNITARY ACTIVATION CONTINUUM

Until 1970, I still thought of the activation states that underlie behavior as forming a single continuum. Experimental and casual observations in the next decade, however, while reinforcing the necessity of including activation variations in any general behavior theory, have forced me to challenge the idea of a single underlying intensity continuum.

An influential example of this evidence for revision came from a piece of research in which anxiety was experimentally manipulated and subjects reported their activation states with AD ACLs in each of three anxiety conditions

(Thayer & Moore, 1972). In the moderate-anxiety condition, students reported, as expected, that they were less tired and more energetic than in the low-anxiety condition. But verbal reports in the high-anxiety condition were unexpected and inconsistent with a unitary activation continuum. Although student participants in this condition reported that they were more tense than in the other conditions, they also reported that they were more tired than in the moderate-anxiety condition and less energetic. Thus there appeared to be two activation systems in simultaneous operation. Activation in one system increased as a monotonic function of manipulated anxiety, while activation in a second system showed a curvilinear relationship to manipulated anxiety.

This experiment and others led to a reexamination of the factor-analytic evidence for a unitary activation construct (Thayer, 1978a). Several large-scale studies of AD ACL responses were conducted in which orthogonal and oblique factor rotations were systematically compared. Second-order analyses were also conducted. The results of these studies indicated that General Activation (energetic, vigorous) generally varied in reciprocal relation to Deactivation-Sleep (sleepy, tired). The same was true of High Activation (tense, anxious) and General Deactivation (quiet, placid). Furthermore, second-order analyses showed that these two pairs of factors form two separate second-order factors.

Research from my laboratory does not stand alone in suggesting at least two activation dimensions underlying behavior. For example, following an activation theory with a unitary intensity continuum, how does one explain the existence in anxiety neurotics of simultaneous complaints of anxiety and tiredness? Yet there is good documentation that these two states, at opposite ends of the traditional activation continuum, do exist together (Miles, Barrabee, & Finesinger, 1951). A related phenomenon, although not so well documented, seems to occur when one exercises vigorously. The activating effects of exercise appear to reduce the activating effects of anxiety (de Vries & Adams, 1972). The more we exercise, the less tense we feel.

Sleep-deprivation research offers still another example of multiple activation continua. Although the primary effect of the continued absence of sleep is profound tiredness, early in the deprivation a mixture of tiredness and anxiety is often apparent (Murray, 1965). We also see evidence for two activation systems in psychopharmacology. Hyperactive children act as though they are very anxious and tense; yet they are helped by amphetamines such as Ritalin or even caffeine, drugs that increase arousal (Rosenthal & Allen, 1978). Other pharmacological agents also act on the body as though at least two arousal systems exist. For example, tranquilizers, when they work optimally, reduce anxiety without making a person tired. Barbiturates, on the other hand, act primarily to increase sleep. Each of these examples, and for me particularly the self-report evidence, lead inescapably to the conclusion that there are at least two bodily activation systems.

A NEW MULTIDIMENSIONAL ACTIVATION MODEL

As I presently conceive of it, the body is an energy system in which metabolic processes in their various forms create the potential for energy expenditure. From the most general perspective, energy expenditure occurs on at least two (and possibly several) separate dimensions of activation or bodily arousal. Though peripheral manifestations are similar (Thayer, 1970, 1978b), the central neural substrates of these two dimensions may well involve the reticular activating system and the limbic system (Routtenberg, 1968; Thayer, 1978b). However, the evidence about central processes is unclear. On the other hand, a psychological analysis of conscious awareness, representing as it does a high level of organismic integration, yields two systems that can be characterized roughly as energy-sleep and tension-placidity.

These two activation or arousal systems, which I have designated Activation Dimensions A and B, tend to operate in a positively correlated fashion at moderate levels of energy expenditure and in a negatively correlated fashion at high levels (see Figure 1). That is, moderate increases in tension tend to increase energy, but high levels of tension result in decreased energy. On the other hand, energy peaks are associated with reduced tension. One implication of the negative correlation is that tiredness and low energy leave a person especially vulnerable to heightened fear and anxiety (in the presence of bothersome thoughts and life circumstances). A last theoretical proposition is that low levels of energy expenditure in one system reduce activation in both systems. An example of this occurs when an extremely tired person finally goes to sleep even when personal stress would otherwise create tension-based arousal.

Each of the two activation systems is believed to influence a different set of behavioral processes. Each system also is affected by a different set of internal and external stimuli.

Activation Dimension A

<u>A Circadian Activation Rhythm.</u> Dimension A activation seems to represent variations in wakefulness in the familiar 24-hr cycle of sleeping and waking. This activation continuum has received relatively little attention from psychologists, with the exception of those who have concentrated on such experimental variables as time-of-day and exercise. Activation theorists, as well as those who employ an arousal continuum in their research, have mainly applied their conceptualizations to emotional variations; or they have lumped together wakefulness and emotional variations in a single continuum.

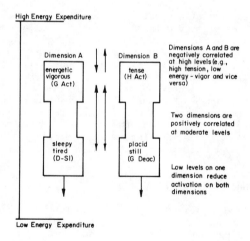

FIGURE 1. A two-dimensional activation model. Dimension A includes General Activation (G Act) and Deactivation-Sleep (D-Sl). Dimension B includes high Activation (H Act) and General Deactivation (G Deac). From "Toward a Psychological Theory of Multidimensional Activation (Arousal)" by R. E. Thayer (1978b), <u>Motivation and Emotion</u>, <u>2</u>, 1-34. Copyright 1976 by Plenum Publishing Corporation. Reprinted by permission.

It is often mistakenly assumed that sleep and wakefulness are merely two dicho-
tomous states. But wakefulness involves continuous and predictable variations
in feelings of energy, vigor, and tiredness. (Continuous variations in the
depth of sleep are well known, but they are not our focus here.) This activation cycle was recently demonstrated in a study conducted in my laboratory. It
involved 25 college students who monitored their activation states with AD ACLs
at 2-hr intervals over two full days (Thayer, 1978b). The study showed that,
on the average, tiredness decreased and energetic or vigorous feelings increased
from morning awakening to a peak about $3\frac{1}{2}$ hr later. This was followed by a low
point in energy feelings at midafternoon to late afternoon, a secondary peak,
and a dropoff before sleep.

Of course, the curve I have just described represents the mean responses of all
the experimental participants, and it is likely that individual differences exist.
For example, morning and evening personality types would probably be represented
by more rapid increases in energy feelings after awakening or less rapid declines
in energy feelings before sleep. Other individual differences might also be
reasonably expected. For example, some people may be more energetic thoughout
the day than others. In fact, it seems to me that one major variation in life-
span development is gradually decreasing absolute levels of daily energy and vigor.

Elsewhere, I have reviewed evidence (Thayer, 1978b) suggesting that the Dimension A activation cycle is endogenous in nature; that is, the cycle continues
relatively independently of environmental events (see also Åkersted, Pátkai, &
Dahlgren, 1977). However, the energy states underlying this cycle or at least
their representations in awareness, are certainly temporarily increased or
decreased by thoughts and experiences. A sudden burst of good luck or an interesting party can bring us from a late-evening tiredness to feelings of energy
and liveliness.

The fact that this biological cycle can be temporarily overridden tends to disguise its importance in our daily lives. I suspect that this is the central
reason that psychologists have studied the circadian energy rhythm as little as
they have. The influence of this rhythm is subtle, and if one is to appreciate
its significance, one must study its effects over many days. Another reason
for neglect of this important predispositional variable is that the cycle can
be modified over a matter of days by alterations of life circumstance (e.g., a
factory worker changing from day to night work; see Åkersted et al., 1977). I
believe that one of the most significant influences in entrainment of the activation rhythm is motor activity. This assumption is reasonable because of the
strong and consistent effects of such activity on energy feelings.

Gross Voluntary Motor Activity. Many years ago, in one of the first systematic
studies of sleep deprivation, Nathanial Kleitman (1963) observed that, after
several days without sleep, the only way to keep the experimental participants
awake was to make them stand up and walk around. It is significant that gross
voluntary motor activity was the only reliable means of counteracting tiredness
and the urge to sleep. Of course, in a general sort of way, animal researchers
have always relied on the absence of motor activity as an indication of sleep.
Moreover, Russian researchers working on sleep therapies found decreases in
gross motor activity to be an excellent index of the passage between wakefulness
and sleep, particularly when adjusted to the idiosyncratic differences among
patients (Andreev, 1960). Decreasing motor activity is even an indication of
the depth of sleep (Cathala & Guillard, 1961; Rohmer, Schaff, Collard, & Kurtz,
1965). Motor activity is somehow integrally related to sleep and wakefulness.

This relationship has been of substantial importance to me because during wakefulness, gross movement is clearly tied to energy feelings. I have published
the results of one study demonstrating that moderate physical exercise reliably

increases feelings of energy and decreases tiredness (Thayer, 1978b), and a number of other unpublished experiments from my laboratory have shown the same results. Never in my experience has a psychological effect been so easily and consistently produced short of using strong drugs or intense stress. These observations strongly suggest that wakefulness, gross voluntary motor activity, and energy feelings are inextricably tied to each other (c.f., Malmo, 1975; Sperry, 1952). In a general sense, they are merely different indications of the same phenomenon -- bodily activation.

The apparently close tie of wakefulness, energy feelings, and motor functions raises important implications too extensive to be discussed in this chapter. But one obvious idea is that changes in the endogenous energy cycle probably would predispose or create preferences for different degrees of motor activity. At least in certain respects, this proposition is self-evident. When we are most tired, exercise is least appealing. This idea is currently being explored in research in my laboratory.

Cognitive Activity. A number of studies have demonstrated the relationship between Dimension A activation states and cognitive activity, particularly a variety of verbal functions. For example, Thayer and Cox (1968) found support for an inverted-U function in performance on a verbal learning task at different levels of General Activation (energy, vigor). A noncomplex task was performed best at highest levels of General Activation, whereas a complex task showed best performance at moderate levels of this subscale. Similarly, Michael Eysenck (1976) found that General Activation scores could be used to predict recall, recognition, and production of verbal material, particularly when level of extraversion was employed as a moderator variable. General Activation scores also predicted performance on a college examination (Wittmaier, 1974). In each of these cases, Dimension A activation variations, as opposed to Dimension B, were the significant predictors.

Dimension B Activation

The second activation system in the multidimensional model is characterized by feelings of tension, anxiety, or fearfulness on one extreme and quietness, placidity, or calmness on the other. Its biological function is discussed later here, but I believe it involves emergency energy mobilization, and it also functions as a warning system.

Research in my laboratory has shown this system to be differentially affected by college examinations, intense white noise, and audience-evaluation anxiety (Thayer, 1967, 1978b; Thayer & Carey, 1974). Each of these affected areas would appear to involve stress to the individual. One other study in my laboratory showed that guided meditation most strongly affected the low activation pole of this system. (General Deactivation).

Activation States and Personality

Depression. The two activation systems described above interact to affect a number of personality functions. One of the first systematic observations of this interaction occurred in a study conducted by Anne Wettler and myself on eight females who complained of chronic low-level depression. This is the kind of condition that creates a great deal of unhappiness for many people in our current society, but which is not sufficiently severe to require professional attention. These women were asked to complete AD ACLs on several days when they felt depressed and on a number of comparison days, which were similar in as many respects as possible to the depression days (same time of day and similar activities), but on which feelings of depression were absent. Statistically significant differences in activation states occurred in both

Activation Dimensions A and B. In each case, depression was accompanied by low energy, high tiredness, and high tension.

Self-esteem. The relationship between activation level and self-esteem was the focus of a study in which 15 college students completed self-evaluation ratings and AD ACLs numerous times over a 7-week period (Rubadeau & Thayer, 1976). One of the clear outcomes of this study was that ratings of self-esteem varied considerably for most experimental participants. This result calls into question the commonly held idea that self-esteem is a fixed trait. For this study, an importatant question concerned the bases of these variations in self-esteem. Dimension A activation (particularly General Activation) was the strongest predictor of self-evaluations. High energy feelings were substantially associated with high self-esteem, and vice versa. High Activation (tension) reports also showed a significant negative correlation, but the relationship was not as strong as the one involving General Activation. Thus, of the two activation dimensions, Dimension A appeared to be th most important predictor of self-esteem variations. It is my guess that activation states are causal variables in changing self-esteem; unfortunately, this type of study does not establish the direction of the relationship. Experimental studies are now being conducted in my laboratory to gain more information about this causation.

Perception of personal problems. From the circle of covariation involving activation states, depression, and self-esteem, one can see that central personality variables have clear-cut relationships with bodily intensity variations. In the experiment to be described, involving perception of personal problems, and in the following experiment on optimism, specific evidence is provided that important ways of seeing the world are substantially influenced by naturally occurring energy variations. Unfortunately, this can only be a preliminary report, because this research is still ongoing.

These experiments incorporate two significant features. First, they give crucial information about causation because they allow an experimental manipulation of activation states through the use of the known circadian activation rhythm and through exercise-produced energy changes. Second, they involve multiple testings on the same subject over many days, thus increasing the meaningfulness of the resultant dependent measures. This design feature is important if one wishes to control the influence of random or unusual environmental effects and to study the more subtle long-term influences of underlying activation states.

Eight specially chosen university students participated in the first experiment. Each person had a fairly serious personal problem, the kind that would be unlikely to change very much over the 3-week period of the study. Their task was to make ratings of the problem based on how serious it appeared at the moment of each rating, its apparent difficulty, and its likelihood of solution. AD ACLs were also completed at each rating time.

Ratings were made five times a day on each of 10 typical days. The daily rating times were specially chosen to maximize known diurnal activation variations and to take advantage of exercise-produced activation changes. Each day, ratings were made once at awakening, again at late morning, at midafternoon to late afternoon, and just before sleep at night. One other rating was made at an agreed on time of day after a 10-minute rapid walk. Mean Dimension A activation ratings verified that late morning and postwalk periods involved higher activation states than did midafternoon periods. Thus the desired activation manipulations were accomplished.

The results concerning problem ratings provide a good indication that this aspect of self-evaluation was influenced by bodily activation in every case. Ratings of the problem's seriousness were sometimes higher and sometimes lower, but 10-day averages showed the same ordinal results in almost every comparison. Seven of the eight participants rated their problems as more serious and less likely to be solved at late afternoon than they were in the morning (p < .05). All eight participants saw the problem as more serious at midafternoon than after the 10-minute walk (p < .05). The obtained data also allowed a second kind of analysis. The best prediction of low concern about personal problems could be made when the absolute level of energy and vigor was greater than the absolute level of tension and anxiety. On the other hand, the problems appeared most serious to the experimental participants when they reported greater feelings of tension than energy or vigor.

Optimism. The following experiment is a variation of the previous one. This research also employed late morning, late afternoon, and walking conditions as a means of manipulating activation states in two ways. Twelve university students completed AD ACLs and ratings of their degree of personal optimism three times a day on each of six typical days. Once again, reported Dimension A activation was significantly higher at late morning and after walking than it was at late afternoon.

The ratings of optimism provide still another indication that activation states influence perception. All of the 12 experimental participants reported being more optimistic at late morning than at late afternoon (p < .05). All 12 reported more optimism after a 10-minute walk than at late morning (p < .05).

STATE-SPECIFIC CONSCIOUSNESS: CHANGING CONCEPTIONS OF REALITY

Some years ago, researchers discovered that learning and recall seemed to be quite dependent on the drug-produced state of the experimental animals under study. These conceptions have since been extended to humans (e.g., Tart, 1975). It is as though the brain operates coherently in a given state of consciousness, but changing states of consciousness do not provide carryover of all information.

The experiments described in the preceding section, on different states of activation or arousal, demonstrate a similar phenomenon. Our relationship with the environment or our personal problems may remain relatively constant. But apparently we view those problems differently, and we feel variously optimistic or pessimistic, depending on the level and balance of our two activation systems. If we are very tired and tense, say at 4 p.m., the world looks bleak and our problems may appear insoluble. However, at 11 a.m. the next morning, when we are energetic and not at all tense, we feel optimistic and we know that we can handle our problems. The same change toward a more positive outlook seems to occur with vigorous physical exercise.

What is happening here? There is no experimental evidence to support this explanation, but I believe that we often evaluate future personal demands by incorrectly projecting our present state of capability into the future. The process goes something like this. We consider a problem that will require vigorous action to deal with, and we ask ourselves, "Will I be able to meet this demand?" Through introspection, we find ourselves very tired and without energy, and the inevitable answer is, "No." It is as though we are saying, "I am so tired that I can't do anything." Here is where the crucial cognitive error occurs. Instead of recognizing that in the future we won't always be tired -- that there will be periods of vigor when solutions are more likely to be obtained -- we mistakenly assume that our present feelings will last indefinitely. I believe that this process occurs so rapidly and at such a low level of conscious awareness that we do not even recognize what is happening.

THE BIOLOGICAL FUNCTION OF TWO ACTIVATION SYSTEMS

It appears that in some way, the function of the activation systems is to mediate, or tune those parts of the nervous system which have responsibility for directional aspects of behavior. Also it seems clear that, in some larger sense, energy expenditure and conservation are integrally involved. For example, it is probable that the sleep-wakefulness cycle (probably Dimension A activation) has as its function the necessary mobilization and expenditure of energy for survival and propagation, alternated with periods of conservation. Of those necessary life functions, gross voluntary motor activity seems to have central importance, and it requires some of the highest expenditures of energy. Furthermore, variations in this motor system apparently are closely related to wakefulness and to the conscious representation of Dimension A activation.

At this time, neither the biological function of the Dimension B system, nor the function of the interaction pattern between the two activation systems is entirely clear. Some educated guesses, however, can be made. I have maintained that Dimension B activation is associated with emergency energy expenditure. Compared with Dimension A activation, tension, anxiety, or fearful feelings are differentially influenced by various stressors (e.g., loud noise, audience evaluation, and exams). Furthermore, similar patterns of physiological arousal are associated with both activation systems (Thayer, 1970; also see Thayer, 1978b, for a longer discussion of this point).

There is one aspect of bodily arousal which is differentially associated with the two activation dimensions. Gross voluntary motor activity is closely related to Dimension A, but only indirectly related to Dimension B activation. Although muscle tension is clearly a part of the syndrome of anxiety, directed or voluntary gross motor activity (e.g., running, vigorous walking, and exercise) is most closely related to Dimension A activation.

If one assumes that Dimension B activation is correlated with stress-related arousal but not directly with gross motor activity, and if one assumes that tension is an unpleasant psychological state, then two biological functions are suggested for this system. The first function is preparation for physical activity. An aroused person (e.g., increased cardiovascular and autonomic activity) would seem to be more ready for vigorous and directed gross motor activity than would a quiescent person. The second biological function must not be neglected, however, for it undoubtedly has critical survival importance. Tension, anxiety, and fearfulness act as a warning system. We are made aware of imminent danger, and that danger is kept within our awareness over time by these unpleasant feelings.

With these two biological functions in mind, let us examine the hypothesized interaction pattern between Activation Dimensions A and B. At moderate levels of energy expenditure, the two dimensions are <u>positively</u> correlated. Thus, as a danger stimulus of moderate significance becomes apparent, the person is energized (Dimension A) to provide the necessary counteractive activity. With this kind of danger stimulus, there is still time for a consideration of alternatives, and moderate voluntary motor activity may be sufficient to allay the danger. An example of this positive correlation occurs when anxiety about some forthcoming deadline mobilizes us to energetic action.

However, at high levels of energy expenditure, the two dimensions are <u>negatively</u> correlated. If we are faced with a danger stimulus that may indicate imminent destruction, we must cease all extraneous function, including the motor activity that we have been engaged in, and regard that danger immediately. For example, when terrible news is relayed to us, we immediately cease all activity and orient to the information. At this time, our consciousness is flooded with unpleasant affect (anxiety, fear, and tension, together with a lack of energy and tiredness).[1] With Dimension B dominant, the negative correlation between the two dimensions is apparent.

Next we act. Whether it is fight or flight, we engage in vigorous voluntary motor activity. And when this happens, the feelings of anxiety and fear vanish. Instead, if we were to introspect, we would feel vigorous and energetic, not tired at all. Again we may see the negative correlation between Dimensions A and B, but with Dimension A activation dominant at this point.

Last, very low levels of activation in either system reduce activation in the body as a whole. As an example, when we become extremely tired, we finally sleep -- anxiety not withstanding. This appears to be something of a bodily protective mechanism.

To better understand the interaction of the two activation systems over time, let me outline an imaginary scenario about a person under stress. A healthy well-rested person is informed at 11 a.m. one morning (maximum level of endogenous activation cycle) that he is going to lose his job. Initially, the news may be shocking, resulting in a high anxiety peak and a corresponding feeling of tiredness and low energy. But the already high morning levels of energy and vigor would soon counteract the anxiety and allow effective action. At 4 p.m., however, when the midafternoon "slump" is on him, this person, who is now tired, would be very anxious. At this time the unremitting stress (cognitively mediated) would continue to maintain high Dimension B activation, but the Dimension A activation would be at its diurnal low point, leaving this person increasingly vulnerable to stress. As evening approaches and Dimension A activation rises in its endogenous rhythm, a temporary reduction in tension and anxiety might be expected. But with the approach of night sleep, and the natural drop in energy, anxiety would once again be at its peak.

If this unfortunate person were not able to sleep well that night because of the anxiety, he would probably feel less energetic the next morning, and there would be less counteraction to the tension. Still, due to the endogenous cycle, late morning might well be the least anxious time of the day. In this second day, the afternoon and evening would probably be extremely anxious times. Vulnerability to stress would be greatest here. The only reduction in anxiety would probably occur with better job news, avoidance of thought (cognitive control), or with physical exercise. The exercise would, temporarily at least, raise Dimension A activation and counteract the tension. Continued stress would for a time result in varying degrees of anxiety, corresponding to diurnal variations in energy and vigor.

Finally, at some point in the gradual debilitation of this person (such as sleepless nights and poor nutrition), there would not be sufficient resources for any

---

[1] The evolutionary adaptiveness of reduced motor activity and increased tiredness in the face of significant threat is only one possible reason for the negative correlation between the two dimensions at high levels. I am currently exploring other hypotheses, including one that Dimension B activation in large measure involves anaerobic energy metabolism and the associated rapid depletions, whereas Dimension A involves aerobic energy metabolism, a much more efficient energy supply system. If, in the future, the latter hypothesis better accounts for the negative correlation, it would follow that the inverse relationship between activation dimensions occurs rapidly following significant threat (within minutes), but not immediately. The transformation from tense to energetic feelings following physical activity also would occur quickly, but not immediately.

significant energy expenditure, and the person would enter the phase of systemic deactivation. Here no apparent anxiety would be present. Bothersome thoughts or events would have little or no effect. This stage would offer temporary respite when some needed rest or sleep could occur. It would represent the body's mechanism for sustaining survival. In a thoroughly debilitated person (e.g., long-term illness or incarceration in a concentration camp), this stage may be quite protracted, and little or no anxiety would seem to be present.

Naturally, the extent of the stress would be important in this interaction as well. Low levels of stress may have little or no noticeable effect (subjective tension) except at times of minimal Dimension A activation, whereas intense stress might produce tiredness and energy drops even for the person with naturally high energy. Here the only possibility for reducing the tension would probably be vigorous gross voluntary motor activity or cognitive control of the interpretational mechanisms that intervene between stressor and stress reactions (Lazarus, 1966).

MOOD: THE CONSCIOUS REPRESENTATION OF TWO ACTIVATION SYSTEMS

Earlier I argued that conscious awareness represents an excellent organismic integrating system. I believe that this biological characteristic has evolved in part as a means by which a person may recognize potential and real energy deficiencies and by which he can optimize behavior-energy couplings. Viewed in this way, conscious awareness is a useful system for survival and development, and its evolutionary emergence is quite logical.

Consider that tension represents danger, tiredness represents a time for rest or sleep, and energetic feelings, an optimal time for active interaction with the environment. Were we to readily heed internal signals of our states of activation, we might change our lives by scheduling stressful experiences during high energy times, and we would probably use physical exercise much more as a counteraction to stress-produced tension. Also, were we aware enough of our bodily signals to note their circadian rhythmicity, we would probably be less discouraged by a view of our problems taken when we are tired, for example, late at night. Instead, we would recognize the fact that in a few hours or a day, things could look different.

Two Activation Dimensions or More?

Although it could be argued that all emotional variations may be represented within the two proposed dimensions, particularly in conjunction with cognitive factors (see Schachter, 1964), there really is not sufficient evidence at this point to firmly draw that conclusion. I am especially uncertain about emotional reactions such as sexual arousal and anger. Future research may show that there are several activation dimensions, and several kinds of interaction patterns (see Thayer, 1978b, for further discussion of this point).

REFERENCES

Åkerstedt, T., Pátkai, P., & Dahlgren, K. (1977). Field studies of shiftwork: II. Temporal patterns in psychophysiological activation in workers alternating between night and day work. Ergonomics, 20, 621-631.

Andreev, B. V. (1960). Sleep therapy in the neurosis. New York: Consultants Bureau.

Cathala, H. P., & Guillard, A. (1961). La reactivite au cours du sommeil physiologique de l'homme. Pathologie et Biologie, Paris, 9, 1357-1375.

Davitz, J. R. (1969). The language of emotion. New York: Academic Press.

de Vries, H. A., & Adams, G. M. (1972). Electromyographic comparison of single doses of exercise and meprobamate as to effects on muscular relaxation. American Journal of Physical Medicine, 51, 130-141.

Duffy, E. (1962). Activation and behavior. New York: Wiley.

Eysenck, M. W. (1976). Extraversion, verbal learning, and memory. Psychological Bulletin, 83, 75-90.

Kleitman, N. (1963). Sleep and wakefulness (Revised and enlarged edition). Chicago: University of Chicago Press.

Lacey, J. I. (1967). Somatic response patterning and stress: Some revisions of activation theory. In M. H. Appley & Trumbull (Eds.), Psychological stress. New York: Appleton-Century-Crofts.

Lazarus, R. S. (1966). Psychological stress and the coping process. New York: McGraw-Hill.

Malmo, R. B. (1959). Activation: A neurophysiological dimension. Psychological Review, 66, 367-386.

Malmo, R. B. (1975). On emotions, needs, and our archaic brain. New York: Holt, Rinehart, & Winston.

Miles, H. H. W., Barrabee, E. L., & Finesinger, J. E. (1951). Evaluation of psychotherapy, with a follow-up study of 62 cases of anxiety neurosis. Psychosomatic Medicine, 13, 83-105.

Murray, E. (1965). Sleep, dreams, and arousal. New York: Appleton-Century-Crofts.

Rohmer, F., Schaff, G., Collard, M., & Kurtz, D. (1965). La motilité spontanée la fréquence cardiaque et la fréquence respiratoire au cours du sommeil chez l'homme normal: Le sommeil de nuit normal et pathologique. Études électro-éncephalographiques. Électroencéphalographie et Neurophysiologie Clinique, 2, 156-183.

Rosenthal, R. H., & Allen, T. W. (1978). An examination of attention, arousal, and learning dysfunctions in hyperkinetic children. Psychological Bulletin, 85, 689-715.

Routtenberg, A. (1968). The two-arousal hypothesis: Reticular formation and limbic system. Psychological Review, 75, 51-80.

Rubadeau, J., & Thayer, R. E. (April 1976). The relationship of self-esteem and self-reported activation level over a seven-week period. Paper presented at Western Psychological Association.

Schachter, S. (1964). The interaction of cognitive and physiological determinants of emotional state. In L. Berkowitz (Ed.), Advances in experimental social psychology (Vol. 1). New York: Academic Press.

Sperry, R. W. (1952). Neurology and the mind-body problem. American Scientist, 40, 291-312.

Tart, C. T. (1975). States of consciousness. New York: E. P. Dutton.

Thayer, R. E. (1967). Activation states as assessed by verbal report. <u>Psychological Reports</u>, <u>20</u>, 663-678.

Thayer, R. E. (1970). Activation states as assessed by verbal report and four psychophysiological variables. <u>Psychophysiology</u>, <u>7</u>, 86-94.

Thayer, R. E. (1978a). Factor analytic and reliability studies on the Activation-Deactivation Adjective Check List. <u>Psychological Reports</u>, <u>42</u>, 747-756.

Thayer, R. E. (1978b). Toward a psychological theory of multidimensional activation (arousal). <u>Motivation and Emotion</u>, <u>2</u>, 1-34.

Thayer, R. E., & Carey, D. (1974). Spatial stimulus generalization as a function of white noise and activation level. <u>Journal of Experimental Psychology</u>, <u>102</u>, 539-542.

Thayer, R. E., & Cox, S. J. (1968). Activation, manifest anxiety, and verbal learning. <u>Journal of Experimental Psychology</u>, <u>78</u>, 524-526.

Thayer, R. E., & Moore, L. E. (1972). Reported activation and verbal learning as a function of group size (social facilitation) and anxiety-inducing instructions. <u>Journal of Social Psychology</u>, <u>88</u>, 277-287.

Wittmaier, B. C. (1974). Test anxiety, mood, and performance. <u>Journal of Personality and Social Psychology</u>, <u>29</u>, 664-669.

7

Genetic Correlates of Personality and Temperament: The Origins of Individual Differences

Pierre Roubertoux

This chapter discusses a behavior-genetics analysis of individual differences relating to temperamental traits. There are at least four reasons why psychologists who study personality and individual differences should concern themselves with genetics.

First, genetics is more concerned than any other discipline with individual differences. Differences between individuals can be seen at all levels in organisms: at a chemical level in the cell, as well as at the physiological level. Furthermore, these differences may be observed for each of the different systems: respiratory, circulatory, endocrine, nervous, and so on. Of course, genetic diversity may be studied and, nowadays, measured on the basis of electrophoresis. Powell (1975) summarized studies carried out on about thirty species; all the studies confirmed the existence of an important genetic variation.

Second, for several years the search for physiological correlates of behavior has been restricted to neurophysiological correlates and pharmacological ones. Without denying the importance of this approach, we must stress that it covers only part of the physiological correlates. Indeed, for roughly twenty years, behavior genetics analysis has allowed us to demonstrate the existence of biochemical and genetic correlates of behavior. This is true for the personality and temperamental traits considered in this volume. It is also true for the markers of the functioning of the nervous system correlated with these traits, such as average cortical potential, and galvanic skin response.

Third, the study of individual differences at the level of behavior is not only limited to measuring these differences and to establishing a factorial structure. Noting the differences is only a first step; and our inquiry is still incomplete if identification of differences is not followed by a search for the origins of these differences. Because of the impossibility of defining environmental factors in an operational way, and thereby constituting identical environments or different environments (with perhaps the exception of the socioeconomic

The research in this paper was supported by the C.N.A.M. (Service de Recherche de l'I.N.O.P.), the E.P.H.E. (Laboratoire de Psychologie Différentielle), the C.N.R.S. (E.R.A. 79), the I.N.S.E.R.M. (A.T.P. 80-79-112), and the Université de Paris V René Descartes (Laboratoire de Psychologie Differentielle and UER Biomédicale des Saints Pères.

H. Leibovici and R. Strong translated the French version into English; we thank them for their help.

level), research in the field of origins of individual differences has been
oriented mainly toward the source of genetic variation. Indeed, genetic analysis
allows us in part to answer the question of the origins of the differences between individuals, since it can define operationally the degree of proximity of
genotypes and, in the case of some species, can sometimes manipulate such proximity. But this does not exclude the possiblity of showing an interaction between the effect of genes and what has long been studied by psychologists -- the
effects of treatments.

Fourth, as Reuchlin (1978) has stressed, individual differences can be interpreted only within the context of a framework provided by general psychology.
On the other hand, Reuchlin insisted on the fact that general hypotheses may be
confirmed with the help of differential methods. The most famous example of
this contribution of differential psychology to general psychology was the construction by Spence and Taylor of a scale allowing us to distinguish individuals
by their anxiety score, thus enabling us to verify Hull's hypothesis concerning
the effect of drive on learning. Because the methods of genetic analysis are
differential, they may provide answers to general questions. For example, the
pedigree method was used to show the coherence of certain categories of psychiatric diagnosis (Carlier & Roubertoux, 1979).

Although the relationship between behavior and genetics has been established
without doubt, the important question is to know what the relationship means.
More often than not, we reason as though we were making a prediction about
behavior when we know the genotype. In fact, it is more complex than that because we must remember that the researcher is making a prediction about behavior
based on a prediction that he has made concerning the genotypes. Now the prediction made on the genotypes provides different information according to the
function of the genetic analysis under consideration.

Three independent functions of genetic analysis may be described:

1. To establish and to describe the mode of transmission of a character.

2. To estimate the genetic components of differences between means for a given
trait.

3. To estimate the genetic components of the variance observed for a trait in
a population.

The interpretation that may be given for genetic or biochemical behavioral correlates differs according to whether the methods used take one function rather
than others as a reference framework. In this chapter, our aim is to discuss
interpretations of genetic and biochemical correlates of temperament traits.
Our discussion is set within the framework of all three functions of genetic
analysis defined previously.

DESCRIPTION OF THE MODE OF GENETIC TRANSMISSION OF A TRAIT

This function of genetic analysis covers several procedures, organized in a
hierarchy:

1. Hereditary determination of the trait to be demonstrated.

2. Genetic mechanisms by which the transmission occurs.

3. Biochemical correlates of the trait and, possibly, establishment of a causal
link between the observed variation on the behavioral and biochemical levels.

The description of an hereditary transmission uses segregation analysis. In this way we test the compatibility of the data with the model.   This has two implications; the compatibility of the model with the data establishes (a) neither the legitimacy of the use of the model, (b) nor the proof that other models (environmental: biological or relational ones, for example) are not incompatible with this data.   The rejection of an environmental hypothesis must therefore be demonstrated separately.

Segregation Analysis for Man: Variants of Activity of the Nervous System

In our species, where planned crosses are impossible, phenotypes resulting from crosses retained after the fact are analyzed. For practical reasons we are forced to analyze discontinuous characters by this method. For this reason, the method has been used for psychiatric disorders (Carlier & Roubertoux, 1979; Roubertoux & Carlier, 1976).   The extension of this to continuous characters, however, is theoretically possible.

Several variants of the activity of the nervous system in humans have been submitted to this type of analysis. Characteristics of electroencephalogram (EEG) activity were first proved to be genetically determined, thanks to the twin method (Vogel, 1957). Next, these same characteristics were submitted to segregation analysis; Vogel (1970) showed that different patterns of the α rhythm followed different modes of transmission. The α rhythm of 8-13 Hz seems to be transmitted polygenetically. The production of a fast α rhythm (16-19 Hz) is probably a dominant character controlled by an autosomic gene, whose frequency is around 0.5% in the population being studied. The amplitude of the α waves would appear to be a genetically controlled polymorphism. Low voltage α is transmitted according to the autosomic dominant mode. The gene can be estimated as being present in 7% of the subjects. The large and regular α waves also follow a dominant autosomic mode of transmission. The gene was present in 4% of Vogel's subjects. The β rhythms are controlled by a polygene. A frontal pattern of 25-30 Hz depends on a dominant gene present in 0.4% of the subjects, whereas the frontal-precentral rhythms (20-25 Hz) obey an analogous mode of transmission, the gene being more frequent (1.4%).

As for the autonomic nervous system, which is part of the physiological reference framework used by both Eysenck and Gray, segregation analysis gives us less information than does analysis of the components of the variation.   In our species, however, we can consider that the activity of dopamine beta-hydroxylase (db-h) is a good marker of the functioning of the central nervous system.   The plasma level of db-h varies from one individual to another in the proportion 1 : 100 .   The deficit in db-h is controlled genetically and is transmitted as a recessive autosomic character.

As far as the indicators of activity of the central nervous system are concerned (such as the monoamine oxydase, MAO, of the platelets), the mode of transmission of the deficit that has sometimes been observed has not been made clear.   The twin method, however, has shown that genetic factors probably play a role in individual variation.   We have little genetic evidence concerning sensitivity to drugs.   For example, Omenn and Motulsky (1975) give us very little information on genetic transmission of sensitivity to drugs and their metabolic bases.

Segregation analysis on the variants of the activity of the nervous system has given poor results.   Several reasons may be given to account for this.   No doubt the most important is the difficulty (technical but not fundamental)

of carrying out segregational analysis on quantitative traits[1] such as personality traits or their physiological correlates. On the other hand, among the
neurophysiological correlates of personality, sensitivity to drugs is suited
to segregation analysis. Furthermore, sensitivity to drugs has been studied
by personality researchers (Claridge, 1967). This kind of study could create
a more direct connection between the study of physiological genetics and of
personality.

Behavioral Correlates of Normal or Pathological Traits

In many species, it appears that genetic analysis of individual differences
could be attempted, starting from known mutations. In our species several
attempts have been made. The problem is to choose a genetic marker such that
one can distinguish the behavioral effect of the gene from the behavioral reaction of the subject to his illness. For example, in Duchenne de Boulogne's
muscular dystrophy, is debility a pleiotropic effect of the gene causing the
disorder, or is debility a reaction of the subject to the disturbance of his
own body? The study of pathological traits of personality associated with
genetic disease poses many questions (Roubertoux, Carlier, Dumont, & Perruchet,
1978).

Such difficulties may be avoided when the phenotype is not identified by the
subject. Thus, Cattell, Bouterline-Young, and Hundleby (1964) endeavor to show
the differences of personality measured by HSPQ for three blood groups (A, B,
and O) and the rhesus factor. Their attempt failed, but other authors have
claimed to have discovered an association between the O group and cyclic temperament traits. We must be cautious in this domain, for a link in a population between a trait and a known genetic marker does not in any way mean that
the trait must be genetically linked to this marker.

Another type of study is an analysis of behavioral correlates of children suffering from genetic disease. A brief overview of the possibilities of this
method is given by Roubertoux et al. (1978). It appears that for children many
genetic diseases are associated with personality disorders; but it is often difficult to know if these disorders are the consequence of (a) a pleiotropic
effect, or (b) a linked gene, or (c) a behavioral reaction to physical disorders, or (d) the treatment given the children. Using this type of analysis,
we have been able to show the effect of a gene to resistance to external inhibition in conditioning. The choice of the gene as an independent variable
was made on the basis of genetic illnesses. The study was carried out on
children with muscular dystrophy. Duchenne de Boulogne's muscular dystrophies
developed either rapidly (DDB I) or slowly (DDB II). Both DDB I and DDB II were
recessive X-linked (80% of cases) and recessive autosomic (20% of cases). The
dependent variable was obtained from delayed conditioning scores.

Using the establishment of the delayed conditioned response as a criterion, no
difference was noted in the establishment of positive conditioned response in
either group of subjects. However, it is interesting to compare the results of
the two groups on the basis of time to recover after the introduction of a
parasite stimulus (light). Several scores of recovery were calculated. All
these composite scores helped classify the subjects in their original groups.

---

[1]In this respect, we should note that there is no link between the observed
form of the variation and the mode of transmission. Indeed, some continuous
characters (such as acid phosphatase of the erythrocytes) are controlled by
a single gene. Inversely, threshold characters that are qualitative can be
determined polygenetically.

One that took into account two disrupting elements helped to identify 90% of subjects. Another, taking three disruptive elements (grouped in two variables) into account, allowed the classification of 97% of subjects on the basis of discriminant functions with two variables and two groups.

These results are difficult to interpret. We will only mention here the fact that the difference between the groups does not seem to be linked to the effects caused by the illness (which are the same in the two groups) but to the effects of the gene.

This method appears to be unsatisfactory because it does not allow us to establish clearly the relationship between genes and behavior. To such difficulties we must add problems that arise because of the low incidence of subjects within the population. The latter problem can be easily overcome when we deal with infrahuman species.

Effects of Allele Substitution (Infrahuman Species)

Several methods may be used. Some consist of the application of segregation analysis to behavior traits by Mendelian crossings. The others involve using possible behavioral effects of mutations. Still others use segregating strains called inbred recombinants. The first set of methods have been rarely used for behavioral characters related to temperament. On the other hand, these methods have produced important results for behavior pathology. The second set of methods uses allelic substitutions and their behavioral effects. A theoretical presentation of this approach was given by Thiessen, Owen, and Whitsett (1970). Different behavioral phenotypes were associated to allelic substitutions affecting morphological characters in Drosophila. For the mouse, behavioral phenotypes such as activity and acquisition of conditional responses were associated with genes of which the linkage group is known. Following a systematic analysis of scores relating to activity in open field, water escape, and activity wheel, it was possible to show that allelic substitution has clearly predictable effects. Thiessen et al. drew the following conclusions:

1. Of the genes tested, 71% affect behavior.

2. Mutations affect behavior in the same way, since in the Thiessen review almost all mutations contribute to the lowering of vigor of subjects.

3. There is behavioral specificity of genes.

The observations reported for our species by Roubertoux et al. (1978) confirm the first and the second conclusions. We disagree with the third conclusion, however. This divergence can be explained by the fact that we worked on mutations which create illnesses. It is probable that the seriousness and generality of brain damage often mask what could be the specificity of the effect of a gene. It must be noted that one of the rare specific effects of a mutation studied which accompany a disease (muscular dystrophy) could be obtained by selecting precisely those subjects for which the neurological damage was the least serious.

In using animals, however, we find that new facilities for study are provided by the existence of inbred strains differing by one allele; this enables us to maintain the genetic background as constant.

The second group of methods envisaged is provided by strains of inbred recombinants. A brief but adequate presentation of this is found in Fuller and Thompson (1978). In the mouse, one locus (Sco, located in the XVII chromosome) was responsible for the modification of exploratory activity by scopolamine.

Differences in the rapidity of learning of active avoidance seemed to be the consequence of an allelic substitution in the Aal locus, located in chromosome IX. Differences between lines in exploratory activity were linked to a locus situated on chromosome IV (Oliverio & Castellano, 1975). The method has been applied to drug tolerance: for example, morphine (Shurster, 1975) and different types of anaesthetic -- Halothane, CO_2, and Flurothyl (Elias & Pents, 1975).

We have discussed at length the methods that allow for the analysis of segregation; at present the available results may seem modest. This method, however, is the only one that will lead to progress in the search for behavioral correlates of underlying biochemical mechanisms. Personality researchers are well advised to consider the use of susceptibility to drugs along with the development of typologies. This will enable an integration qua Claridge of existing theories of personality and bring about a rapprochement between typological taxonomy and genetic analysis.

ANALYSIS OF THE COMPONENTS OF VARIATION

Genetic analysis leads the geneticist to a better knowledge of the genetic origins of differences between individuals. This function is independent of segregation analysis: demonstration of even an important genetic contribution to differences between individuals does not give information on the mode of transmission of this trait.

The genetic analysis considered here seeks, among the sources of variations present within the two populations, those transmitted from ascendants to descendants. The partitioning of phenotype variance into components is explained by Cavalli Sforza and Bodmer (1971) and Roubertoux and Carlier (1976). For each degree of genetic proximity or each type of family relationship, the observed variance results from the addition of genetic and environmental factors -- interaction between genotype and environment -- genotype-environment correlation components and others presented in references cited earlier. A system of equations may be set up with one equation for each kind of family relationship, the resolution of which leads to an estimate of the parameters. This estimate assumes that the parameters are estimated independently; in other words, the genotypes are affected in a random manner in different environments.

The Relative Importance of Source of Variation in Personality Traits in Human Populations: Heritability in Its Broad Sense

One of the most frequent ways of translating the estimated effect of genes in the resemblance between members of a family is to relate that effect to the phenotype variance; we then speak of heritability in its broad sense. To estimate it, we can estimate the part of the correlation that is attributable to genetic factors with respect to the phenotype variation. This statistic, $H = V_G / V_P$, is heritability in its broad sense, or the coefficient of genetic variation. The term V_G contains several genetic components: V_A, additive variance; V_D, due to interaction within locus; I due to interaction between loci. H in the broad sense is not an informative statistic, so it is not used by geneticists. However, it is used by psychologists. We have presented (Roubertoux & Carlier, 1976) a summary of results concerning the estimates of heritability in the broad sense for different personality traits. As far as Introversion is concerned, for the Eysenck Personality Inventory (EPI) the estimates of H are situated between 7% (Canter, 1973) and 53% (Shields, 1962) with a median of 30%. For the scales of the Cattell Personality Inventory (CPI) relating to Introversion, the values are situated between 35% and 49%. The Cattell scales HSPQ, 16 PF in the second-order factor exvia-invia have degrees of genetic determination varying between 0% and 56%, with a median of 31%.

For Anxiety and Neuroticism the extreme values of H are as follows: for Eysenck's scale from 18% to 48%; for the scales extracted from Cattell's tests, from 0% to 69% with a median of 12%.

Heritability in a Narrow Sense for Personality Traits in Human Populations

The equation $h^2 = V_A / V_P$ represents heritability in the narrow sense. The additive variance is a function of the product of the additive value and of a term depending on the frequency of the genes. Additive value is the fraction of genotypical value transmitted by an ascendant to descendants. We must emphasize that the frequency of the genes is that of the genes concerning the trait being considered. Indeed, in a population where the genes concerning the character are fixed, the frequency of genes does not contribute to the variation between subjects. In this case, $V_A = 0$. Thus heritability is null for a trait measured in a population where all the subjects have the same genes for the trait being considered. The same trait measured in a genetically heterogeneous population has a high additive value. This can be explained easily if we consider heritability as a value allowing us to predict the response of a population to a pressure, which we exercise by artificial selection.

Thus, heritability, in our view, is not a characteristic of a trait. It is a characteristic of the trait in a population. It is, in the narrow sense, the effect that the genetic diversity of the population exercises over the observed diversity of this trait. The zero value of V_A / V_P can mean either that the trait has nothing to do with genetics, or that it has a great deal to do with it; but being linked to the survival of the species, the alleles that do not allow good adaptation have all been eliminated. A high value of heritability certainly means that the variation is affected by the frequency of the genes in a given environment, but that the character is not linked to the survival of the species. The calculation of heritability in the narrow sense is possible in experimental populations; in this case, it remains interpretable within the limits that we have defined. In nonexperimental populations (for this reason, in our species) the calculation of heritability in the narrow sense or in the broader sense supposes an unbiased estimate of V_A. Now this assumes that the mating is made by chance, which is what we call panmixy as opposed to homogamy of mating. This supposition holds only if the phenotypic assortive mating is accompanied by genotypic assortative mating. If this really happens, the consequence is to increase the correlation between full brothers and sisters (including fraternal twins) and between ascendant and descendants.

What is the situation for homogamy of mating as regards personality traits? The results are contradictory. It seems that the correlation for Neuroticism may be non null. It then appears clearly that this condition contributes toward making it more difficult to use coefficients of heritability or biometric analyses aiming at a partition of the variance in our species. On the other hand, carefully chosen methods allow us to show that resemblance between individual family members cannot be explained if we consider the role of genetic factors as negligible. The twin method shows that the contribution of genetic variation to the resemblance between family members is probably an important source of variation in the study of different personality traits.

Demonstration of Genetic Effect on Observed Variance by the Twin Method

If we apply the twin method to different tests measuring introversion, we note that, with only a few exceptions (limited mostly to the Cattell scales), the correlations between monozygotic (MZ) twins are higher than the correlations between dizygotic (DZ) twins. The same results hold for the tests of Anxiety and Neuroticism (Meili & Roubertoux, 1975).

The use of the twin method to measure autonomic arousal produces results that
are not easily interpreted. For measures such as those of autonomic arousal,
for which low reliability has been shown, we can only hope to obtain stable correlations when testing a large number of subjects. The populations of twins used
in these studies are low. In addition, considering the diversity of electrophysiological techniques, the diversity of recording situations, the multiplicity
of the parameters, and the arbitrariness of the choice, the results cannot be
added from one study to the next. If we refer to Hume's study (1973) which
bears on a number of subjects, from 19 to 41 pairs of MZ twins and from 30 to
51 pairs of DZ twins, we find 11 values of r_{MZ} which are significantly higher
than r_{DZ} out of 26 calculated values. Within each index group the results are
also contradictory. Consider for example: the higher value of r_{MZ} with respect
to r_{DZ} is not shown in the following cases: (a) skin potential level at 10-s
intervals during the last 60 s. of first rest; (b) skin potential levels during
third rest; (c) skin potential orienting response; and (d) skin potential cold-
pressor recovery. But the differences r_{MZ} - r_{DZ} is present for the skin potential cold-pressor response. In the same study, Hume corrected the arbitrariness
of the choice of indexes by comparing the correlations r_{MZ}, r_{DZ} not on the scores
of the tests, but on factor scores obtained after factorial analysis of the data.
It is unfortunate, however, that the author should have retained varimax factors
known to correspond to a mathematical criterion that does not necessarily have
any psychological meaning. Barring this criticism, Hume shows that differences
between scores in factor I, labeled <u>autonomic</u> balance, are more similar when
individuals are genetically similar. Individual differences for factor II
(<u>arousal</u>) and factor III (<u>EEG components</u>) do not show a similar covariation.

At first sight, therefore, it seems that differences in measures of autonomic
arousal are not accounted for by genetic diversity in the population. A second
interpretation is possible; it has been shown (Meili and Roubertoux, 1975) that
measures of autonomic arousal produced low correlations; for this reason, factor
analysis of these indexes does not allow one to account for a high percentage of
variance. The saturations of variables for these factors are weak -- explained
by the low reliability of these indexes. This does not mean they should not be
used. Low reliability (such as test retest and split half) may result from a
high sensitivity to situational variables. This sensitivity makes them useful
instruments for the analysis of states, but less useful for determining constant
temperamental traits.

So far as the parameters of the EEG are concerned, clearer results have been
reached, probably because there is an operational definition of the states under
which the measurements are made or during which time stimuli are presented.
Thus Lykken, Tellegen and Thorkelson (1974) and Surwillo (1977) have worked on
parameters extracted from a sophisticated analysis of the EEG. Surwillo showed
that the indexes defining the interval histograms of half wavelengths in the
EEG present higher correlations in the MZ twins (median .97 and .71) than in
subjects without parental links (-.30 and -.24, respectively). Though the methodology is insufficient for the geneticist (there was no DZ group), it suggests
the possibility of corroborating the results of Lykken et al. (1974). For example, the alpha frequencies r_{MZ} = .84, and r_{DZ} = .21 show clearly that the variance observed has a genetic component. The alpha attenuation response or alpha
blocking also constitutes a sector of research that is all the more interesting
because it has an important place for students in the neurophysiological basis
of personality (Claridge, 1967, and Nebylitsyn, among others). However, little
work has been done on this subject. A study by Young, Lader, and Fenton (1972)
included a group of 17 MZ twins, but had no DZ group. Hume's results (1973),
though satisfactory from the point of view of genetic methodology, do not show
the effect of sources of genetic variation on the observed variation. There are
contradictions among the results not only because the populations differ in
genetic structure, but also because the trait measured in the two populations

is not the same one (orientation reaction in the first study and visual after-effect in the second one).

Average evoked cortical responses have been used in the study of individual differences (Callaway, 1975). The contribution of the effect of genetic diversity has been shown several times, but the most interesting conclusions are as follows: (a) The sources of genetic variation differ from one sensory modality to another. For somesthesic potentials the correlation between MZ twins is not different from that observed between DZ twins. On the other hand, it is much higher for MZ twins than for DZ for visual and auditory modalities. Several interpretations are possible; but it is likely that that fact of recording at the level of primary areas for somesthetic modalities introduces a marked difference with respect to the other modalities, for which recordings cannot be made on the level of primary areas. (b) The differences $r_{MZ} - r_{DZ}$ are more clearly marked for long duration (90-300 ms) epochs following the stimulus than for the short duration (0-89 ms) epochs. This suggests an effect of different genetic variability according to the segment of the phenomenon recorded. Moreover, such an observation could be made concerning all results of measures submitted to genetic analysis, whether it be of electrophysiological characters or of behavioral observation. These can provide a way of dissociating the different elements of a behavioral process, to the extent that these elements obey a different determination. This then leads us to look for the mode of transmission for each of these elements by segregation analysis.

The gene factor model (Royce, 1973) is an application of the study of components of variation. As Royce and Powell show, it is possible to partition the variance of the factor scores into its components V_G, V_E, $V_{G \times E}$, etc... The results of this procedure (perfectly legitimate) must be interpreted with the greatest caution.

First, consider two variables X and Y, though the reasoning could be generalized to n variables. In the simplest case, where we consider two sources of variation A (effect of the genetic additive value) and E (effect of environment), we obtain the following equation (Falconer, 1960):

$$r_{XY} = \frac{Cov_A + Cov_E}{\sigma_X \quad \sigma_Y}$$

But the gene factor model postulates a model that can be written in a simplified form:

$$E + h^2 = 1$$

$$E = 1 - h^2$$

then

$$r_{XY} = h_X H_Y r_A + E_X E_Y r_E \quad (h^2 \text{ being heritability in the narrow sense})$$

The term r_A is the part of the variance common to X and Y that is due to the effect of additive variance. Thus it appears that a correlation between two variables is due to genetic or environmental factors, or both. For this reason, an observed correlation is not proof of genetic control common to the two variables. We repeat the same argument for environment.

Second, a zero correlation between two variables does not mean that the two variables are genetically independent. Let us consider (Table 1) two variables

TABLE 1. Pleiotropy can lead to strong correlation between two traits X and Y (r_1, r_2) and to null correlation (r_3). The symbols + and − indicate a positive or a negative source of variation.

Locus	Trait					
	X	Y	X	Y	X	Y
1	+	+	+	−	+	−
2	+	+	+	−	−	+
3	+	+	+	−	+	−
4	+	+	+	−	−	+
5	+	+	+	−	+	−
6	+	+	+	−	−	+
Correlation	$r_1 = +1.0$		$r_2 = -1.0$		$r_3 = 0.0$	

X and Y, whose dispersion is controlled by the same series of six independent homozygotic loci (pleiotropy). We see that pleiotropy can lead to a strong correlation, either r_1 positive or r_2 negative. We see also that r_3 is null even though X and Y may be controlled by the same gene. In addition, a weak correlation between X and Y can result from a high value of r_A and a high opposite value of r_E. We see, therefore, that the analysis of factor scores gives us information on the components of the phenotypic resultant of variables. It gives us no information on the genetic mechanism explaining the appearance of a factor. Another approach is then possible. It consists in computing, by an adequate method, the genetic correlation between variables and carrying out an analysis on the genetic correlations. Royce and Powell's aim is to look for the part of genetic variance in phenotypic factorial scores. It is also possible to look for the part of common genetically additive variance for several variables.

GENETIC COMPONENTS OF MEANS DIFFERENCES

This type of analysis enables us to study the genetic origin of differences between groups.

Two different methods are used: one leading to the production of strains that differ for one character by selection, the other aiming to use different inbred strains to study observed phenotypic differences. To know the relative contribution of additive effect deviation due to dominance, several crosses between strains and F_1 are needed.

Use of Methods of Selection in the Study of Temperament Traits in Infrahumans

Among the different methods of selection only the directional methods have been used for behavior. Their advantage over the other methods of analysis of mean components stems from the fact that they presuppose few hypotheses concerning underlying genetic mechanisms. The limits of these methods have been pointed out on several occasions (Roubertoux, 1979). These methodological discussions must be drawn to the attention of the student of behavioral sciences, but go beyond the scope of this chapter.

Studies on reactivity in the open field were first carried out by Hall and Broadhurst, on the rat. More recent studies involve mice. The most striking point is that they all give evidence of a rapid response to selection. The study of correlated responses to selection is interesting in that it leads to the testing of behavioral hypotheses. It has been used by Eysenck (1967) to demonstrate the existence of a general factor of emotional reactivity. Otherwise, the supposed relationship between reactivity and acquisition of a conditioned link with a stimulus was not confirmed by Broadhurst and Bignami (1965).

The study of neurological and biochemical correlates of selection, carried out on behavioral traits, has complex methodology; but this method is effective in the physiological control of certain individual differences in behavior.

Crosses Between Inbred Strains and Temperament Traits in Infrahumans

Another way of analyzing genetic components of means is to use crosses of strains, following a pattern that is sometimes quite sophisticated (Mather & Jinks, 1971). The partition of components of means is based on numerous hypotheses related to underlying genetic mechanisms. In particular, this model supposes that the means differences are due to additive value; and the gap, due to dominance. Tests of adjustment are available.

Royce and Powell (this volume) have presented practical analyses concerning the comparison and the crosses of strains in mice. Unfortunately, the analysis of mean components presupposes subjects genetically homogeneous within the population, differing between populations from this same genetic point of view. Such populations do not exist in our species; thus, it is impossible to know the components of mean differences between ethnic or social groups. For that to be possible we would have to assume that these groups are equivalent to genetically similar strains. Genetic studies of populations bearing on genetic markers do not allow us to retain that hypothesis.

For this reason, it seems that the study of components of differences of means presents above all an interest for the study of the neurophysiological or biochemical correlates of the studied traits.

CONCLUSIONS

The three functions of genetic analysis are independent from one function to the next. On the one hand, it is clear that the twin method and the adoption method do not allow us to demonstrate a mode of transmission, which only segregation analysis can do. On the other hand, analysis of pedigree does not on its own show that the trait under investigation is genetically controlled. The independence of information brought by analysis of components of variation and analysis of components of means is not so well understood by psychologists. Let us take a fictional example. Given four couples of MZ twins (AA', BB', CC', and DD'), separated at birth and placed (for A, B, C, and D) in an enriched environment, and (for A', B', C', D') in an impoverished environment, the trait T

TABLE 2.   Supposed Experiment with Monozygotic Twins Reared Apart in Two
Different Environments Regarding the Measured Trait

	Environment	
Score on a Trait	E	P
1		A'
2		B' C'
3		D'
4		
5		
6		
7	A	
8	B C	
9	D	

Note.   E = enriched environment; P = poor environment.

is then measured in the two populations. The subjects are distributed as indicated in Table 2.

Let us consider that the component of variation (intraclass correlation) is
r_{MZ}= 1.00 . We can say that the sources of postnatal variation are negligible
here. The components of variation are exclusively genetic and prenatal. Consider now the components of the differences between means. The two groups do
not differ genetically, but they differ by postnatal environment. The components of means are exclusively postnatal here. We see then that the components
of means and of variation are two separate pieces of information. Considering
the assumptions of the model of analysis of component means, it seems that the
genetic origin of differences between human groups will remain unknown for a
long time yet.

This chapter was not intended as an exhaustive review of methods and results
corresponding to different functions of genetic analysis. We have attempted to
show how theoretical problems arise when one attempts to integrate behavioral
genetics with the study of personality.

REFERENCES

Broadhurst, P. L., & Bignami, G. (1965). Correlates effects of psychogenetic
   selection. Behavior Research and Therapy, 2, 273-280.

Callaway, E. (1975). Brain electrical potentials and individual psychological differences. New York: Grune.

Canter, S. (1973). Personality traits in twins. In G. Claridge, S. Canter, & W. I. Hume (Eds.), Personality differences and biological variation: A study of twins. Oxford: Pergamon.

Carlier, M., & Roubertoux, P. (1979). Psychoses à manifestations précoces et psychoses à manifestations tardives: Apport de l'analyse génétique. Psychiatrie de l'Enfant, 22, 2, 473-502.

Carlier, M., Roubertoux, P., & Gottesoiener, H. (1979). Les composantes génétiques de la ressemblance entre individus parents. Bulletin de Psychologie, 32, 340, 443-474.

Cattell, R. B., Boutourline-Young, H., & Hundleby, J. D. (1964). Blood groups and personality traits. American Journal of Human Genetics, 16, 397-402.

Cavalli Sforza, L. L., & Boomer, W. F. (1971). The genetics of human populations. San Francisco, CA: Freeman.

Claridge, G. (1967). Personality and arousal. Oxford: Pergamon.

Eleftheriou, B. E. (Ed.). (1975). Psychopharmacogenetics. New York: Plenum Press.

Elias, M. F., & Pentz, C. A. (1975). The role of genotype behavioral responses in Anaesthetics. In B. E. Eleftheriou (Ed.), Psychopharmacogenetics. New York: Plenum Press.

Eysenck, H. J. (1967). The biological basis of personality. Springfield, IL: Charles C Thomas.

Fuller, J. L., & Thompson, W. H. (1978). Foundations of Behavior Genetics (2nd ed.). Saint Louis, MO: Mosby.

Hume, W. I. (1973). Physiological measures in twins. In G. Claridge, S. Canter, & W. I. Hume (Eds.), Personality differences and biological variation: A study of twins. Oxford: Pergamon.

Lykken, D. T., Tellegen, A., & Thorkelson, K. (1974). Genetic determination of EEG frequency spectra. Biological Psychology, 1, 245-259.

Mather, K., & Jinks, J. L. (1971). Biometrical genetics. London: Chapman.

Meili, R., & Roubertoux, P. (1975). La structure de la personnalité. In P. Fraisse & J. Piaget (Eds.), Traité de psychologie expérimental (Vol. V, 3rd ed.). Paris: P. U. F.

Oliverio, A., & Castellano, C. (1975). Exploratory activity: Genetic analysis of its modification by various pharmacologic agents. In S. E. Eleftheriou (Ed.), Psychopharmacogenetics. New York: Plenum Press.

Omenn, G. S., & Motulsky, A. G. (1975). Pharmacogenetics: Clinical and experimental studies in man. In S. E. Eleftheriou (Ed.), Psychopharmacogenetics. New York: Plenum Press.

Powell, R. (1975). Protein variation in natural populations of animals. Evolutionary Biology, 3, 79-119.

Reuchlin, M. (1978). Processus vicariants et différences individuelles. Journal de Psychologie, 2, 133-145.

Reuchlin, M. (1979). Psychologie (2nd ed.). Paris: P. U. F.

Roubertoux, P. (1979). L'Analyse génétique des différences individuelles dans les comportements par les méthodes quantitatives. Thèse d'Etat, Paris V René Descartes.

Roubertoux, P., & Carlier, M. (1976). Génétique et comportements. Paris: Masson.

Roubertoux, P., Carlier, M., Dumont, E., & Perruchet, P. (1978). Behaviors of children with genetic diseases. In D. Walcher, N. Kretchmer, & H. L. Barnett (Eds.), Mutations: Biology and society. New York: Masson.

Royce, J. R. (1973). The conceptual framework for a multifactor theory of individuality. In J. R. Royce (Ed.), Multivariate analysis and psychological theory. London: Academic Press.

Shields, J. (1962). Monozygotic twins brought up apart and brought up together. London: Oxford University Press.

Shurster, L. (1975). Genetic analysis of morphine effects: Activity, analgesis, tolerance and sensitization. In S. E. Eleftheriou (Ed.), Psychopharmacogenetics. New York: Plenum Press.

Surwillo, W. W. (1977). Interval histograms of period of the EEG and the re- action time in twins. Behavior Genetics, 7, 2, 161-170.

Thiessen, D. B., Owen, K., & Whitsett, M. (1970). Chromosome mapping of behav- ioral activities. In G. Lindzey, & D. D. Thiessen (Eds.), Contribution to behavior- genetic analysis. The mouse as a prototype. New York: Appleton-Century-Crofts.

Vogel, F. (1957). Elektroencephalographische Untersuchungen an gesunden Zwil- lingen. Acta genetica (Basel), 7, 334-337.

Vogel, F. (1970). The genetic basis of the normal human EEG. Humangenitik, 10, 91.

Young, O. P., Lader, M. H., & Fenton, G. W. (1972). A twin study of the genetic influences on EEG. Journal of Medical Genetics, 9, 13-16.

II

MEASUREMENT

8

Factor Analysis of Strelau's Questionnaire and an Attempt to Validate Some of the Factors

Michele Carlier

Pavlovian typology was of considerable interest to us 10 years ago, when we were investigating individual differences in learning processes (Gray, 1964; Meili & Roubertoux, 1975; and Strelau, 1970). One of our colleagues (Dumont, 1979) was concerned with demonstrating the existence of transmarginal inhibition in the Pavlovian conditioning procedure. Because Strelau's personality framework is within the tradition of Pavlovian typology, we translated his inventory into French, to explore the relationships between Strelau's construct of strength of excitation (as measured by his Excitation scale) and Pavlov's construct of strength of excitation (as measured by the threshold for transmarginal inhibition). At the same time, we considered it necessary to explore relationships between Strelau's scales and the most important of Western personality factors, namely, Anxiety, Neuroticism, and Extraversion.

Thus this chapter has three parts: First, internal validation of Strelau's inventory; second, comparisons among Strelau's inventory, Eysenck's Personality inventory (EPI), and Cattell's Anxiety scale; and third, construct validation of some factors extracted from the Strelau inventory.

INTERNAL VALIDATION OF THE STRELAU INVENTORY

The Strelau Inventory includes three scales: (a) Strength of Excitation (E), (b) Strength of Inhibition (I), and (c) Mobility (M) (Strelau, 1972). For each scale, parallel-form questions test for internal consistency. There are 44 questions for each of the Excitation and Inhibition scales and 46 for Mobility. In all, there are 134 questions and these were translated by us from the English version into French.[1] Questionnaires were answered by 476 students at the University of Paris X at Nanterre. The students also completed Form A of the EPI and the Cattell Anxiety Scale. Of the 476, only 202 students answered all the questions; our results are based on their data. All were undergraduate, first-year psychology students. As is common in psychology departments, there were more women (172) than men (29).

This research was supported by the C.N.A.M. (Service de Recherche de l'I.N.O.P.), the E.P.H.E. (Laboratoire de Psychologie Differentielle), the C.N.R.S. (E.R.A. 79), and the Universite de Paris X Nanterre.

[1]We would like to thank Dr. T. Klonowicz for agreeing to compare the French version to the Polish version. We would also like to thank Dr. A. Beaudot for helping us to translate the English version into French. One question (item 29) was not well understood by our subjects, and it is excluded from the data.

145

Reliability of the Scales

We have estimated internal consistency because it was impossible to employ the test-retest procedure. The correlations between the two halves of each scale are shown in Table 1. We then factored the correlation matrix of the first half of the whole questionnaire by principal-components analysis. This procedure was repeated for the second half. Then we correlated the factor scores of the first half with the factor scores of the second half. The results are presented in Table 1.

The first and second factors have fair internal consistency, and although we think internal consistency for Factor 3 is not bad, we are certain that Factor 4 has a weak internal consistency.

TABLE 1. Internal consistency of Strelau's questionnaire

I	II
Scales	Factors
E : .73	F1 : .81
I : .75	F2 : .77
M : .66	F3 : .52
	F4 : .32

Note: I - Pearson correlations between the two halves of each scale: Excitation (E), Inhibition (I), and Mobility (M).   II - Pearson correlations between the first four principal components extracted from each questionnaire.   N = 202 .

Factorial Structure of the Inventory

Orthogonal structure. The data were submitted to factor analysis (principal factors with square multiple correlations of each variable with all other variables in the diagonal). The first four factors were rotated to orthogonal simple structure by the Varimax method. The Varimax solution is roughly similar to the principal-factors solution, but the interpretation of the axes is easier with Varimax.

The factor-loadings matrix of the first four rotated factors is given in Table 2; for the percentage of explained variance, see Table 3. The rows have been rearranged for each successive factor from the highest loadings to the lowest loadings (except for the items whose loadings are less than .2). Table 2 also summarizes each item and specifies the scale to which it belongs.

TABLE 2. Orthogonal factorial structure of Strelau's questionnaire

Scale	Item	F1	F2	F3	F4	h²	Response Trait	Summary
E	134	.59	-.01	.31	.07	.44	O	To like assignments involving responsibility.
E	21	.58	-.01	.31	.06	.44	O	To assume responsible jobs readily.
E	98	.56	.19	-.01	.04	.35	O	To feel at ease in numerous or unknown company.
E	66	.53	.17	.21	.00	.35	O	To be quick in overcoming obstacles.
E	32	.53	.11	.00	-.12	.31	O	To take the floor readily at a meeting.
E	130	.53	.03	.02	-.17	.31	O	To like to make public addresses.
E	133	.51	.01	.09	.25	.33	O	To have vigorous movements.
M	119	.50	-.06	-.04	.08	.26	O	To like work that involves talking to people.
M	1	.49	-.11	-.09	.07	.27	O	To make friends easily.
I	128	-.48	-.31	-.27	.02	.40	N	To be thrown out of gear easily.
E	123	-.48	-.23	-.06	.08	.29	N	To have voice failure in a critical situation.
M	85	.48	-.14	.01	.14	.27	O	To be quick in responding to questions.
M	111	.43	-.13	.07	.05	.21	O	To react at once.
M	40	.43	-.05	-.08	.01	.01	O	To be quick in joining in a conversation.
M	93	.41	-.10	.24	.14	.26	O	To be able to perform several operations at a time.
E	106	.41	.33	.02	.15	.30	O	To be able to suppress moods of dejection.
M	55	.41	-.09	-.25	-.24	.29	O	To like frequent changes.
E	102	.36	-.15	.00	-.06	.16	O	To feel an urge to show initiative.
E	122	.36	.28	.18	-.04	.24	O	To be a man of courage.
M	79	.35	-.01	.08	.09	.14	O	To be quick in looking through the newspapers.
M	101	.35	-.09	-.25	.27	.26	O	To like to change occupation frequently.
M	64	.33	.03	-.13	.09	.14	O	To switch from one occupation to another.
I	35	-.33	.23	.19	.05	.20	O	To refrain from talking.
E	105	.32	-.09	-.17	-.07	.15	O	To question a generally accepted view.
M	86	.30	-.25	-.09	.01	.16	O	To speak rapidly.
I	50	.14	.55	.00	.02	.32	O	To restrain the impulse to react.
I	75	.24	.54	-.05	-.30	.45	O	To keep calm in difficult situations.
I	89	-.13	.52	.10	.18	.33	O	To be patient.
M	33	-.28	-.52	.11	.05	.36	O	To be easily upset.
I	120	-.13	.52	.14	-.01	.30	O	To control mimicry.
i	18	-.11	-.51	.08	-.17	.31	N	To be unable to control irritation or anger.

TABLE 2. continued

Scale	Item	F1	F2	F3	F4	h²	Response Trait	Summary
I	110	.01	.49	.09	-.08	.26	O	To be able to argue calmly.
E	94	.26	.49	-.05	-.12	.32	O	To preserve composure.
I	125	-.18	.44	.13	.28	.32	O	To be able to sit quietly for a long time.
E	23	.18	.44	-.08	.10	.24	O	To survive a defeat easily.
I	48	.19	.42	-.04	-.07	.22	O	To keep calm when the situation requires it.
I	5	.02	.42	-.07	-.04	.18	O	To resist temptation.
I	96	.23	.42	-.03	-.12	.24	O	To keep calm when seeing the suffering of a person.
I	27	-.05	.40	.07	.05	.17	O	To keep calm when waiting for some important announcement.
I	108	-.06	.40	-.02	.37	.30	O	To be able to wait quietly.
I	103	-.05	.40	.09	-.06	.17	O	To be able to restrain a smile.
I	112	.12	.37	-.01	-.01	.16	O	To be able to behave quietly.
E	124	.29	.37	.09	.18	.26	O	To be able to overcome despondency.
I	109	.06	.36	.03	.00	.14	O	To abstain from lodging useless complaints.
I	53	.23	.35	-.03	-.27	.25	O	To keep control of oneself when waiting.
I	70	-.11	.35	.12	-.08	.15	O	To refrain from superfluous gesticulation.
I	16	-.08	.34	-.06	-.12	.15	O	To refrain from showing superiority.
I	8	-.22	.33	-.10	.19	.20	O	To be able to wait patiently.
I	59	.22	.33	-.21	-.14	.22	N	To put forward one's arguments.
I	129	-.02	.31	.16	.30	.21	O	To heed the rules in one's milieu easily.
I	36	-.10	-.31	.02	.02	.11	N	To be hot-tempered.
I	2	-.12	.30	.17	.15	.15	O	To be able to wait until signal to do something.
I	10	-.12	.30	.17	.14	.15	O	To keep a secret easily.
E	114	.07	.03	.62	-.03	.39	O	To be able to work with great intensity.
E	61	.13	.00	.57	.03	.34	O	To be able to work hard.
E	82	-.01	-.06	.55	.05	.31	O	To be capable of working uninterrupted.
M	104	.13	.02	.48	.17	.27	O	To get in high gear right away when starting one's work.
E	45	.11	.10	.48	.05	.25	O	To be able to work at night.
M	131	-.01	.11	.47	.09	.24	O	To be quick in starting one's work.
E	7	.06	-.17	.43	-.03	.22	O	To be able to forget fatigue when working.
E	3	.13	.00	.42	.02	.19	O	To recover from work fatigue easily.
E	73	.11	.09	.41	.09	.20	O	To be able to concentrate on work.
E	72	.21	-.08	.37	.15	.21	O	To like strenuous occupations.

148

	No.						Key	Item
E	58	.24	.17	.34	.02	.20	O	To solve problems by oneself.
E	47	-.31	-.13	-.34	.00	.22	N	To give up plans.
M	91	-.28	-.01	.34	.24	.25	O	To perform more than one assignment at a time.
E	97	.20	.29	.33	-.15	.25	O	To be self-reliant.
I	87	.03	.07	.32	.10	.12	O	To be able to work while waiting for guests.
E	81	.16	.00	.30	.01	.12	O	To work after having had little sleep.
E	4	-.06	-.14	-.30	.21	.16	O	To be able to work in adverse circumstances.
M	100	.12	-.07	.03	.69	.50	O	To be able to adapt to other people's way of working.
I	37	.12	-.02	.01	.64	.43	O	To be able to fall in step with a partner when working.
I	90	-.15	.12	.14	.55	.36	O	To be able to adapt to someone else's tempo.
I	30	-.04	.03	.12	.42	.20	O	To be able to adjust one own's gait to someone.
M	54	.35	.05	-.14	.39	.29	O	To get quickly accustomed to a new environment.
M	44	.23	.10	.08	.34	.18	O	To get easily accustomed to a new job.
M	74	.31	-.15	.10	.32	.23	O	To like occupations which call for quick movements.
M	28	.17	-.05	.02	.31	.13	O	To be able to be quick in settling down when on holiday.
I	77	-.25	.23	-.01	.31	.21	O	To be able to wait having done a job.
M	95	.20	-.02	.19	.30	.16	O	To like a job that calls for performing diverse operations.
M	6	.15	.01	.14	.18	.08	O	To resume work easily after a long break.
M	9	-.08	.19	-.09	.18	.08	O	To fall asleep easily at any time when in bed.
M	11	.14	.17	.19	.16	.11	O	To resume work easily after a long interruption.
I	12	.01	.26	.12	.18	.12	O	To stay patient while giving explanations.
I	13	.17	-.02	.26	-.16	.12	O	To like mental occupations.
E	14	-.13	-.07	-.09	-.24	.09	O	To feel bored or sleepy when doing monotonous work.
E	15	-.10	.09	-.14	-.12	.05	O	To fall asleep easily after a strong emotion.
E	17	.28	.11	.01	.05	.09	O	To behave in a customary manner with strangers.
E	19	.27	.28	.02	-.07	.16	O	To control a situation in spite of hardships.
M	20	.03	.03	-.06	.25	.07	O	To be able to behave like others in a group.
M	22	-.09	-.21	.01	-.14	.07	O	To be influenced easily by surroundings.
E	24	.28	.07	.20	.01	.12	O	To talk as freely as usual when wanting to impress someone.
M	25	-.14	-.16	.03	-.28	.12	N	To be irritated by unexpected changes in day's schedule.
M	26	-.03	-.11	.01	-.05	.01	O	To have a ready answer to every argument.
M	31	-.11	.28	-.15	.10	.12	O	To fall asleep quickly when in bed.
I	34	-.06	-.16	.23	-.17	.11	N	To leave a job easily when engrossed in it.
I	38	-.20	.19	.01	-.10	.09	O	To always think twice before deciding on course of action.
E	39	.15	-.04	.15	.05	.05	O	To follow a line of argument easily from start to finish.
I	41	-.14	.13	-.07	.02	.04	O	To refrain from arguing when it is bound to be ineffective.
M	42	.08	.06	.14	.22	.08	O	To like work requiring manual dexterity.
M	43	-.08	.18	-.15	-.10	.07	O	To change mind when confronted with new arguments.
M	46	.25	-.13	-.07	.12	.10	O	To read novels quickly.
M	49	.06	.18	.17	.04	.07	O	To wake up quickly and easily.

TABLE 2. continued

Scale	Item	F1	F2	F3	F4	h^2	Response Trait	Summary
E	51	.01	.10	-.09	-.14	.04	N	To be disturbed by noise when working.
I	52	-.11	.27	-.03	.04	.09	O	To resist telling people the truth, if necessary.
E	56	.19	.05	.23	.08	.10	G	To recover from fatigue of a hard day's work after a night's sleep.
M	57	-.22	-.03	-.11	-.24	.12	N	To avoid occupations which involve different operations.
E	60	.11	-.01	.20	-.18	.08	O	To be willing to rescue a drowning person if able to swim.
I	62	-.24	.29	.03	.03	.14	O	To refrain from making comments when out of place.
M	63	-.22	-.19	-.02	-.28	.16	N	To prefer a permanent seat at work.
I	65	.03	-.19	.03	.03	.04	O	To weigh the "pros" and "cons" in facing crucial decisions.
I	67	-.06	-.20	-.12	-.12	.07	N	To have difficulties in restraining curiosity.
I	69	-.09	.19	.15	.20	.11	O	To easily heed the rules of conduct in public places.
M	71	.20	-.14	-.16	.09	.09	O	To like places full of hustle and bustle.
M	76	.06	.01	.22	.03	.05	O	To be able to get up straight after waking up.
E	78	.21	.27	.01	.08	.12	O	To stay as efficient as usual after witnessing a unpleasant sight.
M	80	.03	-.17	-.02	.05	.03	O	To talk so fast sometimes that it becomes incomprehensible.
E	83	.00	.04	-.08	-.12	.02	O	To be able to work in spite of headache.
I	84	-.07	.14	.25	.24	.14	O	To finish up a job even if being waited for.
M	88	.01	.08	-.29	.02	.09	O	To change opinion in the face of cogent arguments.
M	92	.01	.08	-.02	.01	.01	O	To recover from depression in good humored company.
I	99	-.03	.27	.11	.16	.11	N	To be able to interrupt a conversation at once when time runs out.
E	107	-.03	-.26	.26	-.16	.14	O	To find it hard to fall asleep after a day of strenuous brainwork.
E	113	.15	.16	-.08	.13	.07	O	To submit easily to painful medical treatment.
M	115	.25	-.20	-.17	.11	.14	O	To readily change place when having a rest.
M	116	-.18	-.10	.00	-.29	.13	O	To find it difficult to adapt to a new daily schedule.
E	117	.22	.18	.15	-.15	.12	O	To eagerly offer help in an accident.
I	118	.01	.09	.05	-.03	.01	O	To refrain from excessive shouting or gesticulation at a sport event.
E	121	.21	.00	.03	.13	.06	O	To like occupations which require vigorous movements.
I	126	-.13	.28	.10	.03	.10	O	To control mirth not to hurt someone.
M	127	.21	-.26	-.17	.01	.14	O	To switch easily from sadness to good humor.
E	132	.17	.09	.21	-.01	.08	O	To feel an urge to rescue people in danger.
M	68	.08	-.18	-.18	-.20	.11	O	To be bored by stereotyped operations.

Note. Orthogonal rotated factor matrix. The four factors are: F1, F2, F3, and F4. Before each item number we give the name of the scale to which this item belongs (I, Inhibition; E, Excitation; and M, Mobility). In the 7th column the letter 0 means that the response trait of the item is "yes" (Oui), and the letter N means that the response trait of the item is "no." In the last column we give a brief summary of the item. N = 202 .

150

TABLE 3. Explained variance and percentage of explained variance for each successive orthogonal factor, without and with rotations

Rotation	Factor			
	F1	F2	F3	F4
Without	9.38 (9.49%)	6.99 (7.07%)	4.61 (4.67%)	3.73 (3.78%)
With	7.84 (7.94%)	7.36 (7.45%)	5.11 (5.17%)	4.41 (4.46%)

1. Factor 1. This is easy to interpret as an Excitation factor because the highest loadings are for the Excitation Scale items. It is clear, however, that this factor is not exactly synonymous with the Excitation scale, because it loads on several Mobility items.

2. Factor 2. Interpretation is obvious. It is an Inhibition factor.

3. Factor 3. This seems also to be an Excitation factor. If we compare Factor 1 and Factor 3, the latter appears to load on items that describe working situations. To use Strelau's terminology, we can interpret this factor of Strength in working situations.

4. Factor 4. This is not of interest since it loads only on some items describing situations where people adapt themselves to other people.

Our conclusions therefore are as follows: (a) The existence of an Inhibition factor is confirmed; (b) There are two Excitation factors rather than one; (c) There is no evidence for a Mobility factor; indeed, several Mobility items load on the first of the Excitation factors.

Oblique structure. It is possible that the Mobility factor does not appear because we employed orthogonal rotations. So we decided to test oblique structure. Taking into account the four orthogonal rotated factors, we estimated the centroid of the Excitation items, the centroid of the Inhibition items, then the centroid of the Mobility items. The first factor was rotated through the centroid of the Excitation items, the second factor through the centroid of the Inhibition items, and the third factor through the centroid of the Mobility items.[2] The factor-loadings matrixes of the three oblique factors are given in Tables 4 - 6; for the correlations between factors, see Table 7.

It is easy to interpret the first factor as an Excitation factor, the second factor as an Inhibition factor, and the third factor as a Mobility factor. However, the correlation between the factor of Excitation and the factor of Mobility is high (.58). As we might expect from the orthogonal structure, the correlations between the Inhibition factor and the two other factors are lower (.20 and -.32).

---

[2]We would like to thank Dr. P. Perruchet for writing the computer routine program, following the advice given by Pr. Reuchlin and Pr. F. Bacher.

TABLE 4.   Oblique factorial structure of the Strelau
questionnaire (Excitation scale)

	Factor		
Item	F1	F2	F3
134	.63	-.06	.52
21	.63	-.06	.52
66	.57	.07	.39
98	.47	.05	.42
133	.45	-.02	.54
122	.45	.20	.19
61	.44	.09	.14
114	.43	.13	.06
58	.43	.17	.17
32	.42	-.06	.34
106	.42	.25	.31
97	.42	.24	.01
130	.41	-.14	.34
45	.39	.17	.10
124	.37	.33	.21
72	.36	-.01	.28
73	.36	.16	.13
24	.35	.04	.22
3	.34	.06	.13
82	.30	.07	.05
81	.30	.03	.15
94	.29	.34	.01
117	.29	.10	.06
56	.29	.07	.19
19	.29	.18	.10
132	.27	.08	.12
13	.27	-.05	.08
7	.25	-.08	.10
17	.25	.05	.22
78	.24	.22	.13
102	.23	-.24	.32
60	.21	.06	.19
23	.21	.36	.06
39	.19	-.03	.17
121	.18	.00	.23
105	.12	-.22	.25
113	.11	.12	.14
4	.11	.01	.11
107	.03	-.22	-.02
51	-.04	.04	-.11
83	-.05	-.02	-.08
15	-.14	.04	-.17
123	-.46	-.08	-.29
47	-.46	-.12	-.22

Note.   Three factors (F1, F2,   F3) were
rotated.   N = 202 .

TABLE 5.   Oblique factorial structure of the Strelau
questionnaire (Inhibition scale)

		Factor	
Item	F1	F2	F3
89	.11	.57	-.17
125	.08	.55	-.14
50	.04	.54	-.27
120	.13	.53	-.26
108	.07	.48	.01
110	.19	.44	-.18
27	.12	.41	-.14
129	.18	.41	.04
8	-.12	.38	-.19
2	.10	.37	-.10
103	.12	.37	-.19
10	.10	.37	-.11
77	-.12	.35	-.13
5	.08	.35	-.13
16	.00	.35	-.11
70	.08	.34	-.23
75	.28	.34	-.12
35	-.07	.34	-.30
62	-.08	.33	-.27
90	.03	.33	.12
99	.12	.32	-.03
109	.16	.32	-.06
12	.16	.31	.02
48	.23	.31	-.01
126	.03	.31	-.18
112	.18	.29	-.05
96	.26	.29	.00
69	.08	.28	-.03
52	-.03	.28	-.15
84	.15	.26	.03
38	-.10	.20	-.27
65	-.09	.18	-.02
53	.24	.18	-.06
87	.24	.15	.07
41	-.11	.15	-.15
37	.12	.14	.42
30	.05	.12	.19
118	.06	.08	-.03
34	.04	-.14	-.07
128	-.61	-.22	-.30
67	-.18	-.22	-.05
36	-.14	-.25	.03
59	-.05	-.43	.20
18	-.18	-.47	-.02

Note.   Three factors (F1, F2, F3) were
rotated.   N = 202.

TABLE 6.   Oblique factorial structure of the Strelau
questionnaire (Mobility scale)

		Factor	
Item	F1	F2	F3
85	.34	-.20	.50
1	.29	-.22	.47
55	.15	-.16	.47
119	.34	-.15	.46
100	.12	.11	.46
74	.27	-.09	.46
54	.21	.04	.45
93	.43	-.10	.45
101	.10	-.14	.43
111	.34	-.19	.42
40	.26	-.16	.37
91	.42	.06	.36
79	.32	-.05	.34
44	.27	.15	.33
86	.11	-.31	.32
95	.27	.05	.32
115	.03	-.25	.31
28	.14	.01	.31
46	.20	-.13	.30
64	.19	-.05	.30
127	-.01	-.32	.25
71	.02	-.18	.24
6	.21	.06	.21
42	.17	.13	.16
11	.27	.20	.15
20	.01	.08	.13
80	-.04	-.15	.10
76	.18	.05	.07
49	.20	.19	.02
104	.11	-.01	.02
131	.30	.23	.02
68	-.11	-.27	.01
14	.01	-.18	.00
26	-.05	-.10	-.01
88	-.14	.01	-.01
92	.01	.07	-.02
9	-.05	.22	-.04
33	-.28	-.37	-.04
22	-.13	-.21	-.08
31	-.09	.28	-.13
43	-.11	.13	-.18
116	-.18	-.13	-.26
63	-.24	-.21	-.26
25	-.17	-.09	-.27
57	-.25	-.06	-.29

Note.   Three factors (F1, F2, F3) were
rotated.   N = 202.

TABLE 7.   Intercorrelations between the three oblique factors extracted from the Strelau questionnaire

	Factor	
Factor	1 (Excitation)	2 (Inhibition)
2	.20	
3 (Mobility)	.58	-.32

Note.   N = 202.

CORRELATIONS AMONG THE STRELAU QUESTIONNAIRE, THE EPI, AND THE CATTELL ANXIETY SCALE

The product-moment correlations between the seven scales of the three questionnaires are presented in Table 8.

We make the following observations: (a) The correlation between Anxiety and Neuroticism is as high as the reliability coefficients usually observed for the two scales.   (b) The correlation between Neuroticism and Extraversion is very low, thus confirming Eysenck's model of the structure of personality.   (c) The Excitation scale is slightly correlated with the Inhibition scale and more correlated with the Mobility scale.   This is to be expected on the basis of the factorial structure of the questionnaire, already described.   (d) Each of the three Strelau scales is significantly correlated with Neuroticism, Extraversion and Anxiety; and these results are roughly similar to those of Strelau (1970). In particular, Strelau notes that Extraversion correlates "not only with strength of the excitatory process but also with mobility of nervous processes" and asks if Extraversion is "truly a homogeneous factor" (p. 23).   In fact, our results seem to show that it is only the Excitation and Mobility scales that are not independent.

We also submitted the EPI and the Anxiety scale to factor analysis (principal factors).   The structure of the EPI is confirmed, in that two orthogonal factors are extracted, Neuroticism (the first) and Extraversion (the second); see Carlier (1980).   With regard to the factorial structure of the Anxiety scale, we take the first factor into account without rotation, and then calculate the factor scores in the four orthogonal Strelau factors, the two Eysenck factors and the sole Cattell factor, for our 202 students.   The intercorrelations between the seven scales of the three questionnaires and the seven factors of the three questionnaires are presented in Table 9.

From Table 9 the following points are clear.

1.   Strelau's Factor 1 of Excitation is highly correlated with Eysenck's Extraversion (.71).   The correlation with Eysenck's Neuroticism is relatively low but significant (-.25) and the correlation with Cattell's Anxiety is higher (-.46).

2. Strelau's Factor 2 of Inhibition is highly correlated with Eysenck's Neuroticism (-.61) and with Cattell's (-.61); that is, Inhibition is inversely related to Neuroticism and Anxiety.

3. Strelau's Factor 3, which we labeled Strength in Working Situations, is correlated with neither Extraversion nor Neuroticism, but has a low but significant correlation with Anxiety.

In summary, therefore, we can conclude that: (a) Strelau's first Excitation factor is roughly similar to an Extraversion factor, and (b) Strelau's Inhibition factor is similar to a Stability factor. In the light of these results, it seems difficult to distinguish, on the one hand, between Extraversion and Excitation and, on the other, between Neuroticism and low Inhibition. Finally, (c) Strelau's third factor, Strength in Working Situations, is novel in the context of Eysenck's personality model.

TABLE 8.   Pearson correlations between the seven scales of the three questionnaires

Scale	Strelau			Eysenck		
	Exc	I	M	Ext	N	L
Strelau						
I	.27*					
M	.45*	-.01				
Eysenck						
Ext	.38*	-.21*	.54*			
N	-.49*	-.48*	-.21*	-.12		
L	.17*	.43*	.00	-.26*	-.31*	
Cattell	-.58*	-.59*	-.25*	-.07	.81*	-.36*

*p < .05

Note.   Strelau's scales are Exc, Excitation; I, Inhibition; and M, Mobility. Eysenck's scales are Ext, Extraversion; N, Neuroticism; and L, Lie score. Cattell's scale is Anxiety.   N = 202.

TABLE 9. Pearson correlations between the seven scales of the three questionnaires and the seven factors extracted after factorial analysis of each questionnaire

| | Factor | | | | | | |
| | Strelau | | | | Eysenck | | Cattell |
Item	F1	F2	F3	F4	F1	F2	F1
Scale							
Strelau							
Exc	.72*	.29*	.52*	.07	-.45*	.44*	-.62*
I	-.08	.89*	.18*	.28*	-.56*	-.20*	-.53*
M	.66*	-.13	.06	.47*	-.13	.57*	-.27*
Eysenck							
Ext	.66*	-.17*	-.15*	.16*	.03	.97*	-.15*
N	-.35*	-.55*	-.07	-.16*	.97*	-.16*	.83*
L	-.08	.34*	.26*	.15*	-.36*	-.23*	-.30*
Cattell	.36*	-.65*	-.18*	-.18*	.81*	-.13	.97*
Factor							
Strelau							
F1					-.25*	.71*	-.46*
F2					-.61*	-.16*	-.61*
F3					-.13	-.10	-.15*
F4					-.15*	.14*	-.13
Eysenck							
F1							.81*
F2							-.21*

* p < .05

Note. Strelau's scales are Exc, Excitation; I, Inhibition; and M, Mobility. Eysenck's scales are Ext, Extraversion; N, Neuroticism; and L, Lie score. Cattell's scale is Anxiety. N = 202.

TEST OF CONSTRUCT VALIDATION

In Pavlov's typology, there are three dimensions (strength, mobility, and equilibrium) and two processes (excitation and inhibition). Pavlov hypothesized individual differences in these dimensions. The Strength of the Nervous System, or the Strength of Excitatory Process, is defined as "the working capacity of the cerebral cells" (Pavlov, cited by Teplov, 1964). One way of measuring Strength is to measure the threshold of transmarginal inhibition. As Gray (1964) writes,

> This concept has been derived from conditioning experiments...
> The magnitude of a conditioned reflex increases with the intensity
> of the conditioned stimulus up to a limiting value of this intensity;
> beyond this limiting value further increases in stimulus intensity
> lead to a decrease in the magnitude of the response... The higher
> an individual's threshold of transmarginal inhibition the greater
> is the working capacity, or strength, of the cortical cells (and,
> synonymously, the strength of the nervous system and of nervous
> activity) in that individual. (pp. 161-162)

In his model, Strelau uses Pavlovian concepts but applies them to everyday situations. Our intention was to test the hypothetical relationship between Strength of Excitation as measured in a conditioning procedure and the Excitation factors extracted from the Strelau questionnaire. In our experiment, the threshold of transmarginal inhibition was measured during eyelid conditioning. The Conditioning Stimulus was a tone of 1800 Hz ranging from 15 to 105 dB in seven steps (15, 35, 45, 60, 75, 90, and 105 dB). The Unconditioned Stimulus was a puff of nitrogen. The interstimulus interval was 0.5 s and the intertrial interval about 7.0 s. There were 43 subjects in Dumont's study (1979)[3], but unfortunately only 18 answered the Strelau questionnaire, and the results presented here are based on their data.

The distribution for threshold of transmarginal inhibition for this group was: 35 dB (1 subject), 45 dB (3 subjects), 60 dB (5 subjects), 75 dB (0 subjects), 90 dB (8 subjects), and 105 dB (1 subject). In the light of this distribution, two groups were constructed, one with a low threshold (25-60 dB) and one with a threshold (90-105dB). For the 18 subjects, factor scores were calculated for the four orthogonal Strelau factors. The means and standard deviations for the factor scores for both groups are given in Table 10. We also give the t values for the differences between means.

According to the hypothesis we should observe a significant difference between the two groups on the basis of the Excitation factors (Factor 1 or Factor 3).

The results do not provide confirmation for the hypothesis. The only variable that discriminates the two groups is Inhibition (Factor 2).[4]

These data corroborate the hypothesis put forward by Gray (1964) according to which neuroticism is most likely related to the Strength of the Nervous System.

---

[3]Dumont (1979) gives a detailed description of this experiment, which was designed by P. Roubertoux and E. Dumont. All the members of the team (P. Roubertoux, P. Perruchet, M. Carlier, and E. Dumont) were involved in the collection of data. The experiment lasted for about 9 hours per subject.

[4]Taking into account the scores in the Excitation scale, the difference between the two groups is also nonsignificant.

TABLE 10. Means, factor scores, and standard deviations for the low-threshold and for the high-threshold groups

| | Group | | | | |
| | Low threshold | | High threshold | | |
Factor	$\overline{X}$	σ	$\overline{X}$	σ	t
F1	-.095	1.01	-.128	.43	.08
F2	-.244	.84	.431	.53	1.89*
F3	.448	.91	.215	1.05	.50
F4	-.289	1.00	-.322	.99	.07

* $p < .05$

Note. t values for the differences between means are also given. N = 18.

However, in 1967 Gray aligned himself with Eysenck's point of view and stated that the Strength of Excitation was not related to neuroticism but rather to extraversion-introversion. The fact that our results are not in line with this latter interpretation may be explained in at least two ways. First, the dimensions studied employed Strelau's Excitation and Inhibition, and not Eysenck's Extraversion and Neuroticism. Secondly, the intensity of the Unconditioned Stimulus eliciting the eyeblink reflex was chosen here so that it would produce an eyeblink equal to the spontaneous reaction. This procedure is atypical since normally only one intensity of the Unconditioned Stimulus is used for all subjects in a group. The procedure used by Dumont (1979) is more appropriate for the theoretical framework underlying the study. However, this procedural difference makes comparisons across studies difficult.

The significant difference observed between the low and high threshold groups for the Inhibition factor is contrary to expected outcome. Replication is thus required before conclusions may be drawn.

CONCLUSIONS

A factorial analysis of Strelau's questionnaire was performed for 202 subjects. Four orthogonal factors were extracted, the first two of which are interpreted as Excitation and Inhibition. Mobility did not appear as an independent factor. A correlational analysis between the Strelau and Eysenck questionnaires shows Excitation to be roughly similar to Extraversion-Introversion and Inhibition to Neuroticism-Stability. Using a conditioning procedure, an attempt was made to determine the relationship between threshold of transmarginal inhibition (Pavlov) and Excitation factors extracted from Strelau's questionnaire. The results confirmed neither Eysenck's nor Strelau's claims, but rather supported Gray's hypothesis that people with low thresholds of transmarginal inhibition are more neurotic, that is, have lower mean scores on the Inhibition factor.

REFERENCES

Carlier, M. (1980). Note sur la structure factorielle de la forme francaise du questionnaire de personnalité d'Eysenck (E.P.I.). Revue de Psychologie Appliquée, 30, 253-258.

Dumont, E. (1979). Relations entre l'intensité de la stimulation et l'intensité de la réponse dans le conditionnement. Unpublished doctoral dissertation. Thèse de Troisième Cycle, Paris.

Eysenck, H. J. (1967). The biological basis of personality. Springfield, IL: Charles C Thomas.

Gray, J. A. (1964). Pavlov's typology. New York: MacMillan.

Gray, J. A. (1967). Strength of the nervous system, introversion-extraversion, conditionability and arousal. Behavior Research and Therapy, 5, 151-169.

Meili, R., & Roubertoux, P. (1975). La structure de la personnalité. In P. Fraisse & J. Piaget (Eds.), Traité de psychologie expérimentale. Vol. V, Motivation, emotion et personnalité. Paris: P.U.F., p. 183-287.

Strelau, J. (1970). Nervous system type and extraversion-introversion. A comparison of Eysenck's theory with Pavlov's typology. Polish Psychological Bulletin, 1, 17-24.

Strelau, J. (1972). A diagnosis of temperament by nonexperimental techniques. Polish Psychological Bulletin, 3, 2, 97-105.

Strelau, J. (1975). Pavlov's typology and current investigations in this area. Nederlands Tijdschrift voor de Psychologie, 30, 177-200.

Teplov, B.M. (1964). Problems in the study of general types of higher nervous activity in man and animals. In J. A. Gray (Ed.), Pavlov's typology. New York: Macmillan.

9

The Temperament Inventory: Relationship to Theoretically Similar Western Personality Dimensions and Construct Validity

Kirby Gilliland

Soviet nervous system typology, as a distinct approach to personality classification, has not been studied widely within Western personality psychology. Many researchers (e.g., Cattell, 1972; Eysenck, 1972; Gray, 1964) have discussed the need for more investigations integrating the findings of these two approaches; to date, however, little integrative work has been accomplished. The development of the Temperament Inventory (TI; Strelau, 1972), a psychometric inventory of nervous system typology properties, has stimulated some of this needed research. This chapter presents recent studies of the relationship between TI scales of nervous system typology and popular Western personality dimensions, plus a study designed to offer more direct construct validity for the Strelau scale.

NERVOUS SYSTEM PROPERTIES

Nervous system typology grew from Pavlov's (1927) theory of classical conditioning and the belief that types of nervous activity, and presumably personality types, are based on complexes of basic properties of the nervous system. Teplov (1964) and, more recently, Nebylitsyn (1972; see also Teplov & Nebylitsyn, 1969) have revised Pavlov's theory of nervous system properties (i.e., typology) to include both primary and secondary properties.

The four primary nervous system properties include strength, mobility, dynamism, and lability. (Each of these primary properties can be applied to either excitatory or inhibitory neural processes, thereby yielding eight separate indexes of nervous system functions.) The strength property refers to the endurance or working capacity of the nerve cells. Traditionally, the term <u>strength of the nervous system</u> has referred to <u>excitatory</u> neural process strength with reference to inhibitory neural process strength stated as such. Mobility is believed to reflect the speed in substituting one neural process for another, that is, the ability to relearn or recondition rapidly. Lability represents a property that mediates the generation or termination rate of nervous processes. The fourth property, dynamism, reflects the speed and ease of conditioned response formation manifested in the initial adaptation capacity of the organism (see Nebylitsyn, 1972, for a more complete description of these properties).

The author would like to extend appreciation to Dara Andress, Bruce Saunkeah, and Chris Rice for their help in data collection and to Dick Rubrecht for his invaluable assistance in equipment construction.

Secondary properties of the nervous system include the balance (or equilibrium) of the excitatory and inhibitory processes of any of the specific primary properties; thus, there are twelve possible indexes of nervous system functioning. Only a few of these indexes have received systematic study, with strength of the excitatory process being the most popular.

The various methods for measuring nervous system properties (as outlined by Nebylitsyn, 1972) are characteristically perceptual or psychophysiological and are often complex, posing problems for those researchers needing quick, efficient measurement methods for use with a large number of subjects. Strelau (1972) presented a possible solution to this problem by developing a psychometric scale of the following nervous system properties: strength of the nervous system (excitatory), strength of the inhibitory process, mobility, and equilibrium (of the excitatory and inhibitory strength property). Both the internal consistency and reliability of the Ştrelau TI were reported as being within acceptable limits, with validity established through comparison of the scale scores to an external observational diagnostic rating technique. As yet, there is no evidence that the TI has been used within Western personality research.

The purpose of this chapter is to report on attempts to further compare and integrate Soviet and Western personality research. Three studies are reported that attempt to establish construct validity for the newly developed Strelau TI. Two of the studies compared nervous system typology to popular and theoretically comparable Western dimensions of personality. The third study attempted to directly compare the TI measure of strength of the nervous system to a popular Soviet psychophysiological measure of this dimension.

STUDY 1

Attempts to relate indexes of nervous system typology to Western personality dimensions have concentrated mainly on the apparent similarity between strength of the nervous system and extraversion/introversion (see Eysenck, 1967). Eysenck contends that introverts and extraverts differ in cortical arousal as a function of differences in reticular activating system activity, which leads to differential task performance. It has been hypothesized (Eysenck, 1966, 1967; Gray, 1967) that introverts correspond to weak nervous system types, whereas extraverts have greater correspondence to strong nervous system types.

Evidence for a parallel relationship between nervous system typology and extraversion/introversion grows from the apparent similarities in task performance across the dimensions. Weak nervous system types and introverts have lower sensory thresholds and faster reaction times as compared with strong nervous system types and extraverts, respectively (Buckalew, 1973; Nebylitsyn, 1960; Nebylitsyn, Rozhdestvenskaya, & Teplov, 1960; Shalling, 1971; Siddle, Morrish, White, & Mangan, 1969). Extraverts and strong nervous system types also perform more poorly on attention-type tasks (see Gray, 1964) and suffer the detrimental effects of fatigue of vigilance task performance sooner (Bakan, Belton, & Toth, 1963; Yermolayeva-Tomina, 1960) than do introverts or weak nervous system types, respectively. In addition, the administration of caffeine has a similar directional effect on performance for both dimensions. Caffeine causes a behavioral shift toward the introverted end of the extraversion/introversion dimension (Eysenck, 1967; see also Gilliland, 1977) and toward the weak nervous system end of the nervous system strength/weakness dimension (Nebylitsyn, 1972).

In perhaps the only study to use a direct measure of nervous system strength, the electroencephalogram (EEG) variant of extinction with reinforcement, Frigon (1976) found that introverts were initially more highly aroused than were extraverts, as evidenced by longer alpha-blocking responses (conditioned responses, CRs) during baseline conditioning. The introverts then exhibited a significant decrement in CR during extinction with reinforcement trials. Extraverts showed no significant decrement in CR response and are thus more like strong nervous system types. These results constitute the only well-controlled study supporting the relationship between nervous system strength and extraversion-introversion, using a direct measure of strength of the nervous system. It should be noted that White and Mangan (1972) found no relationship between these dimensions and that Mangan and Farmer (1967) actually found the opposite, a relationship between introverts and strong nervous system types. In both these studies, the indirect nature of the nervous system measures may account for the discrepant findings (see Frigon, 1976).

One other study has shown a relationship between strength of the nervous system and extraversion-introversion in a slightly different manner. On two occasions, Strelau (1970) administered an early form of his TI, along with the Maudsley Personality Inventory (MPI), as a measure of extraversion and found that the correlation between strength of the nervous system and extraversion was approximately $r = .46$ (Ns = 78 and 159). However, the MPI is rarely used as a measure of extraversion, the Eysenck Personality Inventory (EPI) or the more recent Eysenck Personality Questionnaire (EPQ) being preferred measures. Unfortunately, the correlation between the "Extraversion" scales on the EPI and EPQ appears to be only approximately $r = .65-.70$, raising serious questions concerning the comparability of these scales (see Gilliland, 1977). The purpose of Study 1 was to compare the scales on the TI to the scales on the EPI and EPQ, with special interest in the relationship between extraversion and strength of the nervous system.

Method

Subjects were 63 introductory psychology students at the University of Oklahoma. Each student completed the EPI, the EPQ, and the TI (as a measure of nervous system properties).

Results and Discussion

Table 1 presents the correlation matrix for the derived scales. Of the extraversion scales, only the EPQ scale correlated in a manner consistent with Strelau's (1970) earlier findings. Both the EPI and EPQ Neuroticism scales had significant negative correlations with nervous system strength, a finding also consistent with Strelau's data.

Two other findings were noteworthy. First, the correlations between the EPI and EPQ "Extraversion" scales were quite low, considering that these scales are assumed to be measuring the same construct. Secondly, there were relatively high correlations among the scales of the TI, suggesting that a single factor may be underlying all of them. If the underlying factor happens to be the strength dimension, this finding would support the common practice of concentrating on strength of the nervous system in assessment and research.

STUDY 2

The second study was an attempt to explore the relationship between nervous system typology and another Western personality dimension, sensation seeking. Sales and Throop (1972), using kinesthetic aftereffects as a measure of augmenting or reducing, found that strong nervous system types appeared to reduce the impact of stimuli, whereas weak types augmented stimuli. It has also been shown that, compared with weak nervous system types, strong nervous system types exhibit less boredom tolerance, arrive earlier for a laboratory experiment (presumably, an index of stimulation seeking), construct more stimulating hypothetical social

TABLE 1. Correlations between the Eysenck Personality Inventory (EPI), the Eysenck Personality Questionnaire (EPQ), and the Strelau Temperament Inventory (TI)

Scale	EPI Ext	Imp	Soc	Neur	Lie	EPQ Ext	Neur	Psych	Lie	TI Exc	Inh	Mob	Equil
EPI													
Extraversion (Ext)		.54*	.70*	-.32*	.15	.65*	.05	-.04	-.02	.22	-.16	.35*	.36*
Impulsivity (Imp)			.23	.05	.20	.22	.20	.03	.08	.02	-.21	.17	.22
Sociability (Soc)				-.38*	-.01	.69*	-.05	-.03	-.02	.22	-.11	.14	.31*
Neuroticism (Neur)					-.36*	-.31*	.50*	.05	-.09	-.39*	-.02	-.23	-.33*
Lie						.11	.03	-.29	.08	-.07	-.16	.11	.06
EPQ													
Extraversion (Ext)							-.09	.00	.01	.42*	.32*	.19	.12
Neuroticism (Neur)								.06	-.19	-.36*	-.29	-.24	-.08
Psychoticism (Psych)									-.06	.12	-.03	.13	.16
Lie										-.14	-.03	-.34*	-.13
TI													
Strength of Excitation (Exc)											.41*	.51*	.53*
Strength of Inhibition (Inh)												.20	-.53*
Mobility (Mob)													.28
Equilibrium (Equil)													--

*p < .05

situations (Sales, Guydosh, & Iacono, 1974), and self-regulate increases in stimulation during tracking task performance (Eliasz, 1973).

A well-recognized measure of sensation seeking is the Sensation Seeking Scale (SSS: Zuckerman, Kolin, Price, & Zoob, 1964), which has the following four subscales: Thrill and Adventure Seeking (TAS), a measure of desire to engage in activities involving danger or risk; Experience Seeking (ES), the desire to seek new experiences through nonconforming means; Disinhibition (DS), the need to disinhibit social behavior through drinking or partying; and Boredom Susceptibility (BS), an aversion to repetitive experience or restlessness in unchanging environments.

Zuckerman (1978) has alluded to a possible relationship between those high on sensation seeking and strong nervous system types, with low sensation seekers corresponding to weak types. The purpose of Study 2 was to explore the relationship between the SSS subscales and indexes of nervous system typology, as measured by the TI.

Method

Subjects were 58 introductory psychology students, who were administered both the Zuckerman SSS (Form V) and the Strelau TI. All SSS subscale scores were standardized as recommended by Zuckerman (SSS Form V Manual).

Results and Discussion

Table 2 presents the correlation matrix for the various subscales. No significant relationship was found between any nervous system property scale on the TI and the total score of the SSS. Significant correlations were found between TAS and strength of the nervous system, strength of the inhibitory process, and mobility. Significant correlations were also found between ES and strength of the nervous system and mobility. Although these correlations were statistically significant, they were in a range (r = .30) of questionable practical importance. Their significance becomes all the more tenuous when one considers that the average intercorrelation of the SSS subscales is approximately r = +.32 . Thus, it appears that, at best, only a slight relationship exists between selected SSS subscales and indexes of nervous system typology on the TI.

STUDY 3

Little information exists regarding the validity of the Strelau Temperament Inventory. The original validity data cited by Strelau (1972) was based on a comparison of the TI scales with indexes of nervous system properties, based on observational assessment techniques. Compared with psychophysiological techniques, the observational assessment method is a highly indirect means of measuring nervous system typology. Even methods employing reaction-time tasks, which are much less indirect than the observational technique, have been criticized for their inaccuracy (see Frigon, 1976).

The purpose of Study 3 was to explore the construct validity of the TI through comparison of strength of the nervous system, as measured by the TI, and the EEG variant of extinction with reinforcement. It was predicted that weak nervous system types would show a significant decline in conditioned alpha-blocking response over trials during extinction with reinforcement, while the strong types would show no decline or an increase, that is, a predicted Typology-group × trials interaction.

TABLE 2. Correlations between the Strelau Temperament Inventory (TI) and the Zuckerman Sensation Seeking Scales (SSS)

Scale	TI				SSS				
	Exc	Inh	Mob	Equil	TAS	ES	Dis	BS	Total
TI									
Strength of Excitation (Exc)		.58*	.44*	.53*	.33*	.28*	.00	-.01	.21
Strength of Inhibition (Inh)			.25	-.37*	.30*	.18	-.09	.00	.11
Mobility (Mob)				.23	.34*	.31*	.06	.16	.26
Equilibrium (Equil)					.06	.11	.10	-.03	.11
SSS									
Thrill and Adventure Seeking (TAS)						.30*	.29*	.37*	.63*
Experience Seeking (ES)							.29*	.31*	.71*
Disinhibition (Dis)								.24	.70*
Boredom Susceptibility (BS)								--	--
SSS total									--

* p < .05

Method

From a larger pool of introductory psychology students who had completed the TI, 10 students were randomly selected from those who scored one-half of a standard deviation above and below the mean (M = 58.8; SD = 10) on the strength scale. Each of the 20 students was administered the EEG variant of extinction with reinforcement (see Frigon, 1976, or Nebylitsyn, 1972, for a complete description of this EEG measurement technique). As in any alpha-conditioning study, a certain number of subjects are eliminated because they fail to produce alpha or fail to habituate. In this study, four persons were eliminated and were replaced by further random selection.

Procedure

The students sat in a darkened room in a reclining chair approximately 5m from a projection screen. Electrodes (Beckman 214410) were placed transoccipitally at locations 01 and 02, with interelectrode resistance maintained below 15 Kohm. The raw EEG output was fed through an active band-pass filter (8-13 Hz), which would acknowledge an alpha event only on the third successive alpha wave. Once this criterion was met, a millisecond timer (Hunter 220C) was initiated, which recorded the time duration of alpha events during each conditioned stimulus interval (CS, 70 dBA SPL tone, 5 s duration). Intertrial intervals were programmed on a filmstrip-switching apparatus that initiated the CS and unconditioned stimulus (UCS) durations, which were controlled by repeat-cycle timed (Lafayette 51012). Tones were presented by a speaker from an audio generator (EICO 378). The visual stimulus (UCS) was the "Star in Field" figure-ground problem projected from a control room to the screen in the testing room.

Each person was given a number of CS habituation trials to a criterion of 3 successive trials with evidence of no alpha blocking. Fifty conditioning (CS-UCS) trials followed to ensure development of the CR. The CR was the amount of alpha blocking during the duration of the CS. Differential conditioning trials followed to a criterion of 3 successive trials of the differential stimulus (500 Hz; 50 dBA SPL tone) which produced no evidence of alpha blocking. The intertrial interval for the habituation, conditioning, and differential conditioning phases was 15-20 s. The CR baseline phase consisted of 15 trials with trials 3, 11, and 15 being CS-only trials. The average of the CR magnitude on these trials was considered baseline data. During the 48 trials of extinction with reinforcement (average intertrial interval = 4-5 s), 12 trials were CS-only trials. Due to the great variability in CR response, these 12 trials were blocked in sets of 3 trials each forming the 4 postbaseline test trials.

Results and Discussion

These data were analyzed with a 2 (Nervous System Type) × 5 (Trials) analysis of variance with repeated measures on the last factor. The predicted interaction of nervous system type and trials was not significant ($F(4,72) = 1.69$), nor was there a significant main effect for nervous system group; $F(1,18) = 1.44$. The main effect for trials was significant ($F(4,72) = 4.07$, $p < .01$), indicating a significant decline in CR across trials.

Unfortunately, these results did not offer construct validity for the TI. This may be the result of a failure of the TI to accurately predict strength of the nervous system, or a failure to adequately classify typological categories using the EEG variant of extinction with reinforcement, or both. The procedures used in applying the EEG variant of extinction with reinforcement were the same as those described by Frigon (1976), Nebylitsyn (1972), and Teplov and Nebylitsyn (1969). In fact, a secondary analysis of these data was performed in which the 20 subjects were classified according to introversion-extraversion scores instead of the strong-weak nervous system dimension. The results of this analysis, while not statistically significant, resembled those data presented by Frigon (1976), which were analyzed in much the same manner. On the basis of these data, one must conclude that caution should be exercised in the use of the TI as a measure of nervous system strength.

DISCUSSION

The pioneering attempt by Strelau (1972) to produce a psychometric scale of nervous system typology was ambitious and laudable. The data presented in these studies, however, question the validity of the Strength of Nervous System scale. The low correlations with theoretically similar Western dimensions of personality, as well as the lack of similarity to the results of the EEG variant of extinction with reinforcement technique, presented a lack of evidence for construct validity.

The most plausible explanation for this discrepancy is that the rational scale-construction method used to develop the TI may have led to assessing areas of behavior not mediated by the strength dimension. Since the psychophysiological tests of strength of the nervous system tend to be quite direct, little attention has actually been paid the many possible manifestations of strength of this property outside the laboratory setting. Thus, the social manifestations of strength of the nervous system on which any psychometric scale would depend may not be clearly understood. Similarly, a second factor could be that the TI Strength of Nervous System scale may be measuring some constellation of other factors as well. This would allow for trends in the right direction with regard to the correspondence of this scale to theoretically similar dimensions, but would diminish any direct comparison to other referents of nervous system strength.

REFERENCES

Bakan, P., Belton, J. A., & Toth, J. C. (1963). Extraversion-introversion and decrements in an auditory vigilance task. In D. N. Buckner & J. J. McGrath (Eds.), Vigilance: A symposium. New York: McGraw-Hill.

Buckalew, L. W. (1973). Relationship between a physiological and personality index of excitability. Physiological Psychology, 1, 158-160.

Cattell, R. B. (1972). The interpretation of Pavlov's typology, and the arousal concept, in replicated trait and state factors. In V. D. Nebylitsyn & J. A. Gray (Eds.), Biological bases of individual behavior. New York: Academic Press.

Eliasz, A. (1973). Temperament traits and reaction preferences depending on stimulation load. Polish Psychological Bulletin, 4, 103-114.

Eysenck, H. J. (1966). Conditioning, introversion-extraversion and the strength of the nervous system. In V. D. Nebylitsyn (Ed.), Symposium 9, 18th International Congress of Psychology. Moscow.

Eysenck, H. J. (1967). The biological basis of personality. Springfield, IL: Charles C Thomas.

Eysenck, H. J. (1972). Human typology, higher nervous activity, and factor analysis. In V. D. Nebylitsyn & J. A. Gray (Eds.), Biological bases of individual behavior. New York: Academic Press.

Frigon, J. (1976). Extraversion, neuroticism, and strength of the nervous system. British Journal of Psychology, 67, 467-474.

Gilliland, K. (1977). The interactive effect of introversion-extraversion with caffeine induced arousal on verbal performance. Dissertation Abstracts International, 37, 5855-5856.

Gray, J. A. (1964). Pavlov's typology. Oxford: Pergamon Press.

Gray, J. A. (1967). Strength of the nervous system, introversion-extraversion, conditionability, and arousal. Behavior Research and Therapy, 5, 151-169.

Mangan, G. L., & Farmer, R. G. (1967). Studies of the relationship between neo-Pavlovian properties of higher nervous activity and Western personality dimensions: I. The relationship of nervous strength and sensitivity to extraversion. Journal of Experimental Research in Personality, 2, 101-106.

Nebylitsyn, V. D. (1960). Reaction time and strength of the nervous system. First communication: Typological differences in the way in which the "law of strength" takes effect when stimulus intensity is varied. Dokl. Akad. pedagog. Nauk, RSFSF, No. 4, 93-100.

Nebylitsyn, V. D. (1972). Fundamental properties of the human nervous system. New York: Plenum Press.

Nebylitsyn, V. D., Rozhdestvenskaya, V. I., & Teplov, B. M. (1960). Concerning the interrelation between absolute sensitivity and strength of the nervous system. Quarterly Journal of Experimental Psychology, 12, 17-25.

Pavlov, I. P. (1927). Conditioned reflexes (G. V. Anrep, Ed. & Trans.). Oxford: Oxford University Press.

Sales, S. M., Guydosh, R. M., & Iacono, W. (1974). Relationship between "strength of the nervous system" and need for stimulation. Journal of Personality and Social Psychology, 29, 16-22.

Sales, S. M., & Throop, W. F. (1972). Relationship between kinesthetic after-effects and "Strength of the nervous system." Psychophysiology, 9, 492-497.

Schalling, D. (1971). Tolerance for experimentally induced pain as related to personality. Scandinavian Journal of Psychology, 12, 271-281.

Siddle, D. A. T., Moorish, R. B., White, K. D., & Mangan, G. L. (1969). Relationship of visual sensitivity to extraversion. Journal of Experimental Research in Personality, 3, 264-267.

Strelau, J. (1970). Nervous system type and extraversion-introversion. A comparison of Eysenck's theory with Pavlov's typology. Polish Psychological Bulletin, 1, 17-24.

Strelau, J. (1972). A diagnosis of temperament by non-experimental techniques. Polish Psychological Bulletin, 3, 97-105.

Teplov, B. M. (1964). Problems in the study of general types of higher nervous activity in man and animals. In J. A. Gray (Ed.), Pavlov's typology. Oxford: Pergamon Press.

Teplov, B. M., & Nebylitsyn, V. D. (1969). Investigation of the properties of the nervous system as an approach to the study of individual psychological differences. In M. Cole & I. Maltzman (Eds.), Handbook of Contemporary Soviet Psychology. New York: Basic Books.

White, K. D., & Mangan, G. L. (1972). Strength of the nervous system as a function of personality type and level of arousal. Behavior Research and Therapy, 10, 139-146.

Yermolayeva-Tomina, L. B. (1960). Individual differences in the ability to concentrate attention and strength of the nervous system. Vopr. Psikhol., No. 2, 184-195.

Zuckerman, M. (1978). Sensation seeking. In H. London & J. Exner (Eds.), Dimensions of personality. New York: Wiley.

Zuckerman, M., Kolin, E. A., Price, L., & Zoob, I. (1964). Development of a sensation-seeking scale. Journal of Consulting Psychology, 28, 477-482.

10

The Vando R-A Scale as a Measure
of Stimulus Reducing-Augmenting

Gordon E. Barnes

In 1967 Asenath Petrie proposed a theory of individual differences in stimulus intensity modulation. She classified these differences as follows: (a) stimulus augmenters, people who are sensitive to pain and environmental stimulation; (b) stimulus reducers, those not sensitive to pain or environmental stimulation; and (c) moderates, those in the middle of this dimension. Petrie's work stimulated a good deal of research on stimulus intensity modulation. This research was reviewed by Barnes in 1976.

In Petrie's original work, the Kinesthetic Figural Aftereffect task was used as a measure of stimulus intensity modulation. Because of certain difficulties with this task, particularly with test-retest reliability, other investigators have proposed using averaged evoked responses (Buchsbaum & Silverman, 1968) or strength of the nervous system measures (Sales & Throop, 1972) to measure stimulus augmentation-reduction. All these techniques suffer from the drawback that they are cumbersome to administer. In 1969, Alan Vando developed a paper-and-pencil test of stimulus reducing-augmenting (R-A) called the Vando R-A Scale. Because of the simplicity with which the Vando scale can be administered, it provides a potentially useful substitute for the other more cumbersome techniques for measuring stimulus intensity modulation.

In developing his original test, Vando (1969) selected 54 items from a larger item pool that discriminated best between people who were high in their levels of pain tolerance and those who were low. The split-half reliability for this test reported by Vando was .89, and the test-retest reliability was .74. Vando demonstrated the validity of the R-A scale by finding support for his hypotheses that stimulus reducers would be more tolerant of pain (r=.839), more extraverted (r=.648), less hypochondriacal (r=-.596), feel less guilty (r=-.404), smoke more (r=.348), and sleep less (r=-.593) than would stimulus augmenters. A copy of the Vando R-A Scale is included in Appendix A. Scoring instructions for the test are provided in Appendix B.

RELIABILITY

In the seven studies conducted to date where reliability coefficients have been computed, the alpha coefficient of reliability for the Vando scale has ranged

Based on an invited paper, "Stimulus Intensity Modulation, Drug Use and Sensation Seeking," presented at the International Conference on Temperament, Need for Stimulation and Activity, Warsaw, Poland, September 11-14, 1979. During the presentation of this paper the author was supported by a National Health Research Scholar Award (6607-1155-48).

171

from .69 to .87. The median reliability found to date has been .79. This seems satisfactory. No further data are available on the test-retest reliability of the scale.

CONVERGENT VALIDITY

Campbell (1960; see also Campbell & Fiske, 1959) has identified two major types of validity: convergent validity and discriminant validity. To show convergent validity, one must show that a test correlates highly with variables that are theoretically related. To show discriminant validity, one must demonstrate that a test does not correlate highly with variables that are theoretically unrelated. Most reported research using the Vando scale is more relevant for determining convergent validity than for determining discriminant validity.

Pain Tolerance

The most critical variable with which the R-A scale should be correlated is a person's level of pain tolerance. Vando (1969) found an incredibly high (r=.839) correlation between R-A scores and pain tolerance in his female sample. In the closest replication of this study, M. Janisse and M. Dumoff (personal communication, January 1978) obtained a significant (p<.01) correlation (r=-.38) between a person's R-A scale score and his report on the severity of subtolerance level cold-pressor pain in a sample of 48 male college students. Augmenters reported that the cold-pressor pain was more severe than did reducers.

Extraversion-Introversion

Vando reported a correlation of .648 between R-A scale scores and Eysenck's measure of extraversion-introversion in his female sample. In their male sample Janisse and Dumoff (personal communication, January 1978) found a correlation of .48 between stimulus reducing and extraversion. Reducers appear to be more extraverted in both male and female samples.

Need for Approval

Vando hypothesized that augmenters should be easier to socialize than reducers because of their greater sensitivity. He predicted and obtained a significant correlation between guilt feelings and scores on the R-A test (r=-.404). Vando's hypothesis that augmenters may be more highly socialized is supported by the significant correlation (r=-.28) between R-A scale scores and the Marlowe-Crowne Social Desirability Scale found by Barnes and Vulcano (Note 3). Augmenters are apparently more concerned about social approval.

Optimism-Pessimism

In "Civilization and Its Discontents," Freud (1933-1961) outlined the basic sources of man's dissatisfaction. One of the major sources for pessimism and dissatisfaction is the state of one's own body. Because of the augmenters' greater sensitivity to pain, Barnes and Vulcano (Note 2) predicted and obtained a significant correlation (r=.32) between a measure of optimism-pessimism and the Vando R-A Scale. Augmenters are more pessimistic than reducers. Augmenters experience more pain and consequently have more basis for pessimism concerning their bodies. The augmenters' greater pessimism is not restricted to their health and the state of their bodies, however. Augmenters are also more pessimistic with respect to other people. Augmenters in the Barnes and Vulcano Study scored higher (r=-.27) than did reducers on the Rosenberg (1956) scale measuring misanthropy or lack of faith in people.

Ego Strength

Hartman (1955, 1964) hypothesized an association between a strong ego and the ability to reduce or control incoming sensation. Recent writers on the concept of the ego have suggested that there are a number of ego functions (e.g., Bellak, Hurvich, & Gediman, 1973) of which the stimulus barrier or ability to control incoming sensations is one. On the basis of these hypotheses, a correlation between high ego strength and stimulus reducing might be expected. In two studies using the Barron Ego-Strength Scale (Barnes, 1980), significant positive correlations between stimulus reducing and higher ego strength ($r=.34$ and $r=.28$) were obtained.

Locus of Control

To the best of my knowledge, no one has ever made a prediction concerning the relationship between stimulus reducing and augmenting and locus of control. The findings in the Barnes and Vulcano study (Note 2) are not too surprising, however. Augmenters were found to score in the external direction ($r=-.27$) on the Reid and Ware (1974) measure of internal-external locus of control. The correlations with the subscales of the test are particularly informative. Augmenters perceive that they have much less control over themselves ($r=-.57$) than do reducers; but there is no difference in their scores on the fatalism subscale ($r=.07$) and little difference in their social system control subscale scores ($r=-.21$). In retrospect, these results provide strong support for the validity of the R-A test. Augmenters, because they cannot filter out environmental stimulation as effectively, feel that they are not as much under control as reducers.

Sensation Seeking

In developing his test, Vando assumed that since stimulus reducers are chronically understimulated they will try to compensate for this condition by increasing their activity and engaging in behaviors that provide more sensory input, such as talking more, participating in contact sports, and taking stimulant drugs. A similar prediction is advocated and supported by the Sales (1971) research, in which stimulus reducers scored higher on a variety of sensation-seeking measures. It is interesting to note that Zuckerman and his colleagues have made the exact opposite prediction; that augmenters will be sensation seekers (e.g., Zuckerman, Murtaugh, & Siegel, 1974).

Research using the Vando R-A Scale consistently supports the Vando (1969) and Sales (1971) hypothesis that stimulus reducers are high sensation seekers and attests to the validity of the Vando scale. High positive correlations (.46 and .65) have consistently been found between the R-A scale and Pearson's (1970) External Sensation Seeking Scale (Barnes & Hoffman, Note 1; Kohn, Barnes, & Hoffman, 1979). Positive correlations (between .21 and .36) with Pearson's Internal Sensation Seeking Scale have also been found consistently. Reducers have also scored higher on the related concept of risk taking ($r=.49$, $r=.54$) in two studies (Barnes & Hoffman, Note 1; Kohn, Fox, et al., 1979). In general, the groups that have scored highest on the Vando R-A test, indicative of being stimulus reducers, have been high-sensation-seeking groups, such as prisoners and pinball players.

Drug Use

Petrie (1967) hypothesized that augmenters would prefer depressant drugs, such as alcohol, and that reducers would prefer drugs that would stimulate, such as tobacco. Initial research conducted by Petrie supported this hypothesis.

In constructing the R-A scale, one of the criteria that Vando (1969) used to validate his scale was that reducers should smoke more cigarettes per day than augmenters. In his female sample, Vando obtained a significant correlation between the R-A scale score and mean number of cigarettes smoked (r=.348).

In research using the Vando scale, the contention that reducers should prefer stimulating drugs has generally been supported, although these results have not always been consistent. In the Barnes and Fishlinsky (1976) study, for instance, the prediction that reducers would smoke more than augmenters was supported in the female sample (as it was in the Vando study) but not in the male sample. In the Barnes and Fishlinsky research, no support was found for the Petrie prediction that augmenters would crave cigarettes more in low arousal situations.

Research on marijuana use (Kohn, Barnes, & Hoffman, 1979; Kohn, Fox, et al., 1979) has generally supported Vando's prediction that reducers would be more likely to smoke marijuana than would augmenters. In addition, research has shown that reducers have more favorable attitudes toward marijuana use than augmenters have (Kohn, Fox, et al., 1979) and are less concerned about the risks involved in marijuana use than are augmenters (Kohn, Fox, et al., 1979). Reducers also have been found to report greater use of psychedelics and amphetamines in our research (Kohn, Barnes, & Hoffman, 1979).

With respect to the second half of the Petrie (1967) hypothesis (i.e., that augmenters will prefer depressant drugs such as alcohol), the evidence has been less supportive of the validity of the Vando scale or of Petrie's theory. In two studies comparing the scores of alcoholics and nonalcoholics on the R-A scale (Barnes, 1980), it was found that alcoholics did tend to be augmenters, but not any more so than other people their own age. We also found that heroin addicts, in a methadone maintenance program, did not tend to be more augmenters than a nonaddicted comparison group (Kohn, Barnes, Fishlinsky, Segal, & Hoffman, 1979). In addition, the self-reports on narcotic use in our prison sample (Kohn, Barnes, & Hoffman, 1979) did not correlate significantly with R-A scale scores. The prison study also showed that, contrary to expectation, reducers tended to use barbiturates more than augmenters did (r=.18).

Another method for determining convergent validity is to compare scores on a test for different contrasted groups. The means on the R-A scale for several groups are presented in Figure 1. In general, the scores for males are higher than the scores for females. Petrie (1967) noted that there were more extreme cases of perceptual reduction found in male samples; therefore, this finding is not inconsistent with stimulus intensity modulation theory. In the male sample, the highest-scoring group tested were prisoners. This result is consistent with findings by Petrie, McCulloch, and Kazdin (1962) and Compton (1967) that juvenile delinquents tended to be reducers. Other high-scoring groups have included college pinball players (Barnes & Hoffman, Note 1) and students partially selected for being high marijuana users (Kohn, Fox, et al., 1979). The lowest-scoring male group tested has been a group of alcoholics undergoing treatment (Barnes, 1980).

In the female sample, the Vando (1969) sample scored higher than other groups tested thus far. Because this group included student nurses, the scores could have been inflated. Nursing is a high-sensation occupation that should be preferred by stimulus reducers. The lowest-scoring female group has been an alcoholic group (Barnes, 1980).

In general, these findings support the validity of the Vando scale. It should be noted, however, that some of the differences between groups could be accounted for by age differences. Older people become augmenters on the Vando scale (e.g., Barnes, 1980); and the alcoholic samples plotted in Figure 1 were older than the adult comparison groups.

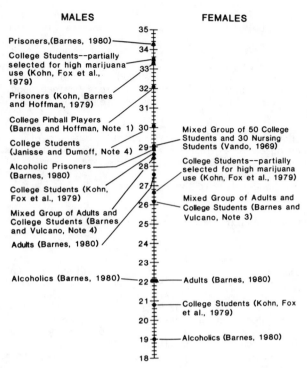

FIGURE 1. Vando Reducer-Augmenter (R-A) Scale Scores. Maximum score = 54; high scores reducers; samples with means broken down according to sex included.

DISCRIMINANT VALIDITY

As has been previously mentioned, to demonstrate validity it is not sufficient to show that a test correlates highly with what it is supposed to measure. It must also be shown that it does not correlate too highly with unrelated variables. One particularly important aspect of discriminant validity concerns the possible test contamination by response set variance. Two of the most notable types of response set contamination include acquiescent responding and giving socially desirable responses. Acquiescent responding is more of a problem when items are worded in an agree-disagree format with all items keyed in the same direction. This problem is not present in forced-choice-type scales like the R-A test, in which the items are not keyed in the same direction.

Social desirability content in paper-and-pencil tests is more difficult to eliminate. To examine the social desirability component in the R-A test, the Barnes and Vulcano (Note 3) study was carried out. In this study, R-A scale scores were correlated with Marlowe-Crowne Social Desirability Scale scores. In addition, subjects (84 males, 93 females) were asked to complete the R-A test under two different instructional sets: normal and faking good. Results showed that the R-A scale had a correlation of -.28 with the Marlowe-Crowne Scale. Augmenters gave more socially desirable responses. The R-A scale item correlations with the Marlowe-Crowne Scale were also computed. None of the items had a correlation over .25 with the Marlowe-Crowne Scale. This suggests that there is a small social desirability component in the R-A scale. As noted earlier, this social desirability component is consistent with stimulus intensity modulation theory and reflects more than simply a response style. The results of analyses comparing subjects' responses under normal and fake-good instructional sets were consistent with the correlational results. Under instructions to fake good, subjects gave responses that were more in the stimulus-augmenter direction (F=54.55; df=1,175; p<.001).

It is unlikely that the relationship between stimulus augmenting and socially desirable responding could explain away the validity data that have been presented on the R-A scale. In fact, stimulus augmenters, who usually give more desirable responses, score lower than reducers on such positive traits as optimism, ego strength, and internal locus of control.

IMPLICATIONS FOR STIMULUS INTENSITY MODULATION THEORY

If the Vando R-A Scale is a reliable and valid measure of stimulus intensity modulation, as it indeed seems to be, then there are several implications for stimulus intensity modulation theory that can be derived from the results just presented. First, strong support has been found for the Vando (1969) and Sales (1971) hypothesis that stimulus reducers are sensation seekers. In addition, the results suggest that only part of Petrie's theory concerning drug-use preferences is supported. Reducers consistently score higher on the self-reported use of stimulant drugs than do augmenters. With respect to depressant drugs, however, more research seems to be required. The hypothesis that stimulus augmenters should prefer depressant drugs such as alcohol has not received much support in our research.

Research with the R-A scale has shown that augmenters have lower ego strength, are more pessimistic, and feel that they have less self-control than reducers. A person's style of stimulus intensity modulation seems to be a pervasive personality characteristic that affects a person's life style, adjustment, and general outlook on life.

REFERENCES

Barnes, G. E. (1976). Individual differences in perceptual reactance: A review of the stimulus intensity modulation individual difference dimension. The Canadian Psychological Review, 17(1), 29-52.

Barnes, G. E. (1980). Clinical alcoholic personality characteristics. Journal of Studies on Alcohol, 41(9), 894-910.

Barnes, G. E., & Fishlinsky, M. (1976). Stimulus intensity modulation, smoking and craving for cigarettes. Addictive Diseases: An International Journal, 2(3), 479-484.

Barron, F. (1953). An ego-strength scale which predicts response to psychotherapy. Journal of Consulting Psychology, 17(5), 227-233.

Bellak, L., Hurvich, M., & Gediman, H. (1973). Ego functions in schizophrenics, neurotics and normals. New York: Wiley.

Buchsbaum, M., & Silverman, J. (1968). Stimulus intensity control and the cortical evoked response. Psychosomatic Medicine, 30(1), 12-22.

Campbell, D. T. (1960). Recommendations for APA test standards regarding construct, trait and discriminant validity. American Psychologist, 15, 546-553.

Campbell, D. T., & Fiske, D. W. (1959). Convergent and discriminant validation by the multitrait-multimethod matrix. Psychological Bulletin, 56, 81-105.

Compton, N. H. (1967). Perceptual characteristics of delinquent girls. Perceptual and Motor Skills, 24, 596-598.

Eysenck, H. J. (1973). A short questionnaire for the measurement of two dimensions of personality. Eysenck on extraversion (pp. 31-36). Rexdale, Ontario: Halstead Press.

Freud, S. (1933/1961). Civilization and its discontents. In J. Strachey (Ed. and trans.), Standard edition of the complete psychological works of Sigmund Freud (Vol. 21). London: Hogarth Press. (Original work published 1933.)

Hartman, H. (1955, 1964). Comments on the psychoanalytic theory of the ego. Essays on ego psychology. New York: International Universities Press.

Kohn, P. M., Barnes, G. E., Fishlinsky, M., Segal, R., & Hoffman, F. M. (1979). Experience-seeking characteristics of methadone clients. Journal of Consulting and Clinical Psychology, 47(5), 980-981.

Kohn, P. M., Barnes, G.E., & Hoffman, F. M. (1979). Drug use history and experience seeking among adult male correctional offenders. Journal of Consulting and Clinical Psychology, 47(4), 708-715.

Kohn, P. M., Fox, J., Barnes, G. E., Annis, H. M., Hoffman, F. M., & Ejchental, B. (1979). Progressive development of a model of youthful marijuana use. Representative Research in Social Psychology, 9, 122-139.

Pearson, P. H. (1970). Relationships between global and specified measures of novelty seeking. Journal of Consulting and Clinical Psychology, 34, 199-204.

Petrie, A. (1967). Individuality in pain and suffering. Chicago, IL: University of Chicago Press.

Petrie, A., McCulloch, R., & Kazdin, P. (1962). The perceptual characteristics of juvenile delinquents. Journal of Nervous and Mental Diseases, 134, 415-421.

Reid, D. W., & Ware, E. E. (1974). Multidimensionality of internal versus external control: Addition of a third dimension and nondistinction of self versus others. Canadian Journal of Behavioural Science, 6(2), 131-141.

Rosenberg, M. (1956). Misanthropy and political ideology. American Sociological Review, 21, 690-695.

Sales, S. M. (1971). Need for stimulation as a factor in social behaviour. Journal of Personality and Social Psychology, 19(1), 124-134.

Sales, S. M., & Throop, W. F. (1972). Relationship between kinesthetic aftereffects and strength of the nervous system. Psychophysiology, 9(5), 492-497.

Vando, A. (1969). A personality dimension related to pain tolerance. Unpublished doctoral dissertation. New York City: Columbia University.

Zuckerman, M., Murtaugh, T., & Siegel, J. (1974). Sensation seeking and cortical augmenting-reducing. Psychophysiology, 11(5), 535-542.

REFERENCE NOTES

1. Barnes, G. E., & Hoffman, F. Pinball playing, risk-taking and sensation seek-
    ing. Unpublished manuscript, available from authors at the University of
    Manitoba, Faculty of Human Ecology, Winnipeg, Manitoba, Canada, R3T 2N2.

2. Barnes, G. E., & Vulcano, B. Optimism-pessimism: Measurement and possible
    causes. Unpublished manuscript, data available from authors at the University
    of Manitoba, Faculty of Human Ecology, Winnipeg, Manitoba, Canada, R3T 2N2.

3. Barnes, G. E., & Vulcano, B. Comparin two different techniques for measuring
    social desirability. Unpublished manuscript, data available from authors at
    the University of Manitoba, Faculty of Human Ecology, Winnipeg, Manitoba,
    Canada, R3T 2N2.

APPENDIX A.   VANDO R-A SCALE

INSTRUCTIONS: Following you will find a series of paired statements which you
are asked to regard as choices. In some cases you will dislike both choices.
In other cases you will find the choices neutral. No matter how the item strikes
you, however, you are asked to choose between them. In each case you are to
decide which of the alternatives you prefer in comparison to the other alternative and then to indicate your selection by drawing a circle around the (a) or
(b) to the left of the statement. It is important to answer all items. Do not
skip any. It is best to work as rapidly as possible.

1.
   (a) see a war drama
   (b) see a situation comedy

2.
   (a) play sports requiring endurance
   (b) play games with rest stops

3.
   (a) raunchy blues
   (b) straight ballads

4.
   (a) jazz combo
   (b) 1001 strings

5.
   (a) stereo on too loud
   (b) stereo on too low

6.
   (a) own a goldfish
   (b) own a turtle

7.
   (a) conservatism
   (b) militantism

8.
   (a) too much sleep
   (b) too little sleep

9.
   (a) danger
   (b) domesticity

10.
   (a) passenger car
   (b) sports car

11.
   (a) have several pets
   (b) have one pet

12.
   (a) be a shepherd
   (b) be a cowboy

13.
   (a) motorcycle
   (b) motor scooter

14.
   (a) see the movie
   (b) read the book

15.
    (a) cocktail music
    (b) discotheque music

16.
    (a) do research in the library
    (b) attend a classroom lecture

17.
    (a) a hot drink
    (b) a warm drink

18.
    (a) a drum solo
    (b) a string solo

19.
    (a) too much exercise
    (b) too little exercise

20.
    (a) loud music
    (b) quiet music

21.
    (a) prepare medications
    (b) dress wounds

22.
    (a) a driving beat
    (b) a nice melody

23.
    (a) hard rock music
    (b) regular popular music

24.
    (a) like athletics
    (b) dislike athletics

25.
    (a) unamplified music
    (b) electrically amplified music

26.
    (a) smooth-textured foods
    (b) crunchy foods

27.
    (a) wake-up pill ("upper")
    (b) sleeping pill ("downer")

28.
    (a) speed
    (b) safety

29.
    (a) rock music
    (b) ballads

30.
    (a) soccer
    (b) golf

31.
    (a) excitement
    (b) calm

32.
    (a) a family of six
    (b) a family of three

33.
    (a) thrills
    (b) tranquility

34.
    (a) play contact sports
    (b) play noncontact sports

35.
    (a) live in a crowded home
    (b) live alone

36.
    (a) share intimacy
    (b) share affection

37.
    (a) games emphasizing speed
    (b) games paced slowly

38.
    (a) thinking
    (b) doing

39.
    (a) competitive sports
    (b) non-competitive sports

40.
    (a) emotionally expressive, somewhat unstable people
    (b) calm, even tempered people

41.
    (a) be a nurse on an acute care ward
    (b) be a nursing operator

42.
    (a) be a NASA scientist
    (b) be an astronaut

43.
   (a) be a stuntman
   (b) be a propman

44.
   (a) a job which requires a lot of
        travelling
   (b) a job which keeps you in one
        place

45.
   (a) climb a mountain
   (b) read about a dangerous
        adventure

46.
   (a) body odors are disgusting
   (b) body odors are appealing

47.
   (a) keep on the move
   (b) spend time relaxing

48.
   (a) have a cold drink
   (b) have a cool drink

49.
   (a) being confined alone in
        a room
   (b) being free in the desert

50.
   (a) security
   (b) excitement

51.
   (a) continuous anesthesia
   (b) continuous hallucinations

52.
   (a) water skiing
   (b) boat rowing

53.
   (a) hostility
   (b) conformity

54.
   (a) traditional art (e.g. Renoir)
   (b) abstract art (e.g. Picasso)

APPENDIX B.   SCORING INSTRUCTIONS FOR THE VANDO R-A SCALE

Total score should be out of 54.

1. Score: A = 0, B = 1

2. Reverse score (i.e., A = 1, B = 0) the following items:

1	17	29	39
2	18	30	40
3	19	31	41
4	20	32	43
5	22	33	44
9	23	34	45
11	24	35	47
13	27	36	48
14	28	37	52
			53

This version of the test includes two minor changes to the Vando scale:

1. Item 27 – original item offered a choice between alcohol use or a mind-
    expanding drug.

2. Item 54 – original item simply listed Renoir and Picasso.

11

Biological and Psychological Correlates of Impulsiveness and Monotony Avoidance

Daisy Schalling and Marie Åsberg

This chapter is concerned with research on two personality traits, impulsiveness and monotony avoidance. We have focused on these particular traits because they appear to be potentially fruitful as intervening variables in theoretical analyses of the relationship between behavioral and biological measures.

H. J. Eysenck has been the pioneer in research on biological bases of personality. The present version of his personality theory (Eysenck, H. J., 1967) includes three basic dimensions, extraversion, neuroticism, and psychoticism, assumed to reflect individual differences in the functioning of ascending reticular system, the visceral brain, and hormonal release patterns, respectively. People high in extraversion are described as sociable, outgoing, carefree, and impulsive; those high in neuroticism as nervous, moody, restless, and excitable; those high in psychoticism as aggressive, cold, cruel, and bizarre. Various correlates of these dimensions have been investigated by Eysenck and his group. Extraversion, as measured by Eysenck's inventory scales (Eysenck Personality Inventory, EPI, and Eysenck Personality Questionnaire, EPQ), has been studied in relation to various neurophysiological, perceptual, and motor measures; to conditioning; and to drug effects (Eysenck, H. J., 1967).

EXTRAVERSION AND IMPULSIVITY AND SOCIABILITY

There is much evidence that extraversion is not a homogenous dimension. As defined by Eysenck, extraversion covers two tendencies that may not even be closely related: a preference for company (sociability) and a tendency to act impulsively on the spur of the moment (impulsivity). Interestingly, these two aspects of extraversion were clearly conceptualized as two separate personality traits by the Swedish psychiatrist and personality theorist Henrik Sjöbring (1913-1973). In Sjöbring's (1973) terminology, extraversion-sociability is called stability, and extraversion-impulsivity is called solidity. High sociability corresponds to low stability, high impulsivity to low solidity.

In a series of studies in which the Eysenck extraversion scale was subdivided into impulsivity (E_i) and sociability items (E_s), our group has repeatedly obtained evidence for the heuristic value of measuring the two components

The research reported has been financially supported by grants from the HSFR (the Council for Research in the Humanities and Social Sciences) and from the Swedish Medical Research Council (21X-4545, P21-4676).

181

separately. The items E_i and E_s consistently load in different factors (Schalling, 1975; an example is given in Table 1).

The terms E_i and E_s are often related to external variables in opposite directions. Thus, in an early study by Schalling and Holmberg (1970), criminals had significantly higher scores in impulsivity and significantly lower scores in sociability than did matched normal controls. This result explains the inconsistent findings obtained in studies testing Eysenck's original hypothesis that criminals are extraverted. In line with our findings, Blackburn (1975) concluded from his studies on criminal groups that sociability and impulsivity should be conceptualized as two orthogonal dimensions, having loadings on both extraversion (E) and neuroticism (N).

TABLE 1.   Rotated factor loadings of personality inventory scales in a group of students (N = 133)

| Variable [a] | Factor | | | | h^2 |
	I	II	III	IV	
N (EPI)	-.11	-.90	-.05	.15	.85
V (MNT)	-.44	.78	.11	.03	.83
E_i (EPI)	-.83	.19	-.06	-.27	.79
Sol (MNT)	.70	.06	.38	.28	.71
E_s (EPI)	-.13	.30	-.19	-.79	.77
Stab (MNT)	.35	.11	-.06	.79	.77
Lie (EPI)	.22	.25	.75	.00	.67
SD (MCSD)	.03	-.09	.89	.08	.80
Proportion of total variance	.33	.23	.12	.09	.77

Note. From Psychopathic Behavior: Personality and Neuropsychology by D. Schalling, 1975, paper presented at a conference on psychopathic behavior, Les Arcs. Copyright 1975 by D. Schalling

[a] The variables are as follows: From the Eysenck Personality Inventory (EPI): Neuroticism (N), Extraversion-Impulsivity (E_i), Extraversion-Sociability (E_s), and Lie.   From the Marke-Nyman Temperament schedule (MNT): Validity (V), Solidity (Sol), and Stability (Stab). In addition, a short version (SD) of the Marlowe-Crowne Social Desirability (MCSD) scale was included.

In a discussion with Eysenck, Guilford (1979) has strongly argued for measuring impulsivity separately. He regarded extraversion as "a shotgun marriage between impulsivity and sociability." He identified impulsivity with his own variable Rhathymia (impulsiveness as opposed to seriousness and self-restraint). Recently, Sybil and Hans Eysenck have also worked with impulsivity scales. In a factorial study (1977) they included items "traditionally used to measure impulsiveness" and found a general factor, Impulsiveness "in the broad sense," which correlates with both extraversion and psychoticism. This factor could be broken down into Impulsiveness "in the narrow sense" (correlating with neuroticism and psychoticism) and three other impulsiveness subscales (Risk-taking, Nonplanning and Liveliness). The best items from these scales have later been used to create a new impulsiveness scale, which is now being used together with a short version of the Zuckerman Sensation Seeking Scale (SSS), denoted Venturesomeness, and an empathy scale, the IVE inventory (Eysenck, S. B. G., & Eysenck, H. J., 1980).

Of the two components of extraversion, impulsivity appears to be more consistently associated with biological correlates. This applies also to solidity, the corresponding dimension in Sjöbring's personality model, as measured by the Solidity scale of the Swedish personality inventory (MNT) (Johnson, Metcalfe, & Coppen, 1975). Solidity and E_i are strongly correlated and tend to load on the same factor (Table 1). Both scales have repeatedly been associated with measures of pain tolerance and with other psychophysiological and neuropsychological measures, for example, catecholamine excretion and sensory thresholds (reviewed by Schalling, 1977, 1978). In our view, such associations between a personality trait and a series of biological measures are highly important, since a personality construct firmly anchored in biological correlates is likely to have a reasonable stability over time and to manifest itself in many different situations.

Some examples are given here of a research strategy aimed at establishing the construct validity for two new inventory scales designed to measure aspects of impulsivity.

CONSTRUCTS AND MEASUREMENT

The consistent psychophysiological findings obtained with the Solidity scale made it important to analyze the item content of the scale and compare it to other existing impulsivity scales. This work has been carried out in our group for some years (in collaboration with Gunnar Edman, Anne-Sofie Rosén, and Birgitta Tobisson, and with the assistance of two psychology students, Gerd Wredenmark and Tord Nilsson). The work resulted in the construction of two new scales, an Impulsiveness scale (I) and a Monotony-Avoidance scale (M) with 20 items each. In further developments, 10 items from each have been selected to form short scales, with a 4-point scoring system (Table 2). They are included in an inventory for research purposes, KSP, intended for use in psychiatric patients as well as nonclinical samples (Schalling, 1977, 1978).

In our scale construction work, we first studied the various clinical and common sensical meanings of the term. Closest to our conception of the term impulsivity is that of Shapiro (1965), who defines impulsive style as a tendency to act on the spur of the moment, without planning and without a clear sense of decision or wish -- "as if the regular executive apparatuses are bypassed." Lack of restraining control on behavior is emphasized, rather than strong urges.

Our item analyses of early impulsivity scales resulted in the following conceptualization of three clusters of content. The numbers refer to the item numbers in the KSP inventory of the Impulsiveness scale items.

1. Acting on the spur of the moment, impulsively, without previous planning or experience of intention (8, 20, 48, 127).

2. Rapid decision-making, without consideration of alternative action, preference for speed rather than carefulness (30, 62, 81, 101).

3. Carefreeness, "rhathymia," taking each day as it comes (68, 113).

Some of the Solidity scale items corresponding to these content clusters are: "Do you more often make up your mind quickly rather than working out a decision slowly and carefully?" "Would you describe yourself as a rather happy-go-lucky person who is not always careful and methodical?" "Do you often sleep on a problem before making a decision?" and "Do you follow the inspiration of the moment and start things which you will later find difficult to manage?" The Solidity scale included another type of item -- thrill seeking and difficulty in tolerating boredom: "When you get bored, do you like to do something exciting?" "Do you prefer change and excitement to security and peace?" and "Do you light-heartedly make provocative statements because you like to shock people?"

This item content is similar to that in the SSS by Zuckerman (1971). We had translated the SSS scales into Swedish but found them difficult to give to patients, because there was some emphasis on extravagant activities and dangerous sports like parachuting, which were beyond the experience of most Swedish psychiatric patients. A content analysis of Solidity and SSS items resulted in two clusters of content. The numbers refer to item numbers of the Monotony-Avoidance scale items.

1. Need for change and novelty, avoiding routine (2, 22, 44, 84).

2. Seeking thrill and strong stimuli, preferring unusual activities and people (28, 54, 73, 102, 109, 130).

Items covering these contents were collected and subjected to item analyses. We avoided the more unusual and deviant contents that would make the scale less appropriate for use with psychiatric patients and older people. The resulting scale was denoted Monotony Avoidance, thus emphasizing what is avoided not tolerated, rather than what is wanted or needed. We wanted to leave open the possibility that what is measured is a difficulty to stand boredom, which may express itself in preference for wild parties, sexual debauches, or drug use, referred to in SSS items, but presumably also in hard work and efforts. A relationship between sensation seeking and striving for achievement has been reported (Blankstein, Darte, & Donaldson, 1976).

We have given these scales both to psychiatric patients and normal healthy people, in whom were collected various biological data (measures of monoamine metabolites in cerebrospinal fluid, as well as neuroendocrine and psychophysiological measures) in a long-term joint project at the Department of Psychiatry of the Karolinska Hospital.

Construct Validity

The construct validity of the two scales I and M has been studied by correlating them with other scales, the validity of which is known to some extent. We describe here the patterns of correlations with EPI and EPQ (including the Extraversion, E, Neuroticism, N, and Psychoticism, P, scales), with anxiety scales and with control scales (Lie, L, and Social Desirability, SD) (see also review by Schalling, 1975).

The two scales I and M are positively correlated in all samples, although the correlations are not high and not always significant, most often around 30 - 40. Both scales correlate with Eysenck's "Extraversion," and more highly with E_i

TABLE 2.   KSP Impulsiveness and Monotony Avoidance items

No.	Item

Impulsiveness

8	I have a tendency to act on the spur of the moment without really thinking.
20	When I have to make a decision, I "sleep on it" before I decide. (F)
30	I usually get so excited over new ideas and suggestions that I forget to check if there are any disadvantages.
48	I often throw myself too hastily into things.
62	I am a very particular person. (F)
68	I think it is quite right to describe me as a person who takes things as they come.
81	I usually "talk before I think."
101	When I'm about to make a decision I usually make it quickly.
113	I take life easy.
127	I consider myself an impulsive person.

Monotony Avoidance

2	I am always keen on trying out things that are all new.
22	I like leading a quiet and organized life. (F)
28	I prefer people who come up with exciting and unexpected activities.
44	I have an unusually great need for change.
54	I try to get to places where things really happen.
73	I almost always have a desire for more action.
84	In a way I like to do routine jobs. (F)
102	I like doing things just for the thrill of it.
109	To be on the move, traveling, change and excitement -- that's the kind of life I like.
130	When listening to the radio, I want it really loud, so that I can feel "turned on."

than with E_S. This applies especially to Impulsiveness. In many samples, Monotony Avoidance correlates almost at the same level with Sociability as with Impulsivity. Correlations with N are low and nonsignificant. Monotony Avoidance is significantly positively correlated with P in many samples (especially in criminals and smokers). The correlations with Lie and Social Desirability scales are negative and sometimes significant.

Correlations with the anxiety scales used are mostly low. Highest and often significant are the negative correlations between Monotony Avoidance and the Psychic Anxiety scale, measuring worrying and sensitivity. The correlations between the Impulsiveness and Monotony Avoidance scales and Swedish translations of the Zuckerman SSS and the EPQ in a group of students are shown in Table 3. Monotony Avoidance, but not Impulsiveness, was positively correlated with the SSS scales, especially with General SSS and Boredom Susceptibility. The correlations between the SSS and EPQ scales are in agreement with those found by S. B. G. Eysenck and Zuckerman (1978). Thus, Monotony Avoidance seems to reflect psychopathy-related traits in normal people, like thrill-seeking, low conformity, and low anticipatory anxiety (Schalling, 1978).

TABLE 3. Correlations between the KSP Impulsiveness (I) and Monotony Avoidance (M) scales, and the Zuckerman Sensation Seeking Scales (SSS) in a group of 40 students

Scale	SSS					KSP	
	Gen.	TAS	ES	Dis.	BS	I	M
EPQ							
E	.11	.03	−.02	.22	.06	.37***	.41***
(E_i)	.24	.13	.07	.11	.10	.40***	.46***
(E_s)	.10	−.03	.02	.31**	.12	.25	.31**
P	.48***	.21	.67***	.30*	.49***	.24	.12
N	.06	−.20	.29*	.18	.17	.28*	.11
Lie	−.14	.05	−.41***	−.25	−.42***	−.20	−.28*
KSP							
I	.20	.05	.23	.13	.05	−	.31*
M	.50****	.23	.31**	.41***	.51****	−	−

Note. General SSS (Gen.), Thrill and Adventure Seeking (TAS), Experience Seeking (ES), Disinhibition (Dis.), Boredom Susceptibility (BS), and the Eysenck Personality Questionnaire (EPQ): Extraversion (E), Extraversion-Impulsivity subscale (E_i), Extraversion-Sociability subscale (E_s), Psychoticism (P), Neuroticism (N), and Lie scales.

   *   p < .10

   **   p < .05

  ***   p < .01

 ****   p < .001

In a study on young delinquents, subjects with high testosterone levels had significantly higher scores in Monotony Avoidance than did those with low levels
(Mattsson, Schalling, Olweus, Löw, & Svensson, 1980). A similar association has
been reported by Zuckerman (1979) for the SSS.

The Impulsiveness and Monotony Avoidance scales have also been given to twins
(Theorell, de Faire, Schalling, Adamsson, & Askevold, 1979). The dizygotic/
monozygotic intrapair variance ratio was significant for Impulsiveness ($F=4.57$,
$p < .05$) but not for Monotony Avoidance. Both scales were significantly related
to psychophysiological changes during a stressful interview.

Neuropsychological Models

The item content in the two scales Impulsiveness and Monotony Avoidance, the
patterns of correlations obtained, and the clinical observations on which Sjöbring
(1973) constructed his solidity dimension, as well as those described by Shapiro
(1965), suggest some neuropsychological models, from which testable inferences
can be drawn that may prove fruitful for the continued exploration of these personality dimensions. The first model is expressed in terms of information processing and hypothetical underlying central nervous system processes, the second
in terms of arousal and vigilance and neurophysiological and neurochemical
activation processes.

The first model suggests that a person's position on the impulsiveness variable
is related to the extent to which his or her behavior, cognition, and acts are
determined predominantly (a) by immediate, holistic processing of sensory input,
attending to its physical properties (high impulsive), or (b) by semantic categorization and analysis of input, by stored content (memories), and by anticipa-
tion and comparison of outcomes of alternative possible actions (low impulsive).
The cognitive style of highly impulsive persons is described by Shapiro (1965)
on the basis of long clinical experience and projective methods, as follows:

> The impulsive person's attention does not search actively and analyt-
> ically. We may add that his attention is quite easily and completely
> captured; he sees what strikes him, and what strikes him is not only
> the starting point of a cognitive process, but also, substantially,
> it is its conclusion. In this sense, his cognition may be called
> passive (pp. 150-151).

Thus, the attention of the more impulsive person may be caught more easily by
what happens around him (acting on the spur of the moment); whereas the less
impulsive person, with his greater involvement in processing of past events and
future projects, is less easily distracted.

A person whose mental contents are more dependent on present or recent sensory
input (short-term memory) than on additional cognitive processing and stored
memories of past events may be more prone to seek out a constantly changing environment or strong stimuli, to maintain an optimal level of stimulation or input.
He would be a sensation seeker, high in Monotony Avoidance.

These differing cognitive styles, assumed to characterize persons high and low
in Impulsiveness and Monotony Avoidance, are strongly reminiscent of the modes
of information processing considered to be associated with right and left brain
hemisphere functioning, respectively. Hemisphere differences in dealing with
visual-spatial versus language stimuli, and in parallel versus serial processing
are well established. There is also growing evidence, however, suggesting that
the right hemisphere is more involved in the preliminary holistic processing of
input, whereas the left hemisphere is more involved in the processing of stimuli

in terms of description systems already existing in the cognitive repertoire, for example, in dealing with linguistically coded material (Goldberg, Vaughan, & Gerstman, 1978; Levy, 1974). It has further been suggested that short-term storage proceeds in the right hemisphere, whereas the semantic or abstract analysis which is assumed to be a prerequisite for long-term storage is predominantly a left hemisphere function (Nebes, 1974). Kinsbourne (1973) has suggested that control of attention is dependent on a balance of reciprocal inhibition between the two hemispheres.

Individual differences in the activation of the two hemispheres in information processing have been described, for example, by Gur (1978). Studies on cerebral laterality and its implications for psychiatry have recently been reviewed by Wexler (1980). There is also some evidence that predominance of right or left hemisphere activation may be related to personality style. Using lateral eye movements as an indicator of immediate hemispheric activation after questions, Smokler and Shevrin (1979) found evidence of more right hemisphere activation in hysterical subjects than in those with an obsessive-compulsive style. Hysterical personality traits are closely related to the dimension of solidity (Sjöbring, 1973) and impulsiveness (Shapiro, 1965). The cognitive style in highly impulsive people is consistent with assumptions of a lower involvement of left hemisphere processing, that is, reduced efficiency in recording of information in terms of linkage with verbal symbols and stored mental content.

One of the predictions that may be drawn from this model is that people who score high on impulsivity scales will tend to rely less on semantic aspects in the processing of stimuli. This was indeed true in a study of generalization of autonomic responses to word stimuli (Schalling, Levander, & Wredenmark, 1980). Such responses may generalize along two dimensions, phonetically (similarity of sound, e.g., hat-cat) or semantically (similarity of meaning, e.g., cat-animal). Students with high scores in the Impulsiveness and Monotony Avoidance scales generalized significantly more along the phonetic dimension.

The second neuropsychological model associates impulsive behavior with deficiencies in cortical and brain stem activating systems, leading to a proneness for low cortical arousal and difficulties in maintaining appropriate vigilance levels in monotonous situations (reviewed by Schalling, 1976, 1978). These activating systems are related to frontal lobe functioning (see, e.g. Luria, 1966). A marked increase in impulsivity has been described in patients with frontal lobe lesions, for example, in the classical study by Rylander (1939). More recent evidence suggests that lower vigilance after frontal lobe lesions (and in impulsive individuals?) may be an effect of interfering with the coeruleo-cortical noradrenergic fibers. These fibers enter the cortex at the frontal pole and innervate large areas of cortex (Morrison, Molliver, & Grzanna, 1979).

It is evident that both models for the neuropsychology of impulsivity have as yet insufficient bases in replicated empirical data. Like the neurochemical model for sensation seeking presented by Zuckerman (1979), they are intended to provide guidelines for the design of studies aimed at testing various inferences that can be drawn from them.

RELATIONSHIPS WITH BIOGENIC AMINES

The validity of the assumption that impulsiveness and monotony avoidance are useful as intervening variables between behavior and brain functioning would receive considerable support if they were shown to correlate with neurochemical measures. A group of such measures that have attracted considerable interest during recent years are estimates related to the turnover of biogenic amines (e.g., dopamine, noradrenaline, and serotonin). These monoamines serve as neurotransmitters or neuromodulators in the central nervous system; and there is much evidence that they are involved in the control of basic neuropsychological processes, such as attenuation of sensory input, attention, memory, and sensitivity to pain (Costa, Gessa, & Sandler, 1974; Krauthamer, 1975; Ungerstedt, 1979).

Although turnover and concentration of transmitter amines in the brain cannot be studied directly in man, it is possible to study their metabolites in the cerebrospinal fluid, or the enzymes involved in their synthesis or degradation (e.g., monoamine oxidase, MAO). This MAO activity can be measured in various peripheral tissues, including blood platelets, which are easily accessible. To some extent, the use of platelet MAO activity rests on the assumption that it reflects MAO activity in the brain, which is not yet proven. Although differences between certain categories of psychiatric patients and controls have been found both for platelet MAO activity (Murphy & Kalin, 1980) and for spinal fluid monoamine metabolites (Åsberg & Träskman, in press; Goodwin, Webster, & Post, 1978), most studies show a considerable overlap between normal and pathological groups. It thus appears that the biochemical variables may not be directly related to psychiatric illness as such, but rather to a constitutional vulnerability, which may lead to illness or breakdown, provided some other factors (psychosocial or somatic) are present (Coursey, Buchsbaum, & Murphy, 1979; Zubin & Spring, 1977). This has led to an increased interest for personality measures.

Murphy et al. (1977) obtained platelet MAO activity levels in 30 normal men and 65 normal women, who also completed two personality inventories, the Minnesota Multiphasic Personality Inventory (MMPI) and the Zuckerman SSS. For the men, negative correlations were obtained between MAO and SSS Disinhibition (-.51, p < .05), Boredom Susceptibility (-.34, p < .05), and General SSS (-.45, p < .05) scales. For the women, in contrast, the correlations were mostly positive.

Schooler, Zahn, Murphy, and Buchsbaum (1978) analyzed SSS results in a random sample of 93 subjects from a population of 375 college students, on whom MAO levels had been measured. For the 46 men, they replicated the negative correlations with the General SSS scale (-.52, p < .001) and with Boredom Susceptibility (-.41, p < .01). In addition, there was also a negative correlation with Experience Seeking (-.43, p < .01). The correlations were negative also in the female group.

From the same population of 375 students, Coursey et al. (1979) selected subjects with MAO levels representing the lower and upper 10% and studied their MMPI scores. The low-MAO males scored in the more pathological direction in 7 of 8 MMPI scales and had significantly higher scores in the Hypochondriasis, Hysteria, and Psychopathic Deviate scales.

The authors studied differences between high- and low-MAO students in many other respects also, analysed on the basis of clinical interviews. Among the findings were more smoking, drug taking, suicide attempts, convictions, and lefthandedness in the low-MAO subjects, who were also very sociable.

The KSP scales have been used in two further studies of platelet MAO activity. Perris et al. (1980) studied 24 consecutively admitted patients (men and women) hospitalized for depressive illness, and found significant negative correlations between Monotony Avoidance and platelet MAO activity (rank correlation, -.40, using beta-phenyletylamine, PEA, as substrate; -.55, with tryptamine, TRYPT, as substrate in the enzyme assay). There was no association to Impulsiveness.

In a recent study from our group (Schalling, Åsberg, et al., 1980), we obtained platelet MAO measures from a group of 40 male students -- 20 psychology students and 20 law students (mean age 28, range 20-49 years). Blood samples were obtained by a single venipuncture in the morning, and platelet MAO activity was determined at the Department of Pharmacology in Umeå University by Professor Lars Oreland, using both PEA and TRYPT as substrates. The MAO values were correlated to scores in the E, N, and P scales from the EPQ, the Zuckerman SSS scales IV, and the KSP scales, including the I and M scales. The correlation between the MAO measures and the EPQ scores in E, N, and P were all low and nonsignificant. Correlations between MAO and the I and M scores are shown in Table 4.

Both scales showed negative correlations with MAO. The correlations with M were significant for both substrates, whereas those for I were nonsignificant. When the group was subdivided, however, into high- and low-MAO groups (27% of the sample in each extreme group) and a middle group with moderate MAO levels, analysis of variance showed that there was a significant interaction between MAO and I scores ($F = 6.79$, $p < .01$). Figure 1 shows that both low and high MAO subjects had elevated I scores, most prominantly for low-MAO subjects. The correlations between MAO and the SSS scales were mostly negative, but significant only for Disinhibition (Table 4).

The consistent finding in four different subject groups of an association between aspects of impulsivity and sensation seeking, and platelet MAO activity, strongly supports the hypothesis of a biological basis for these particular personality traits. Unfortunately, little is known about the significance, in terms of brain functioning, of reduced platelet MAO activity.

It has been suggested, among others by Oreland (1980), that low platelet MAO may reflect some constitutional weakness of monoamine systems in the brain. The suggestion was based on (relatively weak) correlations between MAO activity in human brain and brain levels of serotonin and its metabolite 5-hydroxy-indole acetic acid (5-HIAA) (Adolfsson et al., 1978). This suggestion has received some support from the finding of positive correlations between platelet MAO activity and spinal fluid concentrations of the dopamine metabolite, homovanillic acid (HVA) and 5-HIAA in normal controls, but not in psychiatric patients (Oreland et al., 1980).

TABLE 4. Correlations between monoamine oxidase activity (MAO) in platelets with beta-phenylethylamine (PEA) and tryptamine (TRYPT) as substrates, and KSP inventory scales and the Zuckerman Sensation Seeking scales (SSS IV) (N = 40)

	KSP		SSS IV				
Substrate	I	M	Gen.	TAS	ES	Dis.	BS
MAO (PEA)	−.14	−.33*	−.24	.02	−.20	−.24	−.07
MAO (TRYPT)	−.06	−.30*	−.25	.03	−.20	−.26*	−.11

*p < .05

Note. The KSP scales are Impulsiveness (I) and Monotony Avoidance (M). The SSS IV scales are General SSS (Gen.), Thrill and Adventure Seeking (TAS), Experience Seeking (ES), Disinhibition (Dis.) and Boredom Susceptibility (BS).

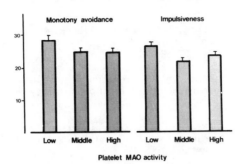

FIGURE 1. Mean scores in the KSP Impulsiveness and Monotony Avoidance scales in a group of 40 students, subdivided on the basis of monoamine oxidase (MAO) values in a low-MAO group (N = 11, 27%), a moderate-MAO group (N = 18) and a high-MAO group (N = 11).

Studies of the relationship between spinal fluid monoamine metabolite concentrations and personality are in progress in our group, and preliminary findings suggest a relationship between the concentration of HVA and Monotony Avoidance.

Several researchers have suggested a connection between lateralization of hemispheric function and brain monoamine turnover (Glick, Weaver, & Meibach, 1980; Mandell & Knapp, 1979; Oke, Keller, Mefford, & Adams, 1978; cf. also the increased incidence of left-handedness in low-MAO people found by Coursey et al. (1979). Such studies may contribute to the testing of the proposed models for the neuropsychological correlates of impulsiveness and monotony avoidance.

REFERENCES

Adolfsson, R., Gottfries, C. -G., Oreland, L., Ross, B. -E., Wiberg, Å., & Winblad, B. (1978). Monoamine oxidase activity and serotonergic turnover in human brain. Progress in Neuro-Psychopharmacology, 2, 225-230.

Åsberg, M., & Träskman, L. (in press). Studies of CSF 5-HIAA in depression and suicidal behaviour. In B. Haber (Ed.), Serotonin - Current Aspects of Neurochemistry and Function. New York: Plenum.

Blackburn, R. (1975). An empirical classification of psychopathic personality. British Journal of Psychiatry, 127, 456-460.

Blankstein, K. R., Darte, E., & Donaldson, P. (1976). A further correlate of sensation seeking. Perceptual and Motor Skills, 42, 1251-1255.

Costa, E., Gessa, G. L., & Sandler, M. (Eds.) (1974). Serotonin: New Vistas. New York: Raven Press.

Coursey, R. D., Buchsbaum, M. S., & Murphy, D. L. (1979). Platelet MAO activity and evoked potentials in the identification of subjects biologically at risk for psychiatric disorders. British Journal of Psychiatry, 134, 372-381.

Eysenck. H. J. (1967). The biological basis of personality. Springfield, IL:
Charles C Thomas.

Eysenck, S. B. G., & Eysenck, H. J. (1977). The place of impulsiveness in a
dimensional system of personality description. British Journal of Social and
Clinical Psychology, 16, 57-68.

Eysenck, S. B. G., & Eysenck, H. J. (in press). Impulsiveness and venturesomeness:
Their position in a dimensional system of personality description. Psychological
Reports.

Eysenck, S. B. G., & Zuckerman, M. (1978). The relationship between sensation-
seeking and Eysenck's dimension of personality. British Journal of Psychology,
69, 483-487.

Glick, S. D., Weaver, L. M., & Meibach, R. C. (1980). Lateralization of reward
in rats: Differences in reinforcing thresholds. Science, 207, 1093-1095.

Goldberg, E., Vaughan, H. G., & Gerstman, L. J. (1978). Nonverbal descriptive
systems and hemispheric asymmetry: Shape versus texture discrimination. Brain
and Language, 5, 249-257.

Goodwin, F. K., Webster, M. H., & Post, R. (1978). Cerebrospinal fluid amine
metabolites in affective illness and schizophrenia: Clinical and pharmacological studies. In E. Usdin & A. J. Mandell (Eds.), Biochemistry of mental
disorders. New Vistas, NY: Dekker.

Guilford, J. P. (1977). Will the real factor of extraversion-introversion please
stand up? A reply to Eysenck. Psychological Bulletin, 84, 412-416.

Gur, R. C. (1978). Individual differences in hemispheric activation: Implications
for cognitive style, personality and psychopathology. Brain and Language, 5.

Johnson, A. L., Metcalfe, M., & Coppen, A. (1975). An analysis of the Marke-
Nyman Temperament scale. British Journal of Social and Clinical Psychology,
14, 379-385.

Kinsbourne, M. (1973). The control of attention by interaction between the
cerebral hemispheres. In S. Kornblum (Ed.), Attention and performance, Vol. 4
(pp. 239-256). Elsevier: North Holland.

Krauthamer, G. M. (1975). Catecholamines in behavior and sensorimotor integration: The neostriatal system. In A. J. Friedhoff (Ed.), Catecholamines and
behavior. Vol. 1, Basic neurobiology (pp. 59-87). New York: Plenum Press.

Levy, I. (1974). Psychobiological implications of bilateral asymmetry. In
S. J. Dimond & J. G. Beaumont (Eds.), Hemisphere function in the human brain.
London: Elek Science.

Luria, A. R. (1966). Higher cortical functions in man. New York: Basic Books.

Mandell, A. J., & Knapp, S. (1979). Asymmetry and mood, emergent properties of
serotonin regulation. Archives of General Psychiatry, 36, 909-916.

Mattson, Å., Schalling, D., Olweus, D., Löw, H., & Svensson, J. (1980). Plasma
testosterone, aggressive behavior and personality dimensions in young male
delinquents. Journal of the American Academy of Child Psychiatry, 19, 476-490.

Morrison, J. H., Molliver, M. E., & Grzanna, R. (1979). Noradrenergic innervation of cerebral cortex: Widespread effects of local cortical lesions. Science, 205, 313-316.

Murphy, D. L., Belmaker, R. H., Buchsbaum, M., Martin, N. F., Ciaranello, R., & Wyatt, R. J. (1977). Biogenic amine-related enzymes and personality variations in normals. Psychological Medicine, 7, 149-157.

Murphy, D. L., & Kalin, N. H. (1980). Biological and behavioral consequences of alterations in monoamine oxidase activity. Schizophrenia Bulletin, 6, 355-367.

Nebes, R. D. (1974). Hemispheric specialization in commissurotomized man. Psychological Bulletin, 81, 1-14.

Oke, A., Keller, R., Mefford, I., & Adams, R. N. (1978). Lateralization of norepinephrine in human thalamus. Science, 200, 1411-1413.

Oreland, L. (1980). Monoamine oxidase activity and affective illness. Acta Psychiatrica Scandinavica, 61 (Suppl. 280), 41-46.

Oreland, L., Wiberg, Å., Åsberg, M., Träskman, L., Sjöstrand, L., Thorén, P., Bertilsson, L., & Tybring, G. (1980). Platelet MAO activity and monoamine metabolites in cerebrospinal fluid in depressed and suicidal patients and in healthy controls. Psychiatry Research.

Perris, C., Jacobsson, L., von Knorring, L., Oreland, L., Perris, H., & Ross, S.I., (1980). Enzymes related to biogenic amine metabolism and personality characteristics in depressed patients. Acta Psychiatrica Scandinavica, 61, 477-484.

Rylander, G. (1939). Personality changes after operations on the frontal lobes. Copenhagen: Munksgaard.

Schalling, D. (1975). Psychopathic behavior: Personality and neuropsychology. Paper presented at a conference on psychopathic behavior, Les Arcs.

Schalling, D. (1976). Anxiety, pain and coping. In I. G. Sarason & C. D. Spielberger (Eds.), Stress and anxiety, Vol. 3 (pp. 49-71). Washington, DC: Hemisphere (Wiley).

Schalling, D. (1977). The trait-situation interaction and the physiological correlates of behavior. In D. Magnusson & N. S. Endler (Eds.), Personality at the crossroads. Hillsdale, NJ: Lawrence Erlbaum.

Schalling, D. (1978). Psychopathy-related personality variables and the psychophysiology of socialization. In R. D. Hare & D. Schalling (Eds.), Psychopathic behavior. Approaches to research. Chichester: Wiley.

Schalling, D., & Holmberg, M. (1970). Extraversion in criminals and the "dual nature" of extraversion (No. 306, Reports from the Psychological Laboratories). Stockholm: The University of Stockholm.

Schalling, D., Levander, S. E., & Wredenmark, G. (1980). Generalization of conditioned SC responses to homonyms in impulsive subjects: Arousal and hemisphere specialization in the processing of verbal input. Unpublished manuscript.

Schalling, D., Åsberg, M., Oreland, L., Askanas, I., Pfannschmidt, W., & Tiberg, B. (1980). Platelet MAO activity and personality variables. Unpublished manuscript.

Schooler, C., Zahn, T. P., Murphy, D. L., & Buchsbaum, M. S. (1978). Psychological correlates of monoamine oxidase activity in normals. Journal of Nervous and Mental Disease, 166, 177-186.

Shapiro, D. (1965). Neurotic styles. New York: Basic Books.

Sjöbring, H. (1973). Personality structure and development. A model and its application. Acta Psychiatrica (Suppl. 244).

Smokler, I. A., & Shevrin, H. (1979). Cerebral lateralization and personality style. Archives of General Psychiatry, 36, 949-954.

Theorell, T., de Faire, U., Schalling, D., Adamsson, U., & Askevold, F. (1979). Personality traits and psychophysiological reactions to a stressful interview in twins with varying degrees of coronary heart disease. Journal of Psychosomatic Research, 23, 89-99.

Ungerstedt, U. (1979). Central dopamine mechanisms and unconditioned behaviour. In A. S. Horn (Ed.), Neurobiology of dopamine. New York: Academic Press.

Wexler, B. E. (1980). Cerebral laterality and psychiatry: A review of the literature. American Journal of Psychiatry, 137, 279-291.

Zubin, I., & Spring, B. (1977). Vulnerability -- A new view of schizophrenia. Journal of Abnormal Psychology, 86, 103-126.

Zuckerman, M. (1971). Dimensions of sensation seeking. Journal of Consulting and Clinical Psychology, 36, 45-52.

Zuckerman, M. (1979). Sensation seeking: Beyond the optimal level of arousal. Hillsdale, NJ: Lawrence Erlbaum.

12

Sensation Seeking: Measurement and Psychophysiological Correlates

J. A. Feij, J. F. Orlebeke, A. Gazendam, and R. W. van Zuilen

People need arousal and variation in their lives, but this need is apparently stronger in some people than in others; there are also differences among people in the ability to tolerate high levels of arousal. Hence, there seem to be stable differences in what is called sensation seeking, and there are different ways in which this sensation-seeking tendency expresses itself. This chapter is concerned with the measurement and the origin of differences in sensation seeking. First, the literature concerning the nature of the sensation-seeking concept is reviewed. Next, results from some of our own research are summarized. Finally, an attempt is made to integrate the evidence from different fields of research.

THE SENSATION-SEEKING DIMENSION

More than 20 years of research have been devoted -- primarily by Zuckerman and co-workers -- to the verification of the central hypothesis that people show characteristic and stable differences in preference for strength and variety of stimulation. Zuckerman and Link (1968) described the sensation-seeking dimension as follows:

> The low sensation seeker seems to need order and predictability in his environment. He values social affiliation and is willing to give in to others to maintain stability. The high sensation seeker needs change in his environment, independence from others and probably needs others primarily as an audience to his experience. He tends to be impulsive and labile. (p. 425)

At the core of this definition is Zuckerman's (1969) postulate:

> Every individual has characteristic optimal levels of stimulation and arousal for cognitive activity, motoric activity and positive affective tone. (p. 429)

Individual differences in the optimal level of stimulation are considered to be dependent on several factors, such as the balance between excitation and inhibition in the nervous system, age, and adaptation following exposure to prolonged stimulation. The possible biological bases of differences in sensation seeking are discussed later in the chapter.

Paper presented by the first author at the international conference on "Temperament, need for stimulation and activity," Grzegorzewice, Poland, September 1979.

Several self-report questionnaires of the sensation-seeking tendency have been developed by Zuckerman and his co-workers. The first Sensation Seeking Scale (SSS) (Zuckerman, Kolin, Price, & Zoob, 1964) consisted of 54 forced-choice items measuring the optimal level of stimulation. Guided by suggestions from Farley (1967) and Zuckerman and Link (1968) that the sensation-seeking concept is multidimensional, several later versions have been constructed, including the SSS form IV (Zuckerman, 1971). This questionnaire has been used frequently for research in English-speaking countries, and has served as a model for our own test-construction activities. Zuckerman's SSS-IV consists of forced-choice items measuring four separate dimensions of sensation seeking (identified by means of factor analysis). These dimensions are as follows:

1. Thrill and Adventure Seeking (TAS): a measure of the desire to engage in sports or other activities involving speed or danger. A representative item is "I would like to take up the sport of waterskiing."

2. Experience Seeking (ES): seeking of new experiences through the mind and senses, and through an unconventional, nonconforming life style; for example, "I would like to hitch-hike across the country."

3. Disinhibition (DIS): the desire to find release through social disinhibition, going to parties and having a variety of sexual partners; for example, "I like wild, uninhibited parties."

4. Boredom Susceptibility (BS): dislike of repetition of experience, routine work, predictably dull or boring people, and restlessness when things are monotonous; for example, "I get bored seeing the same old faces."

A number of items of the SSS-IV feature in a general Sensation Seeking Scale, that is, items with a significant loading on the first principal component. Zuckerman, Bone, Neary, Mangelsdorff, and Brustman (1972) have reported that the intercorrelations among the scores on the four specific scales are of moderate size (about .30 to .40). In other words, although the scales have a certain amount of common variance, they also have a considerable proportion of unique variance. Since the scores on several scales were found to be related to different phenomena, Zuckerman (1974) suggested that the dimensions of sensation seeking are perhaps evidence of different genotypes.

Other Personality Questionnaires and Behavioral Correlates

Insight into the meaning of sensation seeking as a stable personality trait can be gained by studying the relations with other personality traits and behavioral variables. Sensation seeking has been associated with psychopathic deviance and hypomania, as measured by the MMPI (Minnesota Multiphasic Personality Inventory, Pd and Ma scale, respectively). The Pd scale is a measure of social nonconformism, impulsiveness, egocentrism, and antisocial tendencies; the Ma scale measures energy, overactivity, and impulsiveness. These relationships are consistent with Quay's (1965) view that psychopathy should be seen as a pathological form of stimulation seeking. Studies relating SSS scores with Cattell's 16PF test (Gorman, 1970; Jacobs, 1975; Zuckerman et al., 1972) have provided a similar picture of the sensation seeker as relatively nonconformist (low on 16PF-G and high on 16PF-M and Q1), dominant (high on 16PF-E), and extraverted (high on 16PF-F and H). Furthermore, sensation seeking scores are positively correlated with Eysenck's extraversion scales (Bone and Montgomery, 1970; Farley & Farley, 1970; Kilpatrick, Sutker, & Dell Smith, 1976), but independent from neuroticism or anxiety (e.g., Bone, Montgomery, Sundstrom, Cowling, & Calef, 1972). Zuckerman (1974) summarized:

The general trait picture defines sensation seeking as an uninhibited, nonconforming, impulsive dominant type of extraversion. Certain features of the SSS embody one or more of these traits more than others. (p. 103)

Zuckerman (1974, 1979) has reviewed many findings that contribute to the validity of the sensation-seeking scales. Characteristic differences between persons with high and persons with low sensation-seeking scores include differences in variety of sexual relations, sexual excitability, experiences with drugs, preference for strange experiences (such as sensory deprivation or hypnosis), and preference for risky sports. Sensation seeking is related to preference for spiced food, use of alcohol, and smoking. Similar findings have been reported for extraversion by Eysenck (1967). Finally, there are relationships of sensation seeking with job preferences, preference for abstract versus concrete fields of study, and study habits.

This evidence nicely corresponds with the description of the typical impulsive person as described by Kipnis (1971). It should be noticed that in Kipnis' study, impulsiveness was assessed by a questionnaire that is, according to the present authors, actually a measure of sensation seeking. Sensation seekers (or, in Kipnis' terminology, impulsive subjects) are, in comparison with low sensation seekers (low impulsive people), characterized as (a) nonconformist; (b) not very susceptible to feelings of guilt, shame, and fear; (c) not very susceptible to influences of others; and (d) strongly responsive to social stimuli. Moreover, impulsiveness (sensation seeking) is related to a tendency toward antisocial behavior. Impulsive persons show a preference for careers involving social interaction and underachieve in studies that require attending to the same intellectual problems (e.g., mathematics) for a long time.

To summarize, the sensation seeker is someone who has a strong need for varied and new experiences in many areas, does not easily adapt himself to conventional social norms and values, and pursues his independence from others. Sensation seeking is related to social extraversion, impulsiveness, and psychopathy, but unrelated to anxiety. Furthermore, there is strong evidence for a biological basis of sensation seeking.

Biological Basis of Sensation Seeking

Constitutional factors, such as the excitation-inhibition balance in the nervous system, are probably important determinants of individual differences in the optimal level of arousal or stimulation.[1] Concerning this postulate, Zuckerman's theory is highly similar to Eysenck's (1967) neuropsychological theory, which concentrates on the personality dimension extraversion-introversion. Since Zuckerman's theory is of a more recent date than Eysenck's, a brief discussion of the latter will be presented first.

Eysenck (1963, 1967) postulated that more introverted people have a lower optimal level (or preferred external level) of stimulation than the more extraverted. Introverts are more sensitive to weak stimulation than are extraverts; at the same time, however, they are relatively hypersensitive to strong, quickly repeated, and noxious stimuli. These differences are probably accounted for by differences in receptor, ascending reticular activating system, cortex feedback

---

[1] The concepts of "optimal level of arousal" and "optimal level of stimulation" are, in the opinion of the authors, not interchangeable. Their precise relationship, however, is still unclear.

mechanisms that control stimulus input and the level of cortical activation. An implication of this paradigm is, according to Eysenck (1967), that there is

> a certain degree of stimulus hunger (sensation seeking, arousal seeking) in the extravert and a certain degree of stimulus aversion in the introvert. (p. 110)

Testable deductions from this theory include a relatively low tolerance for pain stimuli in introverts, and a relatively low tolerance for sensory deprivation together with a high rate of operant stimulation seeking behavior in extraverts. Evidence for these predictions is generally supportive, although not always unequivocal (see Feij, 1979).

A similar theory has been presented by Sales and co-workers (Sales, 1971; Sales, Guydosh, & Jacono, 1974). In Sales' opinion, the optimum level of internal evoked stimulation tends to be similar for all people. Some people (reducers), however, have a nervous system that dampens down incoming stimulation; they need stronger, more complex, or more varied stimulation to reach the internal optimum level than do augmenters, who possess a nervous system that enhances incoming stimulation.[2] It should be noticed that the assumption of a similar internal optimal level of stimulation is different from the position held by both Eysenck and Zuckerman. It has frequently been suggested (e.g., Sales et al., 1974) that the augmentation-reduction dimension (Petrie, 1967) and the dimension of weakness-strength (in excitation) of the nervous system (Teplov, 1964) have a common substratum. Characteristic of the strong nervous system, then, would be a chronic input reduction, leading to a strong need for stimulation and extraverted or sensation-seeking behavior.

Using this type of theory as a frame of reference, Neary and Zuckerman (1976) have tested the prediction that the electrodermal orienting response (OR) on new stimuli would be greater for persons with a high score on the general SSS than for low-scoring persons. The hypothesis was verified using simple and complex visual stimuli and 70-dB tones, and the results were interpreted as indicating a relatively high arousability in sensation seekers. The prediction, however, that sensation seekers would also show a relatively rapid OR habituation, as a consequence of a strong inhibition of arousal, was not borne out.

Considering Zuckerman's and Eysenck's theories together, there appears to be one -- at least terminological -- contradiction: in Eysenck's model, introverts are characterized by strong chronic excitation, or high arousability, but Zuckerman sees high arousability as a property of sensation seekers (i.e., extraverts). There are more of these terminological or conceptual obscurities within this field of research. It should be clear that many of these controversial issues would disappear if arousability were to be more appropriately defined, that is, if questions were to be taken into consideration such as "arousability with respect to what -- weak or strong stimuli?" There is, for instance, another contradiction apparent, and this concerns the relationship between the augmentation-reduction dimension and personality. In Eysenck's theory, extraverts are reducers and introverts are augmenters (assessed by the Kinaesthetic Figural Aftereffect, KFA; Petrie, 1967). In a study by Zuckerman, Murtaugh, and Siegel (1974), by contrast, high disinhibitors (i.e., extraverts) appear to be augmenters, whereas low disinhibitors (i.e., introverts) are reducers (assessed by the cortical averaged evoked response (AER) on stimuli of increasing intensity). It seems that the meaning of augmentation and reduction is dependent on the intensity of stimulation

---

[2]In this case, augmentation-reduction is operationalized as a score on the Kinaesthetic Figural Aftereffect (KFA) test of Petrie (1967).

used: moderately intense (tactile) stimuli in the KFA task, stimuli of high intensity in the AER method.[3]

Following an earlier suggestion of Buchsbaum (1971), Zuckerman et al. (1974) made a comparison between the AER amplitudes on visual stimuli of different intensities for people with high scores and for those with low scores on the various subscales of the SSS-IV. Zuckerman et al. found that persons with high disinhibition scores had AERs that increased with intensity of stimulation, while the AERs of low disinhibitors tended to decrease. The slope of the AER-stimulus intensity function was not related to the scores on the other SSS subscales, nor was it related to extraversion. The authors concluded that protective transmarginal inhibition is absent in people who have high scores on the disinhibition scale, which corresponds with the absence of effective inhibition in their behavior. These people are probably characterized by a strong nervous system, as conceptualized by Teplov (1964): they possess a neural set-point that permits them to accept and process higher levels of stimulation before their corticoreticular inhibitory threshold is reached. The conclusion that high disinhibitors may have a strong nervous system fits in with the results of a study by Orlebeke (1972), showing that there is a specific relationship between strength of the nervous system and 16PF-F (surgency), that is, a personality trait akin to disinhibition. Hence, it appears that the personality traits of surgency and disinhibition, strength of the nervous system, augmentation, and transmarginal inhibition are all related to the same mechanisms of input modulation.

Concerning the theory linking stimulation seeking and chronic hypoarousal (e.g., Quay, 1965; Eysenck, 1967; Hare, 1970; and Farley, 1973), Zuckerman (1974) has taken a somewhat different position. For example, Zuckerman pointed out that student subjects with high SSS scores have not been found to be physiologically hypoaroused. Moreover, the OR study of Neary and Zuckerman (1976) shows that the sensation seeker is more, rather than less, aroused by the presentation of new stimuli of moderate intensity. Obviously, high and low sensation seekers do not differ in initial level of arousal, but rather differ in the amount of variation of stimuli needed to maintain their level of arousal.

There is reason to believe that the need for strong and varied stimulation has a biological base. This need is characteristic of many kinds of behavior, such as adventure and thrill seeking, rejection of conventional norms and authority, and drinking and smoking. It seems wise, however, to keep in mind that sensation seeking is a multidimensional concept. Consequently, Zuckerman's (1974) suggestion must be reiterated: the various expressions of sensation seeking might have a different genotype.

RESEARCH WITH DUTCH SENSATION-SEEKING SCALES

In the course of a broad research project, aimed at the study of physiological correlates of personality traits, a self-report questionnaire was constructed measuring four traits: extraversion-introversion, emotionality, impulsiveness, and sensation seeking (Feij, 1979). The sensation-seeking scale (which is comparable with Zuckerman's General Sensation Seeking Scale from the SSS-IV) consists of 21 Likert-type items, whereas the Zuckerman scales consist of forced-choice items. The items are for the greater part (about 45%) of the TAS type. Satisfactory homogeneity indexes were found in two student samples ($\alpha = .83$ and .80, respectively). The retest-reliability after an interval of 3 weeks was .81.

---

[3] Buchsbaum and Silverman (1968), however, have reported a certain amount of common variance between AER and KFA augmentation-reduction.

Personality Correlates

As would be expected, moderately positive correlations (ranging between about .30 and .40) are usually found between the sensation-seeking score on the one hand and scores on extraversion and impulsiveness on the other. Sensation seeking is unrelated to a person's level of trait anxiety or emotionality.

The construct validity of our general SSS has been investigated in several studies, a summary of which follows.

First, a factor analysis was carried out on the intercorrelations among the scores on the four scales of Feij's questionnaire and the scores on two well-validated Dutch questionnaires: the Amsterdam Biographic Questionnaire (Wilde, 1963), measuring social extraversion, neuroticism, and psychosomatism; and the Achievement Motivation Test (Hermans, 1967), measuring intellectual achievement motivation, negative fear of failure (debilitating anxiety), and positive fear of failure (facilitating anxiety). These tests were administered to 90 students. A varimax rotation on four factors was carried out, and the result is presented in Table 1.

TABLE 1. Varimax Rotated Four-Factor Solution

Variable	Factor				h^2
	I	II	III	IV	
Neuroticism	.82	.02	.26	.14	.75
Social extraversion	−.09	.83	.05	.28	.77
Psychosomatism	.44	−.09	.25	−.18	.30
Achievement motivation	−.06	.04	−.68	.23	.52
Fear of failure (negative)	.70	−.09	−.31	−.40	.75
Fear of failure (positive)	−.19	.07	−.07	.71	.54
Extraversion	−.09	.81	.10	−.12	.69
Emotionality	.65	−.10	−.14	−.21	.50
Impulsiveness	−.24	.28	.44	.16	.36
Sensation seeking	.17	.26	.39	.14	.27
Eigenvalue	2.44	1.52	.85	.65	5.45
Percent of variance	24.40	15.20	8.50	6.50	

Note. Factor I = anxiety, Factor II = extraversion, Factor III = lack of constraint, and Factor IV = fear of failure.

The first two factors are designated anxiety and extraversion, respectively.
The fourth factor is a specific fear-of-failure dimension. The factor of interest here is Factor 3. The positive pole of this factor represents a weak achievement motivation, a strong sensation-seeking tendency, impulsiveness, and low fear.
This factor can be labeled lack of constraint and is apparently related to weak
superego strength, that is, low acceptance of conventional norms and values.[4]
This cluster of traits is characteristic of the psychopathic type as described
by Kipnis (1971). Concerning the loadings (with opposite sign) of sensation
seeking and achievement motivation (i.e., a specimen of a conventional value) on
one factor, it is interesting to re-examine the results of studies of Gorman
(1970), Zuckerman et al. (1972), and Jacobs (1975), indicating that there is a
stable pattern of relations between sensation seeking and scores on Cattell's
16PF scales. In all these studies, sensation seeking was related to a typical
profile of 16PF scores, including dominance, weak superego, bohemian introversion,
and radicalism. In a previous factor analytic study (Feij, 1974), it was demonstrated that the achievement-motivation scale had a significant loading on a
superego factor that was determined by the very same 16PF subtests.

Recently, colleagues in the Department of Clinical Psychology of the Free University (Bats, Cassee, Gazendam, Slot, & Beenen, 1979), carried out a factor analysis
on the correlations among several tests that were administered to 100 applicants
for psychotherapy. Results indicated that the general sensation-seeking scale
had positive loadings on two factors: an extraversion factor and a constraint
factor loaded by three subscales of the Stern's Activities Index. These subscales were change (i.e., unorganized, changeable behavior), supplication (autonomy vs. dependency of others), and deference (a rebellious attitude vs. sub-
mission to superior others). Hence, it appears that sensation seeking is related
to two largely orthogonal dimensions: social extraversion and lack of constraint
(independency, or rejection of conventional norms and values). Similar conclusions have been drawn by Zuckerman (1974) and Kipnis (1971).

Considering the relationship between sensation seeking and acceptance of norms
and authority, the following observation seems well worth mentioning. In Feij's
questionnaire there is one item bearing upon a person's perception of the way he
has been brought up: "I was rather strictly brought up." It was found that the
average sensation-seeking score was higher for people who endorsed this item (N=145)
than for those who did not (N=301): t=2.08, p<.05. One explanation of this relationship might be that sensation seekers have experienced their otherwise normal parental home as rather restrictive because of their low tolerance of authority.
Another interpretation, however, could be that a strict pattern of upbringing
stimulates the development of sensation-seeking behavior.

Behavioral Correlates

The relationship between the general sensation-seeking scale and several variables that may be viewed as indexes of the need for stimulation or arousal (e.g.,
smoking, coffee, and amount of sleep) has been studied.

Need for smoking and coffee. In three samples of sophomores (Ns = 254, 111, and
129), higher sensation-seeking scores for heavy smokers (persons who report

---

[4]Most personality theorists (e.g., Cattell, Eysenck, and Royce) agree that
introversion-extraversion, anxiety or neuroticism, and superego are the most
important dimensions of personality. Somewhat different labels for the third
dimension are sometimes used. For instance, Eysenck (1977, p. 407) views
superego as the opposite pole of psychoticism. Tellegen (1979, personal
communication) uses the term "constraint."

smoking more than 15 cigarettes per day), than for moderate or nonsmokers (p < .01) were found. Amount of smoking was also related to extraversion (compare Eysenck, 1965), but his relationship was weaker and significant in only two samples. The relationship between the need for coffee (assessed by one global questionnaire item: "I can't do without coffee in the morning") and personality was studied in two samples. It could be demonstrated in one of the samples (N = 254), that people who endorsed this item were higher in sensation seeking (p < .01) than were those who indicated no strong need for coffee.

Sleep habits. Furthermore, the relationship between the sensation-seeking score and self-reported sleep habits was investigated. Persons in two samples (Ns = 254 and 111) were asked to estimate (a) their habitual amount of sleep, (b) their preferred amount of sleep, and (c) their minimum amount of sleep needed. It could be expected that sensation seekers, because of their need for stimulation, frequently engage in situations that are rich in (social) stimuli and that prevent them from sleeping. Furthermore, a negative relationship between sensation seeking and need for sleeping might be predicted from theories concerning arousability or strength of the nervous system (see Vando, 1970), because a strong nervous system is one that can withstand long and concentrated excitation without passing into an inhibitory state. In both samples, there was a small, but significant, negative correlation between the sensation-seeking score and the habitual amount of sleep (rho = -.26, p < .01, and rho = -.18, p < .10, respectively). [5] Sensation seeking was also consistently related to minimum amount of sleep needed (rho = -.18, p < .01, and rho = -.23, p < .01, respectively). Impulsiveness and extraversion were also related to sleep habits, but the relationships were weaker. Similar trends have been reported by van Doornen (1978). Moreover, the study showed that sleep habits are related to emotionality (high-emotional persons needed more sleep than low-emotional persons).

In other words, there are at least two largely orthogonal factors accounting for differences in amount of sleep: emotionality and sensation seeking. Perhaps sensation seekers frequently seek out situations that satisfy their need for strong stimulation, so that little time is left for sleeping, at least during the night; other results of the study indicate that high sensation seekers sleep more frequently in the daytime than do low sensation seekers. The evidence that sensation seekers feel well with relatively little sleep suggests a biological explanation. The hypothesis of a biological foundation of the relationship between sleep and sensation seeking fits in with the results of a study reported by Coursey, Buchsbaum, and Frankel (1975), showing that sensation seekers are more efficient sleepers than are low sensation seekers. Coursey et al. found a correlation of .68 between the score on Zuckerman's general SSS and percentage of efficient sleep (defined by electroencephalogram (EEG) parameters).

In short, sensation seekers seem to sleep for relatively short periods, and they need little sleep; but when they sleep, it is sound. Future research should attempt to answer the question of whether there is a link between biological and social explanations of the relationship between personality and sleep habits.

A Psychophysiological Study

The previous research was carried out with the Dutch version of the general SSS (Feij, 1979). After the construction of this test, a multidimensional SSS was

---

[5]There are all sorts of confounding variables that might have a deleterious effect on the correlations. High sensation-seeking subjects may be expected to fall asleep quickly, once they have decided to go to bed, or when the situation is boring.

developed. Taking the alternatives of the forced-choice items of Zuckerman's
SSS-IV as point of departure, an item pool was composed, consisting of 65 Likert-
type items. The items were administered to a sample of 129 undergraduate students. A factor analysis on the intercorrelations among the items of this preliminary SSS yielded four principal factors, which were rotated with a varimax
procedure. The rotated factors were similar to the four dimensions of sensation
seeking outlined by Zuckerman: disinhibition (DIS), thrill and adventure seeking (TAS), boredom susceptibility (BS) and experience seeking (ES). Next,
factor scales were composed with reasonably high internal consistencies (α coefficients
between .74 and .84). The intercorrelations among the scales were of moderate
size (the mean r was .31 for males and .36 for females). The scores on the four
scales were significantly correlated with the aforementioned general scale (r was
.68, .63, .36, and .45 for DIS, TAS, BS, and ES, respectively).

Several psychophysiological experiments have been carried out with these scales.
One such study is reported here (see also Orlebeke & Feij, 1979).

The present study is concerned with the relationship between the disinhibition
dimension and differences in reactivity of the nervous system as shown by the
galvanic skin response (GSR) and the phasic heart-rate reaction to stimulation.

Among the several dimensions of sensation seeking, disinhibition seems to be the
trait with the most marked biological basis (Zuckerman, 1979). As Zuckerman
et al. (1974) have demonstrated, disinhibition is related to the reaction of the
central nervous system (viz, augmentation or reduction of the AER) to stimulation of varying intensity; whereas other sensation-seeking dimensions, or generalized sensation seeking are not related to it. Disinhibition might therefore be
related to "strength of the nervous system," as conceptualized by Teplov (1964).
Following this assumption, high disinhibitors are people with a nervous system
that enhances stimulus input and that can endure intense stimulation. Low disinhibitors, on the contrary, possess a nervous system that dampens strong stimulation by generating "transmarginal inhibition," or by responding defensively.

Neary and Zuckerman (1976) have reported a positive relationship between the
score on the general sensation-seeking scale and the amplitude of the GSR to
the first of a series of stimuli (visual stimuli in one study, tones in another).
They concluded that people with a strong sensation-seeking need are characterized
by a high degree of excitability of the central and autonomic nervous systems.
Unfortunately, their study was not designed to answer the question whether GSR
is related to one or more of the specific dimensions of sensation seeking, and
especially whether there is a positive relationship with disinhibition. Would
such a relationship be expected? The answer to this question is dependent on
several factors (e.g., the stimulus intensity which is used).

The GSR is frequently supposed to be one manifestation of the orienting response.
According to Sokolov (1963), the orienting reflex (OR) is a complex, nonspecific
reaction, resulting in optimal adaptation of sensory systems to stimulation, and
augmentation of stimulus input. As pointed out by Orlebeke (1973), the GSR amplitude is not necessarily a pure measure of the orienting response. In some cases,
a large GSR must be viewed as an indication of a defensive reflex (DR) -- an
involuntary response to strong or painful stimulation, or a reaction aimed at
input reduction. It is possible to discover whether a GSR can be interpreted
either as an OR or a DR by the simultaneous registration of the phasic heart-
rate change following the presentation of the stimulus. Graham and Clifton (1966)
have demonstrated that the OR manifests itself as a short heart-rate deceleration
and the DR as a heart-rate acceleration.

Following this line of reasoning, the following predictions were tested:

1. People with a high disinhibition score are those who possess a strong nervous system, and their reactions to stimuli of a certain critical level of intensity will be predominantly input enhancing. By contrast, low disinhibition people possess a weak nervous system and will show input reduction. This difference will be observed in the heart-rate reactions: High-disinhibition persons will react with a short heart-rate deceleration (OR), and low-disinhibition persons with heart-rate acceleration (DR).

2. The GSR amplitude will not differ between high- and low-disinhibition people because both orienting and defensive reactions can result in a large GSR. It should be noted that, although disinhibition will be unrelated to GSR amplitude, a positive relationship of GSR with sensation seeking as a generalized trait is to be expected.

3. People with a strong general sensation-seeking need will be strongly reactive to new stimuli; they will thus show relatively large initial GSRs, extending the results of Neary and Zuckerman (1976).

Forty-nine psychology students (26 males and 23 females) participated as subjects in the study. These students were selected on disinhibition (DIShigh or DISlow) and emotionality (EMOhigh or EMOlow) from a larger sample of 135 students. The DIShigh subgroup consisted of 14 students scoring in the upper quartile of the distribution in the larger sample; the DISlow subgroup consisted of 11 people scoring in the lower quartile. The number of subjects in the EMOhigh and the EMOlow subgroups was 9 and 15, respectively. The selection of subjects was carried out in such a way that only people with average emotionality scores (2nd and 3rd quartiles) were placed in the DIShigh or in the DISlow subgroup, whereas those in the extreme emotionality groups had average inhibition scores. That is, the effects of disinhibition and emotionality could be measured independently of each other. The level of emotionality was controlled in this way, since there is strong evidence that emotionality (or neuroticism) is related to physiological reactivity. Because the main focus in this chapter is on disinhibition, the results concerning emotionality are not reported here (see Orlebeke & Feij, 1979).

As a consequence of this method of selection, the total sample did not only consist of subjects with extreme DIS scores, but also of those with moderate DIS scores (viz, subjects with low and high emotionality). The variance of disinhibition scores was therefore sufficiently large to justify (parametric) correlational analysis in the total sample, in addition to comparisons between extreme DIS subgroups. The mean and standard deviation of the disinhibition score in the total sample were almost identical to the values obtained in the larger group of students from which the sample had been selected. This was also the case with the scores on other measures of sensation seeking to be used for additional correlational analysis in this study: thrill and adventure seeking (TAS), boredom susceptibility (BS), experience seeking (ES), and a general measure of sensation seeking (see the previous section).

Method. A series of 10 tones of 80 dB and 1000 cps was presented to each person, with an irregular intertrial interval (mean ISI, 1 min). This stimulus intensity was chosen since it has been demonstrated (among others, by Orlebeke & Passchier, 1976) that around this stimulus intensity a shift from phasic heart-rate deceleration (OR) to heart-rate acceleration (DR) is found. Skin conductance and heart rate were continuously monitored with a Beckman polygraph. GSR amplitude and habituation speed (that is, the number of trials to reach the criterion of two successive nonresponses) were measured. The GSR was measured in μMho's × 1000. The GSR amplitude was converted into Δlog C, that is, a measure that is relatively independent of the prestimulus conductance level. The phasic heart-rate reaction was measured in beats per minute on a $\frac{1}{2}$-sec basis during 5 sec after

stimulus onset. Because first response effects were of prime importance, only
the first three trials were analyzed.

Results. A comparison between the heart rate and skin-conductance responses of
the DIShigh and the DISlow subjects showed that the initial GSR amplitude and
the average GSR on the first three trials did not differ for either group. Although there were no differences in GSR amplitude, the prediction concerning a
difference in heart rate was verified. The mean phasic heart-rate change of
people with high and low DIS scores, respectively, is shown in Figure 1. The
reactions are averaged across the first three trials.

Analysis of variance yielded a significant DISlow/DIShigh × trials × time interaction ($F_{(20/420)}$ = 1.61, p < .05). As is apparent from Figure 1, subjects in
the high disinhibition group react with heart-rate deceleration (OR), and those
in the low-disinhibition group with heart-rate acceleration (DR). This difference
was highly significant for the first trial (see Orlebeke & Feij, 1979). There was
no difference in prestimulus heart-rate level between the disinhibition groups.
Support for the view that the GSR of the low-disinhibition people can be interpreted as a defensive response comes from another result of this study, namely,
a higher rate of GSR habituation for people in the high-disinhibition group than
for those in the low-disinhibition group (t = 2.56, p < .01). Slow habituation
is a characteristic of the defensive reflex.

Product-moment correlations (in the total sample) between the several measures of
sensation seeking, the amplitude of the GSR on the first three stimuli, and speed
of GSR habituation are presented in Table 2.

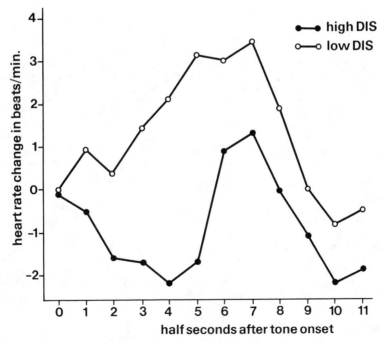

FIGURE 1. Mean heart rate change for both subjects with high disinhibition
scores and for those with low disinhibition scores.

TABLE 2.   Product moment correlations between measures of sensation seeking,
GSR's on the first three trials, and number of trials to habituation

SSS measures	GSR (Δlog C)			Trials to habituation
	Trial 1	2	3	
DIS	.08	-.05	.14	-.20
TAS	.28*	.05	-.04	-.33*
BS	-.12	-.13	-.07	-.16
ES	-.08	-.24	.06	-.16
General SSS	.28*	.01	-.01	-.22

*p < .05,   two-tailed

Note.   The sensation-seeking scale (SSS) measures are disinhibition (DIS),
thrill and adventure seeking (TAS), boredom susceptibility (BS), and experience seeking (ES).   GSR = galvanic skin response.

As Table 2 shows, there is a significant correlation between the general sensation-seeking score and the amplitude of the GSR on the first stimulus. This is
a replication of the result of the Neary and Zuckerman study. Of the specific
sensation-seeking subscales, only TAS was significantly related to the initial
GSR amplitude. By contrast, the other sensation-seeking dimensions were unrelated to GSR. For instance, the correlation between the DIS score and GSR was
only .08 .   The TAS scale was also the only scale that significantly correlated
with the number of trails to reach habituation. It should be noticed that initial
GSR amplitude and habituation rate were independent ($r = .08$). Furthermore, it
is worth noting that a higher rate of habituation for high than for low sensation
seekers was predicted by Neary and Zuckerman, but this prediction was not borne
out in their study.

These results provide evidence that the TAS dimension is related to the strength
of reactions to novelty of stimulation, whereas the DIS dimension specifically
relates to reactivity to intensity aspects of stimulation, or, in other words, to
protective inhibition (cf. Zuckerman et al., 1974). Consequently, the results of
this study are supportive of the suggestion of Zuckerman (1974) that the various
dimensions of sensation seeking might have a different genotypic foundation. The
DIS dimension seems to be specifically related to the capacity to tolerate high
stimulus intensity, or to the threshold of transmarginal inhibition, which is a
measure of the strength of the nervous system.

CONCLUSIONS

Considering the results of the present research as a whole, there is strong evidence supporting the following conclusions:

1. Sensation seeking, viewed as a broad and general personality trait, is related to extraversion and impulsiveness, but unrelated to anxiety. Sensation seekers do not easily internalize conventional norms and values; in contrast, they seek independence from others (cf. Kipnis, 1971; Zuckerman, 1974). This tendency toward independence might account for the finding that sensation seeking is related to perceived stringency of education. Perhaps sensation seekers view the way in which they have been brought up as rather strict, because of their anti-authoritarian attitude.

2. There is a relatively high degree of stimulus hunger in sensation seekers, shown, for example, by a large amount of smoking and a strong need for coffee. Moreover, sensation seekers sleep relatively little, probably as a consequence of frequent social activities during the night. The fact that sensation seekers also need little sleep might be accounted for by biological factors, such as a strong nervous system -- the capacity to endure long-lasting or intense stimulation.

3. A biological foundation of sensation seeking is strongly suggested both by Zuckerman's work and the results of the present research. It is now clear that general sensation seeking, and perhaps thrill and adventure seeking, is related to initial GSR amplitude or reactivity to the novelty aspect of stimulation. By contrast, the disinhibition dimension is apparently related to the intensity of stimulation. In the study of Zuckerman et al. (1974), disinhibition was related to AER augmentation, and in the study described here, it was related to the OR-DR continuum, or to the perception of the stimulation intensity. Both phenomena bear upon transmarginal inhibition and strength of the nervous system.

From this summary, it should be clear that sensation seeking is a pervasive trait, since it is related to many kinds of experience and behavior.

It is tempting to speculate about the way in which these findings concerning the physiological correlates of sensation seeking on the one hand, and complex experience and behavioral correlates on the other, could be incorporated into a developmental model of the sensation-seeking tendency. From an interactionist point of view, differences in sensation seeking should be considered in relation to biological factors in the individual and in external environmental stresses and opportunities. One possibility is the assumption of inborn differences in the threshold of responsiveness to novelty or intensity of stimulation, that form the basis of differences in curiosity and influence the perception of the social environment as more or less restrictive. It can be postulated, then, that some children tend to perceive their social environment as restrictive and avoid this restrictive pressure; whereas other children easily adjust. This difference in reaction to restrictive pressure might account for differences in internalization of norms and values presented by parents and other authorities.

The only way to gain clarity in this respect is to carry out longitudinal studies. Thomas and Chess (1977), for instance, have studied the development of several functional temperament characteristics, some of which seem relevant here: adaptability (i.e., responsivity to new or changing stimuli) and threshold of responsiveness (i.e., intensity level of stimulation that is necessary to evoke a particular response). It is suggested that future research should attempt to integrate the evidence concerning the sensation-seeking tendency in adolescents and adults with results of studies on the development of functional temperament characteristics in children.

REFERENCES

Bats, G., Cassee, A.P., Gazendam, B., Slot, W., & Beenen, F. (1979). Psychologische testvariabelen als predictoren voor indicatie bij psychotherapie. Nederlands

Tijdschrift voor de Psychologie, 34, 331-346.

Bone, R. N., & Montgomery, D. D. (1970). Extraversion, neuroticism and sensation seeking. Psychological Reports, 26, 974.

Bone, R. N., Montgomery, D. D., Sundstrom, P. E., Cowling, L. W., & Calef, R. S. (1972). Relationship of sensation seeking and anxiety. Psychological Reports, 30, 874.

Buchsbaum, M. S. (1971). Neural events and the psychophysical law. Science, 172, 502.

Buchsbaum, M. S., & Silverman, J. (1968). Stimulus intensity control and the cortical evoked response. Psychosomatic Medicine, 30, 12-22.

Coursey, R. D., Buchsbaum, M. S., & Frankel, B. L. (1975). Personality measures and evoked responses in chronic insomniacs. Journal of Abnormal Psychology, 84, 239-249.

Eysenck, H. J. (1963). Experiments with drugs. New York: Pergamon.

Eysenck, H. J. (1965). Smoking, health and personality. New York: Basic Books.

Eysenck, H. J. (1967). The biological basis of personality. Springfield, IL: Charles C Thomas.

Eysenck, H. J. (1977). Personality and factor analysis: A reply to Guilford. Psychological Bulletin, 84, 405-411.

Farley, F. H. (1967). Social desirability and dimensionality in the Sensation Seeking Scale. Acta Psychologica, 26, 89-96.

Farley, F. H. (1973). Implications for a theory of delinquency. In T. J. Myers (Chair), The sensation seeking motive. Symposium conducted at the 81st meeting of the American Psychological Association, Montreal.

Farley, F. H., & Farley, S. V. (1970). Impulsiveness, sociability, and the preference for varied experience. Perceptual and Motor Skills, 31, 47-50.

Feij, J. A. (1974). An investigation into the meaning of the Achievement Motivation Test: I. Questionnaire correlates. Nederlands Tijdschrift voor de Psychologie, 29, 171-190.

Feij, J. A. (1979). Temperament: Onderzoek naar de betekenis van extraversie, emotionaliteit, impulsiviteit en spanningsbehoefte. Lisse, The Netherlands: Swets en Zeitlinger.

Gorman, B. S. (1970). 16PF correlates of sensation seeking. Psychological Reports, 26, 741-742.

Graham, F. K., & Clifton, R. K. (1966). Heart rate change as a component of the orienting response. Psychological Bulletin, 65, 305-320.

Hare, R. D. (1970). Psychopathy: Theory and research. New York: Wiley.

Hermans, H. J. M. (1967). Motivatie en prestatie. Amsterdam: Swets & Zeitlinger.

Jacobs, K. W. (1975). 16PF correlates of sensation seeking: An expansion and validation. Psychological Reports, 37, 1215-1218.

Kilpatrick, D. G., Sutker, P. B., & Dell Smith, A. (1976). Deviant drug and alcohol use: The role of anxiety, sensation seeking and other personality variables. In M. Zuckerman & C. D. Spielberger (Eds), Emotion and anxiety. New concepts, methods, and applications. New York: Wiley.

Kipnis, D. (1971). Character structure and impulsiveness. New York: Academic Press.

Neary, R. S., & Zuckerman, M. (1976). Sensation seeking, trait and state anxiety, and the electrodermal orienting response. Psychophysiology, 13, 205-211.

Orlebeke, J. F. (1972). Aktivering, extraversie en sterkte van het zenuwstelsel. Assen: van Gorcum.

Orlebeke, J. F. (1973). Electrodermal, vasomotor and heartrate correlates of extra-version and neuroticism. Psychophysiology, 10, 211-212.

Orlebeke, J. F., & Feij, J. A. (1979). The orienting reflex as a personality cor-relate. In H. D. Kimmel, E. H. van Olst, & J. F. Orlebeke (Eds.), The orienting reflex in humans. Hilsdale: Erlbaum.

Orlebeke, J. F., & Passchier, J. (1976). Organismic, stimulus and task determin-ants of phasic and tonic heart rate and skin conductance changes. Biological Psychology, 4, 173-184.

Petrie, A. (1967). Individuality in pain and suffering. Chicago: University Press.

Quay, H. C. (1965). Psychopathic personality as pathological stimulation seeking. American Journal of Psychiatry, 122, 180-183.

Sales, S. M. (1971). Need for stimulation as a factor in social behavior. Journal of Personality and Social Psychology, 19, 124-134.

Sales, S. M., Guydosh, R. M., & Jacono, W. (1974). Relationship between "strength of the nervous system" and the need for stimulation. Journal of Personality and Social Psychology, 29, 16-22.

Sokolov, E. N. (1963). Perception and the conditioned reflex. London: Pergamon.

Teplov, B. M. (1964). Problems in the study of general types of higher nervous activity in man and animals. In J. A. Gray (Ed.), Pavlov's typology. London: Pergamon.

Thomas, A., & Chess, S. (1977). Temperament and development. New York: Brunner/Mazel.

Vando, A. (1970). A personality dimension related to pain tolerance. Dissertation Abstracts International, 31, 2292-2293.

Van Doornen, L. J. P. (1978). Psychologische determinanten van het hartinfarct. Re-port of the Department of Physiological Psychology, Vrije Universiteit, Amsterdam.

Wilde, G. J. S. (1963). Neurotische labiliteit gemeten volgens de vragenlijst-methode. Amsterdam: Van Rossen.

Zuckerman, M. (1969). Theoretical formulations: I. In J. P. Zubek (Ed.), Sensory deprivation: Fifteen years of research. New York: Appleton-Century-Crofts.

Zuckerman, M. (1971). Dimensions of sensation seeking. Journal of Consulting and Clinical Psychology, 36, 45-52.

Zuckerman, M. (1974). The sensation seeking motive. In B. A. Maher (Ed.), Progress in experimental personality research (Vol. 7). New York: Academic Press.

Zuckerman, M. (1979). Sensation seeking: Beyond the optimal level of arousal. Hilsdale: Erlbaum.

Zuckerman, M., Bone, R. N., Neary, R., Mangelsdorff, D., & Brustman, B. (1972). Who is the sensation seeker? Personality and experience correlates of the sensation seeking scales. Journal of Consulting and Clinical Psychology, 39, 308-321.

Zuckerman, M., Kolin, E. A., Price, L., & Zoob, B. J. (1964). Development of a Sensation Seeking Scale. Journal of Consulting Psychology, 28, 477-482.

Zuckerman, M., & Link, K. (1968). Construct validity for the Sensation Seeking Scale. Journal of Consulting and Clinical Psychology, 32, 420-426.

Zuckerman, M., Murtaugh, T., & Siegel, J. (1974), Sensation seeking and cortical augmenting-reducing. Psychophysiology, 11, 535-542.

III

DEVELOPMENTAL ISSUES

13

The Behavioral Study of Temperament

Alexander Thomas and Stella Chess

The investigation of the significance of individual differences for psychological development and functioning can be approached on many levels -- genetic, biochemical, neurophysiologic, behavioral, intrapsychic, and environmental. In any one study, consideration of the interaction of two or more of these separate levels may be desirable, or even necessary, even if the major focus of interest is on one dimension.

INITIAL CONCEPTUALIZATIONS

Our own research interests over the past 25 years in the issue of individual differences have emphasized the behavioral level of investigation. Behavior can be described objectively, descriptively, and concretely. The formulation of categories of behavioral organization and criteria for their rating can be done by inductive content analysis of the empirically gathered data. With this approach, an a priori commitment to any specific conceptualization of the origins of individual differences in behavior, whether genetic, biochemical, neurophysiological, or psychophysiological, becomes unnecessary.

On the other hand, it is true that any systematic study of behavior, as with the investigation of any natural phenomenon, must start with some set of theoretical constructs. We have used the term temperament to refer to the how of behavior. It differs from ability, which is concerned with the what and how well of behaving; and from motivation, which accounts for why a person does what he is doing. This conceptualization of temperament is similar to previous formulations by some other workers, notably Cattell (1950) and Guilford (1959). With this formulation, temperament defines the way in which a person behaves, rather than the level of performance or the motivation of the behavior. Two children may dress themselves with equal skillfulness or ride a bicycle with the same dexterity and have the same motives for engaging in these activities. Two adolescents may display similar learning ability and intellectual interests, and their academic goals may coincide. Two adults may show the same technical expertness in their work and have the same reason for devoting themselves to their jobs. Yet, these two children, adolescents, or adults may differ significantly with regard to the quickness with which they move; the ease with which they approach a new physical environment, social situation, or task; the intensity and character of their mood expression; and the effort required by others to distract them when they are absorbed in an activity.

INTERACTIONIST VIEW

Our study of behavior, from the beginning, has been predicated on a firm commitment to an interactionist concept of the developmental process (Thomas and Chess,

1957). In other words, temperament is never considered by itself, but always in
its relationship to, or interaction with, a person's abilities, motives, and external environmental stresses and opportunities. This interactive process produces certain consequences in behavior, which then interact with recurrent and
new features of the environment to reinforce certain previous patterns, or at-
tenuate some, or produce new behavioral characteristics, or all three. To analyze
this constantly evolving process of development requires the view that new behaviors or personality attributes that appear at new age-stage developmental
periods may represent older patterns in new form, as is commonly assumed, but
may also constitute the emergence of qualitatively new psychological characteristics. This leads to the concept that the developmental process may show discontinuities as well as continuities, a formulation which has been emphasized in
a review by Sameroff (1975). (Sameroff uses the term transactional as equivalent
to the term interactionist.) The general formulation of the interactionist position is elegantly stated by Schneirla and Rosenblatt (1961, p. 230).

> Behavior is typified by reciprocal stimulative relationships ...
> Mammalian behavioral development is best conceived as a unitary system
> of processes changing progressively under the influence of an intimate
> interrelationship of factors of maturation and of experience -- with
> maturation defined as the developmental contribution of tissue growth
> and differentiation and their secondary processes, experience as the
> effects of stimulation and its organic traces on behavior.

For human psychological development, both Freud and Pavlov formulated the begin-
nings of an interactionist approach. One of the major achievements of the psychoanalytic movement has been the demonstration of how much that had previously been
labeled as heredity or constitutional was really the result of the interaction
between the young child and his effective environment. Pavlov, on his part,
showed how biology and life experience are integrated in the formulation of the
conditioned reflex. But neither Freud nor Pavlov could develop the logic of a
dynamics of interactionism. With the limitations of their biological position
and the absence of knowledge regarding the social nature of the developmental
process, only the first steps were possible.

As a consequence, formulations of human psychological development were dominated
either by simplistic linear concepts of drive reduction derived primarily from
psychoanalytic theory, or stimulus-response paradigms reflecting Pavlovian animal
conditioning data, or static personality trait concepts arising from academic
psychological studies. A number of developmental psychologist, however, did
suggest formulations that emphasized an interactionist model (Lewin, 1935;
Murphy, 1947; Sears, 1951; Stern, 1927). The most definitive statement in this
period preceding the late 1950s came perhaps from the Russian psychologist
Vygotsky in the early 1930s:

> We believe that child development is a complex dialectical process
> characterized by periodicity, unevenness in the development of different
> functions, metamorphosis or qualitative transformation of one form into
> another, intertwining of external and internal factors, and adaptive
> processes which overcome impediments that the child encounters (1978,
> p. 73).

The dichotomization of biology and culture, of heredity-constitution and life
experience, however, continued to dominate much of psychiatric and psychological
thinking until recently. Thus, when we began, in the mid-1950s, to explore the
possible significance of the infant's own intrinsic behavioral style on later
development, our psychiatric colleagues, with few exceptions, assumed we were
returning to some outdated and discredited constitutionalist view. Polite, un-
convinced nods met our insistence that the polarization of constitution and

environment as mutually exclusive forces was artificial and mechanical, that the influence of constitution could not be understood without a simultaneous considera- tion of the influence of environment, and vice versa.

The past ten years, however, has witnessed a dramatic change. Leading research workers in developmental psychology and longitudinal behavior studies (Bell, 1968; Clarke and Clarke, 1976; Kagan, 1971; McCall, 1977; Murphy & Moriarity, 1976; Rutter, 1972; Sameroff, 1975; Spanier, Lerner, & Aquilino, 1978; Vaillant, 1977) have helped to bring a dynamic interactionist viewpoint into the mainstream of psychological and psychiatric theory. These workers have all emphasized, from the findings of their own studies and their reviews of the literature, that developmental processes cannot be understood in terms of linear, static models. All affirm the necessity of "a dynamic interactional conception of individual and social changes across the life-span, social contexts, and history" (Spanier et al., 1978, p. 328).

This interactionist view of behavior development has been reinforced by data from the fields of neurobiology and neurochemistry on the reciprocal relationships among brain, behavior, and environment. Mammals raised without exposure to pat- terned visual stimuli are subsequently deficient in the ability to learn visual discrimination habits (Riesen, 1960). Rats kept in a lively environment show distinct changes in brain anatomy and chemistry compared with animals kept in isolation (Bennett, Diamond, Krech, & Rosensweig, 1964).

Psychological processes can influence the susceptibility to some infections, to some neoplastic processes, and to some aspects of humoral and cell-mediated immune processes, and these psychosocial effects may be related to hypothalmic activity (Stein, Schiavi, & Camerino, 1976). There is impressive evidence that behavioral events can alter neurochemical function and that altered neurochemical function can change behavior (Barchas, Akil, Elliot, Holman, & Watson, 1978). These find- ings of necessity come primarily from animal studies, but they affirm the validity of the interactionist conceptualization of development.

GOODNESS VERSUS POORNESS OF FIT

In analyzing the nature of the temperament-environment interactive process, we have found the concept of goodness of fit and the related ideas of consonance and dissonance to be useful. Goodness of fit results when the properties of the environment and its expectations and demands are in accord with the organism's own capacities, characteristics, and style of behaving. When this consonance between organism and environment is present, optimal development in a progressive direction is possible. Conversely, poorness of fit involves discrepancies and dissonances between environmental opportunities and demands and the capacities and characteristics of the organism, so that distorted development and maladap- tive functioning occur. Goodness of fit is never an abstraction, but is always goodness of fit in terms of the values and demands of a given culture or socio- economic group.

It should be stated that goodness of fit does not imply an absence of stress and conflict. Quite the contrary. These are inevitable concomitants of the develop- mental process, in which new expectations and demands for change and progressively higher levels of functioning occur continuously as the child grows older. Demands, stresses, and conflicts, when consonant with the child's developmental potentials and capacities for mastery, may be constructive in their consequences and should not be considered as an inevitable cause of behavioral disturbance. The issue involved in disturbed behavioral functioning is rather one of excessive stress resulting from poorness of fit and dissonance between environmental expectation and demands and the capacities of the child at a particular level of development.

The concept of goodness of fit has also been applied by Dubos (1965) as a measure of physical health.

> Health can be regarded as an expression of fitness to the environment, as a state of adaptedness .... The words health and disease are meaningful only when defined in terms of a given person functioning in a given physical and social environment (pp. 350-351).

IMPLICATIONS OF THE INTERACTIONIST VIEW

An interactionist view emphasizes that behavioral attributes must at all times be considered in their reciprocal relationship with other characteristics of the organism and in their interaction with environmental opportunities, demands, and expectations. The consequences of this process of interaction may in turn modify or change selective features of behavior. The new behavior may then modify or change recurrent or new environmental influences. In addition, new environmental features may emerge independently or as the result of the previous or ongoing organism-environment interactive process. The same process may modify or change abilities, motives, behavioral style, and psychodynamic defenses.

Development thus becomes a fluid, dynamic process that may reinforce, or modify, or change specific psychological patterns at all age periods. Such a concept of development can be called homeodynamic, in contrast to those formulations that conceptualize the interplay or organism and environment as achieving one or another form of homeostatic equilibrium.

The interactionist approach must be distinguished from the simpler and essentially static interactive model. (The apparent similarity of the two words is one reason some workers prefer the term transactional to interactional.) The interactive model attempts to overcome a unidimensional approach, in which, for example, only heredity-constitution or environment is emphasized, by creating a two-dimensional structure of an additive nature. Good constitution plus good environment leads to a good outcome; poor constitution plus poor environment leads to a poor outcome. Intermediate outcomes are the result of a good-poor combination. Sameroff (1975, p. 290) pointed out:

> [This model] is insufficient to facilitate our understanding of the actual mechanisms leading to later outcomes. The major reason behind the inadequacy of this model is that neither constitution nor environment are necessarily constant over time. At each moment, month, or year the characteristics of both the child and his environment change in important ways. Moreover, these differences are interdependent and change as a function of their mutual influence on one another.

Stimulus input, the characteristics of central nervous system organization, and behavioral output are all complex and multifaceted. None of these can be encompassed by simple bipolar drive-reduction or stimulus-response models. The effect of any stimulus depends on many factors, and so does the significance of the behavioral output. Thus, for example, someone's choice to sit alone or in the front or back of a room, can have many different meanings, which cannot be subsumed under a bipolar rating scheme such as extraversion-introversion. Furthermore, the behavior itself may have feedback effect on the stimulus.

An interactionist view also demands that the social context of behavior must not be ignored or narrowed or distorted, as happens in drive-reduction, stimulus-response, and static global trait psychology. Behavioral data must at all times be gathered and analyzed within the specific content of the environmental situation in which it occurs. A priori hierarchical judgments of the relative importance of specific behavioral styles, norms, individuals, family constellations, and socio-cultural judgments must be avoided. Specific characterizations of behavior in specific contexts are necessary, rather than global labels and ratings, whether of the child, the parent, the family, or people in the larger social environment. The evaluation and analysis of behavioral constellations at any age period re-quires "the delineation of those <u>specific</u> attributes of parental attitudes and practices and of other intra- and extrafamilial environmental factors that are interacting with the specific consequences for psychological development" (Thomas, Chess, & Birch, 1968, p. 184).

LONGITUDINAL BEHAVIORAL STUDIES

We have pursued our investigation of temperamental individuality and its func-tional significance for normal and deviant psychological development through several longitudinal studies. Cross-sectional studies are considerably more economical and markedly less time consuming, but their effectiveness is primarily limited to the delineation of group trends and comparisons. "The cross-sectional approach can never satisfy the objective of a study which requires the measure-ment of the change in a trait through time in a given individual" (Kodlin & Thompson, 1958, p. 8).

The New York Longitudinal Study (NYLS) is our first and most intensively studied group. Sample collection was begun in 1956 and completed 6 years later. Of the original 138 subjects, 5 were lost to the study in the first few years; the re-mainder are still being followed. The families are of middle- or upper-middle-class background, and almost all parents were born in the United States. There are 85 families involved; many have two or more siblings enrolled in the study. Data collection was begun in all cases in early infancy.

To obtain a population of contrasting socioeconomic background, we initiated a second longitudinal study in 1961 of 95 children of working-class Puerto Rican parents. These families were mostly intact and stable; 86 percent lived in low-income public housing projects (Hertzig, Birch, Thomas, & Mendez, 1968). This group has also been followed longitudinally since early infancy, with the same approach to data collection and analysis as in the NYLS.

In addition, two longitudinal samples of deviant children were gathered and fol-lowed. One sample comprised 68 children born prematurely, with birth weights ranging from 1,000 to 1,750 g. Fifty-five percent of the boys (16 of 29) and 36% of the girls (14 of 39) had clinical evidence of neurological impairment at 5 years of age (Hertzig, 1974). The other sample comprised 52 children with mildly retarded intellectual levels but without gross evidence of motor dysfunc-tion or body stigmata (Chess & Hassibi, 1970). The first group has been followed from birth, the second from age 5-11 years, with similar protocols for data col-lection and analysis of behavioral characteristics as in the NYLS.

A special population of 243 children with congenital rubella resulting from the rubella epidemic of 1964 has also been evaluated behaviorally with similar methods (Chess, Korn, & Fernandez, 1971). This group has been of special inter-est because of the large numbers with physical, neurological, and intellectual handicaps, including many with multiple handicaps.

METHODS OF DATA COLLECTION

The parents were the primary source of information on the child's behavior in infancy. As the child grew older, behavioral data were obtained through teacher interviews in nursery and elementary school; direct observations in the school setting and during psychometric testing at ages 3, 6, and 9 years; and direct interview with each youngster and parent separately at age 16-17 years. Academic achievement scores were gathered from school records. Whenever anyone in contact with the child suspected that there was behavioral disturbance, a complete clinical evaluation was made. Special tests such as perceptual evaluations were carried out as indicated.

All data, whether obtained from parent or teacher or by direct observation of the child, were described in factual, descriptive terms with a concern not only for what the child did but how he did it. Statements about the presumed meaning of the child's behavior were considered unsatisfactory for primary data, though they often provided useful insights into special attitudes or judgments of the teacher or parent. When such interpretative statements were made, the interviewer always asked for a description of the actual behavior. Special emphasis was placed on the child's first response to a new stimulus (e.g., first bath) and his subsequent reactions to the same stimulus, until a consistent long-term response was established. The sequence of responses to new stimuli, situations, and demands, whether simple or complex, provided especially rich information on a child's individual temperament pattern.

Our original methods for data collection involved semistructured interviews with parents and teachers. In recent years, questionnaires for the infancy and 3-7-year-old age periods have been developed by Carey and ourselves (Thomas & Chess, 1977). These protocols have already been used by a number of research centers in various countries. Other temperament questionnaires for the childhood period, based on our categories, have been developed by other workers as well (Garside et al., 1975; Graham, Rutter, & George, 1973; Persson-Blennow, & McNeil, 1979). Carey has also just completed questionnaires for the 1-2- and 8-10-year-old age periods; and we have developed one for the early adult period.

DATA ANALYSIS

Nine categories of temperament were established by an inductive analysis of the parent interview protocols for the infancy period in the first 22 children studied. Item scoring was used, a 3-point scale was established for each category, and the item scores were transformed into a weighted score for each category on each record. (The various questionnaires have used 4-7-point scales.)

1. Activity level: The motor component present in a given child's functioning and the diurnal proportion of active and inactive periods. Protocol data on motility during bathing, eating, playing, dressing, and handling, as well as information concerning the sleep-wake cycle, reaching, crawling, and walking, are used in scoring this category.

2. Rhythmicity (regularity): The predictability or unpredictability, in time, of any function. It can be analyzed in relation to the sleep-wake cycle, hunger, feeding pattern, and elimination schedule.

3. Approach or withdrawal: The nature of the initial response to a new stimulus, be it a new food, new toy, or new person. Approach responses are positive, whether displayed by mood expression (such as smiling and verbalizations) or motor activity (such as swallowing a new food, reaching for a new toy, and active play). Withdrawal reactions are negative, whether displayed by mood expression (crying, fussing, grimacing, and verbalizations) or motor activity (such as moving away, spitting new food out, pushing new toy away).

4. Adaptability: Responses to new or altered situations. One is not concerned with the nature of the initial responses, but with the ease with which they are modified in desired directions.

5. Threshold of responsiveness: The intensity level of stimulation that is necessary to evoke a discernible response, irrespective of the specific form that the response may take or of the sensory modality affected. The behaviors are those concerning reactions to sensory stimuli, environmental objects, and social contacts.

6. Intensity of reaction: The energy level of response, irrespective of its quality or direction.

7. Quality of mood: The amount of pleasant, joyful, and friendly behavior, as contrasted with unpleasant, crying, and unfriendly behavior.

8. Distractibility: The effectiveness of extraneous environmental stimuli in interfering with or in altering the direction of the ongoing behavior.

9. Attention span and persistence: Two categories that are related. Attention span concerns the length of time a particular activity is pursued by the child. Persistence is the continuation of an activity in the face of obstacles to the maintenance of the activity direction.

Three temperamental constellations of functional significance have been defined by qualitative analysis of the data and factor analysis. The first group is characterized by regularity, positive approach responses to new stimuli, high adaptability to change, and mild or moderately intense mood that is preponderantly positive. These children quickly develop regular sleep and feeding schedules, take to most new foods easily, smile at strangers, adapt easily to a new school, accept most frustrations with little fuss, and accept the rules of new games with no trouble. Such a youngster is aptly called the Easy Child, and is usually a joy to his parents, pediatricians, and teachers. This group comprises about 40% of our NYLS sample.

At the opposite end of the temperamental spectrum is the group with irregularity in biological functions, negative withdrawal responses to new stimuli, nonadaptability or slow adaptability to change, and intense mood expressions that are frequently negative. These children show irregular sleep and feeding schedules; slow acceptance of new foods; prolonged adjustment periods to new routines, people, or situations; and relatively frequent and loud periods of crying. Laughter, also, is characteristically loud. Frustration typically produces a violent tantrum. This is the Difficult Child, and mothers and pediatricians find such youngsters difficult indeed. This group comprises about 10% of our NYLS sample.

The third noteworthy temperamental constellation is marked by a combination of negative responses of mild intensity to new stimuli with slow adaptability after repeated contact. In contrast to the difficult children, these youngsters are characterized by mild intensity of reactions, whether positive or negative, and by less tendency to show irregularity of biological functions. The negative mild responses to new stimuli can be seen in the first encounter with the bath, a new food, a stranger, a new place or a new school situation. If given the opportunity to reexperience such new situations over time and without pressure, such a child gradually comes to show quiet and positive interest and involvement. A youngster with this characteristic sequence of response is referred to as the Slow-To-Warm-Up Child, an apt if inelegant designation. About 15% of our NYLS sample falls into this category.

As can be seen from these percentages, not all children fit into one of these three temperamental groups. Individual children manifest varying and different combinations of temperamental traits. Also, among those children who do fit one of these three patterns, there is a wide range in degree of manifestation. Some are extremely easy children in practically all situations; others are relatively easy and not always so. A few children are extremely difficult with all new situations and demands; others show only some of these characteristics, and relatively mildly. For some children, it is highly predictable that they will warm up slowly in any new situation; others warm up slowly with certain types of new stimuli or demands, but warm up quickly in others.

It should be emphasized that the various temperamental constellations all represent variations within normal limits. Any child may be easy, difficult, or slow-
to-warm up temperamentally; have a high or low activity level; have distractibility
and low persistence or the opposite; or have any other relatively extreme rating
score in a sample of children for a specific temperamental attribute. Such an
amodal rating, however, is not a criterion of psychopathology, but rather an
indication of the wide range of behavioral styles exhibited by normal children.

The body of the NYLS quantitative scores of the nine temperamental categories
for each of the first five years of life was subject to factor analyses to determine whether meaningful groupings of the categories could be derived statistically.
The Varimax solutions proved to be most useful, and three factors were developed.
One of these, Factor A, met the criterion of relative consistency over the five-
year period. This factor included approach/withdrawal, adaptability, mood and
intensity. The scores for Factor A were normally distributed for each of the
five years.

It is significant that the cluster of characteristics composing Factor A corresponds closely to the cluster developed by qualitative analysis, which identifies
the Easy Child and the Difficult Child. In this qualitative categorization,
which was completed before the factor analysis was done, the Easy Child corresponds to high Factor A plus regularity, and the Difficult Child to low Factor A
plus irregularity.

It has been possible to identify each of the nine categories of temperament in
each child at different age periods in the preschool and early school years in
all the study populations, as follows: The New York Longitudinal Study, the
Puerto Rican working-class children, the mentally retarded group, the premature
sample with high incidence of neurological damage. The children with congenital
rubella, and the Israeli kibbutz group. In addition, these temperamental characteristics have been identified in a number of populations studied by investigators at other centers in this country and abroad (these other studies are
reported in subsequent chapters). It is clear, therefore, that these behavioral
traits occur ubiquitously in children and can be categorized systematically.

FUNCTIONAL SIGNIFICANCE OF TEMPERAMENT

A number of studies from our own research unit and from other centers have
demonstrated that temperamental characteristics, in interaction with environmental variables, play an influential role in behavior disorder development, in the
dynamics of parent-child and other interpersonal relationships, and in school
functioning. The completed studies are detailed in our recent volume (Thomas &
Chess, 1977). A large number of ongoing projects will undoubtedly contribute
additional significant data in the near future.

The major findings can be summarized briefly. Children with the Difficult Child
pattern are the most vulnerable group to the development of behavior problems in
early and middle childhood. Their intense negative withdrawal reactions to new
situations and their slow adaptability, together with biological irregularity,
make the demands of early socialization especially stressful for these children.
Seventy percent of this group in the NYLS developed clinically evident behavior
disorders (a mild reactive behavior disorder in most cases) before 10 years of
age. With parent counseling and other therapeutic measures, where indicated,
the great majority recovered or improved markedly by adolescence.

In children with physical handicaps or mild mental retardation, the Difficult
Child group is at even greater risk for behavior problem development than are
nonhandicapped children (Thomas & Chess, 1977, Ch. 5). Children with this

temperamental pattern are also vulnerable to psychiatric disorder if they have a mentally ill parent (Graham et al., 1973). Infants with colic are also more likely to be difficult children temperamentally (Carey, 1972).

Behavior disorders can develop with any temperamental pattern, however, if demands for change and adaptation are made that are dissonant with the particular child's capacities, and therefore excessively stressful. Thus, the distractible child is put under excessive stress if expected to concentrate without inter-ruption for long periods of time, the persistent child if his absorption in an activity is prematurely and abruptly terminated, and the high-activity child if restricted in his possibilities for constructive activity (Thomas, Chess, & Birch, 1968). Teachers can underestimate the intelligence of the Slow-To-Warm-Up Child or the low-activity child, with unfavorable consequences for the learning situation (Chess, Thomas, & Cameron, 1976).

Our findings and those of others on the importance of temperament in the develop-mental process do not imply that temperament is always a significant variable in the ontogenesis and course of every behavior disorder, interpersonal disturbance, or school malfunctioning. In some instances, temperament may play a crucial role, in other cases it may be somewhat influential, and in still other instances it may play a minor or even insignificant role. In this regard, temperament is no different from any other single organismic or environmental factor. Whether it be the level or style of cognitive functioning, the goals and aims of the child, the characteristics of the mother, or the nature of the school situation, the significance of these factors for the developmental process in any child cannot be decided a priori, but must be determined on the basis of all the concrete information available in the specific case.

ORIGINS OF TEMPERAMENT

A number of studies have explored the question of the origins of our nine temper-amental categories. Our review of these studies (Thomas & Chess, 1977) suggests an appreciable, but by no means exclusive, genetic role in the determination of temperamental individuality in the young infant. Prenatal or perinatal brain damage does not appear to influence in any striking fashion. The data also indicate that parental attitudes and functioning, as shaped by the sex of the child or special concerns for a premature infant, at the most have a modest etiological influence on temperament. Sociocultural factors appear to have some importance, and special idiosyncratic perinatal characteristics such as chronic anxiety preceding or at least starting in pregnancy may also be significant.

Korner (1973) has suggested that behavioral sex differences in the neonate may result from the actions of hormones in utero in sensitizing the organism's central nervous system. It may be that prenatal variations in hormonal activity or other chemical or physiological influences on the developing brain may play a highly significant role in the etiology of temperamental individuality. This hypothesis still remains to be tested.

CONSISTENCY OF TEMPERAMENT OVER TIME

As we originally began to observe clinically and impressionistically the phenom-enon of temperament, we were struck by the many dramatic evidences of continuity in people we knew, sometimes from early childhood to adulthood. It was tempting to generalize from these instances to the concept that an adult's temperamental characteristics could be predicted from a knowledge of his behavior style in early childhood. Such a formulation, however, would be completely at variance with our fundamental commitment to an interactionist viewpoint, in which behavioral development is conceived as a constantly evolving and changing process of organism-environment interaction. All other psychological phenomena, such as intellectual competence, coping mechanisms, adaptive patterns, and value systems, can and do change over time. How could it be otherwise for temperament?

In considering the data on the consistency of temperament over time, certain methodological problems should first be mentioned. A number of the difficulties in attempting to predict later psychological development from infancy data have been discussed by Rutter (1970). These include: (a) the amount of development still to occur, that is, the fact that most psychological development takes place after early infancy; (b) modifiability of psychological development by the child's subsequent experiences; (c) effects of intrauterine environment on the characteristics of the young infant and disappearance of these effects over time; (d) the effects of differing rates of maturation, which may make for wide variations in different children in levels of correlation between infancy and later measures; and (e) differences in the function being tested in infancy and maturity, so that a test in infancy may not measure the same attribute as a test in later childhood or adult life.

With regard to temperament scores, Rutter points up several specific methodological problems, such as the reliance on adjectives parents use in describing children's behavior, the possibility of selective bias in determining which episodes of behavior the parent or other observer reports, and the problem of separating the content from the style of behavior. Most important, he feels, is the effect that the changing context of the child's behavior might have on the biological ratings.

In addition to these issues raised by Rutter, several other methodological problems regarding the determination of consistency over time have been apparent in the NYLS. A child's characteristic expression of temperament may be blurred at any specific age period by routinization of functioning. Thus, an infant who shows marked withdrawal reactions to the bath, new foods, and new people may, a year or two later, show positive responses to these same stimuli because of repeated exposure and final adaptation. If, at that time, he experiences few new situations and stimuli, the withdrawal reaction may not be evident. Adaptation and routinization of activities may, in the same way, blur the expression of other temperamental traits, such as irregularity, slow adaptability, and negative mood expression. Limitation of opportunity for physical activity may lead to frequent restless movements that may be interpreted as high activity or even hyperactivity. The procedures for quantitative scores necessarily rely on routine judgments and scoring approaches, which can preclude the identification of meaningful subtleties in the developmenal course of individual children. Specific single items of behavior may sometimes be significant in indicating temperamental consistency from one age period to another, but quantitative scoring methods can hardly give proper weight to the importance of such functionally significant items.

Finally, the issue of consistency of temperament over time cannot be studied globally. One or several temperamental traits may show striking continuity from one specific age period to another and the other attributes may not. At other age periods, the reverse may be true: The originally consistent traits may not show the correlations, whereas other attributes may now do so. The factors affecting the identification of continuity over time are so complex and variable as to create all kinds of permutations in the patterns of correlations.

As we have traced the consistencies and inconsistencies of temperament in our NYLS subjects from early infancy through adolescence, five patterns have been evident: (a) clear-cut consistency; (b) consistency in some aspects of temperament at one period and in other aspects at other times; (c) distortion of the

expression of temperament by other factors, such as psychodynamic patterns;
(d) consistency in temperament, but qualitative change in temperament-environment
interaction; and (e) change in a conspicuous temperamental trait. Any child may
show a combination of several of these five possibilities, that is, consistency
over time with one or several temperamental traits, distortion in another, and
change in several others.

It seems clear that temperament does not necessarily follow a consistent, linear
course. Discontinuities over time are certainly, to some extent, the results of
methodological problems in data collection and analysis. Much more important,
however, are the functional, dynamic reasons that determine continuity or dis-
continuity over time. Our categorization of temperament for any person is
derived from the constellations of behaviors exhibited at any one age period.
These behaviors are the result of all the influences, past and present, that
shape and modify these behaviors in a constantly evolving interactive process.
Consistency of a temperamental trait or constellation in a person over time,
therefore, may require stability in these interactional forces, such as environmental influences, motivations, and abilities.

IMPLICATIONS FOR FUTURE RESEARCH

The behavioral approach to the study of temperament has proved fruitful in the
delineation of functionally significant categories and in the formulation of
appropriate methodologies for data collection and analysis. Practical applications of the findings within the goodness-of-fit interactionist conceptual model
have been valuable in the treatment and prevention of behavior disorders (Burks &
Rubenstein, 1979; Thomas et al., 1968) and in the promotion of positive school
adaptation (Chess et al., 1976). Correlative studies of the relationships of
the behavioral ratings of temperament and the neurophysiological measures of
individual differences presented in a number of chapters in the present work
would be very useful, as would correlations with significant biochemical and
psychophysiological valuables.

Studies from other centers have already suggested other temperamental categories
and constellations beyond our nine categories and three constellations (Graham
et al., 1973; Plomin & Rowe, 1977). Comparisons of temperamental patterns and
their functional significance in different societies may prove a fruitful method
of intercultural behavioral studies (Super & Harkness, 1984). And the
development of reliable, economical questionnaire instruments for rating temperament in childhood, adolescence, and adult life should enhance substantially
the further study of individual differences and their functional significance.

REFERENCES

Barchas, J. D., Akil, H., Elliot, G. R., Holman, R. B., & Watson, S. J. (1978).
  Behavioral neurochemistry: Neuro-regulators and behavioral states. Science,
  200, 964-973.

Bell, R. Q. (1968). A reinterpretation of the direction of effects in studies
  of socialization. Psychological Review, 75, 81-95.

Bennett, E. L., Diamond, M. C., Krech, D., & Rosensweig, M. H. (1964). Clinical
  and anatomical plasticity of brain. Science, 146, 610-619.

Burks, J., & Rubenstein, M. (1979). Temperament styles in adult interaction:
  Applications in psychotherapy. New York: Brunner/Mazel.

Carey, W. B. (1972). Clinical application of infant temperament measures. Journal of Pediatrics, 81, 823-828.

Cattell, R. B. (1950). Personality: A systematic and factual study. New York: McGraw-Hill.

Chess, S., & Hassibi, M. (1970). Behavior deviations in mentally retarded children. Journal of the American Academy of Child Psychiatry, 9, 282-297.

Chess, S., Korn, S., & Fernandez, P. (1971). Psychiatric disorders of children with congenital rubella. New York:Brunner/Mazel.

Chess, S., Thomas, A., & Cameron, M. (1976). Temperament: Its significance for school adjustment and academic achievement. New York University Educational Review, 7, 24-29.

Clarke, A. M., & Clarke, A. D. B. (1976). Early experience: Myth and evidence. London: Open Books.

Dubos, R. (1965). Man adapting. New Haven: Yale University Press.

Garside, R. F., Birch, H., Scott, D., Chambers, I., Tweddler, E. G., & Barber, L. M. (1975). Dimensions of temperament in infant school children. Journal of Child Psychology and Psychiatry, 16, 219-231.

Graham, P., Rutter, M., & George, S. (1973). Temperamental characteristics as predictors of behavior disorders in children. American Journal of Orthopsychiatry, 43, 328-339.

Guilford, J. P. (1959). Personality. New York: McGraw-Hill.

Hertzig, M. E. (1974). Neurologic findings in prematurely born children at school age. In D. Ricks, A. Thomas, & M. Roff (Eds.), Life history research in psychopathology (Vol. 3, pp. 42-52). Minneapolis, MS: University of Minnesota Press.

Hertzig, M. E., Birch, H. G., Thomas, A., & Mendez, O. A. (1968). Class and ethnic differences in the responsiveness of preschool children to cognitive demands. Monographs of the Society for Research in Child Development, 33, 1-69.

Kagan, J. (1971). Change and continuity in infancy. New York: Wiley.

Kodlin, D., & Thompson, D. J. (1958). An appraisal of the longitudinal approach to studies of growth and development. Monographs of the Society for Research in Child Development, 23, 1-8.

Korner, A. F. (1973). Sex differences in newborns, with special references to differences in the organization of oral behavior. Journal of Child Psychology and Psychiatry, 14, 19-29.

Lewin, K. (1935). A dynamic theory of personality. New York: McGraw-Hill.

McCall, R. B. (1977). Challenges to a science of developmental psychology. Child Development, 48, 333-344.

Murphy, G. (1947). Personality: A biosocial approach to origins and structure. New York: Harper.

Murphy, L. B., & Moriarty, A. E. (1976). Vulnerability, coping and growth. New Haven: Yale University Press.

Persson-Blennow, I., & McNeil, T. F. (1979). A questionnaire for measurement of temperament in six-month-old infants: Development and standardization. Journal of Child Psychology and Psychiatry, 97, 107-113.

Plomin, R., & Rowe, D. C. (1977). A twin study of temperament in young children. Journal of Psychology, 97, 107-113.

Riesen, A. H. (1960). Effects of stimulus deprivation and the development and atrophy of the visual sensory system. American Journal of Orthopsychiatry, 30, 23-30.

Rutter, M. (1972). Maternal deprivation reassessed. Harmondsworth, England: Penguin Books.

Sameroff, A. J. (1975). Early influences on development: "fact or fancy?" Merrill-Palmer Quarterly, 20, 275-301.

Schneirla, T. C., & Rosenblatt, J. S. (1961). Behavioral organization and genesis of the social bond in insects and mammals. American Journal of Orthopsychiatry, 31, 223-253.

Sears, R. R. (1951). A theoretical framework for personality and social behavior. American Psychologist, 6, 476-483.

Spanier, G. B., Lerner, R. M., & Aquilino, W. (1978). The study of child-family interactions -- a perspective for the future. In R. M. Lerner & G. B. Spanier (Eds.), Child influences on marital and family interaction (pp. 327-344). New York: Academic Press.

Stein, M., Schiavi, R. C., & Camerino, M. (1976). Influence of brain and behavior on the immune system. Science, 191, 435-440.

Super, C. M., & Harkness, S. (1984). The infant's niche in rural Kenya and metropolitan America. In L. L. Adler (Ed.), Issues in cross-cultural research. New York: Academic Press.

Thomas, A., & Chess, S. (1957). An approach to the study of sources of individual differences in child behavior. Journal of Clinical and Experimental Psychopathology and Quarterly Review of Psychiatry and Neurology, 18, 347-357.

Thomas, A., & Chess, S. (1977). Temperament and development. New York: Brunner/ Mazel.

Thomas, A., Chess, S., & Birch, H. G. (1968). Temperament and behavior disorders in children. New York: New York University Press.

Vaillant, G. E. (1977). Adaptation to life. Boston: Little Brown.

Vygotsky, L. S. (1978). In M. Cole, V. J. Steiner, S. Scribner, & E. Souberman (Eds.), Mind in society. Cambridge: Harvard University Press.

14

Temperamental Differences in Infants and 6-Year-Old Children: A Follow-up Study of Twins

Anne Mari Torgersen

A recent concern in developmental psychology is the issue of interaction between the child and its environment. The characteristics of the individual child are seen as influencing the caretaker's way of handling the child, and thereby the child's own socialization (Bell, 1968).

Temperamental individuality has been emphasized by a number of researchers as one of the child's own attributes that influence the interactional process. Attempts have been made to measure these processes reliably. Thomas, Chess, and Birch (1968) as well as Thomas, Chess, Birch, Hertzig, and Korn (1963) have provided an outstanding contribution in their New York Longitudinal Study (NYLS). Their concepts have been widely accepted as useful ways to differentiate temperamental individuality in both infancy and later childhood. The study reported in this chapter was based on the NYLS methods of data collection and definitions of the nine temperamental categories. These categories were as follows: activity level, regularity in biological functions, approach/withdrawal to new situations, adaptability, intensity of reactions, sensory threshold, mood, distractibility, and attention-span/persistence (Thomas et al., 1968).

Some researchers have explored environmental factors that influence temperamental attributes, for example, the effect of different experiences during pregnancy on activity in infancy (Sontag, 1962). Others have emphasized the influence of genetic factors on temperamental development; in human research, these are primarily twin studies (Rowe & Plomin, 1977; Scarr, 1966; Wilson, 1972). The present study is concerned with both of these: the twin method is used to study genetic influences on temperamental development. Twins provide an opportunity for estimating the relative contribution of innate and experiential factors. Identical twins share exactly the same genes, whereas same-sexed fraternals vary in their genetic similarity around an average of 50%. Although our key issue is heritability in temperamental development, several environmental factors are also examined in this follow-up study of twins from infancy to 6 years of age.

SAMPLE AND METHOD

Sample in the Infant Study

The subjects were 53 same-sexed twin pairs, which were the total sample of same-sexed twins born in a single town and its surrounding area over a 1½-year period. Thus it was an unselected sample, and the usual distribution among social classes was found. The group included 46 boys and 60 girls. On the basis of questionnaires and blood and serum typing, 34 pairs were classified as monozygotic (MZ) and 16 as dizygotic (DZ); 3 pairs had uncertain zygosity.

Sample in the 6-Year Study

Follow-up data at 6 years of age were obtained on 32 monozygotic twin pairs and
16 dizygotic twin pairs. A total of 91.7% of the twins were between 6 years
3 months and 6 years 10 months at the time of assessment. The age range was
6.1 to 7.8 years. This group included 44 boys and 52 girls.

Method

The twin births were registered by the midwives who delivered the twins. The
midwives also completed a questionnaire concerning the births. In cases where
twins were transferred to the pediatric department, medical information was
sought from the department's records. During the first 4 days after the birth,
the mother was visited to obtain information with regard to family, social background, and psychiatric symptoms. The only criterion used of prematurity was
low birth weight. The birth weights were graded in three categories: (a) less
than 2,000 g; (b) 2,000 to 2,500 g; and (c) more than 2,500 g. Information
about complications in pregnancy was collected by interview with the mothers
shortly after the twin births, in addition to information available from the
hospital's intake records. Pregnancy complications were graded in three categories according to severity: (a) early or late bleeding in pregnancy, other
somatic illness of such a degree that sometimes required hospitalization or
surgery; (b) unusually strong pregnancy complaints; and (c) only mild pregnancy
complaints, or none. Birth complications were graded in terms of the kind of
technical help needed during delivery: (a) total extraction of the baby,
(b) partial extraction of the baby, and (c) spontaneous delivery with no complications. Satisfactory measures of the state of the infant shortly after
birth were not available.

Temperamental assessment. Data on temperament were obtained by semistructured
interviews with the mother in her home setting at two age periods in infancy,
2 and 9 months, and in the follow-up study when the twins were 6 years. As in
the NYLS protocols (Thomas et al., 1963), detailed objective descriptions of the
child's behavior in daily routines were obtained. The object of the interview
was to determine how the child reacted to various situations rather than what
the child actually did. Even if the questions concerned age-appropriate behavioral criteria at succeeding age periods, the definitional identity of each
temperamental category was maintained over time. The interviews were tape recorded and transcribed.

All information relating to temperament in the interviews was evaluated. During
scoring, the mother's description was evaluated on 5-point scales on how typical
a child's behavior was in different situations.

In the infant study the clustering of items to temperamental categories relied
mainly on conceptual coherency proposed by Thomas et al. (1963). All scoring
was performed by the author, who was blind to the twins' zygosity. For inter-
rater reliability and other methodological details, see Torgersen and Kringlen
(1978).

In the 6-year study the same definitions of temperament were used when the items
were constructed and scored. The scoring was done by someone who was not familiar
with the twins or their zygosity. Interview protocols from 20 children were then
rescored by the author to determine interscorer reliability. Items with interscorer reliability lower than 80% agreement within 1 scale point, and also items
impossible to score in more than 70% of the children, were excluded. After
principle components factor analysis within each temperamental category, items
that had factorial loadings lower than .30 were excluded.

Only three of the initial 14 items in distractibility met the criterion of
reliability. The relationships between these three items were also so low
(Cronbach's alpha = .20) that the whole category was excluded from further
analysis. The final number of items within the other temperamental categories
varied from 4 to 9, and the internal consistency within each category was satis-
factorily high (alpha = .64 to .73), with the exception of regularity, which had
a comparatively low internal consistency (alpha = .46). The reason for retaining
regularity for further analysis was that the items in this category were all
highly reliable, and the category also was of special interest because of its
relationship with behavior problems reported by Thomas et al. (1968) and Thomas
and Chess (1977).

Statistical procedures. To find out whether the greater differences in dizygotic
twins than in monozygotic twins are statistically significant, several statistical models have been used. A common method is to calculate the F ratio proposed
by Vandenberg (1966). This is a relationship between the intrapair variances
within the two zygosity groups, with the formula:

$$F = \frac{\sigma^2 \, w \, DZ}{\sigma^2 \, w \, MZ}$$

A more recent critical comment on this statistical procedure has been proposed
by Christian, Kang, and Norton (1974). Usually, the total variance (among-pair
variance, A, plus within-pair variance, W) is the same in MZ and DZ twin groups.
If this is the case, there is no difficulty in using the traditional statistical
analysis employed by Vandenberg. If the total variances are different (p < .20
in a two-tailed F test), Christian et al.'s more conservative genetic estimate
is preferable. This F' has the formula

$$F' = \frac{var_{AMZ} - var_{WDZ}}{var_{ADZ} + var_{WMZ}}$$

This alternative F' ratio has been calculated for all three age levels whenever
it is necessary, according to Christian et al. (1974).

RESULTS

Genetic Influences on Temperament

At all ages, both in infancy and at 6 years of age, the MZ twins were more like
each other within the twin pair than were the DZ twins in all the temperamental
categories studied. To what degree these differences between the two zygosity
groups are statistically significant can be seen in Tables 1 - 3, where the F
ratio between intrapair variances proposed by Vandenberg (1966) are calculated,
and also the F_T ratio of the total variances and the alternative F' ratio proposed by Christian et al. (1974).

For a 2-month-old child (Table 1), the Vandenberg F ratio is statistically significant for three temperamental categories (regularity, threshold, and intensity), whereas for a 9-month-old (Table 2) and a 6-year-old (Table 3) this F
ratio is statistically significant for all the temperamental categories studied.
As can be seen from these tables, it was necessary to calculate the alternative
F' ratio for several of the temperamental categories at all age levels. At 2
months, only one temperamental category called for new calculations; this was
mood, where the F' ratio became statistically significant. At 9 months, the
F ratios for distractibility and attention-span/persistence had to be recal-
culated, which resulted in nonstatistically significant F ratios for these two
categories. Three temperamental categories needed recalculations of their

TABLE 1.   The F values of the twin variance in temperament at 2 months of age

| Temperamental category | F ratio of twin variance | | |
	Within-pair variance, F	Total variance, F_T	Component estimate, F'
Activity	1.52	1.21	
Regularity	4.98***	1.10	
Approach/withdrawal	0.83	1.26	
Adaptability	0.57	1.10	
Intensity	2.55*	1.42	
Threshold	2.82**	1.35	
Mood	1.54	1.90†	2.36**
Distractibility	1.40	1.12	

†p < .20,   two-tailed
*p < .05,   one-tailed
**p < .01,   one-tailed
***p < .001, one-tailed

TABLE 2.   The F values of the twin variance in temperament at 9 months of age

| Temperamental category | F ratio of twin variance | | |
	Within-pair variance, F	Total variance, F_T	Component estimate, F'
Activity	55.26***	1.30	
Regularity	12.86***	1.13	
Approach/withdrawal	6.77***	1.20	
Adaptability	2.28*	1.05	
Intensity	5.32***	1.14	
Threshold	9.90***	1.15	
Mood	3.31**	1.35	
Distractibility	3.94***	1.54†	1.15
Attention span and persistence	4.40***	2.83†	1.68

†p   .20,   two-tailed
*p   .05,   one-tailed
**p   .01,   one-tailed
***p   .001, one-tailed

TABLE 3. The F values of the twin variance in temperament at 6 years of age

| | F ratio of twin variance | | |
Temperamental category	Within-pair variance, F	Total variance, F_T	Component estimate, F'
Activity	11.34***	1.07	
Regularity	4.22***	1.55†	1.06
Approach/withdrawal	8.80***	1.03	
Adaptability	2.23*	1.32	
Intensity	9.56***	1.08	
Threshold	2.91**	1.79†	2.73**
Mood	3.32**	1.87†	1.40
Attention-span and persistence	5.13***	1.07	

$\dagger$ p < .20, two-tailed
* p < .05, one-tailed
** p < .01, one-tailed
*** p < .001, one-tailed

F ratios at 6 years. Of these, both mood and regularity yielded F ratios that were not statistically significant, but threshold maintained its significance. The level of statistical significance varied for the different temperamental categories. Mood and adaptability had comparatively low significance levels at all three ages. Regularity typically had high significance levels in infancy but low at 6 years, whereas activity, intensity, and approach/withdrawal were highly significant both in infancy and at 6 years.

Environmental Factors in the Infant Study

Table 4 shows that there is a weak but statistically significant and negative correlation between prematurity and activity level in MZ twins. The premature child is more passive at both 2 months and 9 months, which may only reflect the fact that premature children develop motor skills more slowly during the initial period after birth than do those of normal birth weight.

Table 4 reveals a weak but statistically significant tendency, showing that both premature MZ and DZ twins have more difficulty in adapting to new situations than do normal twins at age 2 months. This tendency is more clear at age 9 months for MZ twins only. Table 4 also shows that pregnancy complications have a differential effect on the two groups of twins at age 2 months. In MZ twins, a complicated pregnancy is associated with a passive child. In DZ twins, on the other hand, pregnancy complications are related to a high activity level. In addition, MZ twins from complicated pregnancies are apt to show irregularity at 2 months. A complicated birth is related to low threshold in DZ twins and slow adaptability in both MZ and DZ twins; however, this is only significant for the MZ twins at 2 months.

TABLE 4. Relationship between physical factors and temperament at 2 and 9 months of age (N = 106). Temperament category for monozygotic (MZ) and dizygotic (DZ) twins.

Physical factors	2 months			9 months		
	MZ	DZ	Total	MZ	DZ	Total
Prematurity						
Activity	-.28*	-.11	-.22*	-.26*	-.13	-.21
Adaptability	-.19	-.20	-.21*	-.31**	.00	-.19
Pregnancy complications						
Activity	-.28*	.37*	-.07	-.08	.05	-.09
Regularity	-.24*	.18	-.10	-.14	.10	-.12
Approach	.11	.00	.17	.26*	-.05	.12
Birth complications						
Activity	-.01	.21	.02	.03	.38*	.12
Adaptability	-.28*	.35	-.08	-.08	.29	.01
Threshold	-.03	-.40*	-.15	-.13	.04	-.05

 * p < .05

** p < .01

In conclusion, considering the twins as individuals, we can demonstrate a statistical correlation both in monozygotic and dizygotic twins between pregnancy complications and a low degree of adaptability, regularity, threshold, and activity level. Moreover, if we combine the two groups, this tendency often disappears.

By comparing intrapair differences in twin pairs with the different degrees of pregnancy and birth complications, one obtains an impression of the significance of these somatic factors. Table 5 shows that the average intrapair difference in temperament is greater in both MZ and DZ twin pairs at both ages if they are associated with complicated pregnancies. The tendency is most obvious, although not statistically significant, for MZ twins at age 2 months.

The observations show that at neither 2 months nor 9 months was the twin with the lowest birth weight within a pair the more passive. This was unexpected since we previously had demonstrated a correlation between prematurity and activity level. The previously reported relationship between birth weight and adaptability, however, was supported by the fact that the heavier twin within a pair seems to adapt himself more rapidly. This tendency seems to disappear

TABLE 5. Relationship between complications in pregnancy and intrapair differences in temperament at 2 and 9 months of age for monozygotic and dizygotic twins

Degree of complication in pregnancy	Mean sum of differences for each age group		
	N	2 months	9 months
Monozygotic twins			
Severe	7	150.9	147.1
Moderate	7	140.0	112.4
None	20	94.9	127.9
Dizygotic twins			
Severe	6	232.3	380.5
Moderate	2	112.0	318.5
None	8	135.5	326.8

at age 9 months. To have been born as the first or second twin seems to have no significance for temperamental development.

It is of interest to look more closely at those of the MZ twin pairs who were most different in temperament within the pair. At 2 months, 2 of the 34 MZ pairs were exceptionally dissimilar in temperament within the pair. The mean total difference in temperamental score between two twins was about 115, but the total difference in these two twin pairs was 375 and 470, respectively. These pairs deviate radically from the remaining pairs, and accordingly have a strong influence on the average intrapair difference in behavior variables. Both pairs had histories of several pregnancy complications. Somatic condition after birth was poor for both pairs. At the age of 9 months, the intrapair differences in temperament in both pairs decreased to under half the original value. This means that pregnancy and birth complications may have a strong influence on the temperamental reactions of the child during the first months after birth, but then gradually lose their effect. In general one finds also for the DZ twins that extra complications in pregnancy and birth usually lead to large temperamental differences within the pair at age 2 months. There are observations, however, that might provide alternative explanations to the different temperamental scores at the two age levels of 2 and 9 months. The two MZ pairs with the smallest difference in temperamental variables were, for instance, both extremely premature. Equivalent observations were made in the DZ group. The two pairs with the lowest difference in temperament at age 2 months were both premature.

Postnatal Psychological Factors

Objective factors were registered concerning upbringing, such as degree of regulation by the mother of the child's sleeping and feeding habits, her emphasis on the child's physical well-being, time toilet training starts, information regarding breast and bottle feeding, and age when the child started drinking from a cup, and information concerning the degree of social stimulation received by the child.

Table 6 shows that there are some low but statistically significant correlations, for instance, between a strict regulating upbringing and regularity in the child, between physical stimulation and activity level, between physical stimulation and adaptability. The data do not show, however, whether these correlations have any causal significance. It should also be emphasized that the sample size is small for statistical comparisons, and with regard to methods of upbringing, we have not attempted to measure the more emotional aspects of mothering, such as the stability of the relationship.

TABLE 6. Some relations between mothers' treatment of children and temperamental characteristics at 2 and 9 months (N = 106)

Upbringing according to age of child	Temperamental Category						
	Act.	Reg.	App.	Adapt.	Int.	Thr.	Mood
Stress on breastfeeding							
2 months	.07	-.11	-.07	.10	.01	-.20*	.08
9 months	.23**	.07	.06	.26**	.01	.07	.13
Stress on regulation							
2 months	.01	.37**	-.19	.29**	-.05	-.05	.03
9 months	-.03	.41**	-.10	.03	.03	-.02	.00
Stress on cleanliness							
2 months	.04	.22*	-.09	.17	-.07	-.07	.23*
9 months	.10	.22*	-.02	.12	.06	-.13	.00
Early toilet training							
2 months	-.09	-.01	-.08	.01	-.13	.17	.04
9 months	-.17	.14	.19	-.04	-.26**	-.33**	.19
Stress on physical stimulation							
2 months	.22*	-.03	.18	-.13	.28**	.01	-.02
9 months	.44**	-.12	.11	.10	.25**	-.12	-.02
Stress on psychical stimulation							
2 months	.07	-.12	.25**	-.11	.08	-.09	.01
9 months	.34**	-.06	.22*	.10	.13	-.06	.11

*p < .05
**p < .01

Environmental Factors at 6 Years

No effort has been made to analyze which environmental factors influence temperamental development at 6 years. From the genetic analysis of the material, however, it is possible to see that some of the temperamental categories are influenced by environmental factors, shown by a low F ratio. Table 3 shows that regularity, adaptability, and mood are most strongly influenced by environmental factors at 6 years of age.

A low F ratio is caused either by great dissimilarity within the MZ twin pairs, great similarity within the DZ pairs, or both. The intraclass correlations within each temperamental category can tell us which of these explanations is most relevant. The intraclass correlations show how high the correlation is between two twins in one pair, that is, how much alike two twins are within the pair. In the mood category, the intraclass correlations are exceptionally low for both twin groups (Table 7). The differences within the twin pair are high in both twin groups, as demonstrated by a low intraclass correlation. The differences are still higher in the DZ twins, which could mean that mood is influenced by factors that are not genetic and also by factors that are dependent on individual factors that can be different in the same family.

The opposite is true for adaptability. The intraclass correlations are high for both zygosity groups, which means that both MZ and DZ twins are very like each other within the twin pair. This could mean that factors within the family are strong enough to influence both MZ and DZ pairs, and that children belonging to the same family develop the same adaptability trait.

TABLE 7. The intraclass correlations of the twin variances in temperament at 6 years, for monozygotic (MZ) and dizygotic (DZ) twins

	Intraclass correlation	
Temperamental category	MZ	DZ
Activity	0.93	0.14
Regularity	0.81	0.47
Approach/withdrawal	0.94	0.45
Adaptability	0.81	0.68
Intensity	0.95	0.54
Threshold	0.85	0.23
Mood	0.37	−0.06
Attention span and persistence	0.73	−0.27

Sex Differences

Table 8 presents the sex differences in temperament at the three age levels. At
2 months there are no significant differences between the sex groups in any of
the temperamental categories. Boys are more active than girls, but only at 6
years of age. At 9 months and at 6 years, approach and mood at both ages differ
among girls and boys. The mood qualities change from infancy to 6 years. At
9 months the girls show more positive mood, whereas the boys show more positive
mood at 6 years of age.

TABLE 8.   Sex differences in temperament in twins at 2 months, 9 months, and
6 years of age

Temperamental category by sex of child	2 months			9 months			6 years		
	Mean	SD	t	Mean	SD	t	Mean	SD	t
Activity									
Boys	1.05	0.39		1.02	0.48		2.85	0.96	
Girls	0.97	0.29	1.13	1.03	0.42	0.14	3.45	1.07	-2.81**
Regularity									
Boys	1.18	0.36		1.14	0.29		2.96	1.20	
Girls	1.05	0.40	1.59	1.04	0.38	1.41	2.90	1.04	0.29
Approach/withdrawal									
Boys	0.98	0.29		1.34	0.27		3.05	1.28	
Girls	1.09	0.33	-1.74	1.16	0.33	2.80**	2.51	0.96	2.30*
Adaptability									
Boys	0.81	0.31		0.88	0.35		2.90	1.01	
Girls	0.80	0.33	0.18	0.85	0.35	0.40	2.77	0.99	0.59
Intensity									
Boys	0.97	0.45		0.92	0.36		2.87	0.84	
Girls	0.99	0.38	-0.24	0.96	0.35	-0.57	3.11	0.74	-1.43
Threshold									
Boys	0.78	0.32		1.00	0.32		3.41	0.92	
Girls	0.80	0.30	-0.41	0.88	0.36	1.59	3.52	0.83	-0.61
Mood									
Boys	0.75	0.14		0.98	0.19		2.40	1.00	
Girls	0.81	0.17	-1.99	0.90	0.16	2.15*	2.82	0.88	-2.14*
Distractibility									
Boys	1.41	0.40		1.37	0.32		–	–	
Girls	1.51	0.37	-1.29	1.31	0.45	0.77	–	–	–
Attention span & persistence									
Boys	–	–		1.30	0.31		2.73	0.70	
Girls	–	–	–	1.29	0.32	0.13	2.76	0.71	-0.22

*p < .05

**p < .01

DISCUSSION

The results of this study confirm those of other studies concerning the importance of genetic factors in the development of temperamental aspects of behavior (Plomin & Rowe, 1977; Wilson, 1972, 1974). The present study also suggests that the importance of genetic factors differs within the different temperamental categories. The importance of genetic factors also differs from one age level to another within the same temperamental category. At 2 months, genetic factors seem to be of great importance for the development of regularity, at 9 months for regularity, activity, approach, intensity, and threshold, and at 6 years for activity, approach, intensity, and persistence. In contrast, genetic factors seem to be of minor importance for adaptability and mood at all age levels.

For some temperamental categories, genetic factors seem to be of great importance at 9 months, but not at 6 years; for other categories the converse is the case. What can explain this change over years? When the evidence for the importance of genetic factors is high in infancy and low at 6 years (regularity and threshold), it may be that these behavior styles are easily modified by environmental factors despite the strong genetic influence on the early development of the trait. When, on the other hand, the evidence for the importance of genetic factors is stronger at 9 months and at 6 years (activity, approach, and intensity), at least three explanations may be given. First, genetic influence may have been masked in the earlier age because of perinatal environmental influence. Second, an interaction between heredity and environment may be an explanation. Third, our measures may have a low reliability at an early age.

Some evidence has been found supporting the masking phenomenon in the period from 2 to 9 months. In some MZ twins considerable differences in temperamental reaction patterns were observed at 2 months. In a few cases intrauterine and perinatal complications were so clearly dominant that the influence of possible genetic factors on early psychological development may have been masked. A statistical analysis of all zygosity groups showed only weak correlations between temperamental categories and organic factors such as degree of prematurity, pregnancy and birth complications, as well as birth order. One reason for these negative findings could be small sample size. Findings that MZ twins are much more alike in temperament than are DZ twins at the age of 9 months, in contrast to the age of 2 months, seem to show that environment (organic) factors gradually lose their effect during the first months of life. In other words, after a considerable deviation due to pregnancy and birth complications, development returns to its seemingly natural genetic determination.

The differences from infancy to 6 years are easier to explain by means of an interaction theory. The more difference in the twins at infancy, the more different will be the reactions they receive from the environment, and, consequently, the more different will be their individual development (DZ twins). The opposite will occur when the twins are very much alike in infancy (MZ twins). We have only a few data on what kind of influence the twins get from their parents. These gave low, but statistically significant, correlations between temperament and methods of upbringing in infancy. However, the data do not show whether these correlations have any causal significance. When, for instance, there is a correlation between physical stimulation and activity level in the child, the question is still not answered whether this is because physical stimulation creates an active child, or if the active child elicits physical stimulation from the environment. One may suppose that both factors are at work. A third possible explanation of lower F ratios at lower age levels may be that the method has lower reliability at lower age. It is a fact that the assessment of temperament is more difficult at the age of 2 months. Moreover, prematurity leads to delayed growth and accordingly fewer scoring possibilities, which makes it harder to differentiate twins within a pair. Accordingly, in both MZ and DZ pairs, one tends to give members within a pair a more similar score. It is also possible that different aspects of behavior have been measured in infancy and in later childhood; methodologically this is a difficult question.

The sex differences in temperament found in this study were few. That boys were more active than girls only at 6 years and not in infancy suggests that activity is a role-function that boys gradually learn. It seems so even if activity is among the most genetically influenced temperamental categories. Approach may be said to be a kind of sociability, and thus the fact that girls were slightly more approaching than boys both at 9 months and at 6 years may be interpreted as girls being more sociable at these age levels.

It is interesting that the same temperamental categories that were lowest in heritability (low F ratio), namely, mood and adaptability, or were most easily modified by environment, as regularity, are among the same categories reported to correlate with behavioral problems. Thomas et al. (1968) found that children who were referred by their parents because of behavioral problems more often than the other children in their group had the Difficult Child Syndrome, which means negative mood, irregularity, low adaptability, withdrawal, and high intensity. Graham, Rutter, and George (1973) also found that irregularity and low malleability (much like adaptability) were the two temperamental categories that were among the most predictable for developing emotional problems. Furthermore, they found that the only significant difference between the risk group of children of neurotic parents and a control group, was higher negative mood scores in the risk group. It seems thus that some of the temperamental traits (mood, adaptability, and regularity) that are most relevant for the development of behavioral problems are the same as those found in this study to be most influenced by environmental factors.

In this investigation it is primarily the genetic factors that have been studied in detail. The results suggest that genetic factors are highly relevant in temperamental development. However, the study also gives few but clear suggestions on the importance of environmental factors. Unfortunately, it was impossible to analyze adequately which these environmental factors were.

REFERENCES

Bell, R. Q. (1968). A reinterpretation of the direction of effects in studies of socialization. Psychology Review, 75, 81-95.

Christian, J. C., Kang, K. W., & Norton, J. A. (1974). Choice of an estimate of genetic variance from twin data. American Journal of Human Genetics, 26, 154-161.

Graham, P., Rutter, M., & George, S. (1973). Temperamental characteristics as predictors of behavior disorders in children. American Journal of Orthopsychiatry, 43, 328-339.

Plomin, R., & Rowe, D. C. (1977). A twin study of temperament in young children. Journal of Psychology, 97, 107-113.

Rowe, D. C., & Plomin, R. (1977). Temperament in early childhood. Journal of Personality Assessment, 41, 2.

Scarr, S. (1966). Genetic factors in activity motivation. Child Development, 37, 663-673.

Sontag, L. W. (1962). Psychosomatic and somatopsychics from birth to three years. Modern Problems in Paediatrics, 7, 193-256.

Thomas, A., & Chess, S. (1977). Temperament and development. New York: Brunner/Mazel.

Thomas, A., Chess, S., & Birch, H. (1968). Temperament and behavior disorders in children. New York: New York University Press.

Thomas, A., Chess, S., Birch, H. G., Hertzig, M. E., & Korn, S. (1963). Behavioral individuality in early childhood. London: University of London Press.

Torgersen, A. M., & Kringlen, E. (1978). Genetic aspects of temperamental differences in infants. American Academy of Child Psychiatry, 17, 433-444.

Vandenberg, S. G. (1966). Contributions of twin research to psychology. In M. Manosevitz, C. Lindzeg, & D. D. Thiessen (Eds.), Behavioral genetics. New York: Appleton-Century-Croft, pp. 145-164.

Wilson, R. S. (1972). Twins: Early mental development. Science, 175, 914.

Wilson, R. S. (1974). Twins: Mental development in the pre-school years. Developmental Psychology, 10, 580-588.

15

Reactivity and Individual Style of Work Exemplified by Constructional-type Task Performance: A Developmental Study

Ewa Friedensberg

The concern of contemporary psychology with goal-directed forms of human behavior is reflected in problems relating to temperament. One problem is the influence of temperamental features on the effectiveness of action and task performance. This covers studies into the relationship between style of work and some properties of temperament, primarily reactivity.

By reactivity we mean a relatively stable characteristic of a given individual, intensity (magnitude) of reaction. This intensity (or magnitude) is assessed by response of one person compared with the response of other persons to the same stimulus, the assumption being that this stimulus is either of a similar value or neutral for all other persons compared (Strelau, 1974a). Thus understood, reactivity corresponds to the Pavlovian notion of strength of the nervous system, provided that both these terms are considered at the behavioral level (Strelau, 1974a).

On the other hand, the term style of work means the mode of task performance typical of a person which can be assessed on the basis of the relationship between orienting and executive operations (Klimov, 1969; Merlin, 1970)[1] or by the ratio of basic operations to auxiliary ones (Strelau, 1970). The new theoretical approach to temperament (Strelau, 1975) emphasizes the organization of the functional or temporal structure employed in the course of carrying out an operation.

This understanding of style of work was based on Tomaszewski's (1967) theory of action: Tomaszewski, in an analysis of the structure of action from a functional point of view, singled out basic operations -- those directly modifying the result leading to its achievement as well as auxiliary operations modifying it indirectly, such as preparatory, corrective, and controlling actions (cf. Materska, 1972).

Research financed by the Committee for Psychological Research of the PAN Polish Academy of Sciences within the framework of P-70 Problem.

[1]The adherents of the Pavlov concept of types of the nervous system reduce the term of style of action to a permanent system of individual ways and methods of action dependent on the type of the nervous system. They assume the ratio of orientative operations to executive ones as a measure of the ways and methods of task performance, and it is just this aspect of the structure of action that is investigated.

Two principal streams of investigation have contributed to research into the dependence between style of action and reactivity. The first was devoted to the study of style of work when already developed, and it included investigations into the regularities in question in various domains of human activity such as occupation (Klimov, 1969; Kopytova, 1964; Strelau, 1974b), and school work (Baymetov, 1971; Nosarzewski, 1974). These studies largely considered the formal aspect of style: the way in which characteristic action of a given individual was manifested in various types of activity. It was found that highly reactive persons undertake a much greater number of auxiliary operations in relation to basic ones than do low-reactive persons; or, that in highly reactive people, auxiliary operations occupy more time in the structure of the action being undertaken. On the other hand, low-reactive people carry out a smaller number of auxiliary operations in relation to basic ones, or they spend less time on auxiliary operations.

The second type of investigation dealt with the conditions of the development and improvement of style of action; fewer studies have been done in this area. Therefore, knowledge of the developmental aspect of the relationship which is considered in the present study is limited. Research work in this field has been concerned with the development of the individual style of action. Mastvilisker (1967) and Vyatkina (1970) indicated that individual style of action could already be seen in children aged 6; but the manifestation of the style depended on the child's level of mental development. It was found that the relationship between strength of the nervous system and the manner of performing simple instrumental tasks, considered in terms of the ratio of the number of orienting operations to that of executive ones, could be seen only in children with an IQ over 120. In children with an IQ under 120 no difference in the ratio of orienting operations to executive ones were found (Vyatkina, 1970). This regularity was also confirmed by Mastvilisker and Dikopolskaya's studies (1976) carried out among older children of preschool age, required to solve arithmetic tasks. At the same time, attempts were made by these two authors and by others to determine the role of intelligence in the development of the individual style of action (Prusakova, 1974a; Shtimmer, 1974b). They concluded that a particular level of mental development was not a necessary condition for the formation of personal style of action, because children with an average (or even below average) level of mental development could be taught, by purposeful instruction, those task performance methods that were in agreement with their temperamental features. Mental-development level gains importance when we consider the spontaneous formation of the style of action, because it offers the possibility of a clear understanding of task requirements, which, in turn, is a condition for the development of rational task-solving methods (Prusakova, 1974b; Shtimmer, 1974a).

Researchers have thus far suggested that a person's intelligence plays an essential role in the development of the individual style of action; but explorations into the functioning of high- and low-reactive persons under stress have made it clear that emotional factors may depress the effect of intelligence level (as shown in a study into the effect of negative emotions on intellectual and executive processes, Reykowski, 1974). Individual style of work is manifested under a variety of conditions. Yet even where free choice of the mode of task performance is ensured, it cannot be guaranteed that highly reactive persons might not perceive this situation as "threatening" (e.g., fear of negative evaluation by the experimenter). It may be supposed, therefore, that the effect of intelligence level might be greater in highly reactive persons for whom negative emotions could make task performance poorer and change the course of operations (Matveyev, 1965).

Researchers concerned with individual style of action also studied the role of motivation in the style development process (Baymetov, 1971; Klimov, 1969;

Merlin, 1970; Strelau, 1970). Its role in style formation has been expressed by an active search for the most rational patterns of action that both lead to reaching the desired result of action and provide a fit to the temperamental features of a given person (Merlin, 1970; Prusakova, 1974a).

In considering the conditions under which the style of action is developed, researchers also emphasized that individual ways and methods of task performance are themselves shaped in the process of action and that they depend on the current level of a person's knowledge and experience (Baymetov, 1971; Mastvilisker & Dikopolskaya, 1976; Merlin, 1977; Shchukhin, 1964).

A majority of investigations into the relationship between temperamental features and style of action have been carried out at a stage when style was already formed. Such research involved the diagnosis of this relationship in populations of both adolescents and adults. The present study extends the investigation to embrace some younger age groups in an effort to explore the developmental aspect of the relationship under study.

On the basis of evidence available from the literature, two hypotheses were formulated:

1. An individual style at work is formed as the child develops.

2. The effect of intelligence on the formation of the style of work is more pronounced in low-reactive people than in highly reactive persons.

METHOD

Three variables: reactivity level, intelligence level, and individual style of work were measured to verify the hypotheses.

Reactivity level was measured by means of one of the three versions of a Reactivity Rating Scale developed specifically for this purpose. Three parallel versions of this scale were prepared in view of the wide range of the subjects' age. These are 5-point scales that include typical categories of behavior for the given age group with the poles and the central point described.

For example, descriptions of the behavioral dimension <u>resistance to failure</u> (nursery school format) are shown in Table 1.

TABLE 1. A sample 5-point scale showing the behavior dimension of resistance to failure (nursery-school-age boys)

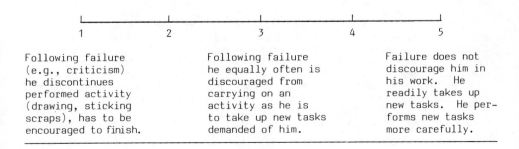

1	2	3	4	5
Following failure (e.g., criticism) he discontinues performed activity (drawing, sticking scraps), has to be encouraged to finish.		Following failure he equally often is discouraged from carrying on an activity as he is to take up new tasks demanded of him.		Failure does not discourage him in his work. He readily takes up new tasks. He performs new tasks more carefully.

The particular scales differ as to descriptions of behavioral categories. These descriptions vary depending on how the given behavior manifests itself at various developmental age levels of the subjects and depending on the number of behaviors assessed. This is due to a lack of certain analogous behaviors in the various age groups.

Reactivity was assessed by childrens' tutors or teachers, who had the best knowledge of their pupils.

A detailed description of this scale can be found in another study (Friedensberg, 1982; Friedensberg & Strelau, 1982).

The next variable studied was intelligence level, measured depending on the subjects' age by the appropriate version of Raven's Progressive Matrices (Hornowski, 1970; Raven, 1965). Individual style of work was studied in an experimental situation where the subject had to solve either the Link Cube test or the Red Block test -- the Link Cube test variation for younger children.

Link's cube consists of 27 wooden blocks differing as to the number of sides painted red. The subject had to use these blocks, of which some have three red sides, some two and some one, and one unpainted block, to build a cube all red on the outside and unpainted inside. The version of this cube for younger children is simpler and consists of 16 blocks with either three or two sides painted red, and the child is to build a "red block."

Conclusions as to individual style of work were drawn from the operations observed, which, as a result of a functional analysis, were classified into basic and auxiliary.

These actions were distinguished on the basis of the criterion of their role in approximating the subject toward his goal (Materska, 1972). In our task a basic action was performed when the subject put the right block in the right place in his construction. The remaining actions were classified as auxiliary since they did not lead directly to the final goal.

Since the latter group was qualitatively heterogeneous, six categories of actions were distinguished here: preparatory, control, corrective, preparatory for control-corrective, searching, and preparing for repetition of basic action. The first three categories had their analogies in the categories distinguished by Tomaszewski (1967), whereas the remaining ones resulted form the three-level structure of the particular construction task used in the experiment.

The auxiliary action categories distinguished here (with the exception of searching actions and preparatory for control-corrective actions) were internally heterogenous; for example, within corrective actions, correct and erroneous ones could be distinguished. The next step consisted in classifying the subjects' actions into the appropriate groups. For example, inserting a wrong block, inserting a good block in the wrong place, and taking out a good block were classified as erroneous-corrective. In view of the constructional nature of the task, boys only, age 6, 8, 10, 13, and 16 years, were the subjects in the study. A total of 184 subjects took part in the main phase of the research work. Preliminary investigations had singled out, on the basis of the quartile deviation criterion, two groups of subjects high- and low-reactive in each group. In the statistical analysis of the structure of action only the auxiliary operations were taken into account, because the number of basic operations (in this specific task) was always constant if the task had been solved correctly. Preparatory, control, and corrective categories were analyzed, as well as such other auxiliary operations that resulted from the specific features of the constructional task used: preparation to control and corrective operations; exploratory operations; and reiterative ones, consisting of the repetition of a basic operation.

The duration of task solving, the total number of auxiliary operations, and the number of errors (with differences in their quality taken into account) were adopted as the task performance level indexes.

An analysis of task performance level was also carried out because it was assumed that the differences in the style of work of low- and high-reactive boys were not accompanied by differences in task performance level.

The following statistical techniques were used: Pearson's coefficient of correlation (r), Student's t-test, Fisher's test (F), the Cochran-Cox test, and the chi square test; $p < .05$ was assumed in all cases as the significance level required.

RESULTS

The analysis began with checking whether there was a correlation-type relationship between intelligence and reactivity level in all age groups. The values obtained for the Pearson coefficients of correlation were small and statistically negligible, which confirmed previous findings in the literature (Shtimmer, 1974a; Vyatkina, 1970). The next step was to establish if there were statistically significant differences between the average results for the various intelligence levels in high- and low-reactive subjects across all the age groups (see Table 2). Statistically significant differences were found between high- and low-reactive persons, in favor of the latter group, in the age groups of 8 and 13 years. In the remaining age groups, no differences in the intelligence levels of the high- and low-reactive subjects were discovered.

TABLE 2. Differences between mean intelligence levels in the groups of high- and low-reactive persons under study (measured by Raven's Matrix)

	Reactivity level	
Age in years	High	Low
6	18.50	22.25
8	23.00*	31.18*
10	37.31	40.84
13	40.25*	48.56*
16	50.11	51.63

*p < .001

The next step in the analysis was to compare task performance index (see Table 3) for high and low reactivity level in each age group.

TABLE 3. Differences between means of task performance level index in high- and low-reactivity groups, by age in years

Age in years	Reactivity level	Task performance index					
		Task performance duration	Total number of errors	Inserting wrong block	Wrong placing of correctly selected block	Removal of correctly selected block	Total number of auxiliary operations
6	High	1539.29	43.57	24.14	12.64	4.79	155.36
	Low	1303.0	36.60	23.55	8.75	4.30	122.00
8	High	1194.41***	38.88**	24.00**	8.18*	6.71**	136.18**
	Low	653.82***	20.24***	12.82**	4.41*	3.00**	79.00**
10	High	1034.38	22.94	17.63	2.13	3.19	124.06
	Low	995.53	20.11	15.84	1.00	3.36	121.00
13	High	1351.88***	33.56***	26.56**	1.75	5.25**	180.31**
	Low	681.67***	14.83***	12.22**	0.61	2.00**	94.00**
16	High	496.94**	7.89	6.89*	0.22	0.78	66.72**
	Low	346.53**	5.11	4.00*	0.53	0.58	39.00**

* $p < .05$ ** $p < .01$ *** $p < .001$

Statistically significant differences between the comparable task performance
level indexes were found both for the high- and low-reactive subjects in the age
groups of 8 and 13 years.

The respective values of all the task performance level indexes (i.e., speed,
errors) were lower in the low-reactive group, indicating superior performance.
In the remaining age groups, the analogous differences turned out to be statistically insignificant with the exception of the three task performance level
indexes (duration of task solving, erroneous corrective operations following
insertion of the wrong block, and total number of auxiliary operations) in the
oldest age group under study.

A comparison of the data for intelligence level and task performance level in
low- and high-reactive persons in the various age groups suggests that the differences in task performance are due to differences in intelligence; the more so
since such a regularity could be noticed when comparing task performance levels
in all age groups, each group divided into two subgroups: those with intelligence
above the median IQ and those below. This comparison has revealed the earlier-
indicated differences in the task performance level as well as new ones concerning
other task performance indexes, in favor of subjects with higher intelligence (see
Table 4). This regularity does not concern the erroneous operation index -- the
removal of the proper block -- and the total number of auxiliary operations in
the age group of 13 years.

Indexes of the functional structure of actions for high- and low-reactive subjects
were then compared across the various age groups. The greatest differences between
comparative index of auxiliary actions between high- and low-reactive subjects were
found in the two lowest age groups (6 and 8 years) and in the 13-year-olds. Higher
indexes (mainly for corrective and control actions) were found in high-reactive
subjects. In the remaining age groups, no differences between high- and low-reactive subjects were found for indexes of functional structure of activity.

In the next stage of the analysis, comparisons were made for the auxiliary operation indexes between successive age groups, separately for high- and low-reactive
persons. Since differences were found to exist in a great number of indexes,
only the general regularities resulting from the comparisons are presented here.
In the younger age groups (6 and 8 years), the corrective operation indexes
dominate, irrespective of reactivity level, in the functional structure of the
operations, but in the age group of 6 years, within this class of indexes the
proportion of erroneous corrective operations is quite pronounced. With subjects'
growth (by 8 years of age), control operation indexes begin to appear. In this
group, compared with that of 10 years of age, the number of indexes concerning
preparation for control and corrective operations increases, but only in the
category of highly reactive persons. Beginning at the age of 10, the number of
corrective operation indexes decreases, and the ones remaining are the correct
corrective operation indexes. At the same time, the group of indexes covering
preparations to control and corrective operations either decreases in number or
even disappears completely. The corrective operation indexes are accompanied
more frequently by control operation indexes.

To determine the effect of intelligence on both the functional structure of action
and task performance level, intelligence level was correlated with the relevant
indexes as a result of correlating performance level and intelligence level indexes. Values of Pearson's correlation coefficient varying from .44 to .80 were
obtained.

Analogous values for the functional structure and intelligence level indexes
varied from .45 to .77. The overwhelming majority of the values of correlation
coefficients is negative; thus, the higher the result obtained in the intelligence

TABLE 4. Arithmetic means for task performance level index in comparable groups with intelligence levels over and below median, by age in years.

Age in years	Reactivity level	Task performance index					
		Task performance duration	Total number of errors	Inserting wrong block	Wrong placing of correctly selected block	Removal of correctly selected block	Total number of auxiliary operations
6	Over median	1040.60**	30.12**	18.53*	8.41	3.17	102.00**
	Below median	1760.00**	48.82**	30.71*	12.28	5.82	170.20**
8	Over median	625.90**	18.13**	11.81**	3.75**	2.56**	81.19**
	Below median	1189.20**	39.72**	24.28**	8.55**	6.88**	131.50**
10	Over median	978.60	18.39	15.17	0.72*	2.50**	116.40
	Below median	1050.00	24.59	18.24	2.35*	4.00**	129.20
13	Over median	682.50**	16.75*	13.56*	0.50	2.68	100.20
	Below median	1276.70**	29.78*	23.78*	1.72	4.27	159.70
16	Over median	341.10*	4.36**	3.52**	0.31	0.52	37.63**
	Below median	501.70*	86.67**	7.23**	0.44	0.83	69.00**

* $p < .05$ ** $p < .01$

test, the lower the value of the relevant index (i.e., the smaller the number of auxiliary operations). If this index has the form of a proportion, it means that the number of auxiliary operations is proportionally smaller in relation to the category being compared, for example, corrective operations (correct and erroneous) considered jointly.

In the high-reactive group, intelligence level correlates with two indexes only; in the low-reactive group, with a total of 21 indexes.

As regards the functional structure of activity, in the groups of highly reactive persons, intelligence level was mostly correlated with a globally smaller number of indexes of auxiliary actions than in contrast with groups of low-reactive subjects.

These results indicate that the effect of intelligence level both on the functional structure of operations and on the task performance level is greater in the low-reactive persons than in the high-reactive ones (this is true for all age levels).

INTERPRETATION AND CONCLUSIONS

On the basis of the results of our investigations[2], we may formulate some general conclusions.

If the high- and low-reactive groups under comparison did not differ in intelligence, then no statistically significant differences in task performance were observed. This is also confirmed by studies of style of action conducted both by Soviet and Polish psychologists, where it has been demonstrated empirically that absence of differences in intelligence is accompanied by absence of differences (between high- and low-reactive persons) in task performance level (Baymetov, 1971; Kopytova, 1964; Strelau, 1974b).

That the high- and low-reactive persons displayed no differences in work output can be explained by assuming that they can employ their (individually specific) mode of performing a given operation. That is, people have a style of action that compensates for all differences in individual abilities depending on temperamental properties (Merlin, 1977; Strelau, 1975). At the same time, the dynamics of formation of the functional structure of operations is more pronounced in younger age groups (6 and 8 years).

In younger children, irrespective of their reactivity level, corrective operations dominate in the functional structure of action, and these operations are accompanied by preparation to control-corrective operations. As soon as checking operations appear, the frequency of both corrective operations and preparation to control-corrective operations decreases. This is connected with the initial prevalence of the trial-and-error method in solving tasks. It is only with the development of the analysis-and-synthesis processes and planning of behavior that corrective operations resulting from them cease to dominate, giving way to checking operations. These, in turn, appear as an expression of deliberate control over the course of the task-solving process, yielding information about discrepancies between the anticipated outcome and the actual one (Kuvshinov, 1979; Salamon, 1964; Wołoszynowa, 1979).

---

[2]A complete specification of the results of study is contained in E. Friedensberg's doctor's thesis entitled "Reactivity and individual style of work exemplified by constructional-type tasks performance development characteristics."

It is suggested here that intelligence has a greater effect on task performance level than reactivity. Success in task performance depends, to a great extent, on the ability to make proper choices and also on the assessment of the result obtained in comparison with the expected result; and success is controlled by the intelligence variable (Merlin, 1970; Vyatkina, 1970).

At the same time, it can be said that the influence of intelligence level on both the functional structure of action and task performance level is more pronounced in low-reactive persons than in highly reactive ones. On one hand, in low-reactive persons the intellectual component, to a small degree, is exposed to the disorganizing influence of emotional factors that may be associated with task solving (compare the studies by Gurievich and Matveyev (1966), concerning the functioning of high- and low-reactive persons under stress). On the other hand, differences in the influence of intelligence level, however, may be due to the low-reactive person's active attitude toward shaping their style of action to make it correspond to their temperamental features. This active attitude probably results from the existing educational system which prefers the style of action typical of highly reactive individuals. Classes are conducted with emphasis on analysis and synthesis of the material to be learned, and the pupils are asked to make synopses. Thus, the educational program is constructed so as to make pupils undertake a great number of auxiliary operations, characteristic of the style of action of highly reactive persons.

The present study has yielded the empirical validation of the hypotheses about the absence of a correlation-type relationship between reactivity and intelligence level and about the nonoccurrence of statistically significant differences in task performance level, between high- and low-reactive individuals, provided that there are no differences between them in intelligence level.

Moreover, a person's style of work develops with age, and changes occurring in the process of its formation concern both the qualitative and quantitative differentiation of auxiliary operations applied.

At the same time, the influence of intelligence level on shaping the style of action is more pronounced in low-reactive persons than in highly reactive ones, which also confirms the second hypothesis put forward in this chapter.

REFERENCES

Baymetov, A. K. (1971). Niektóre czynniki indywidualnego stylu pracy szkolnej uczniów klas wyższych uwarunkowane siłą procesu pobudzenia. (Selected factors of the individual style of school work of higher-grade children dependent on the strength of excitation process.) In J. Strelau (Ed.), Zagadnienia psychologii róznic indywidualnych. (Problems of psychology of individual differences). Warsaw, PWN (Panstvove Vydavneectvo Naukove).

Friedensberg, E. (1981). Reactivity and individual style of work exemplified by constructional-type tasks performance development characteristics. Unpublished doctoral dissertation. Warsaw.

Friedensberg, E. (1982a). Skala ocen jako narzędzie do pomiaru reaktywności. (The rating scale as a tool for measuring reactivity.) In J. Strelau (Ed.), Regulacyjne funkcje temperamentu. (Regulative functions of temperament.) Vroclav: Zaklad Narodovy im. Ossolinskikch.

Friedensberg, E., & Strelau, J. (1982). Reactivity Rating Scale: Reliability and validity. Polish Psychol. Bull., 13, 3.

Gurevich, K. M., & Matveyev, W. F. (1966). O professionalnoy prigodnosti operatorov i sposobakh eye opredelenya. (On the professional fitness of operators and methods of its assessment.) In B. M. Teplov & K. M. Gurevich (Eds.). Voprosy professyonalnoy prigodnosti operativnogo personala energo-system. (Problems of professional fitness of power plant operation section staff.) Moscow: Prosveshchenye.

Hornowski, B. (1970). Analiza psychologiczna skali J. C. Ravena. (Psychological analysis J. C. Raven's scale.) Warsaw: Panstvove Vydavneectvo Naukove.

Klimov, J. A. (1969). Individualnyi stil deyatelnosti. (Individual style of action.) Kazań, IKU (Izdatelstvo Kazahanskogo Universiteta).

Kopytova, Ł. A. (1969). Individualnyi stil trudovoy deyatelnosti naladchikov v zavisimosti ot sily nervnoy sistemy po vozbuzhdenyu. (Individual style of professional activity of leaders depending on strength of nervous system in the range of excitation.) Voprosy Psikhologyi, 1, 25-33.

Kuvshinov, N. I. (1959). Reshenye prakticheskhikh zadach uchashchjkhsya nachalnykh klassov na urokach truda. (Solving practical tasks by pupils from the lowest grades during manual work lessons.) Voprosy Psikhologyi, 4, 48-58.

Mastvilisker, E. I. (1967). Psikhologicheskaya obuslovlennost form reaghirovanya i sposobov deystvya u detey starshego doshkolnogo vozhrasta. (Psychological conditioning of reaction forms and ways of action in children from older pre-school groups.) In V. S. Merlin (Ed.), Tipologicheskhye issledovanya po psikhologyi lichnosti. (Typological researches in personality psychology.) Perm: UOOP (Uralskoe Otdelenye Obshchestva Psykhologov) and PGPG (Permskyi Gosudarstvennyi Pedagoghichevskyi Institut).

Mastvilisker, E. I., & Dikopolskaya, T. E. (1976). Nekotorye uslovya formirovanya individualnogo stila v rechenyi uchebnykh zadach u doshkolnikov. (Selected con-ditions of formation of individual style in solving school tasks by pre-school age children.) In V. S. Merlin (Ed.), Temperament. Perm: PGPI (Permskyi Gosudarstvennyi Pedagoghichevskyi Institut).

Materska, M. (1972). Treść przygotowania teoretycznego a struktura czynności praktycznych. (The content of theoretical preparation and the structure of practical actions.) Vroclav: Zaklad Narodowy im. Ossolinskikch.

Matveyev, W. F. (1965). Psikhologicheskye proyavlenya osnovnykh svoystv nervnoy sistemy u operatorov energosystemy v obstanovke uslovnykh avaryi. (Psycho-logical symptoms of basic nervous system features of power plant operators in contrived break-down situations.) In B. M. Teplov (Ed.), Tipologhicheskye ossobennosti wyzhshey nervnoy deyatelnosti chelovekha. (Typological properties of functions of man's central nervous system.) Moscow: Prosveshchenye.

Merlin, V. S. (1970). Svoystva lichnosti kak sposobnosti. (Properties of per-sonality as abilities.) In V. S. Merlin (Ed.), Problemy experimentalnoy psikhologyi lichnosti. (Problems of experimental psychology of personality.) Perm PPI (Permskyi Pedagoghichevskyi Institut).

Merlin, V. S. (1977). Ravnocennost svojstv obshchego tipa nervnoy sistemi i princip kompensacyi. (Equivalence of properties of general type of nervous system and the principle of compensation.) In A. A. Smirnov (Ed.), Psikhologya i psikhophisyologya individualnykh razlichyi. (Psychology and psychophysiology of individual differences.) Moscow: Pedagogika.

Nosarzewski, J. (1974). Styl pracy umysłowej młodzieży uwarunkowanej siłą układu nerwowego. (Style of youth's mental work dependent on the strength of nervous system.) In J. Strelau (Ed.), Rola cech temperamentalnych w działaniu. (The role of temperamental traits in action.) Vroclaw: Zakład Narodovy im. Ossolinskikch.

Prusakova, M. B. (1974a). K voprosu o tipologhicheski obuslovlennom individualnom stile reshenyi ariphmeticheskikh zadach u mlodshykh shkholnikhov. (In the matter of typologically dependent individual style in solving arithmetic tasks by lower-grade pupils.) In V. S. Merlin (Ed.), Voprosy teorii temperamenta. (Problems of theory of temperament.) Perm: PGPI (Permskyi Gosudarstvennyi Pedagoghichevskyi Institut).

Prusakova, M. B. (1974b). Rol obuchenya v usvoyenyi tipologhicheski obuslovlennogo individualnogo stila pri reshenyi ariphmeticheskhikh zadach uchashchikhsya pyatikh klassov. (The role of teaching in acquiring typologically dependent individual style during solving arithmetic tasks by pupils of fifth grades.) In V. S. Merlin (Ed.), Voprosy teorii temperamenta. (Problems of theory of temperament.) Perm: PGPJ (Permskyi Gosudarstvennyi Pedagoghichevskyi Institut).

Reykowski, J. (1974). Eksperymentalna psychologia emocji. (Experimental psychology of emotion.) Warsaw, KIW (Kshonshka ee Vyedzha).

Raven, J. C. (1965). Guide to using the coloured Progressive Matrices Sets A, Ab, B (revised order, 1956). London: H.K. Lewis.

Salamon, I. (1964). Eksperymentalne badanie rozwoju myślenia dzieci w elementarnej działalności knostrukcyjnej. (Experimental investigation of the development of thinking in children in elementary constructional activity.) Przheglad Psykchologhichny, 8, 20-30.

Shchukhin, M. R. (1964). Nekotorye tipologicheski obuslovlennye razlichya v protekanyi orientirovochnoy ispolnitelnoy deyatelnosti pri usvoyenyi nachalnykch trudovykh umenyi. (Selected typologically dependent differences in the course of orientative and executive activity in the course of acquiring basic professional skills.) In V. S. Merlin (Ed.), Tipologhicheskye issledov issledovanya po psikhologyi lichnosti i po psikhologyi truda. (Typological research into personality psychology and work psychology.) Perm: PGPI (Permskyi Gosudarstvennyi Pedagoghiehevskyi Institut).

Shtimmer, E. W. (1974a). Rol obuchenya v usvoenyi tipologhicheski kharakternogo individualnogo stila u detey doshholnogo vozrasta. (Role of teaching in the acquisition of typologically characteristic individual style in pre-school age children.) In V. S. Merlin (Ed.), Voprosy teorii temperamenta. (Problems of theory of temperament.) Perm: PGPI (Permskyi Gosudarstvennyi Pedagoghichevskyi Institut).

Shtimmer, E. W. (1974b). Sootnoshenye urovnya umstvennogo razvytya po testam Vekslera i sily vozhbuditelnogo processa v starshem doshkholnom vozrostye. (The relationship between level of mental development as measured by Veksler's test and strength of the excitation process in older pre-school age.) In W. S. Merlin (Ed.), Voprosy teorii temperamenta. (Problems of theory of temperament.) Perm: PGPI (Permskyi Gosudarstvennyi Pedagoghiehcvskyi Institut).

Strelau, J. (1970). Indywidualny styl pracy ucznia a cechy temperamentalne. (A pupil's individual work habits and temperamental traits.) Kvartalnik Pedagoghichny, 15, 59-77.

Strelau, J. (1974a). Koncepcja temperamentu jako poziomu energetycznego i char-
akterystyki czasowej zachowania. (The concept of temperament as a power level
and time characteristic of behaviour.) In J. Strelau (Ed.), Rola cech temperamentalnych w działaniu. (The role of temperamental traits in action.) Vroclaw:
Zaklad Narodovy im. Ossolinskikch.

Strelau, J. (1974b). Reaktywność a styl działania na przykładzie wybranych
czynności zawodowych. (Reactivity and style of action exemplified by selected
professional operations.) In J. Strelau (Ed.), Rola cech temperamentalnych w
działaniu. (The role of temperament traits in action.) Vroclaw: Zaklad
Narodovy im. Ossolinskikch.

Strelau, J. (1975). Różnice indywidualne. (Individual differences.) In T.
Tomaszewski (Ed.), Psychologia. (Psychology.) Warsaw: Panstvove Vydavneectvo
Naukove.

Tomaszewski, T. (1967). Aktywność człowieka. (Man's activity.) In M. Maruszewski,
J. Reykowski, & T. Tomaszewski (Ed.), Psychologia jako nauka o człowieku.
(Psychology as a science of man.) Warsaw: KiW (Kshonshka ee Vyedzha).

Vyatkina, L. A. (1970). Tipologicheski obuslovlennyi individualnyi stil v
rechenyi prakhticheskhikh zadach kak pokazatyel obszczikh sposobnostey u
starshikh doshkholnikhov. (Typologically dependent individual style in
solving practical tasks as a measure of general ability in children at
higher pre-school age.) In V. S. Merlin (Ed.), Problemy eksperimentalnoy
psikhologyi lichnosti. (Problems of experimental psychology of personality.)
Perm: UOOP (Uralskoe Otdelenye Obshchestva Psykhologov) and PGPI (Permskyi
Gosudarstvennyi Pedagoghichevskyi Institut).

Woloszynowa, L. (1979). Młodszy wiek szkolny. (Younger school age.) In M.
Żebrowska (Ed.), Psychologia rozwojowa dzieci i młodzieży. (Developmental
psychology of children and youth.) Warsaw, PWN (Panstvove Vydavneectvo
Naukove).

Index